"For anyone wanting to become involved in mul
Multimedia Casebook offers valuab
life experiences to show the bu
challenges of this A CD-RO

"For those with and idea for the perfect multimedia application, this book presents case studies with step-by-step analysis of the creative planning process, costs, hardware and software requirements, and even marketing strategies."

—T.H.E. JOURNAL

0442018193

The
Multimedia
CASEBOOK

Mary Fallenstein Hellman

W. R. James

VAN NOSTRAND REINHOLD
I(T)P A Division of International Thomson Publishing Inc.

New York • Albany • Bonn • Boston • Detroit • London • Madrid • Melbourne
Mexico City • Paris • San Francisco • Singapore • Tokyo • Toronto

Copyright © 1995 by Van Nostrand Reinhold
A division of International Thomson Publishing Inc.
I(T)P   The ITP logo is a trademark under license

Printed in the United States of America
For more information, contact:

Van Nostrand Reinhold
115 Fifth Avenue
New York, NY 10003

International Thomson Publishing Europe
Berkshire House 168-173
High Holborn
London WCIV 7AA
England

Thomas Nelson Australia
102 Dodds Street
South Melbourne, 3205
Victoria, Australia

Nelson Canada
1120 Brichmount Road
Scarborough, Ontario
Canada M1K 5G4

International Thomson Editores
Campos Eliseos 385, Piso 7
Col. Polanco
11560 Mexico D. F. Mexico

Cover Design: W. R. James
Book Design: Mary Fallentstein Hellman
                 W. R. James
                 Chris Grisonich

Cover photos and illustrations courtesy of the companies featured in this book, including Ed Wolkis Photography. Music, graphics, video and animation, supplied by Black Cat Interactive and developers featured in the CD-ROM. Music used in "The Journeyman Project" segment of the CD-ROM is from the original score and supplied by Presto Studios. CD-ROM design by Black Cat Interactive. Macintosh conversion and CD-ROM mastering by Phil Faris and Altura Software. Douglas Adams video intro provided by Reed Exhibitions and *inter*media. Back cover photo by Richard James.

International Thomson Publishing GmbH
Königswinterer Strasse 418
53227 Bonn
Germany

International Thomson Publishing Asia
221 Henderson Road #05-10
Henderson Building
Singapore 0315

International Thomson Publishing Japan
Hirakawacho Kyowa Building, 3F
2-2-1 Hirakawacho
Chiyoda-ku, 102 Tokyo
Japan

1 2 3 4 5 6 7 8 9 10 QEBFF 01 00 99 98 97 96 95

Library of Congress Cataloging-in-Publication Data
Hellman, Mary Fallenstein.
        The multimedia casebook / Mary Fallenstein Hellman, W. R. James.
                p.   cm.
        Includes index.
        ISBN 0–442–01819–3
        1. Multimedia systems--Case studies.   I. James, W. R.   II. Title.
QA76.575.H44 1994
006.6--cd20
                                        94-19345
                                CIP

Contents

To
Otto and Julia Fallenstein
and
Bill and Nila James

Foreword

In *The Multimedia Casebook*, you'll find reviews of twelve distinct cases. The experiences presented are invaluable. The book includes cases with a full spectrum of multimedia applications. Each case provides description, development period, production hardware, production software, cost to develop, etc. In other words, everything you ever wanted to know about the nitty-gritty details of developing multimedia projects. I found each case provided invaluable insight into the successes, as well as pitfalls, of development and production. It seemed as if all the developers had under estimated the time and money needed for the completion of the project.

The authors provide a clear and interesting writing style. I found each case unique and the detail just right. The authors are to be commended for carefully organizing the information into a meaningful presentation of each of the cases.

As a professor of Educational Media and Computers at Arizona State University, I find the cases invaluable for students to understand what is involved in the development and production of a project. Having developed three CD-ROM projects, including a total college course on a CD-ROM, I found this book right on target with detail. If only I would have read this book before doing my projects, I would have saved a lot of time and energy. This book will be recommended reading for all Master's and Ph.D. students in Educational Media and Computers at Arizona State University.

All I can say is enjoy—your future appreciation and understanding of multimedia will be enhanced significantly.

Gary G. Bitter, Ph.D.
Coordinator and Professor
Educational Media and Computers
Arizona State University

Acknowledgments

Writing a book is like having a house guest who was welcomed enthusiastically into your home many months ago, but who now refuses to leave. This guest wakes you in the middle of the night, interrupts meals, and insists on weekends together while taking over your desk, your kitchen table, your life. When the guest finally departs, you're ecstatic. However, hardly a week passes before you start looking around for a new visitor, just one more book, to invite for a brief stay.

Our "house guest" would not have materialized without the help of Waterside Productions and our agent, Matt Wagner, a nice guy who turned our bright idea into a contract for "The Multimedia Casebook."

We turned to multimedia pioneers across the country to collect the real-life stories told in the chapters that follow. Without exception, they interrupted their hectic schedules to talk candidly about this nascent industry, and their roles in it. Without their vision, insight, and gracious cooperation, this book might not have been realized. We also are in debt to a number of industry experts, who willingly shared their observations about multimedia production, even though their projects were not detailed in this book. Kudos are also deserved by the behind-the-scenes public relations executives—particularly Kimberly Rispin, James Yokota, Heather Crosby and Amy Woodward Parrish—who tracked down all the pesky details we needed.

We also would like to express our gratitude to Risa Cohen and Van Nostrand Reinhold for seeing the value of a different kind of "computer book" and helping us through the perils of first time book authoring. And thanks, too, to the rest of VNR's energetic staff, especially Ellen Reavis whose enthusiasm for this project seemed to equal our own, and Chris Grisonich, whose grammar and design skills are evident on every page. We are certain they would join us in thanking Rosa Mitchell, who braved the world of computer-speak to transcribe many hours of interviews, and helped us meet our manuscript deadline.

During the past 18 months, we saw far too little of our friends and family. We thank them for their understanding, and hope this book will answer their questions about what we've been doing. A special thanks to Michael Hellman, Greg LaVance, Joanie Simpson, John Muncie, Sharon Jones, Maureen Chism, Janel Belneki, and Roger and Noriko Ralphs for enduring many a conversation about multimedia, without nodding off.

Aaron Hellman, a young man especially dear to our hearts, managed to avoid most of the turmoil by leaving San Diego for a two-year tour of duty with the Peace Crops in the Dominican Republic. Little did he know when he bought his Mac Plus all those years ago that it ultimately would inspire this book. (See Chapter 12 for details.) We're very proud of him.

We also can't forget our feline family—Bix (our logo cat), Billie, BéBé, Boy, and Josie—who kept us amused, sane, and awake at 6 A. M., over the months we spent writing. And finally we salute each other, knowing that if we can stick together through this adventure, we can make it through anything.

Mary Fallenstein Hellman
W. R. James
San Diego, California

Introduction

In his keynote speech in 1992 at the Seventh International Conference & Exposition on Multimedia and CD-ROM (now known as *inter*media), truth seeker and funny guy Douglas Adams posed *the* question that was on the collective mind of his audience: "What word begins in M and ends in ultimedia? Can any of you work that out?" Knowing, nervous laughter filled the hall. "Because for a while," he went on, "it seemed like that was the only question to which multimedia was definitely the answer."

In those not-so-distant early days, being confused was easy. Even those who had a grasp of this thing called multimedia, with its alphabet-soup of platforms, players, and peripherals had to wonder where it was going. At trade shows, industry experts constantly contradicted each other. While one would cheer that the market for multimedia, especially CD-ROM reference and entertainment titles, had arrived, another would preach doom and gloom, because there were too many platforms or too few multimedia computers to support this new industry. If the subject of multimedia was broached with friends, even the computer literate would yawn; their eyes would glaze over as if Aunt Helen's hernia operation were being described.

What a difference a year made. By early 1993, the "M word" began to make headway. Kiosks and interactive training programs introduced many people to the possibilities of multimedia. Intriguing CD-ROM titles competed for more and more shelf space in computer stores. Buying an MPC did not cost much more than buying a plain old PC. Now a few of our friends were curious about multimedia, and some would even ask for a brief demo on our home computer.

By year's end, multimedia was making headlines. What had been a trickle of stories in trade journals was now mainstream news. Corporate high-flyers saw gold at the end of the information super highway; "500 channels" was their rallying cry. Responsible companies in heretofore niche industries began to converge (or at least attempt to), afraid to be left in the digital dust. They were frantically forming alliances with other like-minded corporate souls. Corporate "heavyweights" like Barry Diller, John Sculley, John Malone, Bill Gates, and others became evangelists of this new media revolution, adding considerable weight and credibility to the new media bandwagon. And those wary friends? We will say only that our collection of CD-ROMs is now a lending library.

Fortunately, beneath the dense cloud of hype, and away from the roar of buzzwords, was an industry already past its infancy. Tumbling prices for computers and peripherals allowed consumers to get more byte for the buck. By early 1994, the real installed base of multimedia-capable machines in homes topped the million mark for the first time, and seven to thirteen million more are estimated to be in use in homes by the end of the year. Now, instead of average sales of 5,000 per title, CD-ROM publishers can expect five to ten times that number. They can even dream of passing the 1 million mark with the next hot game. With the proliferation of new and affordable multimedia authoring and presentation packages, multimedia was within the reach of business executives, educators, and artists, who had begun to use it to communicate as never before. Could it be that a communications revolution even more powerful and far-reaching than the one wrought by desktop publishing a few years ago was in the works?

LET'S MAKE MULTIMEDIA

Yes and no. Even with the "M word" now on everyone's lips, many aspects of multimedia are a mystery to all but a seasoned, scarred few, who had survived on the bleeding edge of these new technologies. Newcomers trying to fathom the how of multimedia—how to do it, fund it, and make money at it—were in for a real adventure. The tools are available but how should they be applied? Do developers need a script? If a person has an idea for a title, how does he or she sell it? Where can you find someone to help you with production? How does one find work on a production? Is there an 800 number for financial backers?

We can relate to this frustration, since we were eager to learn the ins and outs of real-world multimedia production, too. How to program, animate a robot, digitize a video, or any of the other "nuts and bolts" of development could be learned in classes or from books. As a last resort, we could even read the manuals packaged with all our hardware and software. But what we wanted was practical information about application development by real developers, for real clients, for real reasons (and maybe for real money). We wanted to find a dozen or so multimedia Yodas, wizened veterans who know the tricks of the trade and are willing to tell all.

HEY KIDS, LET'S WRITE A BOOK

We diligently roamed the aisles of trade shows, combed through trade magazines, and prowled computer bulletin boards looking for nuggets of multimedia information. Rarely did we find what we were looking for, an invaluable analysis of accomplished applications, not hypothetical tutorials or slick, "no-problem" histories, but in-depth case studies of honest-to-goodness multimedia projects. Our search for a book of multimedia cases proved equally fruitless.

We thought, maybe we should write that book. The rest is history. Our goal was to search out multimedia projects in a variety of areas and compile anecdotal, detailed histories of them. In addition to an analysis of the technical aspects of the production, we wanted to get to know the developers, their backgrounds, motivations and skills. We wanted to chronicle the steps—and missteps— necessary to make a great idea a great multimedia project, and plus share an evaluation of what to do or not to do again. Perhaps most important for us was to put a human face on this new industry, to show the humor, frustration, and joy involved in the creative process. We hoped that when we were finished we would have a reality based, thought provoking, and inspirational snapshot of multimedia development.

Early on, we chose to tell each case history in a similar way, by answering the questions in the categories listed below. This system worked to a point, organizing us and our subjects. But each case proved unique. No two developers followed exactly the same procedures, and no two had the same concerns. The end result is that each segment will not be found in each case study; and some case studies will have a category or two not found in any of the others. Generally, though, this book is organized along the following lines:

• *The Opportunity:* What was the communications goal, and why was multimedia selected to meet it? What steps were taken by client and/ or developer that made proceeding with the project possible?

• *The Team:* Who were the developers, what were their jobs, and where did they get the skills necessary to complete the application? Did they use staff, freelancers, or a company that specializes in multimedia development? How did they manage the stressful process of team and client relations?

• *The Production:* How did the application grow and change during production? How were the needed assets—including illustrations, animation, video, MIDI music, voice audio, interactivity, and graphical interface design—produced? Why was a particular computer platform and authoring system chosen? How was the final product tested? If developer and client had it to do over again, what would they change?

• *Marketing:* If applicable, how is the product or service marketed? How important is packaging and pricing?

• *Financing:* How was this application funded? How are resources allocated during multimedia production? What are the financial options for multimedia developers and their clients?

• *The Future:* What's next for these industry pioneers?

• *At A Glance:* This brief overview includes a list of software and hardware used, as well as the names, addresses, and phone numbers of the pioneering companies profiled.

As we began interviewing, we discovered that the creative process—the inspired pursuit of an idea or dream in the face of daunting challenges and obstacles—was the most fascinating aspect of this project. The stories from this part of the development process, we feel, will be the lasting ones. Hardware, software, and techniques may be obsolete in a matter of weeks, as a result of current technical leaps, but the tales of determination, problem solving, and dedication will never be outmoded.

As you will discover, most of the cases in this book traveled a "rocky" road during development, and not all of the cases have "storybook" endings. This youthful business demands risk-taking without the benefit of standardized procedures or tools. As a result, today's developers, and their clients, learn in the school of "hard knocks," and sometimes they are disappointed when they fall short of their expectations. But we are convinced their hard-won knowledge will serve as an inspriation for those who would follow in their footsteps.

The last case in the book explains how we developed the CD-ROM that accompanies this book. The production of this CD should be an inspiration to all since it is a boring story of an on-schedule, hassle-free development process—not! If by some wild circumstance, this CD-ROM does not boot up or work in your computer, keep changing computers until it does. Once it is up and running, it will provide a wealth of information that didn't fit in this interactive paper edition of the CD-ROM.

SO MANY PROJECTS, SO LITTLE TIME

The most difficult part of completing this book (in addition to missing some episodes of "Star Trek: The Next Generation") was selecting the cases. The problem was not that developers were not forthcoming. In fact, of all the developers we contacted, only one turned us down and he, as it turned out, had a good reason.

Our criteria emphasized diversity. We wanted a full spectrum of multimedia applications that would reveal the promise and power of this industry: international, national, regional, and local projects; educational, business, institutional, and entertainment projects. We wanted to spotlight the "garage" developer, the corporate multimedia division, and most places between the two extremes, just as we wanted both projects done on a "shoestring" budget and those that cost millions. We also wanted to show a variety of platforms and authoring programs, as well as a mix of off-the-shelf software, in action. Finally, we wanted "wanabee" developers of all ages and circumstances, established developers, and those interested in using multimedia in their businesses and institutions to find the book fascinating and helpful.

Those were our aspirations. We hope you agree that the detailed cases that follow are all that and more. The diversity of projects, developers, budgets, and processes, is there. So is the diversity of obstacles that were faced and overcome, everything from lost gigabytes to found credit lines. Do not expect a canned dissertation ahead; these are honest, intelligent professionals talking candidly about the "beast" that is multimedia creation.

We owe them a great debt for their candor and insights. We also had the opportunity to read this book before we started creating the "Casebook" CD-ROM. We vowed to follow their advice and do all the right things to make a multimedia project a success. But we also knew from their experiences, that it probably would not work out quite that way—why should it be any different for us?

Trademarks

Macintosh, Macintosh Quadra, HyperCard and QuickTime are registered trademarks of Apple Computer, Inc.; OS/2 and Ultimedia are registered trademarks and PC is a trademark of IBM Corporation; MS-DOS is a registered trademark and Windows is a trademark of Microsoft Corporation; CD-I is a trademark of Philips Consumer Electronics Co.; Photo CD is a trademark of Eastman Kodak Company; Talking Business Card is a trademark of Galileo, Inc.; Autodesk, Animator, Animator Pro, and 3D Studio are trademarks or registered trademarks of Autodesk, Inc.; CompuServe Information Service is a registered trademark of CompuServe Incorporated; Aldus, Aldus FreeHand and PageMaker are registered trademarks of Aldus Corporation; PhotoStyler is a trademark of Aldus Corporation; Adobe Illustrator, Adobe Photoshop, Adobe Premiere, and PostScript are trademarks of Adobe Systems Inc.; CorelDRAW! is a registered trademark of Corel Systems Corporation; dBase is a registered trademark of Borland International Inc.; Epson is a registered trademark of Epson America Inc., Hewlett-Packard is a registered trademark of Hewlett-Packard Company; SyQuest is a registered trademark of SyQuest Technology; AutoCAD and Autodesk are registered trademarks of Autodesk, Inc.; Multimedia Toolbook is a trademark of Asymetrix Corporation; *inter*media is a trademark of Reed Exhibitions. Other product and corporate names may be trademarks or registered trademarks of other companies, and are used only for explanation and to the owners' benefit, without intent to infringe.

LIMITATION OF LIABILITY
VAN NOSTRAND REINHOLD AND THE AUTHORS OF THE CD-ROM SHALL NOT IN ANY CASE BE LIABLE FOR SPECIAL, INCIDENTAL, CONSEQUENTIAL, INDIRECT, OR OTHER SIMILAR DAMAGES ARISING FROM CD-ROM USAGE EVEN IF VAN NOSTRAND REINHOLD OR ITS AGENT HAS BEEN ADVISED OF THE POSSIBILITY OF SUCH DAMAGES. THE LIABILITY FOR DAMAGES OF VAN NOSTRAND REINHOLD AND THE AUTHORS OF THE PROGRAM UNDER THIS AGREEMENT SHALL IN NO EVENT EXCEED THE PURCHASE PRICE PAID.

SOFTWARE LICENSE
Van Nostrand Reinhold grants you the right to use one copy of the enclosed software program on a single computer system (whether a single CPU, part of a licensed network, or a terminal connected to a single CPU). Each concurrent user of the program must have exclusive use of the related Van Nostrand Reinhold written materials.

The program is owned by the respective author and the copyright in the entire work is owned by Van Nostrand Reinhold and they are therefore protected under the copyright laws of the United States and other nations, under international treaties. You may make no copies of all or any part of the related Van Nostrand Reinhold written materials.

You may not rent or lease the program, but you may transfer ownership of the programs and related written materials if you keep no copies of either, and if you make sure the transferee agrees to the terms of this license.

You may not decompile, reverse engineer, disassemble, copy, create a derivative work, or otherwise use the program except as stated in the Agreement.

By opening the sealed disc package you are agreeing to be bound by the terms of this agreement.

1

"THE 7TH GUEST"

Trilobyte, Inc.

At A Glance

"The 7th Guest"

Developer: Trilobyte, Inc. and Virgin Games, Inc.

Key Personnel: Graeme Devine and Rob Landeros, game concept and design; Rob Landeros, art director; Matthew Costello, script; Robert Stein III, lead artist; Alan Iglesias and Gene Bodio, Phil LeMarbre and Rob Landeros, 3D graphics; Graeme Devine, programmer; David Luehmann, Trilobyte producer; Dr. Stephen Clarke-Willson, executive in charge of production; David Bishop, creative consultant; Robb Alvey and Neil Young, producers for Virgin Games; The Fat Man and Team Fat, musical score; Image Grafx and Rogue River Motion Picture Company, video production; Staunton Studios, sound engineering.

Description: An interactive CD-ROM game built around the story of a haunted house. It includes special effects, thirty minutes of video, and a full musical score.

Development period: January 1991–March 1993.

Production hardware: Networked 486DX machines with 16 MB RAM or better, Apple Macintosh Quadra.

Production software: Autodesk Animator Pro and 3D Studio, Handmade Software's Image Alchemy, Aldus Photostyler.

Cost to develop: $750,000.

Financing: Trilobyte, Inc., Virgin Games, Inc.

Suggested retail price: $99.99.

U. S. distributor: Virgin Interactive Entertainment.

Foreign distributor: Virgin Interactive Entertainment, Ltd.

Awards: Award of excellence, Best Animation/Graphics, Best Programming, Best Adventure, NewMedia Invision Multimedia Awards 1994; Best CD-ROM Game, PC World, 1994; Breadthrough Game, Electronic Entertainment, Editors Choice; Golden Triad Award, Computer Game Review; MVP Award, PC Computing; 1993 BIMA Silver, British Interactive Media Award; Number One Ranked Game, Computer Gaming World Readers Poll; Editors' Choice, Electronic Entertainment magazine.

Future projects: "The 11th Hour," a sequel; an office politics sitcom-style game, a futuristic techno-thriller, a game set in a Scottish castle or ancient Egypt.

Contact: James Yokota, product manager
Trilobyte, Inc.
517 W. 10th Street
Medford, OR 97501
503–857–0614
503–857–0616 (fax)

I t was 11 o'clock in the morning at the Irvine, California head quarters of Virgin Games when the head of the company, Martin Alper, walked into Graeme Devine's office. "Let's go to lunch," he said casually. Minutes later, Devine and Rob Landeros, Virgin's art director, were settled in the back seat of Alper's Rolls Royce, cruising toward a luxurious Orange County restaurant. The two experienced game producers were a little nervous; both assumed the topic of discussion would be their proposal for a state-of-the-art computer game on CD-ROM. They had taken it to Alper after a Virgin committee had "nixed flat out" their idea to explore the potential of multimedia in games.

"Spiritual allies," Devine and Landeros were frustrated by Virgin's then emphasis on video cartridge games aimed primarily at 8- to 14-year-olds. The duo wanted to focus on an older, more mature market—say 14- to 24-year-olds. They wanted to create a more sophisticated game—challenging and cinematic with echoes of the quirky television hit, "Twin Peaks." They also wanted to put it on CD-ROM, even though Virgin's brass dismissed it as "market-less."

Would Alper share their vision of the future of computer games? Would he give them the go-ahead? "We sat down for lunch," Devine remembers, "and the first words he said were, 'well, boys I don't think your future is at Virgin.' "

Alper proved to be right. At that fateful meal, he suggested

Hot Horror: Special effects like this one added to "The 7th Guest's" popularity.

they form their own company to develop the game they envisioned. He said that Virgin would help with start up costs, provided they didn't move more than 90 miles away. Alper added that the gaming giant would give Devine and Landeros a contract to publish the game, as long as they provided a multi-floppy disk version, as well as one on CD-ROM. The parties agreed, and the deal was struck.

Twenty-eight months and more than $750,000 later, Trilobyte, Devine and Landeros' fledgling company, delivered "The 7th Guest," a photo-realistic CD-ROM game with the thrills and chills of a horror movie. Set in a 3-D realistic haunted house, "The 7th Guest" bedevils players with puzzles and games, in each of the mansion's 22 rooms as they unravel the terrifying secrets of its bizarre owner, toymaker, Henry Stauf. A half hour of video with live actors, startling special effects, and a creepy rock soundtrack build suspense in a Gothic environment that hints at virtual reality.

Spiritual Allies: Trilobyte founders Graeme Devine, left, and Rob Landeros, right, shared a vision of computer games.

No wonder ACE Magazine warned, "Get ready to quiver behind the sofa," and PC Review raved, " 'Guest' will completely stun you." Microsoft chairman Bill Gates joined in the applause, hailing "The 7th Guest" as "the new standard in multimedia entertainment. This is the future." Within weeks of its spring 1993 release, "Guest" had become the top-selling computer game in the United States, a ranking it would keep for the rest of the year. By March 1994, worldwide sales of the game, with a suggested retail price of $99.99, topped 1.2 million.

With this ground-breaking achievement to their credit, Devine and Landeros look back on their "lunch of reckoning" and the months of often frustrating work on "Guest" with gallows humor. They laugh out loud when two details of their Virgin deal come up. What about that 90-mile limit, given that Trilobyte's home office is now in rural Medford, Oregon? No problem, they say, touting the clean air and arty population of the town, nestled in the Rogue River Valley 12 miles from Ashland.

As for the promised floppy disk version of "Guest," which ended up filling one CD-ROM and most of another. (That's a gigabyte of stored information or the equivalent of 3,000 360K conventional floppies!) "Well, actually, we were half convinced ourselves then that this could be a floppy," recalled the 28-year-old Devine. "At that point, we didn't have the details fleshed out. In fact, we had no idea that it would be two CD-ROM discs. That came as a shock."

Devine and Landeros had set out to push the boundaries of computer games, but they, and their cohorts, were surprised at the breakthroughs achieved in "The 7th Guest." "It ended up being a lot farther advanced than we originally intended," Devine said. "We planned on getting just so far ahead of everyone else. But, what we did in the end, was like throwing stakes out.... Ours went way off to the right. We were way out there, which is an interesting place to be."

Now, as they work on a sequel, the team once again is trying to look into the future of computer games. "I think we're beginning to merge with a lot of mainstream television, which is becoming our main competition," reflected the 45-year-old Landeros. "Television quality is what the consumer is beginning to expect. I think our job as entertainers is to tell stories. We'll probably experiment with various recipes to find what proportion is game playing and what proportion is pure, passive dramatic entertainment."

THE OPPORTUNITY: The Peak of Hi-Tech Horror

The broad outlines of "The 7th Guest" started to take shape over cups of bad airport coffee following a trade show in New York. As members of Virgin's research and development team, the subject of conversation was computer games. However, unlike their colleagues, who were wedded to Nintendo-type products, Devine and Landeros were determined to test the potential of CD-ROMs.

"Rob and I were talking about doing CLUE as a CD-ROM game, because Virgin had the license to that (board) game," Devine said. "Then we thought, no, no, no, what we really want to do is a cross between CLUE and 'Twin Peaks.' The first episode of 'Twin Peaks' had just aired, and the question on everyone's lips was 'Who killed Laura Palmer?' We thought, wouldn't it be great to do an interactive mystery of some kind with quirky ('Twin Peaks' director) David Lynch-type characters." More coffee; more brainstorming. "Then we thought, no, no, no. What we want to do is a

haunted house game, and we want David Lynch to do the story." Pause. "No, no, no. In the end, what we decided we wanted to do was a haunted house story with David Lynch overtones. And that's how we settled on the theme for 'The 7th Guest.'"

Next, the two producers decided on the tone and feel: cinematic. "At heart, the two of us wanted to make movies," said Devine, who calls "Guest" an interactive drama. "We were movie buffs. We would go to a movie and come out and discuss it like Siskel and Ebert." As they proceeded, their discussions were often connected to films. "We would reference a file by referenc-

ing a movie," Devine continued. "We would say we wanted a claustrophobic feel as in *Alien*, or *The Haunting of Hill House*."

From the initial concept, through scripting and composition of an original soundtrack, to the use of special effects similar to those

Movie-like Screens: Full-motion video and photorealistic settings add to the cinematic feel of the game.

in the *Terminator* movies, "the whole '7th Guest' had a cinematic approach," Devine said. That outlook also influenced the way the game is played; it is "more like controlling the action of a movie than playing an electronic game," according to Devine. Thus, players move in three dimensions through the photorealistic rooms, instead of simply scrolling the screen from side to side. "The difference is striking," he said.

In another departure from most computer games at that time, the Trilobyte team wanted "The 7th Guest" to be a PC game for the whole family, albeit a computer-savvy one, to play at home. "Even our mothers," Devine quipped. "We wanted to get close to something most people are used to, that is, single button clicking around on a television set as they go channel swimming—the most popular computer game out there." This approach meant simplifying "The 7th Guest's" puzzles, Devine said, "in contrast to the classic adventure where you have to pick up a brick out of the third cupboard on the right and use it four scenes later to get yourself out of the window.... And you can't go back to the cupboard to get the brick, so you have to reload the game. We were anxious not to get caught in a loop like this. That was one of the goals of 'The 7th Guest'—there would always be enough information in front of you to finish what there was in front of you."

This goal required some rules, "no inventory, no picking up of objects," for putting the game together. This resulted in some criticism. "People want that stuff; they want complexity," Landeros said. "They want to solve complicated puzzles.... There are certain expectations of what a computer game is supposed to be." To critics, who argue the game is too easy to play, Devine responds, "What we were trying to do was get the whole family involved— the teenage daughter as well as the 12-year-old son. And they sure as heck weren't going to sit around and play something complicated. I mean, the world's complicated enough."

THE DEVELOPERS: Trilobyte's Team

Graeme Devine, born in Scotland, published his first computer game when he was 12. The coin-operated title, written for Atari, was the now-classic "Pole Position" that entertained thousands of early gamers. However, Devine's public school teachers were not amused. "I took a week off to finish up the game. I was happy, and Atari seemed happy," he recalled. "I went back to school with a note. I didn't lie. I didn't say I had the flu, which I should have done. I took it into school, and they said very nice. You're expelled."

The incident didn't dampen Devine's enthusiasm for computer games. During most of the early- and mid-1980s, working as an independent contractor, or for other companies like Atari and Activision, or heading his own firm, IC&D, Devine was associated with more than a dozen titles including "Attack of the Killer Tomatoes," "Metropolis," and "War in Middle Earth." In 1987, he moved

The Trilobyte Team: The founders pose with their staff at their Oregon headquarters.

to the United States to join Virgin Games as a software manager, and eventually he became vice president of research and development.

It was at Virgin's Southern California offices that Devine met Rob Landeros. A California native, Landeros got turned on to computer games in 1983, when he got a Commodore 64. While eking out a living as a freelance artist, Landeros started programming on his Commodore, discovering "that the fun-est game to play was the one you programed yourself," and "that I enjoyed that more than the art I was doing." His vocation and avocation finally merged when he saw top computer artist Jim Sachs demonstrate the game he was creating for Cinemaware, "Defender of the Crown." "That's when I decided I could do that," Landeros recalled. "I quit my job, locked myself up, and came up with a small portfolio of computer art and sent it to Sachs and waited to see if he could get me some work." Instead, Sachs recommended Landeros for a post he had turned down, Cinemaware's art director. Two years later, in 1988, Landeros joined Virgin Mastertronic.

Working together, Devine and Landeros discovered they were on the same wavelength, especially when it came to a vision of the future of computer-based entertainment. Their dream of testing that vision with an interactive drama on CD-ROM led to the lunch with Martin Alper and the deal that set up their independent company, Trilobyte, in 1991.

The Trilobyte partners also were of like minds when it came to selecting a headquarters for their new enterprise. In the early 1980s, Landeros had lived in Ashland, Oregon, home of the renowned Shakespeare Festival. After a conference in San Jose, California, in December 1990, Landeros drove Devine there to take a look. "Ashland was okay," Devine said, "but it really didn't take my fancy. So we went to Jacksonville, because Rob had a cousin there and it was only ten miles down the road." The small town, one of eight historic cities in the state, is rich in history, commerce, culture, and recreation. When Landeros and Devine pulled in, the quaint community was in the midst of its holiday celebrations. "We stepped out of the car, and carolers gathered around and started singing.

And then Father Christmas goes by in a sled. There was someone roasting chestnuts on the corner and all these people dressed up in Victorian garb," Devine said. "I'm pretty attached to Main Street USA at Disneyland, so this immediately took my fancy."

"Actually it was the charm of it—that and not having to spend your life on a freeway in Southern California," Landeros said. "You can buy a house, you can have fresh air, you have seasons and a sense of community.... There's a sense of culture and there are resources to be tapped into...a lot of writers, artists, all kinds of interesting people."

By early 1991, Trilobyte had set up offices in a "quite grand" historic building. It had been a school before its renovation first as a residence for a railroad baron, then a professional office building. Like most multimedia developers, Devine and Landeros realized they could not produce their title alone. They evenually were joined by a team of programmers, office help, and freelance artists, but four men would be tapped to play critical roles in bringing "The 7th Guest" to life.

The first was horror writer Matthew Costello, who was asked to take Trilobyte's bare-bones idea and transform it into a script. The author of a series of horror novels for Berkeley Putnum, as well as the recently released "See How She Runs," Costello also was a game reviewer, who at one time was a contributing editor of GAMES Magazine. "Games have always been a part of my life," said the New York-based writer, "and I've always had a fantasy of someday being involved in a classy horror game." Contacted by Landeros, Costello initially was not too enthusiastic; after all, he had never heard of Trilobyte. The team gave him carte blanche in writing the story, and, as he worked for months on draft after draft, Costello realized the ambitious scope of the project.

To establish the game's cinematic photorealism, Devine and Landeros turned to Robert Stein III. This northern California artist, who studied at three different art schools, is perhaps best known for his distinctive watercolor drawings, which were featured in the mail-order catalogs for the Banana Republic stores in the 1980s. As that decade ended, he was working with Devine and Landeros

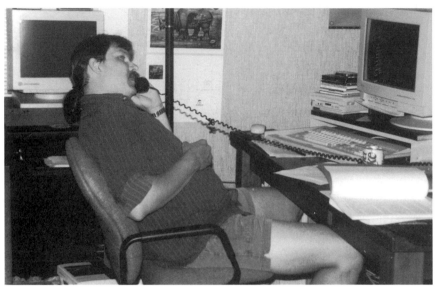

Principal Artist:
Robert Stein worked with the Trilobyte founders at Virgin Games before joining them to create "The 7th Guest."

at Virgin, where his artwork was featured on Amiga games including "Spirit of Excalibur" and "Vengeance of Excalibur." He also designed and animated IBM's "Spot, The Computer Game."

By 1991, Stein was eager to leave Los Angeles, and he took a job with Manley and Associates, a Seattle company producing cartridge games. "After five months, Rob and Graeme called and told me they were forming their own company and moving to Oregon," he recalled. "So I took a trip down (to see them). Back in Seattle, he altered a room he had begun drawing in 3D Studio as a test to suggest "Guest's" haunted house. "I modified the lighting and made the chair move mysteriously," he said, "and sent it down to them." A short time later, Devine and Landeros signed him on as principal artist of "The 7th Guest."

The third member of the team already had carved a specialized niche for himself in the growing computer games industry. George Sanger, better known as The Fat Man, is a nationally-recognized composer of computer game music. Among his 85 credits are the much-admired "Wing Commander I and II" and "Star Trek: 25th Anniversary." A former rock musician who admits he spent more time playing "Missile Command" and "Donkey Kong" than practicing music, The Fat Man is based in Austin, Texas. He remembers, vividly, the day he got a call from Devine. "Nothing has gone wrong for me since that phone call."

The final member of the team was David Luehmann, who served as Trilobyte's producer and liaison with Virgin. Like Landeros and Devine, Luehmann had worked on special projects for Virgin. His role during production of "The 7th Guest" was "...to organize the operation.... Graeme and Rob were really busy with the creative side; they just didn't have time for management tasks." Luehmann scheduled weekly Monday morning meetings to set to-do lists, resolve problems, and focus on areas of the production that needed special attention. Communications with Dr. Stephen Clarke-Willson, the Virgin staff producer initially assigned to the project, were sometimes slow and strained because of Clarke-Willson's demanding schedule and the distance between the two operations. "Our relationship with Virgin wasn't always the best, but for the most part, it was acceptable," said Luehmann, who is now working as a producer with Extreme Entertainment in the Bay Area.

In October 1992, 23-year-old Robb Alvey became Virgin's link to the project. A game player since his teen years, Alvey had worked for Disney Software and a couple of small Japanese Nintendo licensees before joining Virgin. The opportunity to work on "Guest" was a dream come true. "About a month before I joined Virgin, I was at the Chicago Consumer Electronics Show and went to a special sneak preview of 'The 7th Guest.' I saw the whole screening and played the game for about 25 minutes," he recalled. "And I thought, man, I'd give anything to work on a project like this. Then I come to Virgin and I'm told that I have to wrap up 'The 7th Guest.' I was pretty psyched." Since "Guest" was well underway when he came aboard, Alvey focused on the final stages of production, including the tedious compatibility and beta testing.

Normally, as a Virgin Games producer, Alvey would be involved with a project from its conception through its delivery to customers. "Let's say I have an idea," he explained. "I would get these people to do the graphics and these people

Psyched Producer: Working on "The 7th Guest" was a dream come true for Virgin producer Robb Alvey.

to do the programming. And, then I'd take the concept to upper management, pitch it and get it rolling, get the people in gear, and get them the equipment that they need. From there, I pretty much coordinate and organize every aspect of the project from its creative focus all the way through marketing, public relations, distribution, and manufacturing."

When working with developers, he prefers a team approach. "The relationship I build with my developers isn't, 'here, look at this; is it approved or not?' Everything that happens happens along a track that's already been approved. We all sit down, we all know what we want, and as long as we're going along that track, everything is fine."

In the months after Alvey came on board, production on "The 7th Guest" fell behind schedule, fueling some industry skepticism that the much-hyped game might be "vaporware" after all. "Since this was the first game of its kind, we weren't risking sales. But we didn't want to risk quality," Alvey recalled. "So the question was, 'Do we push it out there and have (customer) problems, or 'Do we sacrifice something in the game?' We decided to sacrifice time, and the game came out four months late."

The decision was typical of the high standards of quality and innovation set from the beginning by Landeros and Devine, as the game's chief designers. Costello recalls the collaborative effort "as the best creative experience of my life.... I wasn't prepared for how good this would be." "They gave me a lot of leeway," The Fat Man recalled. "They gave me a lot of support. They told me what they liked...and that sort of set up a direction. Then they let me do what I do." At the same time, "they were extremely quality-conscious and were very clear on the fact that they wanted to make a groundbreaking game," he added. "I think we all felt that. We never lost sight of it."

THE PRODUCTION: A Daunting Haunting

At each step of production, "The 7th Guest" team pushed into uncharted territory, starting with a script that was really an 84-page novella, rewritten more than a dozen times, through the integration of 26 minutes of full-motion video with a complex virtual 3D world, and ending with the manipulation of gigabyte-size files on a relatively small computer network. The process was draining artistically and financially, and, passing their self-imposed December 1992 deadline, the project was not completed until April 1993. In the end, the game Landeros and Devine had originally envisioned had doubled in size to fill two CD-ROMs—an industry first.

Scripting

When Landeros and Devine realized almost immediately that they needed a professional writer to flesh out their "haunted house story with David Lynch overtones," they found him, online, on a bulletin board. Landeros came across New York writer Matthew Costello who seemed perfect for the project. Not only were his horror novels—*Darkborn* and *Beneath Still Waters*—being compared to those of Stephen King, but he also had been a computer games reviewer and editor for GAMES Magazine. "He wrote me out of the blue," Costello recalled.

A Game Novelist: Scriptwriter Matthew Costello had a background in games and horror writing.

The Trilobyte partners provided Costello with the basic structure. "The directions were that there was a toymaker and a house with a room at the top that would hold the secrets of the toymaker. That was the premise," Costello said. "We also talked about a game that we both had played called 'Fool's Errand,' that incorporated puzzles into the matrix of the game." "About the most important thing we said to him, was that there were no constraints on what we could do," Devine remembers. "Just go for anything you want to do in the story, because there's nothing we can't do."

While so much creative freedom caught him off guard, "I didn't expect to have that much latitude," Costello said, he quickly drafted an 84-page novella. The story is about the eccentric Henry Stauf, a small-time hoodlum who becomes a wealthy toymaker after seeing a carved doll in a vision. Later on, he has a vision of a bizarre house, but when he begins to build it, children start to fall ill and die, clutching their Stauf dolls. Stauf closes his business and hides away in the room at the top of his mansion, plotting a way to live forever. As the game begins, six guests are invited to visit the house one stormy night. Each meets a dreadful end. The seventh guest (hence, the game's name) faces a similar demise, unless the player intervenes and foils Stauf's evil scheme.

With a linear story in place, Costello transformed it into a multi-layered interactive script, drawing on his experience writing several board and interactive role-playing games. "In an interactive script, you take the story line and select locations and dramatic scenes so

Storybook Beginning: The story of evil toymaker Henry Stauf sets the scene for "Guest's" games.

that the isolated events are linked together...and each scene has a beginning, middle and end throughout the story," he said. The game's action is based on triggers—"what you

click on, what you do, which puzzle you solve, whether you come back to a room you've already visited." For a player, the result is "...the illusion of freedom, that you are making choices, that you are free to go where you want to go. 'The 7th Guest' has that feel...there's no foot path you have to stay on.... There are many layers, many things that can happen."

Working out of New York, Costello express-mailed each version of the script to Trilobyte's Oregon offices. The long distance working arrangement was smooth, but finalizing the script was not. "It took months," Devine said. "We were in uncharted territory." Thirteen rewrites later, in collaboration with Landeros, all were happy with version 2.1. Rewrites and changes aside, Costello believes the free-wheeling partnership paid off. "It enabled us to get a lot of stuff on the table so that we could pick and choose."

Were Landeros and Devine able to incorporate all of Costello's ideas? "I put in special effects and, later on, they came back and said, 'That's ridiculous. We can't do that,'" Costello said, with a laugh. "Matthew would write about an evil mist making a flopping sound," said Devine, also laughing. "And we'd call him up and ask, 'what does an evil mist look like...and can you make a flopping sound for us.' He also had a lot of tentacles in there. They're tough to do in 3-D, so we had him cut some of them out." Ultimately, artist Stein admitted, Costello's story "was a bit too much for us to incorporate graphically, so we had to whittle it down significantly." Still, the Trilobyte team did manage to incorporate practically every sound effect Costello wanted.

Devine and Landeros' design called for games to be played and solved in every room of the mansion. But which games and puzzles? "We looked around as the game progressed for the various puzzles," Stein explained. "We found quite a few, but we couldn't use a number of them because of copyright problems. So we decided to refurbish and adapt old games without copyrights or to make up our own." Despite their goal of a "game for the whole family," most of the puzzles are devilishly difficult, and are presented, by design, to the player with very few visual or audio clues. For example, in the mansion's kitchen, a cupboard door opens, and players confront shelves of cans, each labelled with a single letter. When properly arranged they form a tongue-twisting sentence that probably has stumped any number of first-time players, and sent them running for help to the clue book in the mansion's library.

The games proved equally difficult to incorporate into "Guest's" storyline and 3-D environment. Stein noted, "We learned to keep the number of moving objects down in the puzzles," he said. "That kitchen puzzle became an astronomical number of moving pieces—something like five hundred renderings—since we had to render the cans moving out and into every possible position on the shelves."

The Soundtrack

Together, the Fat Man and his Team Fat have written over 85 themes for the computer game industry. But none has been as popular—or as technologically advanced—as their eerie soundtrack of "The 7th Guest." Since the game was released, the fifteen cuts with titles like "Dolls of Doom" and "Skeletons in My Closet" have become underground hits with gamers. "One guy E-mailed us that he plays it on his car CD on the way to work every morning," Devine said, with a chuckle.

Such success and cult status was a long time in coming for the lanky Texas native, known as George Sanger to the high school friends he wanted to impress twenty years ago, when he was "trying to be as cool as the Sex Pistols." Frustrated, when he attempted to be a rock music innovator only to find someone else had been there, done that already, he began to connect the rebel spirit of rock 'n' roll and the computer games he loved to play. "It occurred to me that the next big thing wasn't going to be a band," he said. "It was going to be something that kids have an inexplicable affinity for and parents can't understand. At the time, I was spending every moment I could playing 'Missile Command,' 'Donkey Kong,' and 'Asteroids,' and I thought, 'man, this has implications.'"

It did. Around 1981, Dave Worhall, a friend who worked for Mattel Intellevision, commissioned The Fat Man to write music for a game called "Thin Ice." When that company went under, so did the The Fat Man's career as a games composer until his brother's wedding seven years later, when he ran into Worhall again. This time Worhall, a producer for Nintendo, hired him to write music for the cartridge games. Those jobs proved to be a springboard for "Wing Commander" and other titles that are now well-known.

By this time, The Fat Man had hired three other musician-composers, Dave Govett, Joe McDermott, and K. Weston Phelan. All are "...folks who do miraculous work with ridiculous schedules," the Fat Man said. The Fat Man's wife acts as "mission control" for the group that vacations together and races Malibu Grand Prix cars together. "It's like a Monkeys' video all the time," The Fat Man quipped, with characteristic humor.

Devine, who had heard The Fat Man speak at a game developers' conference, recruited him for "The 7th Guest." As they did with Costello, the Trilobyte partners gave the composer minimal direction—a copy of the script with notes scribbled in the margins. "And when I started coming up with weird ideas, they went for them! If you came up with ideas like that for a normal company, they would say...you want what?" The Fat Man said. Devine and Landeros also agreed to take a chance with Roland Sound Canvas and General MIDI, both state-of-the-art, but unproven, computer sound hardware that is not widely available. All but four of the compositions on the soundtrack album are played solely on Sound Canvas, with no additional instruments and only minor signal processing. "I think the successful developers are the ones who can let the creative elements go to those who do it best—let go of the art, the music, the story and give them to people they respect," he said. "I think that's one of the strongest things Rob and Graeme have done."

Music Makers: The Fat Man, in the foreground, poses with members of Team Fat. From the left, they are David Govett, Joe McDermott, and K. Weston Phelan.

The Fat Man and Team Fat worked out of their studio in Austin, Texas, faxing, modem-ing, and FedEx-ing compositions and recordings to Trilobyte. The MIDI music was modemed through an online BBS, for review by the Jacksonville team. The Fat Man would rewrite, or write, some more until Devine and Landeros cried "Enough." "And I'd say, no, no, I gotta write more," The Fat Man recalled. "It's a really great relationship when you have each person saying, 'I haven't done enough for you.'"

The Fat Man believes that the music he writes for a game should "beef up the emotions when the user does something, or, more important, when the user doesn't do something. We drop giant hints on the player." To reinforce the interactivity, he continued, "the music should add to the sense that something has happened when the user is at that point." Not surprisingly, he argued the more music in the game, the better. "I've been writing a lot of looping pieces that are thirty seconds to a minute long. But, it's much more exciting to hear a surprise every three minutes than to hear it every thirty seconds."

While Trilobyte had agreed to house a soundtrack "album" on the second CD-ROM of the game, Virgin at one point considered recording the score as a musical CD. The Fat Man objected, unsure of the CD's audience. As the production wound down and the release date neared, however, the discussion proved almost moot. Unable to get the CD to work, Virgin executives wanted to drop the soundtrack album from the CD-ROM. While The Fat Man lined up expert help, Virgin's technicians agreed to try one more suggestion (Devine had offered this one two weeks earlier) and, just as they were about to give up, the problem was solved.

Interface Design and Navigation

Follow Me: Skeleton hands signal players in "The 7th Guest."

One of Trilobyte's missions, to keep "The 7th Guest" as non-computer as possible, is evident from the moment the game appears on the screen, minus the strip of activity buttons or controls that frame most of their competition. Instead, the player is greeted by a Ouija-type board, called The Sphinx, with controls for most game functions including loading, saving, and quitting.

Once inside the Stauf mansion, with its photorealistic rooms, players maneuver by moving the computer cursor around the screen. As it surveys each room for the "psycho-kinetic" hot spots, where puzzles and special effects lurk, the cursor changes into amusing, animated 3-D icons, created by Landeros to guide the player. For example, a skeleton hand wags its finger if there is no action at that spot, or beckons the player to move to the left, right or deeper into the house. When the player reaches a hot spot, the hand is transformed, depending upon the activity ahead. A drama mask signals a ghostly drama. A throbbing skull, reminiscent of your worst headache, means a puzzle to solve. Chattering teeth, like the windup toy, point to "supernatural" special effects. Finally, an Evil Eye engages the many games and puzzles hidden around the house.

As each puzzle is solved, the player gains access to additional rooms in the mansion. For those who are stumped by a particular brainteaser, there's a Book of Clues in the mansion library. Once all the puzzles are solved and Henry Stauf's secret is revealed, all the mansion's rooms remain open, and players can drop into any one and grapple with the puzzles again. At all stages in the game, players have access to a map of the mansion, accessed from The Sphinx board.

Devine's and Landeros' drive for mainstream appeal has frustrated some hard-core game players, who think the puzzles are too simple to solve. "So the game's easy to play," responded Devine. "Jeeze, that's a terrible thing to say. It's like my car is easy to drive; I don't like it." On the other hand, he admitted that novice players have complained about the difficulty of the puzzles and lack of clues. For them, he promised more online help to aid in solving the sequel's brain-teasers.

3-D Graphics

One hallmark of "The 7th Guest" is the realistic, richly colored 3-D interiors of the haunted mansion. Landeros and Devine originally had envisioned a very different look for the Stauf house: the rooms were to be photographed—in black and white. However, that was before they saw what Robert Stein, and a crew of crackerjack 3-D computer artists, could do.

The Trilobyte partners, in keeping with their cinematic vision, wanted to film an actual Victorian house in the murky style of old horror movies or classic film noir. Luckily, just the house they had imagined, the Victorian Nunan house, stood only two blocks from their office. "We went there and looked around," Devine said. "We were going to get one of those 360-degree cameras and photograph the rooms and use them to move around in. And looking back on it, it would have been wiser to do that because we possibly could have finished on time."

Devilish Cursor:
The game's ghostly icons were created by Rob Landeros

Devine changed his mind when Stein showed him a prototype Victorian room created in Autodesk's 3D Studio. With Stein on board as lead artist, "The 7th Guest" became a major 3-D project and the Nunan house was relegated to the "inspiration" for the haunted house on the game's cover. In retrospect, Devine observed, "if we originally were going to do a 3-D game, we would have chosen a space game. It's a lot easier to do a spaceship in 3-D than a Gothic Victorian house. But we were so taken with the 3-D effects with 3D Studio that we decided to go that route."

As Stein began creating the Stauf mansion's 22 rooms, he knew the job was too big for one person. Landeros quickly joined in, and after some lessons in 3D Studio from Stein, the Trilobyte founder was soon modeling rooms, designing puzzles and creating the 3-D pointers—the throbbing skull and skeleton hand—that are now one of the game's hallmarks. The two partners had planned on animated icons and had assigned a staff artist to design them in a 2-D animation program. "When I saw one, I said, 'let me try that in 3D Studio,'" Landeros said. "We had a model of a skeleton's hand, and I made an index finger with joints so that it would move. It worked out so well, that I realized that we should do all of the icons that way. It was faster. I did that in a matter of hours."

Detailed 3-D: A team of four computer artists created the Stauf mansion's 22 rooms.

Landeros' favorite pointer is the pulsing brain inside a skull. "That didn't take long either," he recalled. "I had a skeleton, so I just chopped off the top of the skull, made this brain, and scaled it up and down to create the throbbing. I already had the eyeballs, and I put those in and rotated them." Using body parts worked well until "...no more icons—all out of parts," he remembered, with a laugh.

Stein focused on the most difficult settings, including the foyer, hallways, dining room, kitchen, library, bathroom, attic stairs, and the game's climatic death scene. He also orchestrated most of the special effects, like the head morphing out of the soup and the hands coming out of the painting. The modeling for the games was divided between Stein, Landeros, and John Gaffey, who also did some of the 2-D work, like the spiders on the foyer's stained-glass door. Three other 3-D specialists from around the country were hired, "Guest" contractors, Gene Bodio and Phil LeMarbre of Boston, and Alan Iglesias of San Diego. They too were given few guidelines for drawing their assigned rooms, a task that could take more than a month for just one interior. "We tried to hire people that had experience and were self-directing," said Stein. "It's hard to find people who work well without supervision. They either go too far, or not far enough. We were lucky to find a good group of competent people."

As the house began to take shape on computer screens, the Trilobyte partners once again changed direction, opting for color instead of black and white. "The black and white version looked really good and spooky," Devine recalled. "When something supernatural happened, like the plant growing in the music room,...it would go from black and white to color and do its ghostly thing. All the actors walking through the house were in color, too. In the end, it would have looked very good, I think."

As with the earlier change of plans, the impressive 3D Studio graphics were a decisive factor. "We became so enthralled with the 3-D background, so attached to them," Devine explained, "that we had to include the color as well." Another reason for the switch was Devine's invention of a program that compressed color images better than those in black and white. "A lot of compression is based on what the human eye can actually see, and Graeme's compression scheme takes away the parts of an image that make the least difference to the viewer," Landeros said. "While these things we do, like compression schemes, are transparent to the user, it is this kind of technology that keeps us ahead of the competition."

To make the transition, Devine also created a proprietary palette management program they called Psychic Palette to maintain color quality throughout the mansion. (Originally named Cyclic Palette, Devine changed it to "physic" because it "looks a few frames ahead and decides what colors it's going to need.") "If you go from a downstairs room, which is basically blue, to a upstairs area that is basically yellow, we had to change the palette to get a good looking image at all times," he said. But as observant game players will notice, there are artifacts of the original concept in the finished "The 7th Guest." "Look around the foyer—all the pictures on the wall are black and white," Devine said.

Both decisions, while key to the game's photorealism, ultimately slowed down production by presenting the team "with problems we weren't prepared for," Devine said. One was the size of Autodesk 3D Studio .3DS files that eventually led Landeros to set specifications for the 3-D contractors. "We had to write a rule book for them," he explained. "These guys were used to just making still images from .3DS files, like a picture or photograph for a hard copy output. They weren't considering that we were going to be making movies out of them. They would make very complicated, high resolution images with a bunch of reflection maps. Some of the files were over 20 megabytes, and just one frame would take 45 minutes to render. So I had to make rules like mesh objects could only have a certain amount of polygons and that we wanted just some 256 colors, not just 24-bit texture map bitmaps."

As the rooms were rendered, Devine noticed "you begin to pick up on the styles in each of the rooms. I could tell who had done what room. Rob uses one set of colors and different textures and Alan Iglesias would use all red and green and had very heavy, big pieces of furniture in his rooms. There's as definite a style in 3-D art as there is in 2-D art."

3-D Artist Alan Iglesias

Alan Iglesias' first contact with Graeme Devine came at the suggestion of a fellow CompuServe user. The computer artist had accidently rendered a 640 x 480 FLI animation file, and, since it was in the days before Animator Pro, there were no off-the-shelf programs to play such a large file. "I got on the CompuServe forum...for the first time...and asked 'is there any way to play it?' and somebody came back and said, 'call this guy Graeme.' So I did," Iglesias remembered. Devine responded by sending Iglesias his Play program, the forerunner to his player program for "The 7th Guest." "Sure enough it worked," Iglesias said.

Introduced to Iglesias' work on a promotional tape for 3D Studio, the Trilobyte partners asked to see more. In early 1991, they asked him to try his hand at a "classic Victorian spooky house," and if they liked it, more work would follow. With only some Xeroxes of Victorian furniture and a description of the room's layout sent from Trilobyte, Iglesias researched the period decor and architecture before rendering his sample room. "They liked it very much," said Iglesias, who wound up working on "Guest" for more than a year, off and on. "One of the best things about working with Trilobyte was the fact that they gave me almost any artistic license I wanted."

Alan Iglesias: This San Diego computer artist worked on "The 7th Guest" interiors for more than a year.

In the end, Iglesias modeled, texture-mapped, and lit, five rooms in the Stauf mansion. He also helped out in other areas of the house, drawing furniture in the foyer and utensils in the kitchen. As he progressed, he sent rendered views to his Oregon bosses, and followed up with phone calls. "They would change stuff here and there; some rooms look exactly the way I gave them to them, other ones are a little different," he said. "When they liked it, I threw what I wanted onto a backup tape and sent it up to them, maps, project files and everything." He was paid a fee, agreed upon in advance, for each room.

3-D Bedroom: File size was a problem on this and other detailed rooms by artist Alan Iglesias

The most difficult part of his assignment was visualizing the rooms, a task that grew easier as he went along. "The last room I did was the Martine Burden room, and by that time, I had it down. Probably the best furniture I ever did is in that room; great wall paper too," Iglesias said. "Best work" was exactly what the Trilobyte team demanded, but they also wanted manageable file sizes and early on the two goals didn't mesh. "One reason the files initially turned out so big was because everybody was trying so hard," he said. "Later on in the project, you learned that you could do your absolute best work and still be as economical as possible."

Since his work on "The 7th Guest," Iglesias said, he's had "offers to work every other day. I'm turning stuff down left and right. It takes something like this to get your name out." So far he's rejected offers to move to both coasts and points in between, opting instead to work for a Colorado game company from his home in San Diego. He's still high on the success of "Guest." "If I were making my living as guitar player," he said, "it would be like getting my first hit."

Video

Another ground-breaking feature of "The 7th Guest" is the movie-like video scenes composited over the photorealistic 3-D world of the Stauf mansion. Unlike many games that confine video to a small window on the computer screen, video in "The 7th Guest" fills the screen in high-resolution 640x480 VGA mode, adding to the desired cinematic feel. Production of the necessary SVHS sequences, however, proved tricky, especially to the inexperienced Trilobyte team. Ultimately, it pushed the production even further behind schedule.

Trilobyte hired two local companies to produce the movie segments. Image Grafx was picked to shoot the video, and The Rogue River Motion Picture Company was to supervise the six-day production, including the auditioning of local actors to play Stauf and his seven doomed guests. While there was no shortage of actors—nearby Ashland is home to an internationally renowned Shakespeare Festival—none knew what to expect at a video shoot for a computer game. "At least they had a script, which was something they could relate to," said Devine.

Since the video was to be superimposed over the already-created 3-D interiors, the actors were positioned on a Chroma Key set, a blue backdrop and props that "drop out" when composited with the computer graphics to allow the 3-D rooms to appear. For example, if a character was to appear to be sitting on a bed in one

Blue Shoot: Use of the wrong color blue backdrop during the video shoot added hours of work for the Trilobyte team.

of the mansion's rooms, the actor was filmed sitting on a box shaped like the bed and painted blue. This kind of set, typical of feature films loaded with special effects or animation, is a challenge for actors, who must visualize where they are in relationship to an invisible 3-D world. In addition, they were required to exaggerate movements and facial expressions. "Because of the video compression we would use, and the fact that the

actors would be (reduced) and appear pretty small at this resolution; we needed them to use lots of body language in their acting, much like in the theater," said Stein. "It came out well, but a little on the corny side."

Landeros and Devine agree. Because of their lack of video experience, the partners gave the production company a free hand. However, in retrospect, they believe they didn't exercise enough control. As a result, the game lacks some of the arty quirkiness they were shooting for. "It was good that we didn't run the show because we wouldn't have been much help anyway," Devine said. "It was bad because we lost a little bit of the vision along the way. We definitely lost the 'Twin Peaks' feel in the acting. The video shoot is closer to a '20s' movie than the feeling we were trying to get."

In the end, the acting turned out to be the least of their problems with the video. "A big, big important lesson," emphasized a rueful Devine, "is when you use a blue screen, make sure that it is the right blue—chroma blue—and not the two shades of cobalt blue we used." "And don't shoot it in SVHS or Hi-8," added a sadder, but wiser Landeros. "It's way too dirty for a project like this. Now we know to use Beta SP or 35mm film." Both mistakes added hundreds of hours to an already over-extended production schedule.

Monumental Cleanup: Unwanted pixels had to be removed from 30,000 frames of video before it could be superimposed over 3-D graphics.

As the background for the video shoot was the wrong blue, a red shift occurred during the digitizing process, making it necessary to clean unwanted pixels out of more than 30,000 frames of video—a monumental task. The task of digitizing fell to Stein, who used a Panasonic AG-7750 SVHS VTR and a Targa Plus 64 board in

a 486/33 computer to transform the SVHS footage into 24-bit JPEG files. He digitized about 1,000 frames at a time, working only at night, because the cleanup team needed his computer during the day. Then they converted the JPEG files into 256-color GIF files, imported them into Autodesk's Animator Pro, and stripped out most of the unwanted blue background using a special routine Devine developed for POCO. Any pixels that POCO missed had to be cleaned out by hand.

"Given the time and money, it would have been cheaper to reshoot," Devine said. Instead, he and Landeros opted to reduce the video from 44 minutes, as originally planned, to 26 minutes. "Maybe, some day we'll release 'The 7th Guest: The Director's Cut'," he added, with a chuckle.

Audio

After playing "The 7th Guest" for an afternoon, certain phrases are bound to echo in they player's mind. For instance, the reverberating "Are you Looooonely?" taunts players at a dead end in the basement maze. By the time they exit, that mocking voice reverberates in their minds.

Landeros says the same thing happens to his crew at Trilobyte. "There are certain catch phrases that keep popping up around the office," he laughingly admitted. That sound effect, he explained, grew out of an afternoon of improvising at a recording studio. "We went there with the actor that plays Stauf (Robert Hirschboeck) and a list of phrases, and we would say 'try this one,'" he said. "There was a lot of improvisation from the actor and from us in the control room."

Were they having fuuuuuun? Landeros paused, then replied, "There were moments of fun, but most of it was work. If we were having fun, we didn't know it at the time."

Speaking of Stauf, the late Vincent Price was Trilobyte's first choice as narrator. "We negotiated with him and his initial price was reasonable," Stein said. "Then his agent tripled the price. And we had to get Virgin and Nintendo to split the cost with us. Nintendo would do it, but Virgin wouldn't. So we didn't get Vincent Price. Now he's passed on and that's too bad."

Image Processing

As all the components of "The 7th Guest" came together in Trilobyte's Ashland office, Devine and Landeros should have been celebrating. Instead, they remember the closing months of 1992 and early 1993 as "a very depressing time for us all." Missing their self-imposed deadline of December 1992 strained the young company financially. The size of the game they were creating burdened their staff and inadequate computer system. "Those were dark and gloomy days," Devine said. "There was a big tunnel there, and there was no light at the end of it."

Stein rendered the 3D Studio, .3DS files of the mansion, and special effects to TGA files, and then converted them to JPEG to save hard disk space and time. It was grinding work. It took 40 seconds to grab, JPEG and save each frame, enabling him to capture only 2,000 frames in a 24-hour period. "We used a series of batch files that would tell the VTR to do a pre roll, so that it rolls back five seconds on the tape, and then rolls forward and captures the frame. Then we used Image Alchemy to JPEG the frame and compress it. The batch file deletes the original Targa and moves the JPEG file somewhere else....That whole process takes 40 seconds." Devine wrote elaborate batch file programs to automate as much of the process as possible. By the time they finished, Devine boasted, "We are the king of batch files. We've even thought about writing a book on how to write batch files."

Devine's VDX tool basically compressed the files, did pallet calculations, overlaid the video, created fades and transparencies, and combined sound files. The team usually worked on 30 to 100 frames at a time. Manipulating the huge files took its toll on production time. "It slowed us down a lot," stressed Devine. "We were generating thousands and thousands of these frames. When Trilobyte started, we had a 500-megabyte hard drive on our server, and by the time we finished, we had six gigabytes across our entire network. We were growing from where we had no network, to a small network, to a large sophisticated network. We had no network experience before that."

As the production neared the end, file size and file management were the biggest problems, according to Landeros. "We were transferring gigabytes up and down the line from one machine to the next," he said. "Then we would send them back down. It took a lot of time compressing frame-by-frame, and every frame had to be processed at least three different ways." "The other great problem was keeping track of it all," admitted Devine. "We had to back-up systems, label cassettes, and log them using sensible names."

Finishing Throes: Special effects, like the two below, were rendered in Trilobyte's Oregon offices.

The seemingly impossible job of keeping the complex project moving and organized fell to "7th Guest" producer Dave Luehmann. Working from a progress chart for each room, Luehmann devised a to-do checklist and went over it with the technical crew each morning, making certain each task was assigned. He even ended up doing a little bit of everything himself. "Graeme and Rob were really

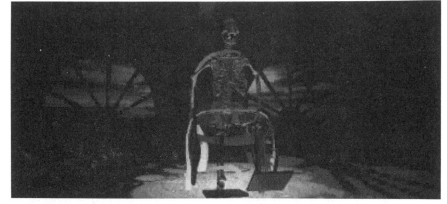

busy on the creative side and just didn't have time for management tasks," Luehmann said. "I would get all that in-hand and then get involved with scripting one of the rooms or sometimes answering the phones—whatever I thought needed a little extra attention."

As each of the large VDX files was finished, logged, backed-up, and stored, every major player on the crew began the interactive authoring process using a scripting tool, called GROOVIE, also of Devine's design. Each programmer was assigned a segment of the game to script. When a segment was finished, Luehmann, Devine, and Landeros checked it, and assigned the scripter another segment until, at last, the game was ready to be tested.

But that was then. For the sequel, "The 11th Hour," the Trilobyte team is using video techniques and off-the-shelf software tools that have simplified production. Needless to say, all of the video was shot in Beta SP with the proper chroma blue backdrop; then it was transferred to a videodisk for digitization. "The quality of digitization from Beta is hundreds and hundreds of percent better" emphasized Devine. The production team then used Adobe Premiere to convert the digitized video into QuickTime movies. Each is about three minutes long and weighs in at a hefty 700 megabytes. "Nowadays Adobe Premiere does the Chroma Key work as well," pointed out Devine. In Premiere, they added the audio track and then compressed the movies using Trilobyte's own QuickTime compression CODEC, VDX. The authoring still was accomplished with GROOVIE, via a Novell network of twelve 486s and three Quadras with nearly five gigabytes of storage.

Although some of Devine's ground-breaking proprietary software has been replaced by easier-to-use and more advanced off-the-shelf varieties, he continued to advance the proprietary tools they still use. Among the store-bought software used in the production now at Trilobyte is Adobe's Premiere and Photoshop, Autodesk's 3D Studio and Animator Pro, Paint Alchemy, PhotoStyler, and Altimira Composer. For projects after "The 11th Hour," Trilobyte will do its 3-D work with the same software and hardware used to create the special effects in the film *Jurassic*

Park, according to Stein: "We just purchased three seats on Alias software which was the high-end software used to do *Jurassic Park*. When you purchase this high end stuff, you buy it by the seat because you can't just buy a box of software and let everybody in the office run on it. They've got a protection program so that it only works on one machine at one time, to make sure you pay for everyone that is using it. This software costs $30,000 a pop."

Testing

With the labor-intensive production behind them, the Trilobyte team faced a lengthy, laborious testing period that, Devine said, "raised the silliest issues—but we addressed them all. It took bloody forever." In addition to consumer testing, "The 7th Guest" faced computer compatibility tests and debugging procedures that often went on around the clock, for days at a time.

Both Virgin and Trilobyte rounded up people of all ages to play the game to evaluate playability, interfaces, and puzzles. "Where we had problems was with the puzzles," Devine recalled. For example, in the mansion's dining room, players are challenged to remove pieces of cake to leave behind five contiguous pieces with the right mix of scary decorations on the frosting. "Initially, for that puzzle, you had to draw out the route to the piece of cake you wanted to get," he explained. "We didn't find that hard because we knew what we were doing. But we lost some people who looked at the puzzle and couldn't get what was going on. So we changed the puzzle to match what the players actually expected."

Alvey said that the majority of customer complaints are about not being able to get the game to work. "That's because it's a high-end product and we realize that it's just not going to work on all PCs," he explained. Virgin hired several outside testing firms to run

GROOVIE Programmer: Graeme Devine's scripting tool, GROOVIE, was used in the authoring process.

the game on 60 to 70 different PC configurations. "But PCs are really like a hacker's dream come true," he continued. "The parts come from all over the world. It's hard for us to sit down and say this is going to work on this PC, because they're all different." In addition to the outside testing, Alvey said he "literally had people

Not a Piece of Cake: Testing showed some players didn't know how to solve the cake puzzle.

testing the game 24-hours a day. Toward the end of the project, in early April, there was a period of two to three weeks straight where I and a team of four other people basically slept here. We had sleeping bags, pillows and blankets." Up in Jacksonville, Devine was pulling all-nighters, too, fixing the faults that Alvey and his testers found and modeming the changes to Virgin's offices. "We went through something like 80 discs that we had to burn, and that process, from the time we'd get a revision from Graeme, until we could make a new disc, takes about an hour. That's when we would sleep."

Despite the compatibility review, when the game was finally released, Virgin's customer service lines were jammed with calls. Alvey attributes the overload on the vast number of "Guest" sales, as compared to the company's previous PC titles. "When we had PC titles that were selling about 70,000 units, we only needed four or five customer service people," he said. "But with '7th Guest' selling 700,000 units and more, we had to quadruple our staff." To this day, Virgin's troubleshooters get an assist from "Guest's" creators. "We're both on CompuServe and GEnie every night talking to customers. And we have another employee here who is on America Online," Devine said. "It's taken a good deal of time."

MARKETING: By Word of Mouth

From the beginning, Virgin Games never had high expectations for Trilobyte's CD-ROM game. After all, Devine and Landeros were on their own because the publisher had very little faith in the future of this new technology. "They would cite Commander CD-TV and its miserable sales, and the Philips CD-I system and it's miserable non-appearance, and they would say it's never going to work," Devine recalled. But that was before "The 7th Guest's" record-setting sales. "Now, we're their heroes," chortled Landeros.

In many ways, the game's success reflects the growing popularity multimedia has with consumers. Before "The 7th Guest" appeared on the market, the sales leader among CD-ROM games was "Sherlock Holmes," which had been released three years earlier by Icom Simulations (which was acquired by Viacom), and it had sold only 35,000 units. Since then, the number of home computers with CD-ROM drives had climbed steadily, building demand for CD-ROM titles. At the same time, anticipation of Trilobyte's game had grown to a fever-pitch among avid game players as a result of trade-show previews and well-placed computer magazine promos. "Because of the word-of-mouth on this game—the hype was so strong that we could have put the game in a brown paper bag and it would have sold," Alvey observed in retrospect.

In advance of the game's release, though, Virgin's marketing plans and the funds allocated for packaging and promotion were modest at best. "We had a pretty strict budget," Alvey said. "We were looking at a CD-ROM game...and the CD-ROM market out there just isn't that big. What we were hoping was to sell 70,000 units at the most. So we were thinking, we could spend $10 on the box for the game, but do we really want to do that. It was a big question." At the same time, as production of "The 7th Guest" slipped further and further behind schedule, skepticism within the company—and within the industry—mounted. "For a while, 'The 7th Guest' was really the stealth project from Virgin," Alvey said. "Here are these guys in Oregon. Were they going to pull through? Was 'The 7th Guest' going to be a reality or was it going to be Virgin vaporware? Everyone was telling us, it will never be done; it will never work."

By early 1993, as the game came together, Alvey said "it was almost too late to go back and rethink a lot of things," like the packaging. By the time he was assigned to the project, Virgin and

Trilobyte had agreed to house the two CD-ROMs in a clear jewel case in a box with a four-color sleeve featuring the haunted mansion and other scenes from the game. "Actually, the box cover turned out to be really nice," Alvey said, "but the jewel case I was really disappointed with because there's no cover or anything on it. That could have been a lot better." In contrast, he said, for its release in Great Britain, "The Seventh Guest" is tucked in a box with a maroon cover and gold lettering that resembles "a leather-bound book from the late '40s, or early '50s." Inside are "pages" with illustrations of the toymaker and his doll and the jewel case that holds the CDs and the instruction manual. Opposite that is gatefold, with a picture of a door that opens to reveal a brief video on the making of "The 7th Guest."

Two Jewels: For the game's release in Great Britain, the plain jewel case of the U.S. version had been replaced with more sophisticated artwork.

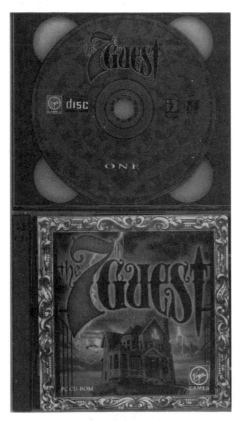

Alvey admits that the video, packaged with the U.S. version as well, was completed and included "as an afterthought," another victim of the hope and skepticism about the game. "In the production stage, we knew we wanted to do something with it, but we didn't know what," he explained. Shot at the last minute, the 15-minute tape is a hodgepodge of interviews with Devine and Landeros, Costello, and The Fat Man that has added to the cult status of all four, while adding "value" for game purchasers.

In the end, the tight budget and muddled marketing did not present a problem. "We were really lucky that the hype on it was so much that we really didn't need to spend the extra money on marketing when it was pretty much self-marketing," Alvey said. That is not unusual, he added, since, compared to their cartridge games, most PC games sell themselves: "For a cartridge product, you have to put in a couple of million dollars to make people notice. For a PC product, it's always a lot less, because it's much cheaper to manufacture and there are so few really awesome games out there.... For a PC game, we put in a quarter- to a half-million dollars for advertising and marketing. And that's really all that's needed, because the audience is much older and there's not that much competition."

In the months after "The 7th Guest" was unveiled, a new wave of anticipation began to build, this time for the Mac version of the game, finally released in December 1993. "We were going to run some special ads, but it was so highly anticipated...that we decided just to put it out there," Alvey said.

Distribution

Given the anticipation surrounding Trilobyte's first title, Virgin's sales force had no trouble placing it with major retail and mail order outlets. Within days after its release, many stores were sold-out and calling to reorder. By the end of 1993, U.S. sales alone had topped 700,000, a record for a CD-ROM game.

While its consumer sales were booming, Virgin executives also wanted to capitalize on the game's success to boost sales of CD-ROM players and thus expand the market for future CD-ROM entertainment titles. "We really wanted to make a product that would sell CD-ROM hardware," Alvey said. "There's so much potential, but people didn't understand what a CD-ROM does, what is the extra added value." As a result, Virgin packaged "The 7th Guest" with the Fusion System, an advanced CD-ROM drive, speakers and sound card put together by MediaVision. By late fall, Alvey estimated that deal had resulted in 150,000 to 200,000 additional sales of Trilobyte's game. "It benefits Virgin, but I think it benefits the entire market," said Alvey who anticipated similar bundling arrangements with hardware in the months to come. "People look at that and say, 'man, this is what a CD-ROM can do.' They want to see full-motion video, to hear Red Book audio, to see incredible graphics. It's unlike anything else that's ever been out there before."

The "bundling" relationship is being recognized independently by some retailers as well. "This is a funny example," Alvey said, "but my dad just bought a new PC that came with a CD-ROM drive from Montgomery Ward. And Montgomery Ward themselves,

Word of Mouth: Comments from industry leaders like Bill Gates helped build interest in the game.

This is the new standard in multimedia entertainment. This is the future."

Bill Gates, Chairman of Microsoft describing Virgin Games CD-ROM Interactive Drama™ The 7th Guest

The 7th Guest
PC CD-ROM

without a deal with Virgin, just bundled '7th Guest' with their system.... It's a game that buyers out there are recognizing will help them sell their hardware." And one game can make all the difference, Alvey believes. "The chairman of Software Etc. told us that ever since 'The 7th Guest' shipped, their CD-ROM hardware sales have gone through the roof."

At the same time, Virgin has relied on its international sales force to place "The 7th Guest" in foreign markets. By the end of 1993, the game could be purchased in France, Germany, and Great Britain, where it has become the largest selling PC CD-ROM game in history—a considerable achievement given that the Amiga is the computer of choice there. Virgin has offices in all those countries, as well as in Japan, where the game became available in late 1993.

FINANCE: Partners with Partners

As business partners, Virgin and Trilobyte started off on a firmer, more equal footing than most game developers and their producer-publishers do. The Trilobyte partners had been valued employees at Virgin and had extensive backgrounds in game development. As a result, they were given a fairly free rein by their former employers to create the company's first CD-ROM title, and enough start up money and equipment to launch their enterprise. As a result, the two companies consider the game a joint venture and share equally its copyright and profits.

The Virgin funding, estimated at $350,000 to 400,000, kept Trilobyte in operation for the first half of the 28 months it took to produce "The 7th Guest." Landeros and Devine financed the remaining half, with considerable help from the giant Japanese game maker Nintendo. "They saw the game early on, when we were at the halfway point—or what we thought then was halfway—and they gave us some cash," Devine said. At that time, Nintendo was planning to develop a new state-of-the-art games platform and wanted to ensure "The 7th Guest" would be available for play on it. Subsequently, Nintendo announced a partnership with Silicon

Graphics Inc. to produce Project Reality, a high-powered, low-priced 64-bit gaming system by late 1995.

Even with the influx of cash from Nintendo and underwriting from Virgin, Landeros and Devine found themselves strapped for money when they failed to finish "The 7th Guest" by December 1992. "We were pretty dependent upon finishing the game on time," Devine said. "And we didn't finish until April." "Actually, we ran out of money toward the end," Landeros admitted. To survive those bleak times, "...we counted our pennies," he said, "and we cross-collateralized (front money) from 'The 11th Hour' to keep us going."

The game's success has resulted in "a very secure environment at Trilobyte," Devine said. After expenses, the two firms split any profits on the game. Trilobyte in turn pays previously agreed upon royalties to Costello, The Fat Man, and Stein. For the composer and script writer, those payments are in addition to the flat fees they charged for their services. "God forbid the royalties don't work out, at least we get something for our work," explained The Fat Man, who also keeps the copyright for his compositions, but grants a producer exclusive use of them for a number of years. For a model, Costello looks to the book publishing industry, where authors typically receive 10% to 15% royalties. "A writer should ask for it, but in this industry, everyone's just finding their way," he added.

After production of a sequel to "The 7th Guest," Trilobyte plans to self-publish their next title. Why are they going out on their own? "Why does a dog lick his balls?" Landeros replied, meaning that they are venturing out on their own because they can.

FUTURE PROJECTS: A Sequel with David Lynch Overtones

After a project as arduous as "The 7th Guest," "anyone in their right mind would have taken a vacation," said Devine, with a knowing laugh. Not the Trilobyte partners. Instead, they went right back to work, not on one, but on two projects.

The first is a sequel to "The 7th Guest," called "The 11th Hour," slated to be finished by fall, 1994 and housed on three CD-ROM discs. In addition, the Trilobyte partners planned a simultaneous release of the new game in versions for the Mac, 3DO and CD-I.

As developed by Costello and other members of "Guest's" creative team, "The 11th Hour" returns to the Stauf mansion more than a half a decade later. Many residents of the surrounding town have secrets connected to the mansion that eventually take them inside the abandoned, crumbling haunted house. "The 11th Hour" begins with a 5–10-minute video introduction and then moves to game playing inside the rooms of the house. However, the story is more linear; the game, more thought-out. "Plus it is 300 times more interactive," Landeros said.

By fall of 1993, all of the video—a total of 66 minutes compared to "Guest's" 26 minutes—had been shot. The video will play full screen at 30 frames a second, Landeros pointed out, "...because Graeme has vastly improved his player. For 'The 7th Guest,' the digitized actors move about a static room so that 90% of the screen remains the same, but to show full movies where all the pixels are moving frame by frame, you need some kind of tremendously clever compression. Trilobyte games will support the video accelerator boards that are coming out, but they will eventually play on computers without the boards." As a result, "The 11th Hour" "is a bigger project than anticipated," he admitted. "It was originally designed to be quick and dirty—just knock it out, and capitalize on the work we did on 'Guest.' But there were things we just wanted to do, like bumping the speed up to 30 frames per second and having more than an hour's worth of video. We just can't help ourselves."

The second project in the works—Trilobyte's first self-published title—is a closely guarded secret. The partners are willing to tell only what it won't be. "It won't be 'The Seventh Guest,' part III," Devine said emphatically. "And it won't be in the horror genre. We're through with that for the time being." "We have our own ideas about what we want to do as an entertainment company,"

Next, A Sequel: Instead of taking a break after finishing "The 7th Guest," the Trilobyte duo went to work on a sequel, "The 11 Hour."

Landeros added. "I think as entertainers, our job is to tell stories. And I think that's the way we want to approach it. But we will probably experiment with various recipes, what proportion is game playing and what proportion is for pure dramatic presentation."

2

WHO KILLED SAM RUPERT?

Creative Multimedia
& InterMagic

At A Glance

"WHO KILLED SAM RUPERT?"

Developers: Creative Multimedia Corporation and InterMagic/Shannon Gilligan.

Personnel: Shannon Gilligan, director, writer and producer; John Calhoun, publisher; Chen-Chi Yuan, executive producer; Phil Marshall, programmer; David Zahn and Anci Slovak, art direction; Christine Goulet, associate producer, video; Gene Regan, software engineer; Collin Bremner, applications engineer; and Steve Munger, quality assurance.

Description: An interative virtual murder mystery on CD-ROM in Macintosh and PC-Windows versions.

Development hours: 6,640.

Development period: Macintosh: January 1992–November 1992; PC conversion: December 1992–April 1993.

Development hardware: Macintosh FX, Macintosh IIFX, Quadra 700, 486/33 PC.

Development software: MacroMind Director, QuickTime 1.1, Photoshop Premier, 2.0, VideoShop, Morph Software, Windows Player.

Cost to develop: $55,000.

Financing: Creative Multimedia Corporation.

Suggested retail price: $39.99.

U.S. distributors: All major software and superstore retail locations and mail order catalogs.

Foreign distributors: Europe: MacZone/PCZone; Computer Bookshop, Ltd.; Kimtec. Mexico: MacZone. Canada: BeamScope; Future Shop. Australia: G&V Advance Electronics. Asia: MacZone; Twilight Express; Dycro, Inc.

Awards: Award of Excellence, gold medal for best adult game, gold medal for best production design, and silver medal for best story/script; *NewMedia* INVISION Awards.

Future projects: "The Environmental Surfer."

Contact: Bill Kelly
              Creative Multimedia Corporation
              514 N. W. 11th Ave., Suite 203
              Portland, OR 97209
              503–241–4351
              503–241–4370 (fax)

It was Sam Rupert's last wine tasting. When it was over, the handsome restaurateur was laid out on his wine cellar floor, flatter than day-old French champagne. A single drop of blood is the first clue that this is going to be a vintage murder case. Whodunit? His jealous wife, or his ambitious mistress? The greedy bartender recently caught skimming the till? The customer who stormed out of his posh eatery earlier that evening? The prima donna chef in a stew over contract negotiations? The press is clamoring for details. The police chief wants the clever perp yesterday. In fact, he's given his new investigator—you—only six hours to find the bad guy, or find a new career.

The clock is ticking. You return to the scene of the crime, hungry for clues. You interrogate likely suspects, squirming as you glance at your watch. You get your hands on the autopsy report, on Sam's diaries, on the restaurant's reservation list for the night Sam sipped his last. Time is running out. A mob of reporters demands to know who killed Sam Rupert. With seconds to spare, you dash into the judge's chambers to request a warrant. The murderer is....Oh no, it's your black cat, strolling across the

Multimedia Murder: "Who Killed Sam Rupert?" is a complex murder mystery aimed at adults.

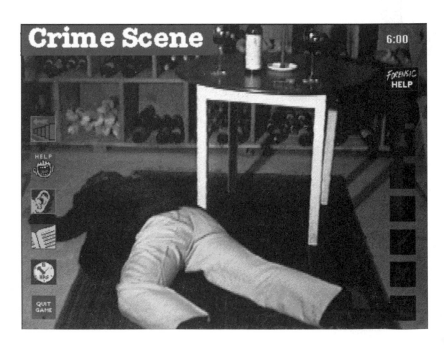

keyboard as nonchalantly as a chorus girl in six-inch heels. The book is closed on this virtual murder case for tonight.

Skilled digital sleuth that you are, though, you know that the brains behind this crime is a former author of children's books who plotted murder and mayhem from her studio in Vermont. You know that she didn't know a pixel from a PICT file until some friends dragged her to MacWorld three years ago. You know too that she's now on Most Wanted lists throughout the multimedia world, where her skill and success with CD-ROM games have been rewarded with many industry kudos.

All these clues point to only one person, Shannon Gilligan. Working with CMC, a Portland, Oregon, publisher of CD-ROM titles, the 34-year-old Gilligan wrote and produced "Who Killed Sam Rupert?" an interactive murder mystery designed to bring out the Sam Spade in just about anyone who installs it into his or her computer. Aimed at adults, "Sam Rupert" challenges players intel-lectually in a race against time to find a killer (although playback on single-speed CD-ROM drives can slow the action to a snail's pace). Produced for about $55,000, the atmospheric game uses full-mo-tion color video, animation, and sound as the case is unraveled.

Since its release in November 1992, sales of "Sam Rupert" have been on a steady rise. By early 1994, almost 50,000 copies had been sold. Six months after its debut, "Who Killed Sam Rupert?" won the Award of Excellence at the *NewMedia* INVISION Awards competition. The game also was honored with gold medals for best adult game and best production design and a silver medal for best story/script. It also has won awards from *MacUser* and *MacWorld* magazines.

Now an "evangelist" for this nascent industry, Gilligan bucked industry trends to become one of the first multimedia developers to market a series of adult-oriented games. In 1993, she released a second CD-ROM title, "The Magic Death." A third whodunit in this "Who Killed ... " series, "The Environmental Surfer," went into production in early 1994. Two more are in the pipeline. Gilligan also typifies the growing number of cross-over multimedia makers who are inspired by the potential of advanced technology and bring to it fresh viewpoints and skills honed in other, compatible disciplines.

Gilligan strives to harness the most up-to-date technology to serve that most ancient art, storytelling. "Multimedia gives the author a method of storytelling that is truly new and revolutionary. The story cannot be created without the help of the user," she said. "On its fundamental level, it is interactive: it involves *you*. And entertainment hasn't been interactive since the days of the oral tradition. Then you could stop the storyteller, ask a question, go off on a new tangent. It's ironic and exciting that multimedia, the most modern of technologies, is helping to return us to our oldest ways of communicating."

THE OPPORTUNITY: Macho No More

By the time she went to MacWorld in Boston in 1991, Shannon Gilligan had already shifted career-gears. After ten years of writing successful children's books, some of them interactive, she asked herself, "What's next?"

Shannon Gilligan: A trip to MacWorld in 1991 transformed this children's book author into a multimedia producer.

The answer was adult fiction, and she had a thriller in mind, set in China. But after a few hours in the product demonstration hall, where multimedia producers and software publishers showed off their latest wares, especially MacroMind Director and QuickTime movies, Gilligan said, she "walked out a changed person." Three years later, she added, "I'm so technologically oriented, and I was really a bit of an anti-technologist for a while...you think this stuff is really hard to understand, it breaks down, it's frustrating—and it is all those things, as we know. But you see the great things it does, and that sort of gets you over the rough spots."

Back in Vermont, Gilligan put her thriller aside, resurrected an on old book proposal, and transformed it into a multimedia prototype that showcased "the possibility of telling a story a different way using technology." The result embarrasses her to this day. "Thank god not too many people saw it; I think that it would have killed my career in the bud, but actually it was excellent learning experience," she said, with a chuckle. "I realized I had to rearrange some mental furniture to write, and design, and tell stories in a new medium. I was still trying to be linear."

With the advantages of computer technology, Gilligan realized, she was no longer limited to the so-called "which-way choices" of her interactive print titles. "You're chasing someone down a hall and you didn't see which way they went. If you go left, turn to page 87; if you go right, turn to page 22," she explained. "The choices were dynamic and participatory, but there wasn't cognitive problem solving that demanded mental and emotional involvement on the part of the reader." In the prototype, though, Gilligan found herself thinking inside the circle, "...and I just said no, no, no, no; it can't be [which way choices] translated onto a disc. It's got to be something more, something that has multiple access from a single point."

That approach suited Gilligan's plan for an adult-oriented mystery that offered players the same choices an actual investigator made on the trail of a real criminal. "I did a fair amount of research into what is available to a detective typically," she noted. "There are suspects, there are the personal effects of the victim, there is the immediate crime scene, there is the larger area surrounding the crime scene. All these elements are basically a part of any murder, even if

37

After reading the small white slip of paper, you bow to the statue, thanking the Buddha. If the weight on your shoulders is your search for Thompson, it seems you're going to find him soon! You smile. The old man from the ja stick booth suddenly appears at your side. "Good fortune, I hope. Ready to go see the head monk?" You nod and follow him to the doorway. Just as you step outside, a chunk of mortar from the wall being repaired comes loose. It hurtles downward, missing the man next to you by inches but hitting you in the skull and killing you instantly.

Was it an accident? Or was the chunk of mortar deliberately dropped? During the police investigation all the witnesses say they could not tell. One thing is certain: your fortune came true—and much sooner than you expected.

The End

Choices and More Choices: Multimedia gave Gilligan many options, compared to the "which-way" choices featured in her children's books.

the body happens to be found in the middle of the woods. There are always clues leading up to it, surrounding it. I tried to duplicate all of those elements in my game." To do that, Gilligan started with a murder and a victim and then "deconstructed the crime, took it apart so there was a multitude of choices, just like what a real detective faces."

That same realism would infuse the rest of the game as well, from the musical score, to the graphics and video, to the typewriter typeface used for text. "I knew that I wanted a gritty, street edge to this," Gilligan noted. Although the script and production pay homage to the private eye classics of the '40s and '50s, Gilligan also was determined that "the story be contemporary. I didn't want to be in the 19th-century. I really wanted to give it an edge." To build suspense, she wanted a "compelling gaming element" like a point system, or a clock to beat, allowing the successful player to "win."

Since she was new to the "religion" of multimedia, Gilligan quickly immersed herself in popular computer games, everything from "Super Mairo Brothers" to "Where in the World is Carmen San Diego?" along with a few parlor games. Although some players have compared "Sam Rupert" to the popular board game CLUE, Gilligan says it was not an inspiration. "I played it as a kid twenty years ago, but it wasn't something that I went and looked at. It wasn't an intentional omission. It just didn't come into my range of vision at the time." Her research did take her into computer superstores, which she found to be "overwhelmingly male-oriented with their war games, and shoot 'em up games and games of domination. They aren't games about using your mind and skills as much as they're about developing computer skills."

With her superstore research fresh in mind, Gilligan concluded that "one reason those games are fairly monotonous is that they are

Gritty Realism: Graphics and all other aspects of the game were designed to build suspense.

fairly monotonous. They are fun to play, but I think they are limited. It's as if they had invented chocolate, but only one kind—no caramel, no apricots dipped in chocolate, only chocolate bars." Instead, the game she had in mind would require different skills to play, "real world skills" such as deduction, analysis, memory, and judgment. "I think that's what content is all about," she added, "and it's why 'Sam Rupert' is different from all those male-oriented video games." Based on fan mail and feedback, Gilligan believes the mystery has a larger-than-average female audience.

Behaving like "an artist," Gilligan agrees that she bucked the trends in computer games in general, and multimedia CD-ROM games specifically. "If my publishers had studied the demographics, they would have told me to do a game for 18- to 34-year-old males," she said. "But I stuck with what I was interested in."

THE TEAM: A Cross-Country Challenge

Before she turned to a life of interactive crime writing, Shannon Gilligan had spent a decade writing for Bantam Books' highly successful "Choose-Your-Own-Adventure" (trademark) series of interactive children's books. A native of Buffalo, New York, who

Virtual Murder Makers: Shannon Gilligan, in the foreground, with members of her team. From left, they are art directors Dave Zahn and Anci Slovak, associate producer Christine Goulet and lead programmer Phil Marshall.

had graduated with a degree in English from Williams College, Gilligan said she "stumbled onto the job" and stayed to author more than 16 titles with their "multiple choices and multiple endings." One, "The Case of the Silk King," was adapted as a prime-time ABC special in 1992. In the process, her interest was peaked by "the power of the interactive process as a means of storytelling and involving someone in the story."

During that time she also tried her hand at mysteries, writing "The History Mystery Series" of unsolved natural or historical mysteries and "Our Secret Gang," a series built around a group of fifth- and sixth-graders who start a detective agency. Gilligan estimates that there are more than two million copies of her books in print. In addition, she "produced" some titles. "I basically came up with the idea and then hired writers and dragged them through the editorial process, often delivering artwork along with the book."

But that was before MacWorld. In the month afterward, she put together a prototype CD-ROM project and began the search for a publisher. One encounter, with an executive of Broderbund, the pioneering multimedia firm known for its children's titles, still makes them both laugh. "He saw the prototype, and it was so bad," Gilligan explained. "It was very funny to have him be honest and say, 'yup, it's terrible...one of the worst things I have ever seen.'" Undeterred, Gilligan continued to pound on publishers' doors, but all turned her down, citing the low installed-base of CD-ROM players at the time. Still she persisted and, "...again, I was lucky," she reflected. "They say that you create your own luck. I don't know how much of that is true, but I tend to believe it."

"Luck" turned out to be a family connection with a West Coast publisher, CMC. Founded in 1987, and based in Portland, Oregon, this company was beginning to make a name for itself with CD-ROM titles for personal computers and Sony's Data Discman "electronic book." So when Gilligan's husband, R. A. (Ray) Montgomery, also a "Choose-Your-Own-Adventure" author, turned to Sony with an idea for an interactive space adventure, the electronics giant referred him to CMC. When Gilligan joined him in Portland to help out on a photo shoot, she broached company execu-

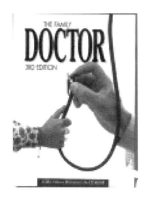

CMC Products:
This Oregon firm was known initially for its medical titles, like the best-selling "The Family Doctor."

tives with her interactive mystery idea. She even summoned the courage to show them her admittedly awful prototype. "At that point, it was as hard for a publisher to find an artist, as it was for an artist to find a publisher," she recalled. "They had seen me produce visual material. And they knew that I could write." And from the prototype, which featured a lot of work done in Photoshop, "they saw I was someone who could take the technology and figure out a way to use it. And that was what multimedia needed, someone who was willing to just throw themselves into it.... So I think they felt, 'well, it's half way there, and, if worst comes to worst, we can take over the computer [development] end.'"

Back in Vermont, Gilligan spent two months outlining three interactive mysteries, at the time thinking that they would be housed on one disc. An equal amount of time was spent hammering out her working relationship with CMC. Gilligan discovered that there are key differences between print and digital publishing. "I just followed my nose...because there are components of development that are not present in a book deal. I was going to have to produce the book as well as write it; traditional print publishing takes care of (production) in-house. I likened it in my mind to the two-step process happening all in one place." So as she devised the plots of the whodunits, she also drafted a detailed proposal of her working relationship with CMC. A contract was finally signed in fall of 1991. "I really have to give them credit," Gilligan said, "because when I sold them the idea, QuickTime was not yet available, (yet) it was instrumental to what I was trying to do...So my hat is off to them for taking that leap, and also for taking a risk on me, since I hadn't produced any video at that point."

Gilligan's determination to use cutting-edge technology was a major selling point with CMC associate publisher, Judith Grillo. "We found Shannon's proposal extremely appealing," Grillo said, "not because we wanted to be in the entertainment business but because of her ability to really utilize the technology that was hot and new and bring us to the next level."

Before its association with Gilligan and her husband, CMC was known primarily for its reference titles, starting with its collection of medical journals on CD-ROM. The product was the brainstorm of one of the company founders, who had worked in underdeveloped countries and appreciated the difficulty in getting and storing up-to-date medical information. Over the years, the firm has expanded and publishes a variety of collections drawn from the public domain, including the complete works of Shakespeare and Arthur Conan Doyle and Audubon's drawings of mammals and birds. Even though there were no retail outlets for its products then, CMC "...was chugging along," Grillo continued. "Doyle placed us in the market, and when Audubon came out, the people who were running the company were known in the industry and already looked upon as visionary.... There was very little that we could do wrong and not get a lot of attention for it."

CMC's breakthrough title turned out to be "The Family Doctor," a consumer medical reference on CD-ROM proposed to the partners by Dr. Allan Bruckheim, developed in-house, and released in June 1991. "It was an enormous hit," Grillo said. Now in its third edition and the recipient of several awards, "The Family Doctor" had sold more than 100,000 copies by the end of 1993. From there, "when they started to believe this market was going to become real," it was a short step from producing to publishing. Montgomery's and Gilligan's titles became the company's first out-of-house projects.

Judy Grillo: A former teacher, Grillo was CMC's director of marketing when the firm produced Gilligan's first title.

The 37-year-old Grillo, a former special education teacher, was new to the company when it began this growth spurt. A summer internship lead to a brief stint in advertising before she joined Computer Information Systems, Inc. as a product marketing manager. She was a product manager in the electronic publishing division of Little, Brown when its new corporate owner Time-Warner folded the undertaking. She knew about CMC from various trade shows and "decided to move from Boston to Portland and look them up." A couple months later, she was hired as director of marketing.

Eventually promoted to associate publisher, Grillo oversaw Gilligan's series, as well as a variety of other multimedia titles, and reviewed proposals for new titles that arrive unsolicited at CMC's Portland offices every day. Before they sign up developers, "we want to make sure they have thought about how multimedia will make the project better than another medium could," she explained. "We want some product definition, a clear idea of what the product is going to do and what its market is. A lot of people just say, 'CD-ROM, yeah, I want to do it.'"

Gilligan, on the other hand, "had done a fabulous job of utilizing multimedia to make her mystery interactive and interesting," Grillo said. "she had a clear role that she wanted to play, and she had real strengths in the creative arena. She did the writing, the casting, the video taping. Her team provided us with an almost complete Macintosh version."

In January 1994, Grillo left CMC to pursue new professional opportunities. With her departure, the marketing of Gilligan's series was passed to William Kelly, a 30-year-old who had worked in newspaper publishing before earning his MBA in 1993. Among his challenges have been building on the success of "Sam Rupert" and establishing an identity for the entire series in what is becoming a crowded market. Still, he said, "every day, coming to work, I'm thankful I've got the coolest job in the world."

Until her move to Santa Fe, New Mexico, in late 1993, Gilligan worked out of her Vermont home, aided by a pair of local graphic artists and a programmer. Still, her first foray into multimedia production would take her three times longer than she initially anticipated. In addition to regular electronic communication with CMC in Portland, she travelled to the West Coast four times as "Sam Rupert" came to life. Reflecting on her working relationship with the Oregon company, Gilligan remembered "they were remarkably generous in their attitude toward me. They kept hands off, supporting me as an artist. Nobody there knew how to deal with a producer, so we were learning our way as we went." As for the long distance separating the two, Gilligan pointed out, "there is a precedent for this—movies go on location, writers write alone in the woods, wherever they may be. Where it is harder is in technology issues, making sure a product tests well on all platforms and with all sound and video drivers. Everybody in the business has problems with those kind of issues."

In fact, what rough spots there were centered on technology. "I think it's hard for publishers to understand that it's almost as if you produce twice—first you produce creative content and then you put it into a technology matrix," Gilligan explained. "And they don't understand that when I send out a product with fifteen bugs in it, I think I'm a genius and they think I'm a slob." The problem is a perception-reality difference," she continued. "As they've come to work with more producers, they understand that I was handing them pretty clean stuff. And, as I've come to work more in this business, I've come to appreciate the frustration they face trying to fix other people's materials. It's one of the hardest jobs in the business."

PRODUCTION: Making Multimedia is Murder

Without any experience, except on her much-maligned prototype, Gilligan moved confidently into the production of her first CD-ROM title. After all, it would be the first of three "virtual murders" she planned on completing in the next twelve months.

Now she laughs at her naivcte, by way of a story she likes to tell of a meeting with two developer wannabees in California. "They were friends of a friend, so I said sure, I would talk to them about title development. I'm chatting away, and I made a joke about once production finishes, production really starts. They laughed and said we know. But later on in the conversation, I asked them when they expected to have their first product out. And they said, 'well, we think that by next year we will have at least two products out.' I almost spit my drink out. It is one of those things you just can't tell someone. Well, you can tell them, but they just won't believe you.

A really good rule of thumb is to come up with a production schedule—make it accurate, give yourself enough time—and then double it...then you are pretty much on the mark."

Scripting

While murder clearly was on her mind, even Gilligan realizes in retrospect that her "Sam Rupert" script may have been overkill. "It was 300 pages long. Single-spaced," she said, with a knowing giggle. "I didn't know any of the conventions of script writing. So I winged it. I really invented a lot as I went along."

At the heart of Gilligan's mysteries is a murder, and that is where she begins her plotting. "I figure out the victim and the style or method of murder," she explained. "That is my kernel or main organizing idea. Then I proceed in a very random way. Sometimes I'll think about what was this person like, why would some-

Too Many Words: Gilligan's script for "Who Killed Sam Rupert?" was 300 pages long.

one want them dead, what kind of enemies could they have." Details are added to flesh out the characters and to add suspense to the subsequent investigation. "Take Sam Rupert," she continued. "He had this complicated personal life, but there had to be other stuff going on in his life, like people who are jealous of him and his money. So let's create a character who stole some money from him and was recently caught. He would look like

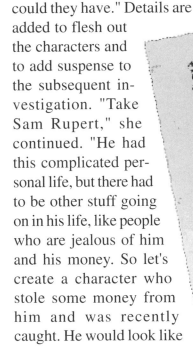
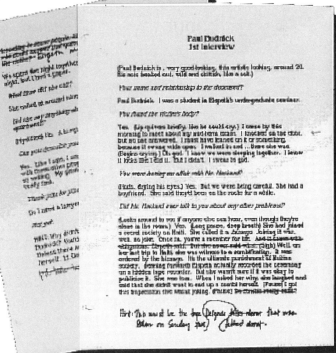

a suspect."

During the months of writing what amounts to richly imagined character sketches, Gilligan solved the crime. "Sometimes I don't know who does it initially," she admitted. "It's not like I come up with the murderer and the victim simultaneously." While she knew that interactive multimedia gave her the option of multiple endings, she drew on her experience as a children's author and opted for only one. "When I had written mysteries for 'Choose-Your-Own-Adventure,' I had always found (more than one ending) contrived, because on some of them, it was implausible that two different people could have killed the one person," she said.

As other parts of the realistic game came into focus, the script, especially the portion for the video interviews with the murder suspects, was constantly refined. "It was a push-pull process," Gilligan recalled. "I would write a first draft of the suspect interviews, and then I would do the crime scene, working out all the clues that you could find there, including lots of red herrings. Then I would go back and work in certain phrases, or little hints into the interviews...or, if I came up with something really interesting—a twist or something in the story—I would go back and adjust or rewrite, add or subtract other places in the story." Keeping track of all the clues was critical "...so that it all fit, it's all interlocking," she emphasized. "If one character says that she left the house at 8 A.M., and in another part of the game, she says that she left at nine—well, that could look like a big clue. You have to make sure that she did leave at eight if you don't want it to be a clue."

In addition to a victim and plenty of suspects, Gilligan also needed some additional characters to help players succeed as digital sleuths. "I needed a judge, and a chief of police," she said. "I also developed a device in the game called Lucie Fairwell, who is the player's assistant and does his (or her) foot work. I could only carry the conceit of you being the detective so far, you can't actually walk into the apartment and look around. So Lucie was always there with the crime-scene team doing that work for you."

On the other hand, Gilligan wanted "to prevent a player from being able to go into a program, go right to the warrant, make a

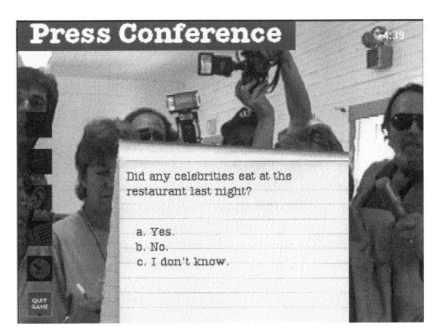

Meet the Press: It wasn't until production was well underway that Gilligan added a press conference to the game.

fluke arrest and be right." But how? The two-tier answer eluded her until the game was well into production. "We really puzzled over this, and finally we came up with the idea of a press conference," she said. "We tried to think what is the test that real detectives face, and frequently what they have to do, especially on a high profile crime, is have a press conference. The press is grasping, aggressive, and stupid and it asks all kinds of impertinent questions that have nothing to do with the case, but you have to answer them anyway." In this portion of the game, the player has to answer seven of ten questions about the crime correctly, before he can reinterview suspects or go before the judge to request an arrest warrant. To stymie repeat players, "there are over 100 possible questions, ten of which are randomly generated from within the program," she continued.

Once the player/detective comes before the judge, he again has to answer several questions, and depending on the answers, the judge's response varies. "So you can have the wrong alibi and the judge will either tell you this is absolutely wrong for this suspect, or he may say, 'I think this is a long shot for this suspect, but I will grant you a warrant anyway.'" After passing these trials, the player learns if he made the right choice: a simple explanation informs him he was wrong, a confession confirms his crime-solving skills. "I suppose we can now do a virtual trial," she added, "but that is the next step."

With script approval in hand, Gilligan remembered using the computer "to draw this elaborate interactive chart, but nobody used it. I think they—my programmer and my graphics guy—were trying to be macho by ignoring it. 'We know what you mean,' they said, 'we know what you mean,'" she said, laughing. "I did do thumbnail sketches to show to my programmer, and there were lots of drafts of the interface design for the first mystery." By the time she began work on the second mystery in the series, though, this free-flowing process gave way to a structured one. "We had a pattern, a paradigm, we were going to duplicate. We pretty much know our way around now."

Video

Gritty and Grainy: Video quality was consistent with the rest of the game's graphic approach.

Before she became a successful multimedia producer, before she was a successful children's author, Shannon Gilligan was fascinated with films and filmmaking. During the summer after she graduated from college, she took an intensive workshop in filmmaking at New York University. Designed for film and television staffers, who got into the business without a film or TV background, the class attracted everyone from "a retired couple who loved film, to producers who had started out as coffee girls, to people like me, who were moping around looking for something to do—and loved film," Gilligan remembered.

Given that love affair, it's not surprising that Gilligan served as casting director, camera person, lighting director, producer, and director of the extensive videos in "Who Killed Sam Rupert?" "No, it wasn't totally cold," she said, putting the video shoot in perspective, "but I was 10 years out of date. I went and looked at my (class) notes and they were virtually useless." Instead, she relied on advice from friends and a few professionals. "The one thing that I had on my side," she explained, "was the limits of QuickTime. I knew that the film quality didn't have to be super good. The frame rate and the graininess were going to eliminate any real need for super high-quality film."

With the script in hand, Gilligan held an open casting call for the actors who would play Sam, Lucie Fairwell, the judge, and the murder suspects. Aware of the active summer theater programs throughout the state, Gilligan distributed notices to theater companies, as well as some newspaper advertising. "I was very, very lucky in casting," she said. "It was the third day of casting, and we still hadn't come up with the professor, and in walked someone who looked like Central Casting sent them over." The only casting problem encountered for both this mystery and its sequel was "casting people of color," she added. "Partly, it is because Vermont is the whitest state in the Union.... It got to the point where I went to a mall and asked every black person I saw if they acted."

Even though Gilligan was working on a shoestring budget, she paid her actors the Screen Actors Guild wage for

Added Impact: Gilligan's use of video makes it appear there is more footage in the game than there is.

an experimental film (although she didn't know it was the standard fee at the time). And despite the small scope of her project, she stressed the importance of getting signed releases from all involved, just as a big budget feature would. "Even on a small production, it is important to make sure that all your legal Ps and Qs are taken care of."

Most of the shoot was set in a Vermont restaurant. "It definitely simplified my life by having all of the suspects for 'Who Killed Sam Rupert' interviewed in one place," she explained. "It was in the office of the restaurant where the murder occurred. Everybody that was a suspect was somehow connected to the restaurant, so it was quite simple and plausible." Video for the second mystery, though, became more complicated because of the variety of suspects. "We felt we had to create different backgrounds for all these different people," she added, "and that involved quite a bit more work, schlepping the camera and the lights around, getting the actors there, and so forth."

Since good lighting is important when shooting video for QuickTime movies, Gilligan consulted with professionals about the lighting and hired someone to place the lights in the restaurant for the shoot. "It is not sophisticated lighting," she said. "I just used high powered halogen lamps bouncing the beams of light off the ceiling or off umbrellas. It gave a nice kind of flat, defused, bright daylight, high-color spectrum light, which is natural looking. A good lighting designer might look at it and say, 'this sucks.' But when you reduce it, when you get the corruption on QuickTime, it is important that it is lit brightly, because there is a tendency in QuickTime to darken the image."

Gilligan shot "Sam Rupert" using a Sony Hi-8 video camera. For the sequel, "The Magic Death," she hired a professional cameraman for some of the video work, but, she noted, "there was just no discernible difference for the money. Lighting had much more to do with the success of the shoot at that level, than the quality of the camera or the camera man." To digitize the video, Gilligan used a Mac IIFX and the MacRecorder for recording the audio. Just as important, she said, was a large hard drive to digitize and manipulate the QuickTime movies.

When the project was finished, "Sam Rupert" contained 45 minutes of QuickTime movies, although it appears as if there are more because Gilligan figured out how to pause the QuickTime images during the suspect interviews. "We actually paused the video while the interviewers were asking the questions and this eliminated about half of video footage," she explained. The use of still images saved disc space as well, since CMC plans, eventually, to put the Mac, DOS, and Windows versions of the game all on one CD-ROM.

As daunting as it was to fit so much video in "Sam Rupert" without slowing the game to halt, Gilligan more than doubled the QuickTime movies in her sequel, "The Magic Death." "It has 110 minutes," she said. "I couldn't believe it."

Audio

As any master of suspense knows, music and sound effects are vitally important in creating atmosphere as a mystery builds to its spine-tingling climax. But in multimedia productions, for the most part, Gilligan believes "sound design is underused and overlooked. It's an incredibly important way of communicating with your audience. It can make up for a lot of rough edges."

For "Who Killed Sam Rupert?" Gilligan turned to professionals for the mystery's distinctive and memorable score and sound effects. The music was written by Pete Scaturro, a San Francisco composer who worked with long-distance advice from Gilligan. Gilligan wanted the music to describe "themes that I wanted, like a fear theme, something suspenseful, something eerie." For the sound effects and design, she lugged her computer to nearby Burlington to work with Doug Lang of Shadow Productions. Working from a list of effects that she needed, they drew some from Lang's sound library and created others.

Witty Menu: Interface buttons are easy to understand—and humorous.

From Beginning to End: Graphics are consistent throughout the game, as these three screens show.

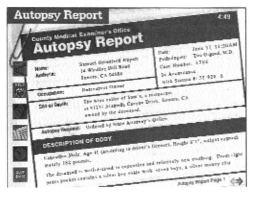

At points in the game, where it is slow going as the computer loads large files, Gilligan turned to sound to fill the time. As the QuickTime movies of the suspect interviews are brought to the screen, players hear the whir of a projector. And as close-ups of the crime scene come into focus, there's the sound of a camera clicking. "Those were my ideas," she said. "I got bored looking at it, and I said 'let's put a sound effect in here so we can kind of jam their circuits.'"

Graphics

From its black-and-white opening sequence to the final credits scrolling down the screen, "Who Killed Sam Rupert?" maintains a look that is both as contemporary as a TV cop show and as classic as a Sam Spade movie. The blend salutes the genre's time-honored conventions and suits "Sam Rupert's" modern-day setting—and method of play.

With some preliminary sketches in hand, Gilligan turned to two "Mac-adept" Vermont graphic designers, freelancers Dave Zahn and Anci Slovak, for help with interface and screen design. "I told them that I wanted this gritty, street feel," she recalled, "but as we talked about it some more, we decided to conjure up some of that '40s film noir detective story look-and-feel. Hence the black-and-white opening, the sound of the typewriting tapping, and continuing with the use of American typewriter throughout as the main typeface."

While Gilligan knew what information was needed on the main interface, she admits she "had no idea how to arrange it." She credits Zahn with organizing the player options on menus designed around pictures of Sam Rupert. "It's an image of the victim alive, like a snapshot out of an album, so you'd be staring him in the face while you were deciding what to do next," Gilligan said. Set into the photo on the left side of the screen, are small icons (buttons) that provide clues, access the player's "case notebook" and reverse the game. On the right side, "typed" onto what looks like a lined page from a notebook, are the key sections of the game, including the report of the murder, the crime scene, the interviews with the suspects, and the press conference. In the top right corner, a digital clock counts down the time left to solve the crime.

In the Same Style: The graphic design in the first and second games in the virtual murder series is identical.

The same flavor of realism extends to a menu that accesses other sources of information about the crime, such as Sam Rupert's diaries, copies of his phone messages, the reservation list at the restaurant, etc. The menu, also on lined notebook paper, is handwritten. So are Rupert's diaries "to give you the feeling that this is someone who really lived and wrote in his notebook and all that stuff." The phone messages, on the other hand, look as if they came off a computer printer, while the reservation list duplicates a computer screen that the player scrolls through. "Because we were delivering a lot of information by text, we wanted variety and interest level, so we used a number of different graphic techniques," Gilligan said. "I was always looking for ways to present information in a lively and engaging way."

Since various elements were added to the game well into production, the interface was changed constantly—up until the final authoring. In addition to the press conference segment, "we also decided to introduce hints," Gilligan said, "This would be an interesting device you'd pay for using a few minutes of time so you could consult with your assistant and find out what she thinks about something. This was added late in the game. So was how to play. We decided we wanted a long walk-through of the entire game and have it be very detailed. All required changes in the interface, as well as additional programming." There also were some deletions—like a "save to disk" icon that allowed players to save the game they were playing, which was dropped in favor of a notice with the option to quit or save.

While the interface of "Sam Rupert" and the subsequent mystery, "The Magic Death" are identical, Gilligan is not satisfied with either. Based on feedback from players and her own preference for simplicity, she said "I'm aiming to come up with some clever ways of cleaning up the interface design. I think there are too many icons. It's just too crowded. Even if players have to figure out where to get help, or get a hint, it's better than having a cluttered screen."

Authoring

As the content of the game changed, and concern about the slow speed of play grew, Gilligan, Zahn, and her programmer, Phil Marshall, found themselves making many changes in the game during the authoring process. To their surprise, when they finally finished, the Windows and Mac versions of "Who Killed Sam Rupert?" filled 250 megabytes each. "It's quite a bit longer and more complex than I had any notion," Gilligan acknowledged.

The three-month-long authoring ordeal was made less painful in many ways with the use of MacroMind Director, a tool that wins high praise from Gilligan. "It is a program that a creative person can understand," she said. "And it is interesting and complex enough that a programmer can really sink his teeth into it." Initially, the focus was on "refining little things," like adding sound effects and animation, smoothing out some of the art work, and reorganizing the interface and icon system to simplify the game's navigation.

Although Director facilitated making the changes in the game, its slowness became a real problem. (The newest version of Director has addressed many of the speed questions, including the addition of a compiler.) "Director has a lot of architecture that you have to bring in, regardless of whether you are using it, and that slows things down considerably," Gilligan explained. "And it is an interpretive language, as opposed to a compiled language. So, first it compiles, then it interprets what it compiles. That whole step is missing when you compile directly. You are preforming certain tasks, it compiles them, and boom, it's done. It can be very, very fast."

Play speed forced the team to make some difficult choices—and resulted in some heated arguments among team members. "A large portion of your customers are going to be playing (the CD-ROM) on much slower computers," Gilligan said. "And so you end up having to eliminate effects that were really neat and wonderful, but you can't afford to have because of the time limits. ... as the producer, I had to deliver a game with a certain level of performance." With that in mind, Gilligan often overruled her art director and cut the overlong credits, some special effects in the opening sequence, and "other neat visuals." They also reorganized certain files to make them smaller and thus faster to load. Some times, though, they added a sound effect or "a throwaway animation" to "create the illusion that something was happening, to hide the slow access times."

During this process, Gilligan felt that she was a good judge of what was too slow or cumbersome in the game. "I have a zero attention span," she admitted with a laugh. "If it is too slow for me, it's probably too slow for most people. You can't count on people having fabulous concentration." At the same time, like so many game producers—and players—Gilligan said she was "really craving better performance. I'm so glad double speed CD-ROM drives are here."

Testing

Debugging was the focus of Gilligan's "completely unscientific" testing process. "Basically, we just kept making discs until we got one that played well and we couldn't find any bugs in it," she explained. Working with Director, Gilligan and her team had alpha and beta discs within weeks after they began programming. "But the distance between beta and gold is quite long and laborious," she continued. "Because you are still fine tuning, every time you make a change you have to debug the whole thing...And every time you find a bug to fix, you have to laboriously and exhaustively go through it again." By the time she went gold, she had concluded, "It's almost as if once the production is finished, the work starts."

What consumer testing she did consisted of "inviting everybody I knew over to play the game, " she recalled with a laugh. "It was very interesting to show it to my completely computer-illiterate friends and see how they reacted. Some really liked it, others didn't like it at all. One of my best friends played it for about thirty-five seconds and said, 'That's very nice, Shannon,' and walked off." While finding bugs was still the objective, Gilligan said, "when anyone had comments, we listened to them. But I don't remember anyone saying anything specific that made me change something."

When the gold disc reached CMC in Portland, it faced more trials. Working with detailed specs, "in-house engineers and technical support people spend days with the product, literally going through every potential 'what if' and user sequence to make sure it's all running the way it's supposed to," Grillo said. CMC also tested the speed functionality and how the disc played on different hardware.

In all, the production of her first CD-ROM took three times longer than Gilligan had estimated. Today her original goal—to complete three mysteries in one year by December 1992—makes her laugh. "I got one mystery done by November (1992), and the second mystery was basically completed in May (1993), but we kept fine-tuning it, and released it in September (1993)." Pre-production of the third mystery began in late 1993. Its estimated release date of fall 1994 would put it in stores in time for the profit-able Christmas sales season.

FINANCE: Going by the Book?

Negotiating a contract for an original CD-ROM title is a little like playing a game for the first time—without a rule book. "There are no models," CMC's Judith Grillo declares, and no one who has been through the process would disagree. While this free-form way of doing business has its drawbacks, it also has a built-in, if limited, flexibility that seems to serve an emerging industry well.

Grillo noted that what prospective developers bring to the negotiating table tends to depend on their background or previous experience, Grillo noted. "You interface with people who are used to the traditional publishing company or the entertainment market, and so they have their own set of expectations," she explained. "You work with people who are musicians, writers, video producers, and everybody has their own perspective." But since there are major differences between those two established industries and multimedia, "there's a lot of imparting of information about the size of the pie and how a project is put together," she continued. "A book person might come in and say that I want 11 to 13 percent (royalty) and that's about all we have to give at this point in time. So we tell them these are the kind of numbers you're going to be seeing, so let's negotiate if you want to do it."

For a developer like Gilligan, who supplies a complete or almost complete title, or one who brings in "major content," CMC works in the 15 percent royalty-base range with a high of 20 percent. Advances, paid against royalties, also vary from project to project, depending on the needs of the developer, the size of the production, and the estimated costs. Grillo puts the range at $5,000 to $25,000, with payments generally made monthly. "First we decide on a total percentage rate of royalties," she said, "and then up front, we'll pay as needed for production costs; and if the developer also needs a monthly payment, it's normally x amount of dollars of prepaid royalties."

When it comes to updating or expanding an existing title, Grillo often finds the negotiations even more of a challenge. " 'The Family Doctor' is now in its third edition," she explained, "and my royalty base is virtually used up. I have very little to work with at this point. So, I'm doing a lot of outright buying of additional material for an annual fee placement. It really puts you in a bind, especially when you weren't the one who negotiated the royalties for the first two editions."

Based on her experiences, Gilligan advises novice developers to "approach any deal not assuming that all rights are on the table. The people paying for the production should potentially get rights like North American rights for all desktop computer platforms. However, world rights for all platforms is something that they are simply not being paid for at this stage of the game. People are doing this for such low advances and working with such tight production budgets, that it really behooves them to keep certain rights. I think that it is much the same model as in any creative endeavor. It is this way in books, it is this way in films...the French rights are French rights, German rights are German rights." Gilligan also calls attention to "the division between the desktop arena and the so-called player arena which like Sega, Nintendo, and 3DO. Some products are not appropriate for both, but some can crossover, and I think developers should be very aware of that."

MARKETING: Pay As You Go

Although Gilligan had some input on the packaging and marketing of "Who Killed Sam Rupert?" the responsibility rested with CMC. And, like the other dimensions of the multimedia industry, methods of bringing a product like this CD-ROM game series to market are evolving.

Packaging

The initial challenge was packaging or "trying to represent a dynamic multimedia product in a flat space," as Grillo described it. The front and back of the box for "Sam Rupert" conveyed some of the game's excitement with four-color photos of screens and inter-active features, but, as Grillo pointed out, most of that promotion is initially lost on potential customers in retail outlets. "Most of the time you go in there and see a spine and only a spine," she explained. "And how much can I put on that one and a half, or two, inches of space that attracts somebody so that they will pull it off the shelf."

Grillo said that currently, the dimensions of the boxes for "Who Killed Sam Rupert?" and other CD-ROM products have been determined by the display space in retail stores. In 1991, when CMC began to increase its marketing through computer stores, "there was a war going on. Everyone wanted to own the packaging for CD-ROMs." While major producers like Compton's New Media and Sony were vying to make their box size the industry standard, retailers cast the deciding vote. "Basically what happened was that the channels...said we don't have floor space, and we're not changing our shelving, so make it a software box." As a result, most CD-ROMs are housed in the same six-inch by nine-inch boxes as most other software. However, Grillo expects that to change. "There's the whole environmental concern with the jewel case," she explained. "The music CDs have now gone full circle as that industry addressed all the issues that CD-ROM is now totally ignoring. I think we'll go through the same phase over the next couple of years, reducing packaging and getting rid of plastic cases and so forth. For now, the software stores are saying this is the size we have...deliver it."

By and large, Grillo believes, the selling of multimedia is "following the same model as the software industry. It started in mail order catalogs at first, and the retail channels, I believe, are just opening up." But to obtain product visibility on a catalog page or a store shelf, producers pay a price. "We're finding that the distributors like Merisel, and the others, basically want you to make a dollar commitment to them for promotion, so that all they have to do is take your product and shelve it. You pay for the marketing; they sell through and take a commission. It's definitely an interesting arrangement at this point in time." While distributors are flexible in

Reaching for Sales: The spine of a game box often is all a potential buyer sees on a store shelf.

their financial dealings with companies like CMC, "it's not like, 'write us a check for $25,000,'" she continued, "but you do certainly have to commit." Displays in computer stores also cost. "You won't get any in-store promotion in virtually any store unless you pay for it," said Grillo, laughing. "Someone can read the spine of your box, if you have given the store a deep discount to start." What if the box front is facing forward? "Even that's something you sometimes pay for," she said.

Selling a Series

Among professionals in this new field of multimedia marketing, CMC's Bill Kelly is in the unusual position of promoting a series of

games. With two titles already selling well in stores, and two more due shortly, Kelly knew he wanted to build on the games' early success. However, he also had to take into account rapid changes in the industry that were shaking up the existing market. "It's an odd climate right now," he explained. "Typical software channels are used to dealing with hundreds of SKUs (or products), all clearly defined. Now we're presenting them with thousands, and potentially, tens of thousands of SKUs that are not so easily distinguished from each other, because they are more content driven, than application driven. So it didn't mean a whole lot to say to them this is a murder mystery series, as it would to a bookstore."

Out of Focus: The cover of this and other games in Gilligan's series tried to promote too many aspects.

His first move was to establish an image for the series by giving it a new name. "The series was being marketed as the 'Virtual Murder Series,' which wasn't as descriptive as we wanted it to be," Kelly said. "So we named it 'Who Killed ...?' to leverage the success of 'Who Killed Sam Rupert?' and present products to the channels that they will know how to handle." The change, he believes, focuses CMC's marketing effort. "We were trying to do too many things—promote Shannon, promote the game, promote the series—and when you spread very limited marketing resources over so many attempts to promote identities, nobody gets identity."

Kelly said that although they will have related titles, each game, for the most part, will be marketed individually. "I think that we made a mistake when, in a couple of packaging formats, we had 'The Magic Death' only available in a bundle with 'Sam Rupert.' Again we were diversifying our market, rather than focusing it, which was counter-productive." In the future, though, he expects to offer value bundles to consumers who purchase the entire series.

Pricing

In today's multimedia marketplace, no one pays the suggested retail price for entertainment software, Kelly said. "It's this weird psychological game that gets played," he said. "We set a retail price on a product and then offer it to a channel at a fifty-five percent discount. Then they mark it up to a competitive price. In a rational world, we'd set our discount strategy differently so that we'd get out of the product what we want, and the channel would get to mark it up to, or near, the suggested retail price. But that's not the way it works."

He said that the pricing "game," which is played throughout the software industry, in part reflects consumer uncertainty. "Most of the purchasers of multimedia software aren't technologiclly savvy. Plus, it's not like a book that you can preview by flipping through it. Even when you get it home and put it on your computer, you can't see what the value of the product is all at once." As a result, so-called bargain pricing is necessary to convince purchasers "to pony up the money, to take the risk," he continued. "If they see the suggested retail price is $79, and they are buying it for $50, then they think, 'well, I don't know exactly what's on it, but at least I'm getting thirty bucks off.' When in reality they aren't, because nobody is going to charge $79."

For publishers like CMC, setting a suggested retail price for one of its products is a complicated process that involves more than getting a fair return on an investment. "We have to be sensitive to competitive issues," Kelly said. "And we have to be forward thinking. If we suspect there's going to be a general price reduction in multimedia, we wouldn't want to trail that price drop, because we wouldn't get any of the long term benefits out of it." CMC also relies on "some assumptions that help us decide how volumes will increase at various prices," he continued. "We have a very good grasp of the economics of bringing out a title, and we're dedicated to running a profitable business...but in the end we set the price we want, knowing what the channel is going to mark it up to."

Distribution

As if marketing multimedia were not difficult enough, software publishers like CMC expect the sales outlets for their products to change dramatically in the near future. "From what we can tell from our strategic thinking, the curious thing is that (the marketplace) isn't all that stable," Kelly said. "Multimedia products are a completely different ball game from what the traditional software channels are used to dealing with. It's also a completely different ballgame from what video, music, and book stores are used to dealing with." In this transition phase, he believes, "companies that are willing to be flexible about their pricing, merchandising, and relationships with the channels are going to survive going forward." In contrast, "companies that go in demanding that everything work as it did before, aren't going to be well respected by the new channels that open up, and they aren't going to get stocked."

To keep a leg up on the competition, Kelly said that publishers also have to be forward-thinking. As examples of CMC's steps in that direction, Kelly points to two sales experiments the company participated in during the 1993 holiday season. One, a joint venture between the distributor Baker and Taylor and Blockbuster Video, offered CD-ROMs for rent, like movies and music videos. The other, led by Apple, placed kiosks that demonstrated CD-ROM titles in bookstores. "We want to develop new channels," he explained, "because that's where we see things going and we want to be there when it gets there."

Admitting to a bias from her background in publishing, Grillo predicted that the multimedia software industry will grow to have more in common with book publishing than the computer software business. "Walk into any bookstore today and look at the shelves," she said. "Yes, you have your top three titles, but you also have specific topics of interest to lots of different people and just because I bought one, doesn't mean I'm not going to buy another in the same category." In addition to a variety of titles on the same topic, like books, multimedia software will be available at a variety of outlets, including discount and department store chains. "The software stores will become limited offers of the top titles," she continued, "and for the range, people will be going to other merchants, whether that's Sears, Wal-Mart or the Price Club, or a book store, or a video-laser disc CD-ROM store."

In the interim, Kelly considers bundling, the packages of software that are included with multimedia hardware like CD-ROM drives, as a valuable way of building a customer base. At CMC, bundling is the responsibility of the company's director of direct sales, but Kelly has no objections to "some well-placed strategic bundles in the first twelve months of a product's release." He theorizes that consumers "spend a lot of time with the bundled software and wait months to absorb their initial investment before they go looking for additional product to buy. So if you have a product that's coming out when they are buying their MPC, and you hit all those buyers with that software upfront, I don't think you've lost anything in the market." And when those consumers return the response card with the software, "we build our user list, and we can direct-market to those people," he added. "Each of those names is worth a certain amount of money."

Kelly believes that currently bundles are an important source of information for consumers about multimedia titles. However, in the future, product reviews may be all important. "These products aren't like books that you can go take a look at, and reviews on books are probably the single biggest driving factor in book sales," he pointed out. "So you can just imagine how important reviews will be for products you can't preview before you buy them. I think reviews are going to be vital to the success or failure of a product going forward."

FUTURE: Faster and Faster, More and More

While Gilligan believes the market for multimedia entertainment like her interactive mysteries "hasn't been given an adequate chance to find itself yet," she believes advances in computer technology and falling hardware prices will build an audience. Proceeding on that assumption, she already has added one title to her now retitled murder series, "Who Killed Elspeth Haskard: The Magic Death," and expects to complete another, "Who Killed Brett Penance: The Environmental Surfer," in 1994. Unlike its predecessors, the third game features a Hollywood star in the video sequences. Actress Sheryl Lee, best known to television fans as Laura Palmer in "Twin Peaks," plays the role of sleuth Lucie Fairwell.

In the ncar future, though, Gilligan expects the most successful interactive games to be modeled after conventional video fare "elaborate shoot-em up games with very little content." She agrees with a friend who theorizes that the industry will divide along the same lines as the motion picture business. "There is going to be the 'hits' kind of development that is going to be West Coast-based, Hollywood-oriented and very big budget...and then there are going to be publishers...that will do a lot of interesting projects with smaller budgets, and only a few hits will come out of that."

Regardless of the publishers' mentality, CD-ROM games need faster play, if they are going to compete with video games for a

Third in the Series: Due out next is "Who Killed Brett Penance: The Environmental Surfer."

mass market. Gilligan acknowledged, "Speed is very much an issue." She noted that the industry predicts double speed CD-ROM players will number only 4.5 million by the end of 1994. "I don't think that 100 kbs drives are a real market; I don't think that it's real software. I think we're talking beyond 300 kbs minimum. It's not too far off, but unfortunately there's still a lot of Windows CD-ROM drives being sold that are 'real dogs'...dumped on the market."

With interactive television on the horizon, Gilligan is intrigued by the prospect of multiple user games that could be played across networks. "I think that requires vast rearranging of the mental furniture," she said. "It's like a space-time continuum...as well as an internally taut game. When you're playing a game, it's a group of people in a defined space beginning at a defined point in time. [For multiple user games], you really have to have games where you can break in at any point in time." Making that creative leap probably "...will come out of a deep level of concentration on retreat somewhere," she said. "I don't think it's something that I'm going to get sitting down with my pen and pad." However, she has begun to

experiment with interactive fiction. " My next project is an elaborate work of fiction that will be completely embracing and take
many hours to play. Plus, I am working on a geopolitical thriller
that incorporates video."

For developers like herself, Gilligan believes her biggest challenge is to invent new models that tap the power of multimedia.
"Here you are not reinventing the wheel every day," Gilligan
stressed. "You are trying to come up with something brand new
and it's exhilarating, and it can be overwhelming. You can have a
great idea, and a great concept, and a mastery of interaction, but
you need to invest a lot of powerful creative energy in coming up
with compelling paradigms. Then you will create a piece of multimedia that is so great it can change the way people live their lives.
This is the definition of all great art."

3

"THE JOURNEYMAN PROJECT"

Presto Studios

At A Glance

"THE JOURNEYMAN PROJECT"

Developer: Presto Studios, Inc.

Key Personnel: Jose Albanil, lead 3-D modeler; Farshid Almassizadeh, lead animator and programmer; Geno Andrews, audio sculptor and 2-D artist; Jack Davis, art director and lead artist; Dave Flanagan, writer and programmer; Eric Hook, public relations and 3-D artist; Michel Kripalani, project coordinator, lead 3-D artist and programmer; Phil Saunders, conceptual design; Greg Uhler, lead programmer and 2-D artist.

Description: "The Journeyman Project" is a time-travel adventure game with photorealistic worlds, interactivity, and a nonlinear plot. It features a branching storyline, a professional music score, and 30 minutes of QuickTime video.

Development hours: 15,000 hours.

Development period: June 1991–January 1993.

Production hardware: (2) Macintosh II, (2) IIci, (4) IIs, and (1) SE/30; (4) Radius Rocket Accelerators, 5 GB online storage.

Production software: Macromedia Director, Electric Image Animation System, Swivel Professional, Infini-D, Macromedia Three-D, Adobe Photoshop, Vision, SoundEdit.

Cost to develop: More than $100,000.

Financing: Loans from friends and family.

Suggested Retail: $79.95.

U. S. distributor: Sanctuary Woods.

Foreign distributors: Too many to list; contact Sanctuary Woods.

Awards: Award of Excellence, gold medal for best animation/graphics, bronze medal for adult games and bronze medal for best production design, *NewMedia* INVISION 1993 Multimedia Awards ; SVM Mac, best entertainment title (France); Apple Japan/Apple Award.

Future projects: "The Journeyman II"

Contact: Eric Hook or Michel Kripalani
Presto Studios, Inc.
P. O. Box 262535
San Diego, CA 92196-2535
619– 689–4895
619–689–8397 (fax)

In the early 1980s, 15-year-old Michel Kripalani begged his fa ther for an Apple computer, promising to learn to program, study harder, and anything else he thought would be convincing. When his father finally agreed and the Canadian-born high school student got his hands on an Apple IIe, all his promises were forgotten—for a time—while he indulged his passion for computer games. "I can remember whole summers in high school and college that were devoted to playing computer games," he said. "That's where the seed was planted."

Days and nights spent with fellow gamers zapping dragons, chasing space villains, and solving puzzles were an education in the state-of-the-art of this new, popular entertainment. "We played board games, war games, space games, adventure games—you name it. We learned what we liked and what we didn't like," he continued. "We all felt we could write a better game."

Realistic Time-Travel: This best-selling game has been likened to an interactive movie.

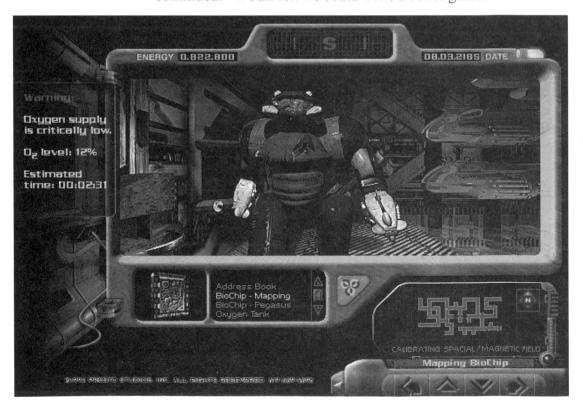

A decade later, Kripalani, and his roommate Dave Flanagan, another gamer, decided to try. Their dream was to create a game that would surpass any done before, including the newly released "Spaceship Warlock," the first Mac game to utilize the vast memory of the CD-ROM and advances in animation and video programming. Eventually, as Kripalani and Flanagan turned their dream into reality, they were joined by six other fellow gamers and computer "wonks" who transformed a two-story home in a northern San Diego suburb, into a computer center and crammed it with workstations, posters, and models of robots and spaceships. Working 90-hour weeks, the group turned to friends and family members for loans to pay living expenses.

Two years and many macaroni and cheese dinners later, this team of twenty-somethings delivered "The Journeyman Project," a 3-D, time-travel adventure game that fills a CD-ROM with photorealistic images, digital video, animation, and an original stereo soundtrack. The scripted tale, with its echoes of "Star Trek" and other science fiction classics, pits an agent for the elite Temporal Protectorate, guardians of the flow of time, against saboteurs who are tampering with the past and jeopardizing world peace.

"It's the closest thing to an interactive movie I've seen yet," a reviewer for *Mac Computing* wrote, giving the game a four and a half star rating out of a possible five. " 'The Journeyman Project' set the current standard for new CD owners," concurred editor James Bradbury of *MacUser*. Judges for the *NewMedia* INVISION 1993 Multimedia Awards agreed. "The Journeyman Project" earned an Award of Excellence, as well as a gold medal for animation and graphics, and bronze medals for adult game and conceptual design.

Fifteen months after its release, "The Journeyman Project," with a suggested retail price of $79.95, had sold more than 100,000 copies in the United States, Japan and Europe. Sales of the Japanese version, released in mid-1993, totaled approximately 10,000 units, making the game that country's top seller in 1993. A PC version, shipped to stores in mid-November 1993, was the "Journeyman's" sales leader in early 1994. And a sequel, "The Journeyman Project II," is due in stores in time for the 1994 holiday sales season.

"A lot of people out there writing computer games are coming purely from a games background," reflected Kripalani, president of the now incorporated, Presto Studios. "What we're going into now is almost like an interactive film. You're dealing with character, with plot, with scenes, things you've never dealt with in games before.... There's always that time with a new technology when programmers are the people who know how to get things done, but in order to get truly aesthetically pleasing work out, you have to get the artists involved."

THE OPPORTUNITY: A Game Like No Other

Photorealistic Settings: Presto Studios wanted every set to look as if it had been shot with a camera.

"The concept of doing a game has been around in my head for a long time," Kripalani acknowledged. But the 25-year-old was determined from the start to create a game that would be a benchmark in the industry. Initially that meant dissecting everything already on the market. "Every quality Mac CD-ROM that was available, I got," he said. "I'd figure out what they did, and I'd see if there was anything

I could use or any technique I could learn. Things like that.... But to really understand this industry, you have to understand a game called 'Spaceship Warlock.'"

"Spaceship Warlock" is a CD-ROM game that was considered state of the art for its graphics and interactivity when it was released in the summer of 1991. However, Kripalani said that he and the other inveterate gamers on the Presto team saw some limitations in that game and an opportunity for themselves.

"The problem was that a two-man team put it together, and because of that, it is limited in scale and the quality of graphics wasn't what we were aiming for," he explained. "It didn't have an interface. It had one image on the screen, and you clicked right on the screen for what you wanted to do.... But the big thing for us was that it wasn't a game. It was linear, a story, but it wasn't a game. So here we were, gamers, with CD-ROM drives and all the right software. And we get it and—it's kinda fun—maybe."

In their drive to surpass the current generation of games, Kripalani drew on his film and video studies at the University of California, San Diego, to derive the skeleton for "The Journeyman Project"—a script that gives the game its movie-like beginning, middle, and end, filled with plot twists, suspense, and challenges for the players. "Most games don't have that type of feel," he said. "Arcade games are strictly shoot 'em up. The standard adventure game is a kind of quest, and you're an adventurer. You wander around randomly for 200 years in dungeons, killing whatever monster steps in front of you, trying to build up your character and stuff. It's not really scriptable. Another standard of filmmaking, key to the envisioned game, was photorealism; thus every image in the game's imaginary settings would look as if it had been shot with a camera. The picture-perfect look would require attention to details such as lighting, point of view, and depth-of-field, all hallmarks of a well-made movie.

Kripalani also wanted to exceed the size—and thus the scope—of all other available games. To do that would mean filling a CD-ROM's 680 megabytes of memory. ("Spaceship Warlock," by comparison, filled less than one-quarter of a CD-ROM.) Working on *Verbum Interactive* magazine, a pioneer interactive magazine on CD-ROM, had convinced Kripalani that a game of 400 megabytes, or larger, was "very do-able. At the same time, we didn't want to be unreasonable about size, either. Some of our original scripts had 10 time zones...and that would have meant 40,000 views. You could see how that would get out of control.... Finally, we went through 'Spaceship Warlock' and counted how many steps you take in the entire game. It came out to 127, which doesn't sound like a lot for something that's supposed to be an epic adventure." (In the end "The Journeyman Project" more than tripled that number.)

Finally, Kripalani wanted to avoid the violence that drives most other computer games. In fact, nonviolence has become a credo of Presto Studios and a standard for all its products. "I had worked for a company [where] my boss was a big environmentalist, and all of his work was based on environmentally sound principles, which actually was interesting, because it showed you could have a whole business stressing what is important to you," Kripalani explained. "[This company] will not do a violent game; we will not do a shoot-out game. Everything we do is going to encourage world peace and nonviolence. It forces us to push, and it makes for a different product than most of what's out there."

THE TEAM: Friends of Friends

The game that Kripalani envisioned clearly exceeded the energy and talents of one or two skilled computer specialists. By mid-1992, when "The Journeyman Project" was entering its most demanding production phase, eight young men with diverse media backgrounds would be working on it almost around the clock, united by a vision of the product, a fascination with computer games, and friendships dating back to their high school days in California. "Did you see *Jurassic Park*? Did you see the special effects credits?" Kripalani asked. "That's what we were doing on a much smaller scale. And it's too much work [for one person]. People say we had too many people, but if you look at the projects that are being done with less, their deadlines are just going out the window."

Although he had toyed with creating a game since his teen years, Kripalani didn't decide to pursue it until after he

Game Players, Game Makers: The Presto Studios team combined a love of computer games with a desire to invent one that was state-of-the-art.

had an internship at the San Diego Supercomputing Center, where he worked on many computer platforms. As a co-founder of MOOV design, Kripalani was the lead programer for *Verbum Interactive* magazine, and became aware of the potential of CD-ROMs as a vehicle for hi-tech games.

At the time, Kripalani was living with Dave Flanagan, a high-school buddy and fellow "gamer" who had graduated with a degree in English from the University of California, Irvine. In addition to a specialty in literature, Flanagan was familiar with several computer platforms and Pascal, BASIC, and Lingo programming languages. He was employed as a computer programmer with Jostens Learning Corporation when he and Kripalani began drafting a script for "The Journeyman Project."

While Flanagan focused on plotting the story and creating "Journeyman's" cast of characters, Kripalani turned to two colleagues from MOOV design to wrestle with technical questions, including the critical interface design. In this early stage of the game's creation, all were still holding down full-time jobs and/or attending college. "The Journeyman Project" was simply an avocation.

A student at the University of California, San Diego, majoring in cognitive science (a curriculum that combines computer studies and psychology in pursuit of artificial intelligence), Farshid Almassizadeh had worked with Kripalani on *Verbum Interactive* magazine. Almassizadeh also had valuable CD-ROM experience as the lead animator on Radius' "Rocket Home Companion" CD-ROM. Rounding out the quartet was Gregory Uhler, also a student at the University of California, San Diego, who was learning visual arts/computer media. During his sophomore year, Uhler was an intern with MOOV design, and later joined the firm full-time to work on *Verbum Interactive* magazine, as well as projects for Proxima Corporation, Chevron, and Yosemite National Park.

Synchronicity helped pull the rest of the team together. "Out of the eight people, we went to four different high schools," Kripalani explained. "Now what happened was one person out of each of those four pairs knew someone in another pair, and then they each pulled in a high school buddy. It's not as if you can put an ad in the paper saying 'Looking for a musician to work insane hours for six months for no pay.' You've got to know someone and say, 'We're doing this cool thing, there's no money right now. But you've gotta trust us, it's gonna work.' You can't do it any other way."

To complete the team, Almassizadeh recruited Jose Albanil, a visual arts graduate from the University of California, Santa Cruz, who had worked with him as the 3-D animator for Radius' "Rocket Home Companion" CD-ROM. Uhler tapped his high school friend, Eric Hook, who had recently graduated from the University of Washington with a degree in economics. Kripalani signed on Jack Davis, who was art director and designer for *Verbum Interactive* magazine. In his early 30s, and thus the oldest member of the team, Davis was a San Diego computer graphics professor and a freelance art director for numerous design studios in Southern California. Davis added Geno Andrews, a composer of television, radio, and film scores, who had created a portion of the *Verbum Interactive* magazine soundtrack.

In addition to the eight principals, who would become the founders of Presto Studios, the team contracted with three industrial designers, who were responsible for the futuristic setting of "The Journeyman Project." The design group was led by Phil Saunders, who had worked at Nissan Design International in San Diego since he was 20. These artists "are futurists," Kripalani said. "When I need a couch, what a couch would be in the year 2318, they can give me front, top, side and three-quarter views.... It was just a coincidence that I found Phil. We were put in touch with him at a time when I really, really needed him."

While each was responsible for a facet of the project, team members often had more than one role. Uhler was the lead programmer, for example, but Kripalani, Almassizadeh and Flanagan also helped to program. Andrews, the project's audio sculptor, and Albanil, its lead 3-D modeler, also served as 2-D artists. To save money, Kripalani became a jack-of-all-trades, even learning to install telephones and Ethernet.

Initially, Kripalani was the only team member working full-time on "The Journeyman Project." A visit to Mac World in January of

1992 in San Francisco, with a prototype and brochure for the game, changed everything. "The excitement level was huge," Kripalani recalled. "It was the catalyst of getting everyone to say this is do-able. There are enough people out here to support what we are doing. Enough people are going to buy the game. And from that point on, we actually started on working to get the project out.... All the production took place from August until November. And we were shipping exactly one year later."

By mid-1992, the other team members had left their jobs to join Kripalani, working full-time on the game and living together in two rented houses in the San Diego suburbs. The decision to risk their livelihoods was traumatic, but necessary. "I had to quit a great job to come do this," Flanagan said, "and it was extremely scary for me...but it was a risk I had to take, to do something for myself instead of for someone else."

As the initiator of the project, Kripalani emerged as its coordinator. "There was a lot of creative energy, but one person has to direct where the group will go," he said. Often, that meant drawing the line for his perfectionist crew in order to keep the project on a demanding self-imposed schedule. "From a business standpoint, there is a point when you've got to say, this is enough. The consumer is going to be very happy with this, and the difference between very happy and elated is not worth another three months, considering that the cash flow isn't going to change."

Decisions about the project were generally hammered out in group meetings that could last for hours, even days. Controversies were resolved by a vote. "The bottom line is that when you have a lot of people discussing, you work through to what the best answer

Multimedia Studio: This house in suburban San Diego County was Presto Studios' home during the making of its interactive game.

Michel Kripalani: A game player since his teen years, he coordinated work on "The Journeyman Project."

is.... When we talked about it enough, the answer showed itself," Kripalani said. There were some drawbacks, though. "Too much input can be a negative thing," Flanagan concluded. "Everyone has an idea...and they are very attached to it. And the more ideas we have, the longer it takes...."

Both agree the group's decision-making will change. "I don't think we'll have the luxury of all that discussing the second time around," Kripalani said. "The first time, though, was kind of idyllic."

THE PRODUCTION: A Dream Becomes Reality

"In the beginning," Kripalani recalled, "It was like staring at a blank sheet of paper." While he and the others knew the broad outlines of the game they wanted to create, they were novices in planning its development and production schedule. The game's nonlinear format made traditional storyboarding unworkable. Flow charts often were ignored in the pursuit of excellence.

"We didn't do a chart of the game itself," Kripalani admitted. "We tried to do a chart of the production schedule, and probably due to the inexperience of the group, and myself, it didn't work out so well. But...the biggest problem was from an organizational standpoint. We didn't have a good flow chart. Because we're all perfectionists, everyone wanted one more day to fix the thing they were working on. By the time we got to the end, the programmers' time was eaten up by everything else, and there was a major crunch."

SCRIPTING

The specifics were months in the making, but the Presto team, from the beginning, set their sights on creating a time-travel game through a three-dimensional, computer graphic world that would deliver a large-scale, hi-tech playing experience.

The idea was initially worked out by Flanagan, who created a futuristic scenario and filled it with protagonists and antagonists: robots, an evil scientist, the agents who guard time. Science fiction buffs get an extra kick out of the game's insider references to science fiction classics, everything from "Star Trek" to "The Hitchhiker's Guide to the Galaxy" series by Douglas Adams. "But," Flanagan said, "I tried to keep it to a minimum because the more references you put in, the more it looks like someone else's work. I tried to be as original as possible but...it's difficult not to invite comparisons, especially in science fiction time travel."

"Slowly the story started to gel," recalled Kripalani. But finding scripting and storyboarding solutions for the complex, nonlinear game required some experimentation. "We tried several different approaches," Flanagan said. "First, we tried doing it online in HyperCard. You could push a north, south, east, or west button, and there was a text screen with a description of the scene. But that became pretty time-consuming, so we dropped that." Finally, Flanagan said, "I wrote a script (describing) exactly what happens in each area....If you walk into this room at this point in the game, this is what you see, and this is what happens. I followed that through for the whole game. And I also did grid maps using MacDraw to supplement the script information. After a few stages of evolution...that worked."

Kripalani believes Flanagan's script gave the game its movie-like qualities of character and plot; but unlike a movie, the game was not outlined scene by scene. "The storyboarding took place in the sketches, which then got put into models," Kripalani said. "That's something we were wrestling with. There's no real easy way to do storyboards when the story isn't linear and you can't go shot by shot. You create an environment, and the user can go anywhere

In the Beginning: The adventure game began with the plot and characters from a detailed script.

in that environment. The environment itself is sketched out and plotted.... Each room has its own environment, its own lighting, its own props, its own interactivity, and maybe a robot. And there was some degree of interactivity with most of the environments."

As animators and modelers attempted to bring "The Journeyman Project's" characters to life in a three-dimensional computer world, technical restraints forced Flanagan to rethink his story "Everything was modeled in 3-D, using Swivel and ElectricImage," he said. "Technically, doing digitized 3-D human beings is almost impossible. You can do objects, environments, and robots, but people, you can't do. Our alternative was to do people by way of digitized video (QuickTime), which is very flat..... So I had to get away from using people in the script."

Interface Design

While Flanagan polished the script, Kripalani, Uhler, Almassizadeh, and Davis spent months confronting the many questions surrounding the game's interface, the critical on-screen template that controls the action and enables the player to navigate in an interactive 3-D world. "We were establishing two things—aesthetic and technical," Almassizadeh recalled. "We had to merge them to make the game look and feel like something that you could play fourteen hours at a time. We actually have beginning shots of the early layouts. Aesthetically, it changed tremendously, but, in the end, the key elements were all the same ones we originally laid out."

"We were looking for several different things in the interface design," Davis said. "One was the layering of information. We wanted to have techno-complexity without interfering with the game play itself.... We wanted a dynamic interface capable of changing or being changed by the player.... We also were looking for tactile response (feedback to the player that a command had been received and was being processed). The problem [of no feedback] was that people were not sure they had actually done something when they pressed a button, and they'd get frustrated if there was any lag time between the pushing and the action.... So we wanted to add responses—sounds or animation—for everything that a player interacts with. (This feedback) not only communicates to the person that they are actually interacting with something, it helps them believe they are inside a futuristic virtual world."

Next, Jeal Choi, a student studying industrial design, sketched the interface with an eye toward merging the group's philosophical demands with their desire for state-of-the-art graphics. "We told him we needed a viewport, movement, a compass, and whatever. He came up with the idea of a left-eye monocular view piece," Kripalani said. The resulting BioTech Interface is both dynamic and high-tech with displays like the message window and BioChip display panel. "We nested the information so that it is available to players who want (to expand their knowledge)," Davis said. "They can get rid of it, if they don't."

The relationship of the BioTech Interface to the on-screen "stage," or window for animation and QuickTime movies, was dictated by CD-ROM drive performance, an issue that influenced a number of project decisions. The larger a CD-ROM animation, or video, appears on a computer screen, the slower it moves. The Presto team opted for speed, filling two-thirds of the screen with the BioTech Interface and the remaining one-third with the movement-filled stage. To give the illusion of greater size, the proportions of the stage were changed to conform to a movie screen ratio of one-to-two instead of a TV-screen ratio of three-to-four. "I've had people say that the movie-ratio stage is twice as big as the TV ratio, just because the proportions are different," Almassizadeh confirmed, with a smile.

Also, the BioTech Interface was designed to utilize a computer screen's built-in black border. "All computer screens have about a

Welcome to the Future: The interface design invites players into a 3-D world and facilitates game play.

ten percent black area around the perimeter that can't be used," said Davis, who made use of this space when he was working on *Verbum Interactive* magazine. "Some developers hide that area with a bezel around the screen. But the edges of our interface are black, and the left hand of the interface fades to black, giving the impression that the interface, which is supposed to be a monocular eyepiece that the player is wearing, is wrapping around the left side. Fading out to black allows us to take advantage of the extra ten percent, and the player perceives it as part of the interface."

As the game evolved, changes in the interface design were necessary. The Presto team originally designed the game with three directional buttons—left, right, and forward. "We had the whole future world gridded out in eight-foot squares and a player would step forward one eight-foot square at a time," Almassizadeh said. "When you indicated left or right, you would turn left or right ninety degrees. Later on we asked ourselves, what if you wanted to go backwards." Since that move would have taken considerable time and effort, Almassizadeh said, "We added one more button for a backwards step."

The team settled on 90-degree turns, which result in 360-degree views of each environment. "In 'Journeyman,' there are 1,600 views. If we were to do in-betweens," said Almassizadeh, "you would need a three-or-four CD-ROM disc set to do it.... Other games lead you through a path because they don't want to render the three other sides, because that's three times the work. We wanted to give the user a chance to look around the environment."

Another change in the interface came when they were down to the wire. "The compass on the top of the interface, originally, used to spin every time you took a step," Kripalani said. "It kind of twirled with a motion blur like it was on a liquid base and had to center itself each time...it was cool. But, it added one second for every time you turned left or right. In a game, where physically turning takes a second, how do you justify taking two seconds to see an animation which they are going to see over and over again? We were four days off from pressing a disc when Geno said, you'd better pull that damned compass [animation] because this is too slow. And we did."

Graphics and Modeling

As decisions about the game's course, and look, were hammered out, the team created a three-dimensional world populated with the characters and environments in Flanagan's script.

"Originally we thought we were going to do a lot of the game in true photography," Kripalani recalled. "We actually figured out how to take pictures with a 35mm camera with a perfectly balanced tripod, but it wasn't really cost effective. Plus, we were having aesthetic concerns about the photographed images conflicting with the computer generated images. It was like going from black and white to color."

Having decided to rely on 3-D computer-created images, along with a small amount of digitized video, a workflow developed. First, conceptual sketches were quickly drawn. Along with Flanagan's 2-D grid maps, they became the basis for final drawings by industrial designers that showed objects and environments from several views. Since he was most familiar with the script and game play, Flanagan monitored continuity.

Increasingly tight deadlines forced industrial designer Phil Saunders to alter his drawing approach. Instead of transforming his futuristic sketches into slick pen and ink renderings, he would give pencil drawings (hastily done in a very short time), to the 3-D modeling crew, who would start work on them immediately. "It was amazing what they could get from those rough drawings," he said.

The multi-angled conceptual drawings were necessary for the lead 3-D modeler, Jose Albanil, and his crew to visualize the object in 3-D space. Often Saunders first explained the drawings to him to give him a better understanding of the artist's vision. Albanil then would break down the scene into simple components to determine which features

Sketches to Start:
To save time, the 3-D modeling team often worked from quick pencil drawings by designer Phil Saunders.

could be created with bump maps or textures rather than labor-intensive modeling. Even with detailed, multi-view drawings, the rendering was difficult. "Even with the latest, greatest technology, three-dimensional design still requires patience and perseverance," warns Albanil. "After all, where is the state-of-the-art, if you're constantly pushing its borders?"

Though it lacked a few advanced features, Albanil stuck with Macromedia's Swivel Pro for most of the game's modeling, because he was familiar with it. "Even if a program has every feature you need, if it's difficult to learn and cumbersome to use, trying to finish a project with it will be like fighting a forest fire with a garden hose. I chose to do the choreography in Swivel for several reasons. First, I work on a 33Mhz 040 Radius Rocket. This makes Swivel's updates tolerable even when working with 10,000 polygons or more. Next, one of the best features of Swivel, and probably the reason I picked it, is its shaded-view rendering abilities."

From Start to Finish: Sketches were modeled and rendered, a time-consuming, headache-inducing process.

Albanil started modeling an object, or environment, by creating the large underlying parts first and then modeling the detail pieces afterward. Generally, the complex looking environments in "Journeyman" were little more than elaborate facades, like old-time Hollywood sets. By only concentrating on the visible aspects of the

3-D objects, Albanil was able to maximize production time. "This is generally a good rule to follow, " he said, "because you can save both modeling and rendering time by ignoring the parts of the model which aren't going to be seen."

In Part: Robots and other moving objects were modeled in segments.

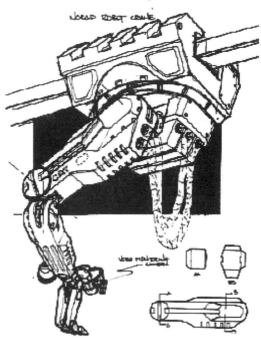

After he modeled its components, Albanil assembled the scene or object for animating and rendering. For objects that move, like robots, he created joints and then locked the pieces together. Having shown the model to the designer to be certain it conformed to his sketch, he would make any necessary adjustments, label the model's parts, and hand them off to Almassizadeh to be animated and rendered.

"Success in 3-D modeling depends on a few simple factors: the proper hardware, the best software for your needs, and being prepared," said Albanil. "Take the time to learn how to use the software. Know its features and limitations. If you know in advance exactly where you are going, and how to get there, you will be able to avoid a lot of headaches later. But have plenty of aspirin on hand anyway, just in case."

Rendering and Animating

As each model was finished, Almassizadeh began the painstaking task of rendering and animating. First, he would apply the elaborate texture, bump, and transparency maps to the models. After test renderings confirmed object placement, animations were choreographed, and lighting was set up for final rendering.

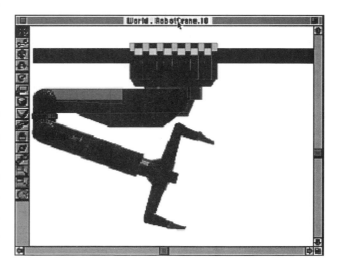

Texture and bump maps, critical to the look of the environments, came from a variety of sources. "We got inspiration from science fiction movies like *Star Wars* and *Blade Runner*," said Davis, who also made regular expeditions to the toy stores for more ideas. "One way (of making maps) was to scan in lots of materials, laying them down on a flat bed scanner. I'd buy little robots or toy ray guns, stuff like that, (scan) them, and turn them into seamless wrapping textures that we could use as part of the greeblies. (Coined during the making of the *Star Wars* movies, "greeblies" is an industry term for the nonfunctional, geometric, and organic-looking appendages hanging from space ships and other futuristic structures.) We also created texture maps by using noise and motion blur to create brushed steel-type effects. We used filtering and texturing to come up with bizarre out-of-this-world effects."

During the modeling and rendering phase, the Presto team used Swivel 3-D Professional, Macromedia 3D, ElectricImage, and Infini-D. Using multiple programs caused difficulties for Almassizadeh, whose job was "to make everything look the same. Kripalani was doing the environments using ElectricImage, and I was forced to use Infini-D...and they don't create the same look. You can render the same image in each program and they look like night and day."

The solution was time-consuming. "Kripalani gave me the backgrounds (from ElectricImage)," Almassizadeh said. "I laid 3-D objects on top of them looking for details in the backgrounds. If he had a light there, then I had to reproduce it in my world. So I was working off of his world. Kripalani and I would plan out everything mathematically and put those lights in the same place in my world."

To avoid this problem in the future, the production team plans to limit the number of modeling and rendering programs. "We're going to try to do everything in one program," said Almassizadeh, "that way we don't have to recalculate all that stuff twice. We most likely will use ElectricImage, although I'm still in favor of Infini-D. In one sense, it made my job a lot easier, because I could actually character-animate everything in Swivel, and then bring it into Infini-

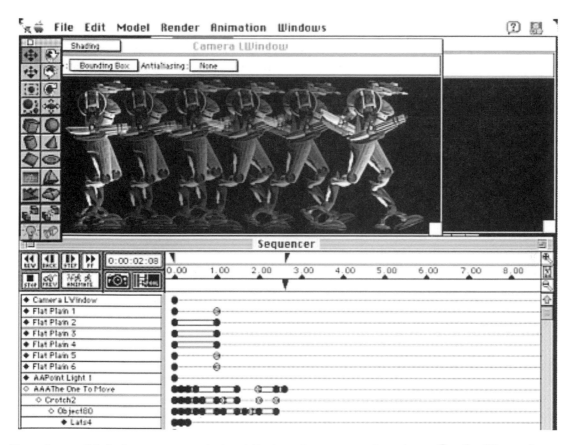

D and wouldn't have to touch it. All the character animation remained the same, no other program does that."

Finishing Touches

The prize-winning graphics and animation in "The Journeyman Project" owe a debt to Davis. Kripalani believes, "He showed us that the level of graphics we were doing was good, but not where it should be...he showed us how to get there."

An important step in that direction was the game's superior Photorealism. Certain that "God is in the details," Davis used Adobe Photoshop to retouch, by hand, each of the 1,600 frames in the game's environments, spending from 5 to 30 minutes a frame, to add realistic shadows, dirt streaks and reflections. "People notice the

On the Move: A variety of programs were used to animate the game's many moving objects.

detail," Kripalani said. "Subconsciously, I think they look at our project, and at others, and they know ours looks better, but they don't know why. You see the same differences in a good quality movie and a B movie."

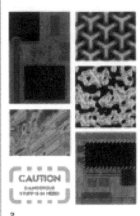

"God's" Touch: Details including a variety of textures were added to heighten the game's photorealism.

Davis, the author of a book on Photoshop, (*The Photoshop Wow! Book*, PeachPit Press, 1993), called on his extensive knowledge to expedite the labor-intensive retouching and compositing process by writing macros to automate the process. Each Photoshop macro, activated by a hot-key, automatically accomplished a number of tasks, including paste the clipboard, transparency, feather, delete, and paste again. The macros were essential since "many of the objects, like the robot, had up to ten composited layers," Davis said.

Video

Interspersed with the computer animations in "The Journeyman Project" is thirty minutes of digitized video shot by the team in less than twenty-four hours. Kripalani's experience in film production was helpful in this improvised phase of the production, which was a little like, "hey guys, let's make a movie."

"I went back to my film books, and I figured out how to do lighting, and I found people to do costuming and makeup," said Kripalani, who transformed the living room of their suburban house into a sound stage. "We did all the shooting (with a rented Hi-8 camcorder) in one day, which wasn't so bad because everything was torso and head shots."

While it seems inspired to have a veteran professional actor play the part of the evil scientist, in reality, casting Graham Jarvis was a lucky coincidence. "The way we got Graham Jarvis, who was our professional actor, so that we could say that we used professional actors," Kripalani remembered smiling, "was that he was Geno's next door neighbor. The fact that he had worked on 'Star Trek: The Next Generation' in a guest-starring role was great. So now in our brochure and packaging, we say, professional actor, as seen on 'Star Trek: The Next Generation'."

According to Kripalani, Jarvis got into the spirit of the shoot. "Doing Graham was pretty funny....He has a beard—or he had a beard. We asked if he minded us doing some makeup on him to make him look like a futuristic scientist. And he says, 'No. Do you want me with or without a beard?' Graham said he had a shoot coming up in a few days and had to shave it off. Of course then the idea comes up...why don't we shave off your beard for you! And so we shaved the middle here and a little over here. And we shot him with this futuristic beard, and we glued things on his head, like cables, and gave him this eye piece...it was fun."

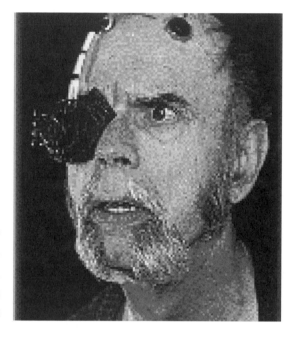

Starring Role:
Graham Jarvis, who appeared in "Star Trek: The Next Generation," played the evil scientist.

The team used CoSA's PACo and QuickTime for video compression and playback. If the sound needed to be in sync with the video, they used QuickTime; if it didn't, they used PACo.

Audio

With the addition of Geno Andrews, an experienced composer of film and television scores, to the Presto team, the professional quality of "Journeyman's" custom music score and special sound effects was a given, Kripalani said. "There wasn't a choice...his biggest thing was wrestling with the programmers to get the music sound quality better in the game. The Mac has a real good sound output, but he wanted it better."

Andrews spent six months on the game's soundtrack, doing whatever it took to get the right effects. "There's this scene where there's a moon pool where submarines go out," Kripalani said. "Geno would fill up the bathtub with water and give someone a microphone by the tub. The wires led from the bath to his bedroom, where he was doing the recording. We were all working on our computers downstairs, and we hear him yelling, 'more waves...a little more splashing.'"

Andrews also was a man of many voices. According to Kripalani, "almost all of the narration in the game was Geno.... He would record himself in the studio and use every effect he knew to twist and tweak it. When he was done, we had something like twenty different voices in the game that were all his."

However, not all the voices were Andrews. "We had a friend come in to do the female voice for the radio opening. Then we had another friend come in to do the Mars-base scene," Kripalani recalled. The Mars base is an old mining company purchased by the Japanese, and we felt that the Japanese would speak English in the future just as poorly as many do today. Rather than get someone who speaks English to speak with a bad Japanese accent, we actually got someone who was Japanese who didn't speak English very well. It was very real and very natural. We felt that it wasn't a cultural slam because we got a Japanese to do a Japanese voice."

Putting It Together: Geno Andrews added sound sequences to the game using sophisticated software.

Andrews' bedroom sound studio was packed with high-end music hardware. He composed the music by keyboard using Vision MIDI software on a Macintosh IIci. The stereo score from the master DAT was reduced to 22kHz mono using Macromedia's SoundEdit Pro. However, the Presto team was so impressed with the quality of the score that they decided to put the full stereo version on the game's CD-ROM for play on the home CD player. "The 'Journeyman' game itself is 400 MEGS, which left 200 MEGS free," Kripalani said. "Since we did the game on compact disc, we did score as CD-quality audio. There are eleven tracks, or about fifteen minutes of full stereo music, and it sounds great."

Authoring

With all of the key elements finished, the programing crew, led by Greg Uhler, using Macromedia Director, tied together the animation, movies, sound effects, music, and interaction. Most of the team had had experience using Director in previous projects. "I really like it as a tool," said Kripalani. "It can be complicated at first, but once you know all of its features, it is very powerful. I taught myself Director when it was a beta version. I don't even know if there was a manual.... At the birth of an industry, there's no one teaching you how to do it. If you can't figure out software, you're nowhere. With time, that will change, but we're not at that point yet. You've got to be a tinkerer."

The Presto programers agreed that Macromedia Director's scripting language, Lingo, was the best off-the-shelf authoring tool available for the Macintosh, although it did have a few drawbacks. Foremost, according to Uhler, was the lack of a compiler, causing Lingo to react slowly, which is especially noticeable in a game environment where speed was essential. Eric Hook, a 3-D modeler who also handled Presto's public relations, pointed out the need "to address the speed issue. If we use Director to run the game, we get a 20 to 30 percent reduction of speed in comparison to custom code. Director may come up with a compiler which may speed it up, or we may get a custom shell written for the next game.... I think we're reaching the limits of what we can do in Director."

Testing

Testing a 400-megabyte game, which can take more than eight hours to play, is a formidable task. "We were beta testing for two and a half weeks, which is actually a short period of time for a project of this size," said Kripalani. "We tested off CD-ROM discs produced from a rented JVC ROMaker. We rented it for about $2,000 dollars for three weeks and were pressing test discs everyday. We pressed 11 alpha discs, eight or nine beta discs, and two versions of what we thought would be the gold master. As we proceeded, each disc became more stable, like disc six, which Greg thought was pretty stable, so we pressed three copies of beta six and tested it. And then we would find a bug, so we would destroy the discs, fix the bug, and press another."

Presto rounded up as many CD-ROM drives as they could find during the last week of testing. "The whole team was sitting around clicking at the interface, looking for bugs," said Kripalani. "You know there were problems in the game. In the game, you could walk into a room, and there's a door you could walk through even though it's closed or maybe you could walk through walls. The only way to find out is for you to physically bump into it. We had to hit every door and wall from every direction. There's a lot of testing in a game like this."

Besides testing for bugs, Presto also did some consumer testing. "We brought in some kids, friends of friends, everyone we knew. We were bringing in people off the street. `Hey do you have 10 or 15 hours to try our game?' " Kripalani said, with a laugh. "We gave them T-shirts and popcorn to sit there all night and play. The young kids liked it, but it wasn't "Nintendo" for them; it wasn't fast enough. That's when we realized that the game would be for ages 12 and up." (Sales information eventually confirmed this observation; the majority of purchasers to date are males 30 and older.)

The consumer testing proved particularly valuable in fine-tuning the game's instructions. Kripalani explained: "We found out what places in the game were not clear, and places where instructions were not evident—like in some arcade games and puzzles within 'Journeyman.' Where we needed to patch in instructions, we just dropped in audio clues.... We realized this was important stuff, if people were going to play the game."

MARKETING: A Game Plan for Sales

In keeping with the company's aim for autonomy, the Presto team initially decided to package and market "The Journeyman Project" on their own, instead of turning it over to an outside publisher. Encouraged by enthusiasm for the game's prototype and discouraged by what they thought were meager royalties offered by game publishers, they boxed and shrink-wrapped the games, made arrangements with individual mail order houses and distributors to sell them, and even filled some mail orders themselves. However, in less than four months after the game's release, Kripalani and his team began to discuss turning marketing over to another company. By then, the manpower, time, and financial demands of selling "Journeyman" had convinced them distribution by the right outside company made dollars and sense.

While the game was still in production, "we went through a lot of research because we understood the concept was that you put together a game and a publisher picks it up," recalled Kripalani. "The numbers we were initially getting back from a publisher did not seem appropriate at all. It didn't seem like there was enough money coming back—like two or three dollars a game." Presto's later calculations, though, proved otherwise. "We were finding that marketing was really distracting from production, and that's what we do best. There is no question that packaging, distribution, and marketing are a full time job for many individuals to support just one product," Kripalani explained. "And there is no question in my mind that the numbers the publishers were talking about were pretty close to appropriate. We looked at our per-disc profit compared to what we were offered by publishers and it was within a dollar or two. By then, we were in a better position to negotiate a better deal than when we were an unknown group of 25-year-olds with a game that might never sell."

In choosing a distribution "partner," Kripalani's foremost concern was "the percentage," Presto's share of wholesale sales income. "We also wanted a company that was going to give us a lot of attention," he continued. "We wanted a company that had something to prove so that they would put in extra effort." Those criteria lead Kripalani to a nearby start up company, located in northern San Diego County. By September, this company had shouldered all of Presto's marketing and distribution, including the conversion of the Mac game to PC and foreign language versions, customer support, and advertising. Within a year, Presto realized it had outgrown its small publisher and moved to a larger Bay area publishing company, Sanctuary Woods.

Even though Presto's profits now are being shared with these distributors, Kripalani believes his company "got a really good deal out of all of this. We already had a successful application when we set this up." Presto's percentage reflects that, he said, though he declined to reveal the specifics of the deal. However, he could point to some emerging industry standards: "If you are an inexperienced group, and you talk to a publisher and want them to put up all the money [to develop your product], you might be able to get 8 or 9 percent. If you go to them with all your material, and you're putting up your own money and are an experienced team, then you can get considerably more—like 25 or 30 percent of the wholesale price, which is about 45 percent of the suggested retail price."

To Market: Presto's staff initially boxed and shrink-wrapped the game.

Packaging

"The box is it!" said Jack Davis, whose wife, Jill, a professional graphic designer, created the game's packaging. "In most store situations, a customer can't play the game. They will be sold based on that box. That's why most game makers are going to invest a good portion of their budget creating great graphics for the box."

"It's very important," Kripalani agreed. "A major computer superstore's buyer came up to us, when we were first showing the prototype, and asked what the box looked like. I told him we didn't have a box yet. He said, `Well, as soon as you have a box to show me and if I like it, I'll buy it.' 'Do you want to see the game?' I asked. He said, 'No. I don't care what the game is. What's going to sell it is the box.' The bottom line is the box is at least 50 percent as important as the game itself. You first have to get the customer to pick up the box. Then you have an opportunity to intrigue them. If you've intrigued them enough, then the $65 price is no obstacle. If you get them to pick up the box, you're halfway there."

The "Journeyman's" four-color packaging showcases its state-of-the-art graphics, including actual screens of the game. "If you go into a store and look at the games, they all have gorgeous air-brushed renderings or photorealistic images. And usually they have absolutely nothing to do with the game," said Jack. "So we made sure that customers knew that what they were looking at was actually a part of the game. We also added our 'unique selling points' or USPs—the music and animation, and a picture of Graham Jarvis, the professional actor, to let them know this was a game with a story."

Jill's job was "to lay out all of those elements without making it a visual pollution," her husband said. Skillfully using type, a grid system, and color, Jill designed the back of the package so that the eye flows from the upper left hand corner, with its prominent quote from the *MacUser* magazine review of the game, into copy that describes the game's storyline. "A good designer is going to be thinking about eye flow." Jack said. "You want to draw them through the information and then, usually in the lower right hand corner, appeal to them to buy. If you don't catch a person within the first second, when they pick it up, with large quotes or graphics, then you've lost them. She designed the box so that when a person picked it up, they wouldn't have the option of putting it down, there was too much to absorb at one glance."

A Box That Sells: Packaging for "The Journeyman Project" called attention to the game's strong points.

Pricing

"The Journeyman Project" entered the market with a suggested retail price (SRP) of $99.99. "We just looked at the industry," Kripalani said. " 'Spaceship Warlock' had come out at $99.99, so we did also." However, based on response from major wholesalers and mail order channels, "...we realized that that was just too much for them to pay. They just weren't into it. So, we went down $20 to [a suggested retail price of] $79.99."

The SRP, Kripalani explained, is important to distributors, who expect to pay approximately 45 percent of that price for the product. They add a small markup before selling it to retailers. The in-store price, which varies from outlet to outlet, generally reflects the extremely competitive market for computer games. More than a year after its release, "Journeyman" generally retails for about $49, Kripalani said. "I've seen it as cheap as $39 or $40, but that's really cutting it close." Though some games continue to be discounted as their time in the marketplace lengthens, Presto has resisted additional price cuts for "Journeyman." "We just didn't want to do discounts, except for that one time," he emphasized. "Normally a game's shelf life is only about six months. So there's not enough time to discount. It's only with CD-ROM titles that we're seeing where sales don't drop off. 'Journeyman' already has had a shelf life of more than a year."

A Sales Pitch: Copy on the back of the game's box concluded with an appeal to buy.

Before opting for future discounts, Kripalani has begun to bundle "Journeyman" with other titles that are packaged with multimedia hardware, such as CD-ROM drives. The exposure he believes will help build the market for the game's sequel, due to be released in late fall 1994. On the other hand, "people really try to low-ball you on bundling deals. They come to you and say, 'we'll sell 100,000 copies of your product but we'll only give you $2 or $3 per disc.' You really have to weigh it out."

Sales

Networking within the infant CD-ROM industry was vital in generating initial sales of "The Journeyman Project," according to Presto's publicist Eric Hook. "We had a very limited budget," he recalled. "So a lot of what we did was talk to people that we know in the industry. The CD-ROM industry is a small and close-knit community. We know all of our competitors, the people that make the discs and the people who publish them. We networked. Apple helped us a lot. Apple put our demo on their sample CD-ROM that they ship with their CD-ROM players. People would go into a computer store, play the demo disc, and see our demo, and then order the game. We still get a lot of calls saying they saw our demo on that disc."

Kripalani agreed that hitching a ride on other companies' discs was a key, early marketing strategy. "Apple and a lot of other companies have been a great deal of help to us. Since CD-ROMs hold so much, people who are doing them have leftover space on their discs. They're looking for cool stuff to make their disc worth more, and we're looking for exposure. So we give them a copy of our 15-megabyte demo and they put it on their disc. That's been our most cost-effective way of marketing."

The first major distribution channel for "Journeyman" was through mail order houses, which accepted copies of the game in exchange for Presto's share of co-op advertising fees. "We do a lot of co-op advertising in the catalogs of companies like MacConnection and MacWarehouse. Fifty percent of all Mac software is bought through the mail and 20 percent of that is bought from MacWarehouse. So between the two, we get good exposure. Many times people see something they want in the catalog and they don't even wait a day. They go to the computer store and buy it. Or, vice versa, they see a demo at a computer store and run home and order it from MacWarehouse.

"We spend from 15 to 20 percent of our gross revenue on [co-op advertising]. We were Educorp's best seller for the last three or four months [spring, 1993]. We were MacConnection's number one best seller in June 1993. They come to you and say you're a best seller and we want to keep promoting your stuff, so you buy more space in their catalog. It's expensive. We give them product in trade to pay for it, and as long as that ad sells that amount of product, plus two or three times that amount, we're set. If we sell four times that amount, then we're totally set because then we're close to our 20 percent."

Convincing some major firms to distribute the game proved to be more of a challenge. "Some distributors saw 'Journeyman' at the CES (Computer Electronics Show)," Hook said. "One was Baker & Taylor. They were pushing our product from the very beginning, knowing that this market was going to take off, and they wanted a foothold. They were one of the first, and they are our top-selling distributor. We were on a waiting list for Ingram Micro. They are very selective. They only carry products that do about $25,000 a month. A Macintosh CD-ROM generally wouldn't be accepted by them, but we finally were, which was a big coup for us. On the other hand, a few large distributors like Merisel turned us down."

Presto also had some difficulty gaining entry into the nationwide computer super stores. "There's just so much shelf space," said Kripalani, "and most stores weren't stocking Mac CD-ROM games, but that's changed, and we're now in the chains like CompUSA." The next step is space on the shelves in small mom-and-pop outlets, including bookstores, and giant warehouse stores like Costco. "We're not complaining; we've done great," he added. "We sold more than 10,000 copies (in the first six months of 1993) and 'way back when,' I said if we can sell 10,000 in the first year, we're going to be fine."

Foreign Distribution

With U.S. sales climbing, Presto set its sights on sales in other countries in Asia and Europe. And as a result, the entire "Journeyman" team wound up with an expense-paid trip to the 1993 MacWorld Tokyo show.

"The Japanese were one of the first to take an interest in the game," said Kripalani. "With Interactive Media Agency, a company in Los Angeles, acting as our agent, we ended up striking a deal with Bandai, Japan's largest toy maker, which has rights to a lot of the old Japanese content like Godzilla movies and Thunderbird television shows. They wanted to get into the CD-ROM market. So they decided, not only to do their own titles, but to buy them from outside developers. They have exclusive Japanese rights, and we make lifetime royalty money. Their marketing budget for their blowout was about $80,000 and part of the marketing budget included flying all nine of us to Tokyo for the MacWorld show. Geno and Greg stayed in Japan for three weeks all expenses paid, and did the Japanese conversion. They hired Japanese actors and rerecorded the script and spoken QuickTime movies, and translated all the on-screen text into Japanese."

Introduced in spring 1993, "Journeyman" broke all sales records for CD-ROM games in Japan, selling more than 5,000 copies in two weeks. By the end of the year, almost 10,000 copies had been sold, making the game the number one bestseller in Japan. The initial licensing agreement prepaid Presto for slightly more than 3,000 units; thus they already have begun to bank royalty checks. In spring of the following year, a version of "Journeyman" was shipped for the NEC 9800 series of computers very popular in Japan.

Japan wasn't the only foreign country to see gold in this CD-ROM game. "We sell the English version in all the big markets," said Kripalani. "France is a big market and we're in England, Italy, Germany, and Australia." By spring 1994, Kripalani said, French, German, and Spanish versions had joined a "Queen's English" version of the game.

According to Hook, selecting foreign distributors was a kind of

The Journey to Japan: Promotion of a Japanese version of the game paid off with record setting sales.

a weeding-out process. "We met most of the foreign distributors at the 1992 MacWorld in San Francisco. They would come by the booth, get excited about the game and say they would like to carry it. We came away from the show with big stacks of catalogs and business cards. So we looked through them and looked for companies that sold products in the entertainment area. Just because a company sells a lot of software doesn't mean that it's going to be your type of software. We've set up tentative exclusive deals with distributors in most of the countries, with two in the UK."

FINANCE: Teamwork Pays Off

Financing a project by an unknown company, always difficult, was even more of a challenge in the recessionary economy of the early 1990s. Yet Kripalani was determined to maintain Presto's financial independence and retain ownership of the game it was creating. He succeeded, thanks to some monetary help from family and friends, and a well-equipped team that was willing to work for free.

"We wanted to stay away from venture capital. And we wanted to own the program outright," said Kripalani. "For investment capital, we went to our parents first and our friends second. That ended up generating everything we needed. We really didn't need much money at first; we took out our first loans in the summer [of 1992], about eight months before we started shipping."

"We offered investors ten percent on their money on an unsecured promissory account," Kripalani continued. "In their eyes, it was secure because we were their kids; in our eyes, we were going over our heads in debt. We ended up rounding up about $60,000; enough for us to pay the rent on the houses and to buy the macaroni and cheese. We didn't have a lot of huge expenses until the final disc pressing."

Kripalani admits that budgeting a project of this scope was hit and miss. "It was tough to estimate the costs, because a lot of this was just so brand new. I thought I had a good idea of costs, but I was off by about 50 percent, because I was just thinking pure expenses like pressing discs. I didn't know how much brochures cost. But if we needed money, we found it. The very last deal we made was with one of our distributors, Educorp. We said, "Here's the final product. We're going to gold disc any day now. Please place your first order. If you do that now and pay us in advance, we'll give you an extra ten percent.' And they pre-ordered 500 discs, which was something like $20,000."

According to Kripalani, one expense that doesn't show up on the balance sheet is labor. "I figure about 15,000 man hours went into the game and the bulk of that in the last six months. For the most part, it was difficult planning, because there were no models to go by and most of us were new to the industry. So we said, 'Let's not worry about the hours or the details, let's worry about what's important—the project. And when we're done, assuming we make any money, we'll split everything evenly.'"

By mid-1993, Kripalani said Presto had enough money in the bank to repay its loans and to pay staff members small salaries. "We asked our lenders if they wanted their money back and most of them said leave it in, but we paid them back anyway," Kripalani noted. As for staff pay rates, he added, "The average student as they graduate from college is making about $24,000 a year, and we're all making

Moving Up: Success made it possible for Presto Studios to move into new offices.

at least that." Remuneration from future projects by Presto Studios, which was incorporated in July 1992, will be divided differently, though, Kripalani said, "It won't be the same. It's already been changed. It's just that some people, by the nature of their jobs, do more work, and they have to be compensated more than everyone else."

Looking back over its history, it becomes obvious how important team dedication was to completion of the project. "If you pay people during the production term," Kripalani explained, "you're looking at $400,000 or $450,000 in salaries. If you add in the computers and equipment, it would be another $100,000. But as it was, our total expenses, without labor and equipment, were around $120,000. Lifetime 'Journeyman' will make on the order of a million dollars. So even if it takes a half a million in pure costs, there's still a half a million in profits."

FUTURE PROJECTS: Closer and Closer to Film

Since the market for PC games is quadruple that for Mac games, naturally a Windows version of "The Journeyman Project" was a priority for Presto. So was development of "The Journeyman Project II." Once again the team decided to play to its strengths. They turned over conversions of the first "Journeyman" and are focusing on creation of the new game.

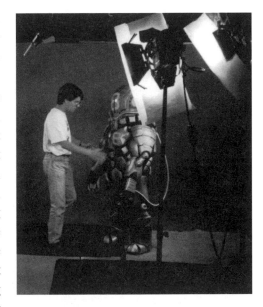

It took Kripalani, Flanagan, and Saunders five months to draft the script for "The Journeyman Project II," which picks up six months after the first game left off. Now, though, instead of working out of make-do offices, they gather to brainstorm in their new headquarters in a modern office complex in north San Diego. Although they are not eating much macaroni and cheese this time around, there are still signs of the good old days. The conference room is outfitted with a futon couch that pulls out into a bed when they pull all-nighters. In the spring of 1994, with release of "Journeyman II" only months away, the pace was already fast and furious. "We are well into graphic production," said Kripalani, who had hired three new people to work with the original Presto team. "And for our large blue screen video shoot [using Beta SP], we had this costume made up in Hollywood that is just insane. We'll have a lot more actors, a lot more video in this one."

On Stage: Kripalani adjusts space suit during the shooting of "Journeyman II."

While "The Journeyman Project" ultimately raised the standard for CD-ROM-based games, today Kripalani said he is "almost embarrassed by it. It's unbelievable how much better the sequel will be. Just to give you an idea of the complexity of the environments, in the first game, the average world had 10,000 to 15,000 polygons. For 'Journeyman II,' we're averaging about 200,000 polygons.

There's a lot more detail in everything." All of that effort is aimed at taking the second game "toward interactive film making. We want people to be really convinced, to have no doubt in their minds that this is real."

"Journeyman," like "Spaceship Warlock," has probably been analyzed screen-by-screen by other aspiring game makers who are determined to best it. Kripalani's goal is to beat them to the punch. "Everyone out there knows that this is a benchmark they will have to surpass. And we're going to surpass it. We want to go leaps and bounds beyond it."

The Sequel: Scenes from "The Journeyman Project II" display state-of-the-art realism.

4

WERNDL, "FEEL AT HOME AT THE OFFICE"

Big Hand Productions

At A Glance

WERNDL "FEEL AT HOME AT THE OFFICE"

Developers: Designed and produced by Big Hand Productions, Inc. Dallas, Texas; Executive Producer, Two's Company, Eindhoven, Holland; Software Engineers, Interactive Resources, Des Moines, Iowa.

Client: Werndl Office Furniture Systems.

Key Personnel: Jay Wolff, producer/director; Lance Lyda, project manager; Troy Harrison, art director; Natalie Ammirato, Brian Barr, Patti Bonham, Troy Harrison, Chris Howay, Lance Lyda, Rajesh Nidwannaya, Don Relyea, Bryan Taylor, and Jay Wolff, graphic artists; Brian Barr, character designer; Brian Barr, Chris Howay, and Steve Ross, animators; Valerie Grant, disc author; Steve O'Brien, audio post production, Cursor Audio; James Neel, audio/music scores, James Neel Productions; Rowan Gibson, copywriter; Peter Barrat-Jones, art director/Europe; Joelle Sandberg, account coordinator/Europe; Steve Dickinson, Bob Lawson, and Rob Arnold, software engineers.

Description: An integrated sales presentation tool on a single interactive compact disc designed for playback on the Compact Disc-Interactive (CD-I) platform. Created entirely in German, it contains the equivalent of 300 transparencies, three minutes of animation, and several self-running audiovisual presentations in full color with stereo sound.

Development hours: "Many standard multimedia work weeks."

Development period: September 1992–January 1993.

Production hardware: Various Macintosh models (IIci to Quadra) with color monitors, Philips CD-I authoring system, SyQuest drives, UMAX transparency scanner, various hard drives, Digidesign sound card, and LaserWriter printer.

Production software: Adobe Photoshop, Macromedia Director, deBabelizer, Adobe Illustrator, Engraver, MacFlow, and Adobe Premiere.

Presentation hardware: Compact Disc-Interactive (CD-I); Portable CD-I Player on-the-road, and CD-I base kiosks in dealerships.

Cost to develop: $120,000.

Financing: Client funded.

Awards: Gold Medal, Sales/Marketing Applications (sales presentation), *NewMedia* INVISION Multimedia Awards, 1993; Finalist, Point of Sale, European Multimedia Awards (EMMA), 1993; Finalist, Best Industrial Presentation/Marketing Program; The CD-I Association Annual Awards, 1993.

Future projects: Annual updates and new product discs.

Contact: Kimberly Rispin
             Big Hand Productions, Inc.
             4514 Travis Street, Suite 220
             Dallas, Texas 75205
             214–526–2888 ☐ 214–526–288 (fax)

It was a dream come true. A young multimedia company landed a major overseas account. The assignment: to create a digital promotion of a major office furniture company and its wares. Done right, it could bring new business, an international reputation, and a niche among the rising stars in a rapidly growing industry. No wonder, Jay Wolff and Chris Howay couldn't say no.

After all, the two college buddies had big ambitions when they formed their multimedia production company, Big Hand, in Dallas two and a half years earlier. Since March 1991, they made their

mark as developers for the then new CD-I player by Philips Consumer Electronics. Both were excited about this affordable, plug-and-play multimedia platform that plugged into a television and did not require a computer to operate. Since CD-I simplified use of CD-ROM business applications in

A Werndl Welcome:
Dunny Bugnugget, an animated Everyman, domimates a menu screen.

the field, Wolff and Howay were confident that it would spur demand for the multimedia presentations, and create work for their young firm.

However, in their wildest dreams, Wolff and Howay could not have predicted that their CD-I work eventually would attract the attention of a Dutch marketing firm, that worked for one of Germany's oldest furniture companies. When two businesses came to Big Hand for a multimedia sales presentation, the opportunity was too good to reject. So what if the presentation had to be in a foreign language, for foreign television, in three months, by a novice Big Hand team, using unproven tools and production techniques? No problem.

Within weeks, in the midst of the holiday season, the dream job had turned into the multimedia version of "The Nightmare Before Christmas." The client changed its mind, twice, about what it wanted. Big Hand's already stretched team had to race to complete a major revision in merely thirty days time. And, with that impossible deadline only days away, fatigue, pressure, and technical trouble combined to gobble up a gigabyte of work.

But, on January 18, 1993, Big Hand delivered "Feel At Home At the Office," an interactive CD-I disc that shows off the wares of Werndl Furniture to potential clients. Included was an overview of the company's history and a complete catalog of its office furniture, plus a witty pitch on the advantages of a well-designed office, told through the antics of an animated worker, Dunny Bugnugget. The sleek colorful interface and graphics echo the old line company's corporate logo, while a specially commissioned soundtrack adds to the modern mood.

The presentation has earned Big Hand a big hand from its multimedia colleagues. In 1993, "Feel At Home At the Office" won the Gold Medal for Best Sales/Marketing Application (sales presentation) at the *NewMedia* INVISION Multimedia Awards. Meanwhile, Werndl's business has boomed, despite the worldwide recession, moving it into the forefront of Europe's furniture makers. Big Hand's business also has increased. It now boasts a client list that includes Southwestern Bell, Mercedes Benz, and Time-Warner. The company's revenue tripled in 1993, topping $1.2 million.

Like many pioneers in this industry, Big Hand's founders often are forced to learn on the job, as they did with the Werndl project. In their drive to make a name, and profit, for themselves, developers take on the unknown, boldly confident that they can solve problems as they arise. In the process, as Big Hand's experience exemplifies, they are charting the brave new world of multimedia production management, as

Big Hand's Home: The firm worked on the Werndl project in this historic building.

they stretch the boundaries of this new form of business communications.

Wolff believes that Big Hand's CD-I projects stand out in the increasingly crowded multimedia field, because of the company's emphasis on design. "It was very evident that, at the beginning of CD-I, the developers were all programmers," he explained. "The design just wasn't there. There were all these big square buttons that said, 'push this'.... Now there are a lot of people out there doing better design, and as a result, we're seeing better and better discs."

From that point of view, the company's decidedly non-technical name starts to make some sense. "We were avoiding the computer approach, because the talent sitting at the computer is much more important—the hand is more important than the mouse," Wolff volunteered. "That's why our stuff looks so different because we hire artists; we don't hire computer people.... We did Right Brain, Left Brain, trying to incorporate computers and design. That became Right Hand, Left Hand; Big Hand, Big Brain; and then Big Dog, Bad Dog; and finally Big Hand...and Big Hand was the one that kept sticking." He paused. "It's not a very good story. But that is how it happened! If you can think of a better one...."

Hand Over Mouse:
Big Hand's logo reflects its emphasis on art, not technology.

THE OPPORTUNITY: Big Hand Across the Ocean

If the naming of Big Hand seems a little convoluted, the company's link up with a client in Germany seems like the invention of a cybernetic Rube Goldberg. Wolff actually started the ball rolling during a trip to Knoxville in February 1991, but neither he nor the Philips' staffers he met in Tennessee could have imagined it at the time. In fact, neither could have dreamed that in a matter of months, he'd be an experienced CD-I developer.

Then partners in a struggling animation business, Wolff and Howay had wanted to spearhead the creation of a new multimedia computer platform to play their clients' software applications in the field. "I was producing animated trade show kiosks on a Macintosh. They required at least 8-bit color, at least 8 MEGS of RAM, and a Macintosh IIx to operate," Wolff said. When his customers rented Macs in different cities, "something would always go wrong. Sometimes the rental company didn't put in the additional 4 MEGS of RAM. Or, kids would mess with the system so that the exhibitors couldn't restart the program." Concerned that these recurring hardware problems would hurt business in the long run, he was determined to find a simple playback system.

Then early in 1991, Wolff and Howay spied a brochure from Philips Interactive Media on the Dutch company's new CD-I player. "It was disc-based," Wolff recalled. "It was portable. It plugged into your TV. It didn't require a computer system. It didn't have a keyboard. It was exactly what we needed and exactly what our clients needed." Wolff was convinced CD-I was the solution to his problem, but convincing the company to let him see and sell it, took some fast talking. Still in the testing stage, and unsure of CD-I's market, Philips then did not have a sales representative in the entire South who could demonstrate its new system for Wolff. "I told them I could sell this today," he said. "I told them I could replace a $12,000 Macintosh with their $2,000 box..... And they were saying it's not really ready, and we don't think the market is all that big or hot right now." Somehow, the youthful Texan made his point; he was invited to Knoxville and spent the day with the Philips product manager. Two weeks later, he had a CD-I player, courtesy of Philips' vice president of sales, who let him use it between trade shows.

One sales presentation later and Big Hand had a client for the new system. Another Texas firm, DSC Communications Corporation, had contacted Big Hand about a multimedia presentation for an upcoming trade show in Geneva. Having shown the DSC executives his previous Mac multimedia projects, Wolff demonstrated some sample CD-I discs, emphasizing that the technology was not on the market yet. DSC was sold on Big Hand *and* CD-I. "It needs to be multi-format....in four languages...and we want all the animation that you are known for," DSC's leaders told Wolff. "There was only one hitch. We didn't know how to make a CD-I disc," Wolff said with a laugh. "Well we were used to it. We've taken a lot of big leaps."

For two frantic months, Big Hand worked with DSC's advertising agency to produce a kiosk disc. "It nearly killed us," said a semi-serious Wolff. "It obviously sucked up all of our time; we were literally doing nothing else." Since the authoring program was still in the very early stages of development, the Big Hand staff worked closely with OptImage, the firm doing the work for Philips. "They actually jumped through a lot of hoops to get it up and running," Wolff said. "It ended up being the largest program ever developed with their software. When we got it finished in the last couple of days, it wouldn't press onto a disc, because it was so big."

As one of the few experienced CD-I developers, it's no wonder Big Hand was tapped to produce a number of CD-I demonstrations that would extend the company's reputation across the Atlantic to Europe. The first was for OptImage, for presentation at the first international conference on CD-I in late October 1991. There, their work impressed the head of Philips Interactive Media of America, who subsequently hired Big Hand to create a point-of-sale demonstration disc for CD-I retailers.

On Halloween Eve, Wolff met with editors of *CD-I World*, a print magazine published by Parker Taylor Co. Over a beer and a handshake, Big Hand agreed to do an interactive version of the magazine on CD-I. The resulting title premiered in March 1992 and scored a big hit with Philips. Disc Manufacturing, Inc. pressed discs for free, then Philips distributed more than 10,000 discs worldwide and company executives credit it with selling more CD-I

Demo Disc:
This sampler for Philips' CD-I system won many fans for Big Hand.

players than any other application.

Meanwhile, Werndl Furniture, a family-run maker of office furniture based in Rosenheim, Germany, under the new leadership of the founder's great grandson, wanted to boost the firm's sales, which then ranked third among the country's office furniture companies. Aware that the sales leaders spend a total of 1 and 2 million respectively on marketing, Werndl's chief executive upped the ante to $3 million and hired a Dutch marketing and communications company, Two's Company, to update its image.

One of Two's Company's strategies was to make a statement about Werndl by using multimedia, primarily CD-I. Why CD-I? Two's Company, it turned out, also represented a giant Dutch company headquartered in its home base of Eindhoven, with branches and subsidiaries all over the world, including Knoxville, Tenn. With none other than Philips Electronics as a major client, Two's Company was working to introduce CD-I on the continent and often used the Big Hand demo disc in its sales presentations. One look at the "CD-I World" disc, and Werndl's leaders were sold on the new technology and Big Hand.

"So (Two's Company) called us," recalled Wolff. "It was real interesting, because I was walking by our operating officer, and said, 'you know we really need to get ready for some overseas business because I believe business is going to come over from Europe and Asia as much as from the U.S.' The next day we got a fax from Two's Company saying, 'Hey we want you to do a CD-I project. Can you guys come over here by Wednesday of next week?'" On Monday and Tuesday, faxes flew back and forth between the two companies, convincing Wolff that the job was almost a sure thing. "We normally don't make $2,000 sales calls," he quipped. "But they obviously needed to shake some hands and see some smiles. I flew to Holland the next day to close the deal. And that's how it started."

THE TEAM: Helping Hands

Since his teen years in Tulsa, Oklahoma, 28-year-old Jay Wolff has been intrigued by technology—not its bits and bytes, but applications. When he was a high school sophomore, he insisted that his parents come with him to look at Apple's Lisa computer. "It was absolutely unaffordable, and I didn't need one," he recalled. "But I was showing them the interface and the idea of the icons, and I said, 'This is going to change the way people use technology.... This is momentous.'"

At the time, Wolff was struggling with career choices. He wanted to study art, but he excelled in science and math and felt "a responsibility to take engineering and stuff and be serious about life." On a full scholarship, he enrolled at Southern Methodist University in Dallas as a computer engineering major. A year and a half later, he had realized, "I don't want to program the thing, I just want to be the best at applying it." At the end of two years, though, he had flunked out of the costly private school.

Helping Hands: Big Hand's team grew during its work for Werndl.

Determined to re-enroll, Wolff had to find a source of income to pay his SMU tuition. His solution was a T-shirt business. It not only brought him much needed cash, but it led to a meeting with a talented SMU freshman majoring in fine arts, Chris Howay. "I had a nice thing going," Wolff said. "It was just before the T-shirt craze, and I started a craze on campus. Chris, who was two years behind me, had designed a shirt for some of his friends, and it was much better than anything I had produced. So I hired him." The two undergraduates soon became best friends, fraternity brothers, and partners in the thriving business.

When he graduated with a degree in economics and finance, Wolff fulfilled a longtime dream and in 1988. He headed for Europe on a "T-shirt company loan." "I took a backpack to travel around with, and a duffle bag of shirts and ties in case I happened to find a job," he remembered. When he called a Mac reseller in Dusseldorf, Germany, to rent a computer to use to write his resume, Wolff ended up joining the firm and selling computer graphics systems to the NATO military forces. "Since showing it to my parents, I have been totally attentive to the Mac," he said, explaining his expertise. "Knowing a little bit before everyone else propelled me to learn a lot more.... Still, I have to admit, I'm one of the luckiest people." In his spare time, Wolff huddled with technicians, "talking about what was possible with the technology, especially with CD-ROMs. I realized that things were happening faster than I had expected. I had these ideas, like everyone else, but here I was in Germany. So, not able to implement anything there, I came home."

Eye on CD-I:
Big Hand co-founder Chris Howay checks CD-I discs for defects.

Back in Dallas, after a year abroad, Wolff again needed cash to pay back his loan from the T-shirt company which was still being run by Howay. He joined a fraternity brother who was doing desktop publishing. "It was that time when businesses were selling computers, but didn't know anything about them," he said. "So our customers started buying Macs from us." Within a year, the company was the fastest growing Apple reseller in the Dallas area, as well as a VAR for forty other high-tech companies. "Our big claim to fame," Wolff remembered, "was the setting up of a $500,000 Macintosh prepress system for Horchow catalogs." The success was heady, but Wolff said it taught him a valuable lesson. "I learned that when you are successful, you will be doing more of what you've been doing. When I understood that, I said, 'I'm going to have to leave to do multimedia. Otherwise it's going to pass me by.' So I quit."

With his commission money, Wolff and Howay formed Big Hand and moved into a nondescript Dallas office building. "He was the one friend of mine, who would always say, 'Hell, yeah, let's do it,'" Wolff said of his partner. "I was always talking about what I ought to do. I should be doing multimedia. I should be working

for myself. And he said, 'If that's what you think, let's do it.'" In March 1990, that was easier said than done, even though the partners' ambition was to create computer graphics and animation. "As we began, basing our new business on a new technology there was a glaring roadblock," Wolff said. "Interactive technology and

Project Managers: Jay Wolff, left, and Lance Lyda took charge of the Werndl project.

multimedia—our business, might was well have been Greek terms in 1990. Nobody knew what the heck we were talking about." Especially conservative financial institutions. To qualify for a $30,000 bank loan to purchase equipment, the partners had to come up with $15,000, which they raised in eight days from family, friends, and even "one new acquaintance."

During its formative years, both Wolff and Howay produced computer graphics and animations for their first projects. But as the company grew, "Chris kept on drawing, and I was answering the phones and handling the clients," Wolff said. "That's basically, how I ended up in my position (as president)." Like any new venture, Big Hand had its financial ups and downs. During one particularly lean time, Wolff admits he was evicted from his home. But, "we've never missed a payday for our employees, and never bounced a paycheck. We're proud of that," Wolff said. "Payday for the owners is another matter. It's scheduled for the first of each month, but in reality is a very 'flexible' date."

For the Werndl project, Wolff exchanged his executive hat for a producer/director's cap, since so few members of the Big Hand crew had the necessary experience. "As president, for the most part I was running the company as opposed to producing projects," Wolff explained. "Our head producer was working on a Philips demo, which was consuming all of his time and all of our artists' time. So I became a producer again." To manage the project, Big Hand turned to newly hired 25-year-old Lance Lyda, a graduate of Texas Christian University with a commercial art degree. He had just moved back to his home state from California, where he had worked as a freelance designer for ad agencies, producing art on his Macintosh. Newly-married to a fellow Texan, he was introduced to Wolff by a friend who leased Big Hand its computers. When one key developer on the Werndl project left the company, Lyda became Wolff's right-hand man, with primary responsibility for asset management.

Wolff served as liaison with the European team. Two's Company's Rowan Gibson wrote the copy, Peter Barrat-Jones was the European art director, and Joelle Sandberg served as account executive. "I would handle day-to-day script problems, changes, translations from German, and things like that," Lyda said. "Jay would handle crisis situations, or anything relating to design." During his early days with Big Hand, being a project manager or producer meant doing "just what ever it takes to make it happen," he said. "It has kind of evolved into a producer-type role, where I'm overseeing projects as they come in.... Now I oversee the total project, insuring that it comes in on time, on budget."

The size and quick turnaround of the Werndl project, plus the two other major projects already in progress, strained Big Hand's resources. When Wolff returned from Europe with the contract in hand, he knew he had to add to his seven-member staff. In the end, art director Troy Harrison would supervise a crew of 10 computer artists who were responsible for the animation and graphics. Three software engineers in Iowa and an in-house disc author rounded out the team. "Everyone, other than the art director, was pretty brand spanking new," recalled Wolff, who along with Lyda assisted with production chores. "When Werndl came in, we

All On Hand: Weekly meetings bring Big Hand's teams together.

had just moved into some new offices and we had seven people," he said. "That was twelve months ago. Now we have twenty."

New business and a much bigger staff dictated changes in Big Hand's development process. "Before, we used to have two or three projects at once and everyone in the shop—all seven to nine people—worked on each one," Wolff said. Now with as many as ten projects in-house at a time, "we have design teams," he continued. "We split the whole studio into small three- and four-man teams so that each team has a couple of projects. The mission of each team is to stay with your group; don't steal talent from anyone else's team. Budget everything as if those three or four people were the only ones who were going to touch the job." The result is "the communications are better, the designs are better, everybody gets along better, and we are able to produce much more."

Currently the small teams see each project through from start to finish; however, Wolff believes Big Hand may outgrow that system in the near future. "We're thinking of setting up a studio to do the design work and then pass it off to production. We may move to that model when we open another branch. We might actually have that group either be the studio or production group."

PRODUCTION: Multinational Multimedia As Easy As *Eins, Zwei ...*

Wolff stayed in Holland for ten days, hammering out a contract and meeting over lunch and dinner with Two's Company staffers on the design and content of the project. By the time he headed back to Texas, most of the details, down to a node map for the program, had been approved. "So I ended up signing the contract and went home," Wolff recalled, never dreaming that the project would change course, not once, but twice, in the hectic weeks ahead.

During the discussions in Holland, Wolff had insisted that the presentation be designed for a single purpose, for sales presentations, or trade show display, but not both. The furniture maker opted for the sales aid. However, as a huge European office furniture trade show grew closer, Werndl set its sights on the CD-I presentation as their exhibit's centerpiece. "But it wasn't being designed by our team to be a trade show disc," moaned Wolff. "A disc designed for a trade show would include animation to attract people. It would need to project a lot of good sound, but we were designing it for a conference room where you don't want to blow people away.

Wanting to make their new clients happy, the Big Hand team scrambled to finish a disc that would work in Werndl's trade show booth, which featured a circle of six large viewing screens with track balls on the exterior and a huge sixteen-screen video wall with a disc player inside that would play the program continually. Via trans-Atlantic phone calls, they learned that the backdrop for the video wall was stone, so they even incorporated that into the screen textures. "But we knew, once the show was over, that this was not the disc we wanted to end up with," Wolff recalled.

During the trade show in Cologne, the Werndl booth "was busy and full of life the whole time," Wolff said. But he and his art

Starting Over: Art Director, Troy Harrison, knew the Werndl disc needed major revisions.

director, Troy Harrison, were downcast. In thirty days, they had to deliver a CD-I disc for sales presentations, and a quick review of the screens in the trade show version of the program convinced them "we had to start over from scratch." "Troy and I went home sick," Wolff continued. "We knew we had to start over because the fundamental design element wasn't working with anything else. And there was this damn stone interface.... Once we pulled that out we were left with almost nothing."

For the next four weeks, Big Hand's Dallas office was a beehive of activity twenty-four hours a day, as they remade the Werndl disc. In the midst of the makeover, the furniture maker notified them that it was dropping two product lines featured in the catalog section of the presentation and adding a new one. "That's why the Werndl product menu is a scrolling menu, because we kept having to redesign it, changing the number of buttons on the screen," Wolff said, with disbelief still in his voice.

On January 18, as previously planned, representatives from Two's Company and Werndl were showing the disc to the entire Werndl sales force in Germany. Miraculously, Big Hand had delivered! If he had it to do over again? "I would stick to my guns," Wolff stressed. "I would not produce a project that served two purposes.... I trust myself now more than I did then." When the focus changed, "I should have just stopped the project and had them sign off on a new project and insisted on a bonus to repeat some of the original design work." Even so, he still believes "it was worth it. It was painful, but it was worth it."

Storyboarding and Scripting

As soon as Wolff returned from his initial trip to Holland, the Big Hand team began to immerse themselves in everything Werndl—history, products, and graphics. Existing photos and artwork were inventoried; company brochures and catalogs were studied for corporate style. At the same time, the script was drafted by the Two's Company copywriter, Rowan Gibson, who wrote in English for the Dallas crew, and then had Werndl translate it into German.

Even though the presentation is predominately in German, some English phrases were left in. "In Germany, it's cool to use English phrases," according to Lyda. "They don't make up new words like we do, like 'sanitation engineer,' and such. If a phrase, or a word, doesn't exist in German, they sometimes keep it in the language that it came from. For some time, English phrases, particularly titles of things, were considered stylish. That's why phrases like 'feel at home at the office,' were left in."

During their early meetings, Wolff and Two's marketing team had shaped Werndl's presentation into four segments: an introduction and history of the company, called "The Spirit of Innovation"; an animated feature that showed how employees are adversely affected by poor office design; a catalog of Werndl's office furniture lines; and an overview of its office design service. Since employee comfort meant greater productivity, "Feel At Home At The Office" was selected as the overall theme.

With the script and artwork in hand, Wolff and his co-workers began the storyboarding process. Section by section, the individual screens were sketched one at a time, and numbered photos were matched to them. Then requests were made for the matching transparencies and photos. Before the trade show in Cologne, Wolff asked for pictures as he needed them. However, during the higher-pressure redesign, he borrowed Two's complete Werndl art file, promising to return all of it when they were done. "That's actually pretty common," Wolff added. "Some clients just bring us a box. It's got slides, all their print material, and a couple of video tapes. And they say this is what we need, but on a disc. So we write scripts and go from there."

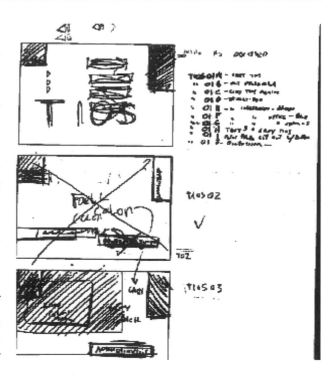

Screen Sketches: Storyboarding for the Werndl sales presentation began with rough layouts like these.

Although Big Hand had a script and did flow charts and story-boards, Lyda, in retrospect, feels that even more planning would have been helpful. "One of the things I would have done back then, and we do this now, is plan more in advance," he said. "We used to get a project and start producing immediately.... We used to just experiment, find what worked and what didn't, redo it until it was perfect and send it to the client. Instead, we now figure the whole thing out: how it works, how it is going to branch, and how it is going to run, before we even go into production. In the past, we used probably twenty percent of our effort planning, with about eighty percent production. Now it's eighty percent planning, twenty percent production. It is substantially easier, and more successful."

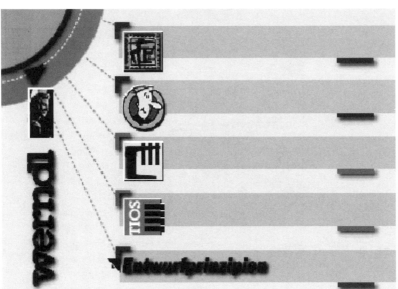

Werndl Interface:
The Big Hand design echoes the furniture maker's catalogs and other print materials.

INTERFACE DESIGN AND NAVIGATION

Big Hand's approach to interface design and interactivity begins and ends with two words: simple and elegant. At the same time, the company strives to identify all new digital presentations with their clients' existing graphic look. "So we try to be unique and innovative and at the same time be very consistent and similar," Wolff said. "That's really the challenge."

Meeting that challenge for Werndl began with an interface design that echoes the company's catalogs and brochures. "We grabbed different items from their print material," Wolff said. "Basically, we used the same kinds of graphic elements they had used...like flat plains, flat colored bars and colored squares. They have this black stripe on their print material, so we put a black rectangle in the (top right) corner of the screen with the word Werndl going up the side vertically." While the graphics may be familiar, the addition of interactive multimedia—animation and video—gives the graphics new life. "So we can take their static brochures and use the same graphic elements," he explained, "but they appear very new and very innovative, because things on our disc are moving as opposed to sitting there on the page."

On the Move:
This draft flow chart is the navigation system for Werndl's program.

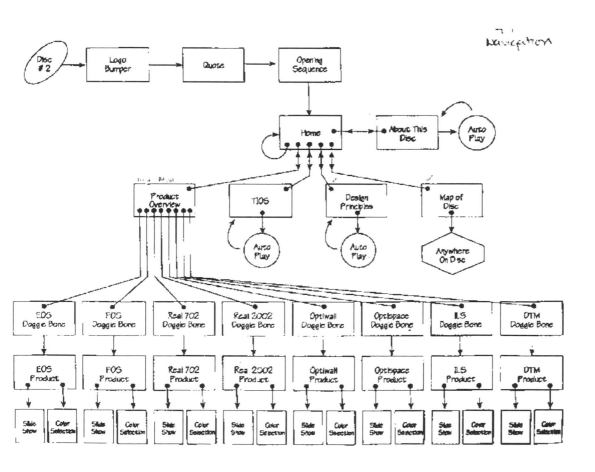

The Werndl project owes much of its award-winning graphic style primarily to art director Harrison and his crew of designers. All were stretched by the freedom and demands of this new medium. Lyda said, "Its a whole different ball game from producing for print, which everybody is used to, and everybody has done. All of a sudden you are not just moving from page one to page six, you are moving wherever you want, whenever you want. Which means that there have to be buttons that can be understood by the user. Sometimes they have to be understood by the user even if he doesn't speak the language that the disc is in." For the Werndl project, he said, that meant "months of research and testing of interfaces and how to put buttons on. We changed up until the last minute."

The finished product—with its menu of color-coded buttons on the right side of the screen—reflects Lyda's philosophy on interface design. "You never close a door on the user. If he goes somewhere, he's got to be able to find his way out.... Especially non-computer types, and a lot of the world is still not computer smart.... If they can't (go where they want to), they are going to get confused, and frustrated, and they are going to walk away from your program." To avoid such "dead-ends" or "black holes" in the Werndl project, Harrison and his team added a small return button to every screen, that takes users back to the main menu. As they move from section to section, a graphic in the upper right corner of the previous screen, and a black bar bordered with a color-coded stripe on the left side, indicate the section they are in. Each section in the Werndl presentation has a distinctive color scheme as well, a "subtle psychological change" that helps users navigate. "The fact

A Way Out:
A button at the top right of every screen takes users back to the main menu.

that you went from one section to another, needs to be made visually, we used color to communicate this," Lyda said.

Wolff shares Lyda's concerns, emphasizing that a user-friendly interface and navigation are critical to the success of any multimedia application. "One of the problems in multimedia, so far, is that there are all of these buttons on the menu that don't have any clear purpose," he said. "If there are more than a few buttons on a screen, they lose their value and functionality. With a smörgasbord of options available, the user ends up being enamored with the technology, but doesn't really get the message you are intending to communicate." And while the technology offers the possibility of layer upon layer of interactivity, Wolff believes in "limiting the depth of the program." In fact, he finds merit in an old-fashioned linear presentation. For example, "it would take you three and a half hours to go completely through the 'CD-I World' disc—it's about five or six layers deep," he said. "You're in one menu, then you're in another menu.... We really learned from those kinds of projects that people got completely lost and didn't get the same value they might have if they were watching a TV show, where they'd get a preview at the beginning, a message and a summary at the end. That's always been a powerful way to present material."

As a result, the company vows never to go more than three layers deep in an interactive project. Sometimes they urge clients to divide their presentation and house it on more than one disc. "This isn't a capacity issue," Wolff emphasized. "Werndl is a good example. Werndl has a lot of information about the company, plus its product catalog on the disc. We are recommending that they split that one disc into two discs, so that the executives who are deciding on this multimillion dollar furniture purchase are always totally focused on one thing. And the salesman can control what they are focused on by which disc he plays." Changing discs is "literally a menu selection," he continued. "We think that's more powerful than putting two buttons on the first screen that ask, 'do you want to talk about the company or the products?' That's interactive design. Some clients think it's graphic design—where to put the buttons. But it's really how to control the psychology of the user."

GRAPHICS

Building the Werndl screens was a learning experience from start to finish for the Big Hand team. Managing what would amount to 5 gigabytes of graphics files would prove daunting. However, that problem paled when compared to coping with the idiosyncrasies of the CD-I system. Again and again, what the designers saw on their computer screens was not what they got on the CD-I's television monitor. "It's kind of good, I think, that we didn't know what we couldn't do," Lyda said, in retrospect, "so we just went ahead and did what most said couldn't be done."

As soon as the transparencies, slides, and negatives of the selected photos began to arrive from Holland and Germany, they were digitized. Initially, a 1200 DPI transparency scanner was used, but it was abandoned in favor of the Kodak Photo CD format because the latter "eliminated a lot of input problems," Wolff said. At the same time, Big Hand's graphic artists began the mammoth job of building over 2,000 screens in Photoshop on their Macintoshes.

About 80 percent of the computer art was created in Photoshop; most of the rest was done using Fractal Design's Painter. Each change on each screen of the CD-I program required a separate Photoshop screen. In addition, every main screen required an identically-sized highlight screen for the menu buttons. "In CD-I, when you pass over a button, it highlights or the button turns another color, creating an area

Lighting Up: Making these buttons hot spots required two screens and plenty of memory.

that is called a hot spot," Lyda said. "Highlighting hot spots is accomplished by using two identical screens with different colored or positioned buttons. So when you travel over the hot spot, the top screen goes transparent, and seamlessly shows the screen behind it with the different button." Since the artists were using alpha channels to create their designs, each screen initially consumed more than four megabytes. "When you multiply that by 2,000, you've got a lot of storage challenges," said Lyda.

As the screens were completed, they were compressed to save space and then stored in a hierarchy system that duplicated the layout of the CD-I program. All of the files for each section were in one folder, sub-folders held each group of screens. Under each master screen were the highlight screens. Quickly, Big Hand's available disc space was overloaded, so the company was forced to add three additional 1.2 gigabyte hard drives to help store, what would amount to, a whopping 5 gigabytes of graphic files for the Werndl project alone. "Storage and asset management are things you don't really think about in the beginning," Lyda admitted. "We've learned a lot since then."

One change devised to reduce the volume of files involved the creation of master screens. At the time, "we used the channels features in Photoshop extensively, where you can create different black and white channels, four selections, load that selection and alter that area. It holds up to sixteen channels, and we would usually fill them all up. Anytime you fill a channel, you add a lot of bytes to the size of the file—around 320K." Lyda soon realized that their storage space was overflowing with screens that were very similar except for a few channel changes. "We now will build a master for screens 1 through 20, for example," he continued. "We build those screens on that fully channeled document, then copy it and save it onto a new one, and then save that. (As a result,) it doesn't have any excess channels on it, you don't have to rebuild it, and it appears as if it has all the channels with it."

Since the graphics were destined for CD-I with its TV playback, the graphics team quickly learned that "what you see on your computer screen is not what you get on the TV," Lyda said. For starters, television resolution is half of most computer screens today. "So you can design something that looks awesome on your 24-bit monitor, convert it to CD-I, play it on the TV, and it looks

More complications: Initially graphics were lost or distorted when Big Hand compressed files to conform to European televison standards.

like hell," he explained. Then there's the fact that a computer screen has different proportions than a television screen and, if that weren't complication enough, the European television standard differs from the American one. As a result, when the computer graphics were converted to CD-I and played on the TV monitor, the edges of the design were lost.

To prevent this, the Big Hand crew framed its computer screens with a thin line; inside it were so-called safe areas for text, animations and buttons. Establishing this template was further complicated as the CD-I had to play on the PAL standard of European television, rather than the NTSC format used in the United States. "We went round and round with that," groaned Lyda, who discovered there were no existing CD-I standards for PAL and no PAL televisions available in Texas. "We were able to author in PAL on our authoring machine, so we could see what it looked like in PAL on our CD-I system. But when we would press a worm, pull it out and play it on our (NTSC) TV, we would have all sorts of images running off our screen." This problem forced the Big Hand team to experiment with different placements of the framed safe area before they solved the pesky problem. The solution? "Since NTSC shifts everything to the left substantially, our safe areas were not at the center of the screen, but off-center to the left," Lyda said. "When you look at some discs prepared for NTSC in Europe, you'll find everything is off to the left hand side of the screen."

A second unforeseen problem was distortion of rectangles and circles that resulted when the graphic screens were compressed vertically from 305 to 280 to conform to PAL television dimensions. "But what we found was, when you are scaling in percentages in between 50 and 100, that Photoshop doesn't really handle it that well," Lyda explained. "When it squishes them, you lose some of your image quality, and we were already having a problem having the full color photographs appear really sharp and crisp." The solution was not to try to distort the overall screen to make the geometric shapes true, but simply distort the specific distorted images, before they were compressed.

Colors also proved tricky to duplicate. "If you've got a red on screen, it's probably going to be red on TV, but you are never exactly sure which shade of red," Lyda said. To compensate, the Big Hand team created their own color palette chart for the project, after some experimentation. "We played the CD-1s we authored on TVs, pulled up beside our monitors and adjusted our Gamma on our computers," Lyda said. After testing every screen, "we made a master palette of all the colors and saved it as a Photoshop file," he continued. "Then while you are working, when you need a color, you get it from there." In addition, some of the colors, especially bright reds, would bleed or look blurred on the TV screen. To solve this problem, Photoshop was used to lower the color saturation level down below 78 percent. "We were pretty lucky with the photographs. They didn't have a whole lot of terribly saturated colors in them," Lyda noted. "And actually deBabelizer now has a function that will go through 24-bit images and take the saturation out of any colors that are too saturated and leave any that aren't alone."

Lyda admits that he and his team were caught off guard by these problems, but they coped. "The best thing is patience," he said "and it takes a lot of it to do this. Some people would say that something goes wrong every day. We think of it as learning something new everyday." And, when working with a new medium, unknowns are a given, he added. "We don't know what we're doing when we start a lot of projects. We are pushing it, we are out there, saying 'yeah, we can do that.' Then we turn around and say, 'how in the world did we do that?' And we did a lot of that with Werndl."

Animation

No one who sees the Werndl presentation can forget the animated segment, starring Dunny Bugnugget, a cartoon everyman who fidgets and fumes at his poorly designed workstation. Like so much of the Werndl project, he too strained the team's resources.

While there were plenty of dry statistics relating comfortable office design to worker productivity, all of the principals in the Werndl project wanted to get that message across without traditional charts and graphs. The furniture makers suggested a 60-second animation. Big Hand artist Brian Barr suggested Dunny, and did a preliminary sketch. "The client just fell in love with Dunny," Wolff said. "They thought it was going to be the greatest thing, and it did end up being wonderful."

Dunny's Maker: Artist Brian Barr created the animated worker to show how office surroundings affect productivity.

Two's copywriter, Rowan Gibson, flew to Dallas to help write the Dunny script. "It was kind of like writing a screen play," Wolff said. "Now Dunny stands up; no, no, no, he leans over on his elbow...like that. They would sketch out characters and scenes, and the scenes were storyboarded according to the script." When that step was done, Barr, along with Chris Howay and Steve Ross, drafted the animation. "It was traditional, single cell, low budget animation. I think Brian used a binder and paper. I mean traditional low budget," Wolff said with a laugh. "He drew a free hand border proportionate to the screen size, and then drew his animation within that border." To achieve the flickering style that adds to Dunny's charm, Barr and his crew had to draw each frame three times, adding slight variations. The total of 1,659 frames "nearly killed Brian," Wolff

Hats On: Barr sketched many hats for Dunny to wear to the office.

recalled. "It was really crazy." Finally, when all the black and white line drawings had been inked, they were scanned, cleaned up in Photoshop, and exported as PICT files into MacroMind Director where they were animated.

With so much enthusiasm for the Dunny animation, Wolff had to struggle to keep the production at a manageable size—and within budget. Originally planned to be 60 seconds long, the completed script instead called for three minutes of animation. When the script was translated into German, the animation grew another 25 percent longer. At ten hand-drawn frames a second, this was a time-consuming and expensive addition. As a result, Dunny's segment was only half-completed by the time of the furniture trade show in Cologne. Back in Dallas, as the presentation was being revised, Wolff convinced everyone involved to hold the animation down to 90 seconds. "We bid for 60 seconds of animation," he reminded his European clients, "and I'm afraid you're going to put people to sleep with three minutes worth. So we cut a lot of material out.... It doesn't matter how good it is, if people don't watch it, it has no value at all."

Hats Off:
The final animation was a hit with Big Hand's client.

Audio

Werndl and Two's had high expectations of the Texas company in every aspect of production, including the audio. Both wanted a score, Werndl theme music, if you will, and for Wolff that meant an original composition, not canned "multimedia music." The resulting theme, composed by James Neel at his music studio in Dallas, was customized for each segment, especially Dunny's animation. "There are changes in instruments and tempo throughout to change the mood," Lyda said. "One area is slow and strong, another is upbeat and lively."

Dunny's theme, a musical counterpoint to his travails at work, was fine tuned by Barr, Dunny's animator and Two's staffer Rowan

Gibson, who literally camped at Neel's studio to brainstorm with the composer. The resulting theme "sounds like Dunny," Barr believes. An attempt to add sound effects to the animation, though, was less successful. "At first we only wanted to implement a couple of funny sound effects," Wolff said. "We thought that his chair should squeak and when he picks up papers, there should be a shuffling sound." But one effect led to another and ended up "grabbing so much attention that Dunny was no longer the centerpiece," he continued. Afraid of audio overkill, all of the sound effects but four—a sneeze, thud, clock ticking and phone ringing—were dropped. However, all of their efforts weren't for naught. In the finished presentation, the sound effects play as the credits roll—to humorous effect.

Though a Texan was tapped to write the score, Wolff decided to record the voice-over narration in Germany, despite the added expense. After all, Wolff did not want his clients to notice a decidedly Texas twang in the reading of the German script. He flew to Frankfurt for the recording by narrators selected by Two's Company and approved by their German client. "There have been other projects where we have used foreign talent out of agencies in the Dallas area, but we did not want any problems on our first project in Europe," said Wolff, who returned days later to the States with DAT recordings of both the German and English scripts.

Conversion to CD-I

Before all of the components of the Werndl project could be transferred to CD-I, everything had to be digitized. The music and narration were mixed in Neel's studio, and the resulting DAT was then re-digitized in a Mac. Video, film, and graphics files were digitized, too. "So we have everything either created on the Mac, or shot on videotape, or film, or recorded, now digitized," explained Wolff. "You duplicate every file in a new format and move them either by Syquest or by network to the authoring system."

The conversion process is accomplished with easy-to-use plug-in export filters from OptImage, makers of the CD-I authoring tool, MediaMogul. "Using the export filters makes converting a Mac file to a CD-I file as simple as saving to a new file format. Then you just call up every file in order of appearance and attach every audio file to the right time code in what we call 'scripts.' You import each image into each script in the right order, add the visual transitions, set the time code, add audio files, fade them up and down in the right places, and set the volume. Then you define the screens that are to be 'menus' and which areas are buttons and how they are supposed to behave."

Time on His Mind:
Lance Lyda felt the pressure of an incredibly tight deadline.

Programming

"You know. There's never enough time to do it the way that you want to do it," according to Lyda.

By the time Big Hand reached the programming stage for the Werndl CD-I disc, the pressure on the team was mounting. They had struggled with a new format, client changes of direction and impossibly tight deadlines. But just as the project was coming all together—on schedule—a major glitch caught the young developers off guard and taught them a valuable lesson. "If I were really smart, and if I were being interviewed by a casebook author or something, I would say, 'yes, we do two copies of everything,'" Wolff said, with rueful irony. "If anybody were going to be reading what I was saying, I would say, 'we make two copies.' Yes, Jay Wolff advises young upstart multimedia companies to make two copies of everything."

The in-house authoring effort, lead by Valerie Grant, got off to a good start, thanks to a helping hand from an Iowa company that tailored off-the-shelf authoring tools to meet Big Hand's needs. Interactive Resources worked with OptImage, a fellow Iowa firm, to create plug-in software for OptImage to compliment MediaMogul. Wolff believed MediaMogul was the best CD-I authoring tool available because of its automatic preview feature which allows instantaneous playback of authored material without compiling it first. "With other (programs), you have to compile into a runtime file and play that back. Then if you want to make a change, you have to go back to the original program, make the change and compile it again," he explained. "With automatic preview, it plays off the hard drive...as if it were running on a CD onto a TV, without pressing a disc." (Now that pressing CDs is so quick and cheap, Big Hand now generally skips this simulation.)

Wolff said that on average he turns to Interactive Resources for at least three plug-ins per project. One essential addition made for the Werndl project made possible the product scrolling in the catalog section. Because of some last-minute changes in the Werndl lines of furniture, the Big Hand team "needed the pieces of furniture to float across the screen in front of everything, instead of (floating in the background) in a window," Wolff said. "With CD-I it's supposedly very difficult to do that, but we went over this with their engineers and they figured it out." Earlier efforts to achieve the same effect took months of programming, Wolff said, "but these guys accomplished the basic task with a couple of weeks of tweaking." The close working relationship between the two companies continues to become closer as the Iowans are opening a Dallas branch at Big Hand. "It's a perfect combination," Wolff said. "They engineer for our platform, and we design for it."

Even without the addition of plug-ins which are not always thoroughly debugged, authoring a CD-I program is tricky business. Ideally, the best approach, Lyda said, "is, in the very beginning, you dummy up the screens, give them to the 'CD-I' author, and they make an alpha version of the project. They check all of the branching and make sure that everything runs correctly and goes where it is supposed to. And then, as you produce the finished assets, you simply drop them off at the authoring station, they replace what was there before. Then toward the end of the project, the authoring is minimal...just some cleanup and touch-ups."

And in the real world? "You know that stuff never happens," he admitted. "Actually, it happens a lot more now; we have the resources and time to do that kind of thing."

But as the deadline neared for the Werndl disc, the Big Hand team members, learning as they went, began working around the clock, oblivious to the approaching Christmas holidays. "I had family coming in for Christmas...and I worked Christmas Eve and the day before. But even before then, working 72 hours straight before going home to take a shower wasn't unusual," Lyda remembered of the month-long authoring process. On Christmas day, the Big Hand team rested except for a solitary Wolff, who, despite pleas from his family, continued to put the Werndl project's pieces together. Eventually, though, the taxing schedule took a crippling toll. "I had set up a computer that I called The Gateway," Lyda continued, "and hooked on to it two or three 1.2 gigabyte drives. Each external hard drive had a part of the program, which had the files divided as they would be on the CD-I disc. I took one of those hard drives off that machine and brought it over to my machine to do some work, set two hard drives up with the same SCSI ID number and completely lost one of the drives."

Had Lyda backed up the more than a gigabyte of finished files? "Oh no, of course not," Lyda said, able to laugh now at what seemed like a disaster then. "Funny, but that was not a word that we used at the time." Blaming the loss on fatigue, Lyda nonetheless credits it with "changing the way we work." They needed to figure out an

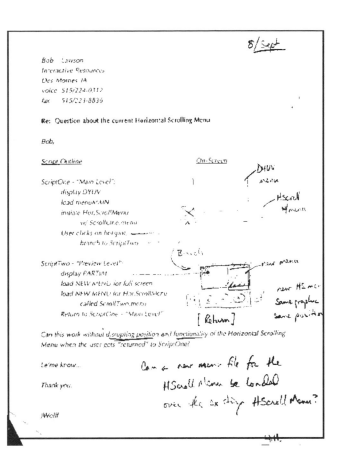

Expert Advice: Big Hand's staff turned to Interactive Resources for help during production of the Werndl CD-I.

effective backup system and a way to manage information. "We have improved (our) systems substantially, and we have a tape backup system now.... We have gone from being stingy with backup tapes to passing them out to whoever wants them at any time. I think they cost $20 a pop, but man, who cares when you have lost $50,000 worth of information."

To rebound from the "big crash," Big Hand had no recourse but to recreate—fast. "What's amazing," Wolff recalled, "is that once it had been produced one time, we learned how to automate the process of rebuilding it. And we rebuilt it literally in days." Re-scanning took about three days. At the same time, two artists prepared files for the automating process, and one computer was set up so that it just created screens. Oddly enough, the lack of a strict file management system actually helped the rebuilding process, Lyda said. "It was actually a godsend," he said.

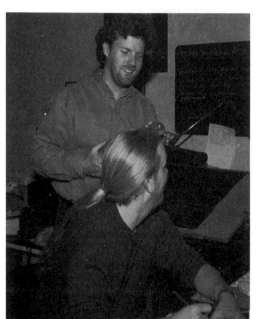

All Hands at Work: Artist, Troy Harrison, confers with fellow animator, Chris Howay.

Since the team was working on more than a dozen different computers without a network, "there was a lot of file duplication, and at the time, that was a problem," he continued. "We managed to retrieve over half the destroyed files from other hard drives; and from there, we went on and even improved those sections that we had lost anyway."

Testing

Testing of the Werndl disc was more difficult than most CD-I applications, not only because of its size and complexity, but also because the entire presentation was in German. Generally, "we press a disc, put it in a CD-I player and just literally beat it up," Wolff explained. "We go though every branch. We view every screen. We reset the machine over and over to make sure it boots up every time." "We also hammer on it," Lyda said. "You click as fast as you can, move things around, interrupt the animation, all that stuff, to make sure that no matter how badly it is abused, it won't crash." Regardless of the platform, Wolff points out, there will be bugs. "The thing you have to remember, when you're developing multimedia is that it is software development. The authoring tools buffer you from actually writing any code, but...there are always problems."

Since Lyda and Wolff were equally fluent in German—each spoke about 10 words—there were only minor corrections made to the on-screen text. A few cosmetic changes later and the disc was pressed for presentation to Werndl executives. Even so, Wolff still considered the disc to be another beta version, unlike some developers who do not press a disc for the client until the project is due. "The hype that you get from the computer companies is that it can be done this way. That's absolutely not the way to do it—to run your company, or to trust in the software and the hardware, because they're in the early development stages right now, no matter what they tell you. We consider everything in beta because it's changing all the time."

Of course, the Werndl disc needed a fix, as Murphy's law reared its ugly head during the debut demonstration to the Werndl board of directors in Eindhoven. "The first word in the presentation was misspelled," Wolff recalled. "It was supposed to be '*Ist*,' and we spelled it '*Its*'.... Even with faxing the files back and forth, the Germans didn't catch it." Because of the tight deadlines, there were no sign-off procedures. Instead, Wolff said, "they just trusted us with the whole thing...they had to."

Finishing Touches

After the bugs are worked out, the errors are corrected and the client is pleased, a CD-I project is still not finished, although many developers then call it quits. "Final details, ranging from the artwork on the face of the disc itself to storage of the project's assets, remain." Wolff emphasized.

For starters, both the packaging and design on the face of the disc must be comparable to the graphics that appear on the screen. "Right now, if done right, we have four-color process capabilities for illustrating a disc," Wolff explained. "You should leave something in the budget for printing beautiful images on the disc, because, in this context, the disc is valuable as a marketing tool whether it's in the machine or not." Like an increasing number of CD-ROM applications, the CD-I should have a disc sleeve and related print materials that explain, among other things, how to navigate the program. "One problem is that clients have a hard time spending an extra five to ten thousand dollars on print material." Wolff noted "But it's a critical element. It should have the same design as the digital presentation. It should have a Disc Map, a Table of Contents and a Help Section."

Disc Details:
Graphics on the CD-I disc function as a marketing tool.

The packaging and instructions help overcome the still widespread unfamiliarity with the CD-I system. "We're all comfortable with print, and a person will open at least the first couple of pages and scan through it before (he or she) will go out and find a CD-I player to play it," Wolff said. "They can then understand the value of what's on the disc...instead of staring at it in bewilderment, wondering what it is.... That's why we think the print material is absolutely critical." And since most offices do not have CD-I players, Wolff recommends advising recipients of the discs to take them to a local electronics store to play them. This may pose some difficulties for clients, but Wolff believes this is a positive part of the message. "Part of the statement is 'look how innovative and cool we are.' We are so advanced, you don't even have the machines to play these yet," he explained. "The clients go, 'oh wow, that's pretty cool.'" And if they don't make the effort to play it? "They aren't going to throw the disc away, to them it's the equivalent of a $13 music CD. So it's going to sit on their desk and remind them daily of our client. That's another reason why the disc itself should be absolutely beautiful."

A final concern once an application is completed is storage of assets, since "a client could want a revision in a year or so," Wolff said. "Their files must be safely organized and stored; and in multimedia, with literally gigabytes of material, that's a major, major problem. Our rule of thumb is that we have five times the number of files in total assets as there are number of files on the finished disc." Clients are given the option to store the files themselves, or to pay Big Hand to keep them safe. When they pick Big Hand for the job, the assets are stored out of the office, generally in a safety deposit site and at one of the partners' homes.

MENÜ 1: HAUPTMENÜ

zu "Spaß am Caravaning+Erklärung".

zu Exponate 1 bis 6 Mercedes-Benz.

zu Service Mercedes-Benz.

zu Grundriß Menü.

zu Film "gebrauchte Caravans".

Questions Answered: Instructions, like these for a Big Hand CD-I project for Mercedes-Benz, are an essential aid for clients.

Hardware

While many innovative multimedia companies leap at the chance to purchase the latest hardware and software, Big Hand does not invest in upgrades until the bugs have been worked out and the prices drop. "We always want second generation equipment," said Wolff, who currently works on Quadras and Centris 650s. "With every round of Macintoshes, there are higher prices in the beginning. And six months later, there's always an improved version.... We like to buy Macs when they are about a year old....one that works with all my software, because the software is the brain of the machine." He added that software compatibility is equally important. "Many little tools do a certain function for us, and we rely on them for our day-to-day production. They don't get upgraded very quickly. So we just buy stuff that's been out for a while and make sure even our incidental software utilities are compatible."

The Big Hand team also uses removable hard drives, rather than a network, to move data from computer to computer. While his employees are connected by AppleTalk, it's "not valuable for moving files around," Wolff noted. "We just put everything on Syquest. The easiest way to move megabytes of files...is to unplug the hard drive, carry it across the room and plug it into another computer." As a result, to facilitate the transfer of files as well as possible repairs, they use external hard drives only. When the company can afford it, they will link up via Ethernet, although, Wolff warns, "the problem with Ethernet is that once you get it connected, you don't want to move your machines and reconfigure."

While many developers have dismissed CD-I as a dead-end platform, Wolff believes it has a future and has committed his firm to develop new CD-I titles—games and education software—"because we believe there is a market out there." He also is keeping an eye on new developments in this fast-changing industry, however. "We know that to tie yourself to one platform is stupid and suicidal," he said "We work on CD-ROM now; we are also looking at 3DO.... We are a design studio, so (the final platform) really doesn't make any difference to us.

FINANCE: Stretching the Envelope

Big Hand was paid approximately $120,000 for the Werndl project. Given all the client changes as the disc took shape, Wolff believes he "could have made a good case" for additional fees, but he decided against it. "The foremost issue was the fact that we had our first European client and the Two's agency has many more clients," he said. "So we delivered, we stayed with our original bid." In the process, "a whole new production crew was trained under fire to produce CD-I," he added. "We had a lot of growing pains to go through, and we were paid to go through them."

While Wolff believes creation of the Werndl disc was "a profitable project," the travails his company experienced illustrate the difficulty of estimating costs for a multimedia job, especially one that stretches the technical envelope. Although it's difficult for clients to accept, Wolff argues that "purchasers of multimedia need to understand that, if someone gives them a solid price, the producers are really taking a risk. Nobody really knows how much this costs, because, truly, until you design it, you don't know what the product contains." When bidding for a job, Wolff says that he takes three factors into consideration. "The quantity of content is number one. `How much do they want to say or how much do they want to show on this disc?' The second one is 'what is the complexity of the material and the message?' And the third is the sophistication of the client...and its expectations. I make a judgement call on whether this needs to be more expensive because I know the client is going to be picky about the color, about the timing."

When a bid is accepted and a contract drawn up, Wolff is careful to sidestep two other potential problems. "One is not defining the contact who has authority for the client" he said. "And the second is when they introduce a third party, a design firm or ad agency, to be involved in the project. This can be valuable or it can be a real runaround." As a result, Big Hand avoids subcontracting with an agency or other representative of the client. "We contract directly with the client and get paid by the client." Unlike many businesses, which accept 30-, 60-, and even 90-day payment terms, Big Hand insists on 30 percent down "before we start designing," 30 percent when production begins, and another 30 percent when the authoring and programs get underway. The final 10 percent is collected upon delivery.

Since multimedia, in all its forms, is becoming increasingly prevalent in corporate communications around the world, Big Hand is experimenting with new client relationships, including a monthly retainer. Currently, a couple of clients view the Dallas company as "their multimedia agency," Wolff said. "We are responsible for all their communications in which they use multimedia. That is a different role than we have ever played before." In the same way that an advertising agency coordinates all of a company's communications, Big Hand "strategizes (with its clients about) how they are going to use technology in their communication, including training, marketing, sales presentations, store kiosks..." and anything else that may be pertinent to a particular project. With this approach, companies move away from what Wolff calls "one-purpose, disposable multimedia" like a kiosk that is used for a series of trade shows and then dismantled. "Instead, (Big Hand's approach) basically lets us focus on long-term applications, and how a disc we may be doing for them now is going to fit into the whole mix." The retainer plan also reduces the seemingly nonstop search for clients. "Multimedia is very exciting and everything," Wolff said, "but when you have to go out and keep finding a new client for every job, it gets a little old."

Other companies, though, may prefer to handle their in-house multimedia production themselves and turn to a firm like Big Hand for "important" presentations or to solve problems. "There are two models of how large companies will do their multimedia

Management Trio:
Left to right, Jay Wolff, Craig Rispen and Steve O'Brien are Big Hand's key executives.

development," Wolff explained. "One group—and I think that this is going to be followed in mass—brings it in-house for training, and then goes to outside developers when they are too busy or their internal structure won't accommodate their 'hot' jobs, (for example, doing a trade show kiosk in a month), like we can." The other model is the company that invests thousands of dollars in the hardware and software needed to develop multimedia but lacks the staff to use it effectively. For these firms, experienced professionals, like those at Big Hand, can offer a solution when a presentation is due, but the in-house developers are not able to deliver. Wolff, in fact, recalls at least two instances when the frustrated client hauled all of their equipment into the Big Hand offices, begging "do the CD-I project for us."

Despite multimedia's long learning curve, Wolff expects more and more companies to make multimedia tools and experts part of their in-house communications' departments. "And I think they are going to get really good at it," he added, "because the authoring tools are getting more sophisticated and easier to use. The expense will be easy to justify as businesses realize how effective multimedia presentations can be," Wolff continued. For example, he cites a CD-I presentation he did for a client that helped them win a several billion-dollar contract. "The executive summary for the presentation was 8,000 pages and our disc was a five-minute piece of their presentation. They left our disc on 20 CD-I players at the prospect's offices for a couple of weeks, so people could sift through the presentation and learn more about it on their own time. It was a hell of a leave-behind."

MARKETING: Keeping Expectations in Hand

Although they have two freelance representatives who scout prospective clients on a commission basis, referrals and repeat customers are the mainstay of Big Hand's business. Key to this success, Wolff believes, is a carefully crafted sales pitch that matches a client's multimedia needs to its budget, giving them maximum bang—mileage and impact—for the buck.

During Big Hand's first year in business, though, Wolff often erred, he believes, by overselling multimedia to potential clients. One instance is still vivid in his mind. "We had this incredible sales presentation, and the client was absolutely floored, their chins were on the table. They saw how multimedia might revolutionize their company, and they (realized) they should have it. We had talked to some big, big people, but basically the project became too large for anyone in the room to have authority over. Then nothing happened." The problem, he admitted in retrospect, was aiming too high. "We thought we were going to land these huge jobs, and because of our thinking at the time, we literally have no clients from that stage of the business," he said. "After about a year, we started recognizing that no one is able to buy these big projects—at least not quickly and easily."

Attracting Clients: Big Hand's award-winning discs and trophies help its marketing efforts.

Today, when Big Hand approaches potential new clients, Wolff aims to keep the first project small. "Now at every (sales presentation), we jazz them up," he said, "and then we talk them back down to the ground. We say, `Let us deliver that first disc, and then we'll go from there.'" By making a client's first multimedia experience a positive one financially, Big Hand gets more business, more often, from that company. "If they blow their whole budget on this awesome multimedia piece for a trade show, then they wait until next year, until the next trade show, to call us," Wolff continued. "We don't want that necessarily. We want to do this trade show, then their directors' meeting, and then maybe a sales marketing tool. So, we often sell down, and it's more effective for us and, we think, much better for the client."

Another Big Hand marketing strategy is to look for ways to enhance each application's value to the client. After establishing the project's primary goal, Wolff said, "we look at the long term needs of our client. We quiz them on what's coming up, and we find out, say, that they have a presentation to their board of directors next month. If that is the case, we tell them, `let's put a little section on the disc (at no charge) that talks about your department and what you have been doing.'" As a result, the board and other company departments are exposed to the power and value of multimedia. At the same time as it satisfies a client's objectives, Big Hand tries to avoid depleting their multimedia budget. "It's a lot better doing it that way," he said, "than doing one massive project where their job is on the line, and if it fails and nobody likes interactivity, they've just dropped $100K. There is a lot of pressure on everyone and we try to cover for the client."

Wolff said that even when clients bring return business, they tend to want a new application, built from the ground up. That approach to multimedia strains independent developers financially since "they literally are custom designing every project." Instead, Wolff prefers to develop ways to integrate multimedia into a client's long-term communications mix. "We don't want it to be just a novel, fun project where a company comes to us, throws some money at an application, gets some nice press for it and then goes back to the old way of doing things."

FUTURE PROJECTS: Reaching into Other Media

From its beginnings, as a two-man animation studio, Big Hand has carved a niche in the emerging multimedia industry with its work on CD-I. However, as the company's founders looked to the future, Wolff said they realized that "we're not a CD-I developer. We're an interactive design studio." And even though they are confident that the mass market multimedia on the horizon is "going to be disc-based, interactive and hooked to your TV," Wolff believes that "our design theories, our metaphors, and policies can all be applied to all interactive platforms."

Among the Big Hand projects currently in the planning or design stages are interactive movies. One is a twenty-minute interactive feature that invites viewer participation throughout the storyline. "It's at a much higher intellectual level than most games," Wolff explained. "Most games depend on which way you choose to go. One way you get shot and die, and one way you don't. It's like rote learning, you just remember which way to go next time. We want you to be thinking along with the character as the plot unfolds." Wolff said the company is seeking a partner, or private funding, in hopes of having the movie in stores by Christmas 1994. Prototypes on CD-I have already been previewed at two electronics shows, but Wolff believes "it would work on any upcoming platform."

Big Hand also is developing two series of children's interactive books. "One series has characters that everybody falls in love with when they see it," Wolff said. "The other takes traditional children's toys that have been around for thirty years and maps them into multimedia. Parents are already familiar with these toys, and they will buy what they played with when they were young even faster than they will buy innovative new things. So we combine the old and the new."

Another new venture, with appeal to the Big Hand founders, is interactive cable, which Wolff expects to be delivered to home televisions via satellite, telephone or cable. "So we'll be designing with two things in mind," Wolff pointed out. "One, it will be on your TV. And two, the user will have control of the program. With those two things in mind, everything we do now applies to interactive cable."

Interactivity greatly enhances traditional media, especially movies, Wolff believes, by "enriching the experience. I believe that a person should enjoy a movie straight through at least the first time. But wouldn't it be wonderful, if you were watching, say, *Dances With Wolves* for the second or third time, you could learn about the costume design; tell me what the feathers in his headdress mean. Or wouldn't it be wonderful, if your eighth-grader could watch

Dances with Wolves, click a button, and learn about that period in American history. How incredible that would be!" Of course, Wolff's ideas will eventually become reality, but even for the pioneers of this industry, the implementation of those big ideas present great risk and challenge, which sounds like a job for Big Hand.

5

TALKING BUSINESS CARD

Galileo, Inc.

At A Glance

Recipient of over twenty national, international and local awards.

TALKING BUSINESS CARD

Developers: Galileo, Inc.

Client: Ed Wolkis Photography.

Personnel: Jackie Goldstein, art direction, design, creative/graphic production; Mike Wittenstein, programming; Ed Wolkis, Ed Wolkis Photography, photography; Andre Boyce, Unit One Productions, music.

Description of project: An introductory portfolio presentation of Ed Wolkis' photography, created for art directors, creative directors of ad agencies, and corporate advertising departments.

Development hours: Approximately 70.

Development period: 8 weeks.

Production hardware: Macintosh Quadra 700, Macintosh IIcx, Isomet PhotoCD, Hewlett-Packard Scan Jet IIc for scanning images.

Production software: Adobe Photoshop, Macromedia Director, Macromedia Director Player for Windows, SoundEdit Pro.

Presentation hardware: Macintosh IIcx or better with 13-inch color monitor.

Presentation software: Run-time version provided with Talking Business Card.

Selling price: $6,500.

U.S. distributor: Ed Wolkis Photography.

Future projects: Versions of the Talking Business Card with added interactivity.

Contact: Jackie Goldstein and Mike Wittenstein, co-presidents
              Galileo, Inc.
              6055 Barfield Road, Suite 200
              Atlanta, GA 30328
              (404) 255-6377
              (404) 255-6301 (fax)
              WEB Page HTTP:\\galileoinc.com

Talking Business Card: Galileo has updated a traditional communications tool for the Information Age.

Ajax First National's new creative director, Linda Smith, is in charge of finding a photographer for her company's upcoming annual report. It is a daunting, and somewhat confusing, task. Her desk is littered with the slick brochures of area photographers. As far as she can tell, most of the photographers could do the work, for about the same rate. She is about to close her eyes and point...when she notices a small floppy diskette among the pile of papers.

Its label announces the "Ed Wolkis Studios: An Electronic Portfolio." Intrigued, she pops it into her Macintosh. Soon, a jazzy tune with James Brown-like flourishes starts to play. She settles back in her chair, and watches the screen come to life with elegant graphics, which focus her eye on samples of Wolkis' award-winning photography. Clever, informative text conveys Wolkis' marketing message. Minutes later, the music and screen fade. "Well," Linda Smith thinks to herself, "I think I'll call Ed Wolkis."

This scenario may be fictitious, but the desire—and need—of small businesses, like Ed Wolkis Studios, to stand out in a field crowded with competitors is not. Making that leap from being just another commercial photographer to the firm that gets the job, sent this Atlanta lensman to a nearby company he believed could help. Within a few weeks, Galileo handed him a floppy disk that would act as a tireless and effective salesman for his services. When targeted at the right market, it becomes a powerful, modern, communications tool with the convenience of an old-fashioned business card.

In fact, Galileo trademarked a name for its version of this digital marketing tool, simply titled the "Talking Business Card." For as little as $2,500, the three-year-old company has helped small- and medium-sized businesses to discover the advantages of a multimedia sales presentation over traditional print media. In an increasingly computer-networked marketplace, many similar standard business tools, such as brochures, newsletters, directories, and catalogs, have been, or are being, retooled with multimedia features for the Information Age. As this product exemplifies, the power of multimedia is not limited to corporations with deep pockets; nor does it require months of around-the-clock work, with sophisticated software, to be unleashed. In fact, a new generation of interactive sales and information products, like the Talking Business Card, puts its capabilities within reach of companies of all sizes, for everyday use. As for independent multimedia developers, this, and related products, could be their bread-and-butter work in the very near future.

Pioneers in several forms of multimedia marketing, advertising, and sales applications, Galileo's partners, Mike Wittenstein and Jackie Goldstein, believe in this product and its versatility, because they have used it successfully to promote their own communications company. "It's the medium itself,—and we're not shy about saying this,—that really draws the attention," emphasized Wittenstein. "It's not just because of our creative abilities and skills. It's that people are interested in multimedia. But so be it, if it's going to bring the buyer closer to the customer's product."

THE OPPORTUNITY: Multimedia In Your Pocket

In 1991, at an Apple users group meeting, Mike Wittenstein slipped a floppy disk into a computer. It contained an interactive multimedia presentation showcasing the capabilities of his newly-formed company, Galileo. The response was encouraging. "It really caught on," said Goldstein, Galileo's co-president. "We eventually started talking about our Talking Business Cards and that was the name we trademarked."

While Galileo is not the first company to distribute its message on floppies to promote its services, or its clients, its founders are helping to position this new tool as a sophisticated alternative to print media. Like an advertisement or a sales brochure, Talking Business Cards are "basically short, one-message presentations," Goldstein pointed out, but they "incorporate audio, video, text, animation, and graphics—anything that can fit on a floppy disk. They are a very good introductory piece for clients who don't want a major presentation, but who want to give multimedia a try. Since it is a fixed size, it also has a relatively fixed budget that fits into most people's budgets pretty nicely."

Not surprisingly, Talking Business Cards are most effective when the targeted market is computer literate, and has machines that will play the message. "It's good for any company that sells a product to computer users, including hardware, software, multimedia peripherals, and office supplies—and for just about anybody whose audience is composed of office workers," Wittenstein said. Take photographer Wolkis, for example. "His audience is creative directors and ad agencies. And he knows that most of those businesses have upscale Macintosh work stations...."

For The Computer Literate: Talking Business Cards appeal to clients whose customers are computer users.

At present, this innovative product equals 20 percent of Galileo's business, as clients come to appreciate the advantages of its digital format. Wittenstein believes that its biggest plus is its "pass-along value," which can land a digital message any place in the digital world. Since they can be downloaded over modems or networks in

minutes, "they start to fly to other places," he said. "Because of the informal digital networks people are starting to create themselves, your message can travel on new channels you don't even know about, and find its way to interested users. One person who had our Talking Business Card message called us from Japan. He didn't have a disk; he just had the file. We still don't know how he got it."

As a result, Galileo encourages clients to think creatively about distribution of their multimedia messages. Wittenstein said that one Talking Business Card user, a real estate company, plans "a bulletin board service where interested parties can order the presentation to be modemed to them to download to their PC. And if it's a broker, guess what happens. He starts showing it to everybody else."

Other clients' messages are added to promotional CD-ROMs, if the targeted audience is right. One example is the "Virtual Portfolio" put out by American Showcase. "It's like a multimedia review," Wittenstein explained. "They have a database of 6,000 qualified buyers of advertising, illustration, and photography who have Macintoshes with CD-ROMs.... They send out that disc for free to these people. Each person who wants to put a presentation on the disc pays a fee per megabyte and the presentation is worked into the main menu system." When Ed Wolkis' sales pitch was included, Wittenstein said, the photographer reached 6,000 potential clients for only $750—far less than the estimated $13,000 duplicating his Talking Business Card and mailing would have cost. "It's an incredible cost-efficiency," he said.

Another advantage to a digital presentation, Wittenstein believes, is that its digital assets can be changed easily and inexpensively to reflect changes in the business or be adapted to print, video, or other media. "We start from a digital point of view, and work with digital assets," he said, "and then 're-purpose' them into different channels. So, for a multiple media campaign, it's really cost effective." And when an address or phone number changes, or a vice president is promoted, or a marketing thrust is redefined, a Talking Business Card can be altered, instead of thrown away. "In print, to gain the economy of scale, you have to order large quantities,"

Wittenstein explained. This often means a business is forced to "live with the message longer than it would like. (Traditional business cards) become dated, get old and stale, and you are still forced to use them, because you paid for them. Talking Business Cards or any digital media can be produced and changed as needed."

In a multimedia presentation, most changes can be made in minutes by creating and substituting a few text or graphic files, according to the Galileo partners. Disks with an outdated presentation are reformatted, and then filled with the latest information. "Each digital sound, graphic, animation, or programming element can be adjusted independently of everything else," Wittenstein added. "So if there is a change in your organization chart ... out with Suzy, in with Johnny, and the disk is ready to go." To make such simple changes, Galileo usually charges an hourly fee. Substantial revisions are given a project price.

Cost and practical advantages aside, most of Galileo's clients have a basic, bottom-line concern. They want to reach and impact their audience. In Wolkis' case, his goal was "to break through the portfolio barrier," he said. "When you're a photographer and work with ad agencies, you call them up, tell them who you are, and three days later they forget about you. So what I wanted was not just a foot in the door, because these people are usually pretty good about seeing you. I wanted agency people to remember my name." When Goldstein first proposed a Talking Business Card, Wolkis did not know what she was talking about, but now he is a fan. "I've sent out over a hundred of them, so far, and the response has been really good," he said. "It's nice when I make a follow-up call on the agency, and say `Hi, this is Ed Wolkis.' And they say, 'Yeah, yeah, you're the Talking Business Card.'"

THE TEAM: Old Friends, New Partners

Wittenstein and Goldstein had moved in the same social circles for years, but, Goldstein recalls, "I never knew what Mike did." When, by chance, she learned of his interest in multimedia, the two started down a path that would lead to the formation of Galileo.

Both had impressive careers in the Atlanta area. As art director for Turner Broadcasting for more than four years, Goldstein was responsible for all print advertising promotions for the network's four stations and two Atlanta sports teams, as well as for all other Turner properties. "Prior to that, I was assistant art director at WSB-TV, the Atlanta ABC affiliate," said Goldstein, who had moved to Atlanta from Cleveland where she had been an art director for an advertising agency. Her honors are numerous: ADDYS (advertising design awards), several gold and silver Broadcast Designers' Association awards, and Broadcast Promotion Directors' awards. She also was a finalist in the International Advertising Festival of New York. In 1989, she left broadcasting to become a creative consultant, advising the FOX Network, The Family Channel, TV Guide, and Coca-Cola, among others.

For five years, beginning in 1985, Wittenstein ran his own consulting firm, Wittenstein and Associates, specializing in providing technology-based telecommunications software solutions for Apple Computers, The Nutrasweet Company, Xerox, and other southeastern companies. "I helped people with automation systems, and with learning to use computers intelligently in the workplace," he explained. "They were really excited about the visual impact that multimedia brings. I had developed a just-in-time (knowledge when you need it so that you can act on it immediately) learning package about

the Macintosh operating system, and I got really interested in being able to use video as a way to teach people. That was really the turning point for me."

Multimedia had caught Goldstein's eye as well, and a mutual friend suggested she contact Wittenstein. "It was a total fluke," she

Mike Wittenstein:
Before forming Galileo, Wittenstein operated a high-tech consulting firm.

remembered. "Mike and I knew each other socially, and I really had no idea what he did. We had a mutual friend who told me that I needed to be in multimedia, and that I should check it out. When I finally agreed to do it, he told me to get in touch with Mike...I went, 'Oh, I already know this guy.' " With books borrowed from Wittenstein, Goldstein learned Photoshop and some other programs. "Eventually, we started getting jobs in-house where Mike would use me as the creative director. One day, we looked at each other and said, 'I think we have a business here.'"

Three years later, Galileo is still a two-person development company, but according to Wittenstein, that is by design. "We are a virtual corporation. If you look at our payroll stubs, there are two people, but if you look at the size of our teams, we work regularly with four to eight people on projects. Jackie and I do most of the Talking Business Cards ourselves because they are pretty straightforward; however, for applications with some really fancy programing in them, we bring in a programer to help us out. Larger projects, training, kiosks, and the like, take more production people." By building teams on a project-by-project basis, Goldstein and Wittenstein believe they can hire the best people for the job, keep their overhead low, and they stay within their client's budget. "Without a large production facility or staff," Goldstein said, "our work can be really flexible, and doesn't look the same. You can always tell a shop that's gotten kind of stagnant, because everything starts to look the same. We've always got new teams, fresh ideas and approaches, and the latest technology."

Jackie Goldstein:
An award-winning art director, Goldstein brings a background in advertising to her multimedia firm.

The company now develops multimedia advertising, marketing, and sales applications for a variety of corporate customers, including AT&T and Coca-Cola USA, as well as for the 1994 Goodwill Games. Since they went into business together, the Galileo partners have designed and built kiosks, and created electronic directories and catalogs, boardroom presentations, and portable sales and marketing systems. The company also helps to design and produce collateral materials, such as brochures and video tapes, to supplement multimedia applications, until they become more familiar in the marketplace. "We know that a multimedia application is only one part of the communications puzzle," Goldstein emphasized.

PRODUCTION: Making Floppy Talk

The making of Ed Wolkis' Talking Business Card illustrates Galileo's approach to this multimedia marketing tool—a melding of new technology and standard communications design. Though the medium is new, the first step is traditional. Target the audience and the message.

After talking with Goldstein, his friend of a dozen years, and seeing Galileo's own Talking Business Card, Wolkis was convinced that this approach could reach his prime market. The trio next brainstormed about creative ways to present his digital message. "The main questions that I always ask are `What does your audience need and want to know? What is most important to them?'" Goldstein said. "In Ed's case, we came up with a concept that the customer is looking for a great photographer with great clients. We wanted to get across certain points—to show he had credibility,

Picture This:
Photographer, Ed Wolkis, featured his new studio as well as samples of his work in his Talking Business Card.

which was established with the quality of his clients, to point out that he had great ideas, and show some examples.... He also had built a beautiful new studio space that...[potential] new clients certainly would be impressed to see." Wolkis also wanted potential clients to know that he had won several awards. The Talking Business card, like an informed third party, could sing his praises "rather than me going in there and kind of bragging, 'yeah, I've won a lot of awards,'" he said.

With an understanding of what to communicate, the Galileo team devised a simple storyline, which pointed out Wolkis' impressive client list,

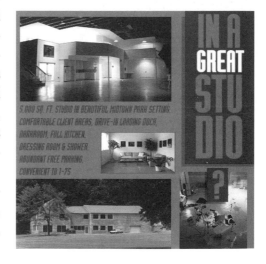

his creative achievements and awards, and his state-of-the-art studio. This message, mixed with music, would star many samples of Wolkis' work. "The images were the most important to him, so we spent a lot of time tweaking them to make sure they were perfect," Goldstein recalled. At the same time, the Galileo team and their client also agreed on a budget, a time frame, and the kind of hardware that would be used to play the Talking Business Card. Finally, they determined what assets—graphics, photos, video, and audio—were available from the client for use in the presentation and what elements needed to be created.

Client List: Wolkis' work for past clients was mixed with music and interactivity.

Because of the limited storage capacity of a floppy disk, Wittenstein said, "you have to be concise and focus in on one thought. That makes it a lot more challenging." Unlike some multimedia developers who expand content to fill the delivery device, Goldstein argues that everything included must support the message. "I don't believe that less is more. And I don't believe that more is more.... I believe that enough is enough," she said. "You want to add things that are important and mean something...that support the message. When you add something and think, 'I really don't need that,' take it away. If there is not enough information, then add until it looks right." She applied the same rule to all multimedia wizardry. "Everything on a screen has to support the message; it can't be there for its own sake. If you are trying to sell bells and whistles, then use every bell and whistle. If you're not, keep (bells and whistles) out of there."

Interactivity

To click, or not to click, is the next question. Although interactivity is a defining multimedia element, its use should not always be taken for granted.

In short, with multimedia presentations like the Talking Business Card, the Galileo team believes a linear approach, with little or no interactivity, may be most effective in getting the message across. "The Talking Business Card is usually someone's first experience with multimedia," said Wittenstein, "and in the projects we have done so far, we've tried to keep interactivity to a minimum...Talking Business Cards, by definition, don't last very long—usually less that five minutes—and you don't want people to get lost in hypertext. If you have ever seen a HyperCard application where there are eight choices and all the screens are different...it's easy as hell not to know where you are."

Some subjects demand some interactivity, however, Wittenstein added. In these cases, helping users to navigate, so they do not get lost or confused is important. For example, for one Talking Business Card which filled two floppy disks, and featured interactive demonstrations of several software programs, "we built a navigational metaphor so that once you click on a section, the button permanently changes color and you know that you have already been there. We try to give the user as many hints as we can along the way," Wittenstein said.

Wittenstein said that interactivity also is appropriate if the customer is going to be making a choice—a red car or a blue car, for example. "Interactivity also can be used for processing data, or initiating action," he said. "You can print out a screen, or a little file embedded in the program, or a questionnaire or order form—just about anything you can imagine. The point is that this is the beginning of a two-way communication." The action can be the next step in the sales cycle, whatever that may be. For example, a potential client may call for more information, or put this card in his or her card file, or print this out, and send it back with a request for a proposal.

Interactivity based on dated schools of thought is a mistake, Wittenstein cautioned. "To make people click a button just to see the presentation—press here to continue—is an old CBT (computer-based training) metaphor that doesn't make any sense. As Jackie said, 'if adding buttons takes away or interferes, then they just don't belong.' "

Graphics

The limited storage on a floppy disk demands that multimedia assets for a Talking Business Card have maximum impact and high quality. "Most of the work on a project is in processing the images, and not the programming," explained Wittenstein. "The trick is making sure that you have solid, consistent images."

Galileo either creates images, or digitizes video, graphics, and photos provided by the client. To digitize video, Wittenstein and Goldstein use RastorOps' MovieTime Media pack. Of the three processes they use to digitize still images: Hewlett Packard's ScanJet IIc desktop scanner, the photo CD, and the drum scanner, the photo CD is the current favorite, based on quality and price. While the office desktop scanner is fast, and provides good resolution, "the photo CD is inexpensive, and gives us a lot higher quality, as well as options for the future," according to Wittenstein. "If we are working with slides, we put them on photo CDs, and we recommend to our clients that they have their images digitized onto photo CDs. It saves us a lot of time and gives the client a chance to use that digital image in the future." The drum scanner, available at a nearby service bureau, is used primarily for odd-sized materials. "We can basically convert any image of any kind," Wittenstein added. "But here's something that will get developers' attention. You can spend $100 to $200 for a high-end drum scan, or you can get the same thing on a photo CD for $2."

Two Storyboards: Goldstein experimented with ways to communicate Wolkis' message.

Since their needs vary from project to project, Wittenstein's approach to hardware purchases is the same as his approach to staffing. "We own a lot of peripherals, a lot of hard-disk drives, and storage devices, as well as a new CD-ROM cutter," he said. Galileo owns the things that give Wittenstein and Goldstein control of the three most important aspects of the development process: the database or asset creation, the project management, and the vision—the look and feel of the project. "We rent a variety of other products based upon what we need to do, particularly sound equipment, because our clients' requirements for that change so much," Wittenstein said. "We do the same with video. We try to own as little as possible."

The photos for Ed Wolkis' Talking Business Card were digitized on the in-house flatbed scanner. In addition, some high-resolution scans were done at a service bureau. "We originally scanned them in 24-bit color, and we also did an eight-bit version of it," Wolkis recalled. "We actually used the eight-bit version because I felt that the difference in quality was not worth the increased difficulty it would take to play the presentation...we would have had to put it on two disks for the 24-bit version."

Goldstein's next challenge was to link the visual elements so they would enhance, not detract from, Wolkis' photos. She began by selecting a typeface. "For Ed's piece, I wanted something pretty modern looking, and easy to read, yet not just straight type. And I wanted the type to be in the same position on each screen," Goldstein explained. "I chose a type face that fit the space, (one that is) very condensed, modern, and stylized. I adjusted the size, so that the word, great—great work, great clients—was always in the same position. And the color of the 'great' stands out, but you kind of ignore that word after a while because it's in the same place on each screen."

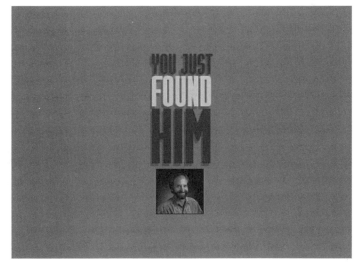

While Goldstein wanted drama in the screen design, she was careful to keep the focus on the images. The first screen sets the tone. The type reads, "Looking for a Photographer," and is stacked in a vertical column, at its base is a photo. Shaped like an exclamation point, the typography conveys excitement, while drawing the user's eye to the object of the presentation—Wolkis' photos. The same format is followed on subsequent screens, which display a half-dozen color photos or more. Other type on the page is screened back "because type is not what we are trying to sell. We are trying to sell the images," she said.

A Dramatic Point: The graphic design and typeface were selected to complement Wolkis' photos.

Audio

The destination platform of each Talking Business Card is an essential consideration in sound design. Macintosh systems, with their built-in speakers, present little or no trouble. However, many PCs are not equipped with sound cards and speakers, and, in general, this rules out the use of audio in the presentation. Ultimately, though, it depends on the client's needs. "If sound is a really important part of the message and the user base supports sound, it definitely goes in," Wittenstein said. While there are methods of getting sound out of built-in PC speakers, the poor quality may detract from the rest of the presentation. "It is a judgment call every time," he admitted.

As the availability of multimedia-capable PCs grows, the problem may disappear. But some of Galileo's clients don't want to wait for that critical point and have found ways to overcome the problem now. One client has gone so far as to subsidize the cost of some multimedia peripherals "because they feel it's important enough to make sure the customer has CD-ROM players and speakers, as part of their regular communications channel. So, instead of the customer paying $400 for a CD-ROM player, the customer pays $200 and gets the (player, a sound card and) speakers as well," Wittenstein said. "They have a vested interest in that particular niche, and want to make sure there is a multimedia communications channel."

Once they establish that audio is necessary, and possible, Wittenstein and Goldstein work with the client to choose the best way to obtain it. Some audio is taken from commercial CDs or DAT tapes. Sometimes, specially created scores are recorded at their own sound studio (although they prefer to use it for voice-over only) or at an off-premises studio. In Wolkis' case, since art directors primarily watch silent presentations on their computers, the team agreed that music would enhance his Talking Business Card, and Wolkis himself commissioned a score. "The music was written by Andre Boyce (head of Unit One Productions). It's real jazzy and funky. It also has a wild kind of James Brown scream in it. Every time a screen changes, it screams at you. It's really fun."

Authoring

Since Wittenstein and Goldstein keep their short multimedia applications simple, they have great flexibility in authoring tools. "The best thing is to have a good sense of what has to be done from the beginning, and then find a software tool to match," said Wittenstein. "In the beginning, there were only a few tools to work with, HyperCard and VideoWorks, which was the predecessor to Macromedia Director. Now there are probably several dozen. So the trick in using the right tool is to know what capabilities you will need up front."

Today, the team primarily uses Macromedia Director and authors on Macintoshes, because "the software is a little more friendly and a little more mature." Other authoring programs are used when needed.

"On the Windows side, we use AuthorWare and Animation Works Interactive," Wittenstein said. "On the Mac side, we use Astound, Persuasion, and AuthorWare.... We are now working with Apple Media Toolkit, and I'm very excited about that, because it will let us produce a title for a Mac and for Windows on the same CD, without having to split the CD into separate Mac and Windows volumes."

Testing and Delivery

Even for small applications like the Talking Business Card, testing is invaluable. When one is completed, Galileo works with individuals or groups from the target audience to check for "consistency of message, operational types of errors, and navigation, as well as the general feeling it creates," said Wittenstein. Because duplicating a small number of disks is easy and inexpensive, he prefers to work with small sample groups. "Let's say your audience is a thousand potential customers. You send out ten or fifteen disks, and get some response, and then you may do that again. Then, when you send out the final version, you have a much surer chance of a successful delivery."

After four to six weeks of production, a master disk is delivered to the client, and, usually, because of strict sign-off procedures, there are no surprises. "Actually, the less time you have for development, the more client involvement is needed," Goldstein said. "We make them sign off at every stage—storyboard, audio. We usually show a sample screen with the typeface and...layout. They sign off on that; we produce the rest of the screens, and they sign off on those." The process can be unnerving for customers, because "they see pieces, and don't always understand how it's going to come together," she added. "But it always does at the last minute. Then they go, 'Wow. I can't believe you really did that.'"

The Galileo team also oversees disk duplication for its clients, since, according to Wittenstein, many details in that process can make or break its effectiveness. "For example, when you pop in a Mac disk, the windows should be open, and the icon should be centered, and have a special logo attached to it, instead of the plain old Mac document or application logo. It also must be named properly, copyrighted, and be equipped with instructions on how to copy it to your hard disk."

Once in hand, the digital message on the Talking Business Cards can be distributed in a variety of ways—ranging from the traditional direct mail, to inclusion on CD-ROMs or in-house computer networks, to uploaded onto computer bulletin boards.

No Surprises: A strict sign-off policy keeps Galileo's clients involved in projects from start to finish.

FINANCE: Advertising For A Model

Galileo's Talking Business Cards have ranged in price from $2,500 to $15,000, but most don't exceed $10,000 to produce. Wittenstein and Goldstein believe that fee is comparable to the cost of traditional promotional items, such as four-color brochures and video tapes. Additionally, a Talking Business Card's assets can be easily converted into either video or print materials. "Instead of paying X dollars for a Talking Business Card and another X dollars for a video, they pay only 1.25 X and have both pieces," Goldstein pointed out.

Citing advertising industry standards, Wittenstein believes the cost of a Talking Business Card compares favorably to the $5,000 to $14,000 fee for preparing an ad for a trade magazine. "And that's not even placing it," he said. The fee for placing a national ad can range up to $15,000. In addition, the team's involvement in distribution of each Talking Business Card protects clients from "just pouring advertising dollars into a black hole," he said. "We spend a lot of time after the fact with a client to make sure that they...are using their electronic advertisement as efficiently as possible...because we want the Talking Business Card concept to be successful...."

Ideally, the price for a Talking Business Card meshes the client's budget with the features he, or she, wants, according to Wittenstein. "We try to educate our clients, so that they know exactly what they are buying, and can communicate to us what they want to spend," he said. In addition to a creative fee, costs are affected by the amount of original work, project management and variety of versions—Mac, CD-ROM, DOS, or Windows—needed. These costs are broken down on a spreadsheet. Throughout this process, the Galileo team is on the lookout for opportunities that gain the customer some extra advantage from the production. Wittenstein explained, "For example, if they are going to do a fifteen-minute presentation, we recommend that they get a video of it done. It's a lot cheaper to do then rather than later."

Fee and billing procedures, Wittenstein and Goldstein concur, are modeled after those of advertising agencies. After all, the businesses are similar; both deliver market analysis, creative development and planning, creation of graphics and audio, and product testing. Goldstein said that some clients, especially ones who have not worked with an agency before, are shocked by development costs. This reaction makes clear communication essential early in the project. "The whole idea is to have a mutual understanding about the proper scope and expected results; if we can do that, then it's clear sailing," she said.

As with most young companies, Galileo has had its financial ups and downs. "Some people don't pay," Wittenstein growled. "It's a pain in the butt. Some people don't know what they want, so we waste a lot of time. We're a lot sterner about the way we handle customer accounts now, and since we have more work, we can afford to pass on people who won't meet our terms. We couldn't do that before, because we were building the company. We had to take what would come.... Along the way some of those people didn't pay, and it cost us tens of thousands of dollars." In one instance, Wittenstein said that the company spent thousands of dollars, assembled a creative team, and devoted 150 hours to a kiosk project, only to learn "the whole thing was bogus. Somebody was just on a little tire-kicking expedition.... That was our biggest disappointment."

In The Market: A sophisticated logo aids Galileo in its search for new clients.

The company now requires customers to agree to specific financial guidelines, before they start a project. Wittenstein said, that for creative work, Galileo uses AIGA standards; for software licensing, guidelines from the Software Publishers Association are used, Wittenstein said. "We normally ask for 50 percent up front, expenses paid upon expense, and 50 percent upon completion. If it's a long-term job, we phase out the payments according to a mutually agreed-upon schedule."

As for the freelance creative team, individual compensation depends upon the job. "For things like writing and photography, a flat fee is appropriate," Wittenstein said. "For programming...we pay on an hourly basis, but we check for milestones and expectations as we go along, so we don't get caught in a black hole."

MARKETING: A Hard and A Medium Sell

Finding new multimedia clients is a challenge for Galileo, as it is for most other multimedia developers. For this firm, the search boiled

down to knowing the marketplace, networking, and informing people about their new venture. In the case of Talking Business Cards, for instance, the partners looked for companies that sold computer-related products, or had customers who had access to computers. "We told everybody what we were doing. We spread some seeds," said Goldstein. "We also thought about who were the more likely players for multimedia.

Then we thought about some really cool things that they could do with it, and pitched the ideas to those businesses." Both methods proved rewarding.

Still, getting clients for Talking Business Cards or other multimedia projects is never easy, according to Wittenstein. "Getting people to change is a hard sell period. Selling them multimedia is a medium sell because people are being approached with something new, it takes a little bit more time than you would expect.... The hardest part for us is finding progressive-minded individuals, with control of their budgets, who have a need for the product. That is difficult, because they're not in any particular level of an organiza-

Practice What You Preach: This is the main screen from Galileo's latest self-promoting Talking Business Card.

tion. Sometimes it is the president of the company who drives the decision down. Other times, it's an influential employee who drives the decision up. In the case of larger, more sophisticated projects, we've been more successful working from the top down. So it's all over the board. I'd say it's tough. Yeah it's tough."

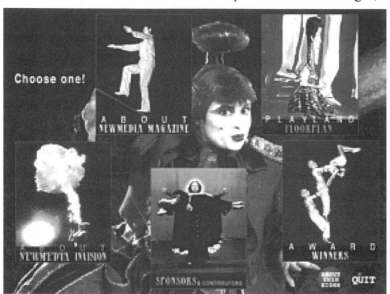

Part of their marketing strategy includes maintaining a high profile in the multimedia industry. Both Wittenstein and Goldstein have been guest lecturers, instructors, judges, panel members, and active participants in a variety of seminars, specialty group meetings, and in-house events. In the last three years, they took part in eighteen such events, including seminars on "Marketing with Multimedia," "Kodak Photo CD and Multimedia," "What Multimedia Can Do For Your Business," and "Multimedia in 30 Minutes or Less." Galileo has also been profiled in various industry-related publications.

An Industry Profile: This menu is from a Galileo-designed kiosk for *NewMedia Magazine* for Comdex in Atlanta.

Why spend so much time on the multimedia speakers circuit? Wittenstein cites three reasons, "The one that's most important is to stay in touch with the market.... The second is improved credibility and exposure for Galileo...people are starting to recognize our name. And the third is to obtain leads."

FUTURE PROJECTS: Electronic Brochures and On-line Newsletters

As a result of its experience, Galileo's most recent generation of Talking Business Cards is increasingly sophisticated and complex—the equivalent of digital brochures. The company also is concentrating on alternative electronic methods to serve its clients' communications needs.

Recent undertakings illustrate this expanded reach and scope. One project was for Digital Communications Associates (DCA), a software development company, which asked Galileo to create a disk to demonstrate the company's software in a user-friendly way. "Instead of sending out disabled software with limited functionality," Wittenstein said, "the demo disk has an interactive, navigational system, which enables a user to tour seven specific features and benefits.... It's a simulation, not the real software, but we animate it to look just like their program, and design it so that every user has a successful experience."

Wittenstein and Goldstein also led a development team that created an on-line multimedia newsletter for a company with a 5,000-station computer network. Every morning, employees load the newsletter into their Macs or PCs, a process that takes 15 seconds. Since the company did not want to invest in sound and video playback cards for the system, there is no sound or digitized video. "The newsletter is on the desktops so it has become a natural part of everybody's day," Wittenstein pointed out. "It's all interactive so you can get just the information you want with full graphics support. We also offer full-text bibliographies as part of the multimedia. So if you're interested in finding more about a subject, you click and can read the entire article or a bibliography."

Eventually, the newsletter will include interactive polling via digital questionnaires which will provide al-

Talking To Art Directors: This screen is from a recent Talking Business Card for a printer. The cut paper art work was scanned, and then manipulated in Photoshop.

most instantaneous reactions to company policy and actions. Wittenstein added, "We are working with this company, and others, to develop a process of polling the entire organization, and having it take a few minutes instead of months and $100,000. The survey will be an addendum to the daily online newsletter." Completed questionnaires will be automatically tabulated.

Regardless of their form or delivery, these multimedia applications have to be based on an understanding of effective communication. "No matter what kind of marketing program you're doing, if you are not communicating well, you are wasting your money," Wittenstein said. "Also, you must understand how to reach a customer's market through electronic delivery. The real challenge right now is figuring out how to get a multimedia message from point A to point B. Sometimes multimedia makes a lot of sense for customers; sometimes it doesn't."

"Multimedia is not an industry, product, or technology that you can touch. It is simply tools and techniques," Wittenstein emphasized. "Tools are the hardware and software. Techniques are how we apply the tools. Multimedia is simply an extension, a toolset that we can use to communicate better in our chosen discipline."

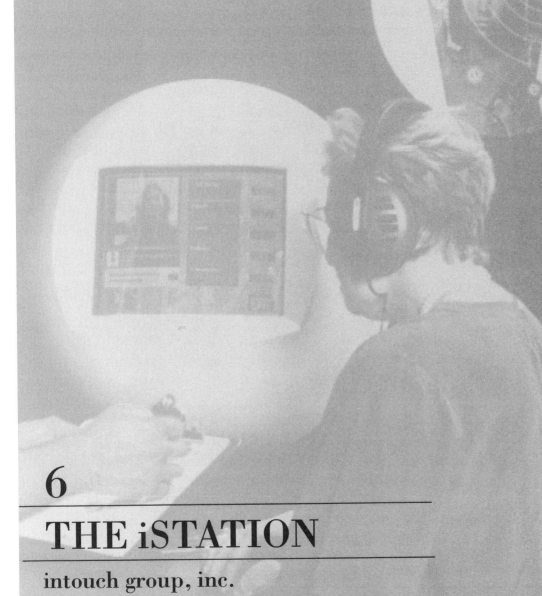

6

THE iSTATION

intouch group, inc.

At A Glance

THE iSTATION

Developer: intouch group, inc.

Personnel: Joshua D. Kaplan, founder and president; Tom Silinski, vice president and chief operating officer; Steve Katz, vice president, product development; and Dick Wingate, vice president of marketing.

Description: An interactive kiosk, with a touch screen, bar code scanner and CD-ROM jukebox. The iStation allows consumers to preview audio CDs before purchasing them. An internal Macintosh computer and modem enable the kiosk to collect data about its users and their music preferences and this information is shared with record companies and retailers.

Development period: 1988-1993.

Production hardware: Quadras and other Macintoshes, Indigo workstations.

Production software: MacroMind Director, Photoshop, MacroMind 3-D, Renderman, Macromedia's MacroModel, Alias Power Animator, proprietary C ++ programming.

Presentation hardware: Macintosh CPU, 24-bit video graphics board, RasterOps Media Time card with DSP for audio, a 14.4 modem, three SCSI-based CD-ROM jukeboxes, Microtouch touch screen.

Development cost: $22 million.

Financing: Start up loans; personal savings, investors.

Awards: Winner, Best Informational POP/Kiosk Display, 1994 Interactive Advertising and Media Awards.

Future projects: Video iStation; ticketing iStation; CD-ROM/games iStation.

Contact: Heather Crosby
              intouch group, inc.
              333 Bryant Street
              San Francisco, CA 94107
              415–974–5000
              415–974–5087 (fax)

T rue story: When you're writing a book, you don't spend much time away from your computer. Breaks are for essential business, like watering the roses, buying coffee and cat food, and watching "Star Trek: The Next Generation." So it's not surprising that the authors of this book had not been in a record store for a while, preferring to save both time and money listening to a college jazz station. But, on a windy Friday night, we pulled into the parking lot of our area Wherehouse to do some research and to check out the new Frank Sinatra album, "Duets." Interestingly enough, the two missions were related.

Information, Please: A listening booth for the computer age, the iStation lets music lovers preview albums.

Inside the door stood one of two very distinctive kiosks in the bustling store. Each looked a little like R2D2—a boxy body topped by a beach-ball-sized head with a computer monitor for a face. Two teenage girls, both wearing earphones connected to the kiosk, were smiling and swaying to music we couldn't hear (and probably wouldn't understand). At the other kiosk, in the center of the store, between racks of CDs and tapes, was a thirty-something woman, also wearing a headset. She touched the screen several times in a row, then closed her eyes and began tapping her foot.

The two teens finally left and it was our turn. After filling out a form which asked who we were and what music we liked, we had been issued a user ID card by the store clerk. We felt a little like DJs as we slipped on the padded headphones and passed the bar code on our card over the scanner on the kiosk's "chin." A silky female voice responded immediately, giving us the option of "previewing" some new releases, or hits from Billboard's top ten, or listening to some albums in every category we could think of from country, to classical, to comedy. A slip of the finger later, and instead of Sinatra, we were looking at a screen full of holiday releases. Oh well, let's try Aaron Neville, we decided, and touched the album cover pictured on the screen. Up popped a choice of cuts from the album.

Hmmm. How about thirty seconds of "Louisiana, Christmas Day?" Within moments, Neville's clear tenor was floating over a Cajun beat. Not bad, we nodded, working our way through "White Christmas" and "O Holy Night."

But we came here to check out Sinatra, so we pushed the exit button. Not so fast. Instead of the main menu, the next screen was dominated by five disembodied hands with their thumbs extended like digital hitchhikers. We had to rate what we'd heard, ranging from thumbs up, most excellent, to thumbs down, dud, by touching one of the waving hands. Thumbs up, we agree.

Now, where was Old Blue Eyes? Probably already on the charts, we guessed, tapping the Billboard icon. Of the eight Billboard categories we were offered on the next screen, we picked Top Pop and there was "Duets." The menu of songs began with Sinatra and Streisand. It was OK. So were his vocal flings with Gloria Estefan and U2's Bono. We exited, after giving Frank a so-so rating. "Duets" was a disappointment, but at least we didn't spend seventeen bucks to find out. We also had found some new music for our annual Christmas bash, and, now, we knew how to start this chapter on the iStation.

Touch Tunes: iStation users touch the kiosk's screen to select an album to preview.

National Release:
After trial runs in four cities, iStations have been placed in record stores around the country.

The brainstorm of Josh Kaplan, a former investment banker and founder of intouch group, inc., the iStation is the computer-age version of the listening booth of the long-ago '40s and '50s. Via a sturdy white kiosk shaped like the letter "i," the international symbol for information, music lovers can take some of the guess work out of buying new recordings by "previewing" a wide range of music from the iStation's CD-ROM "jukebox," with a database drawn from more than 32,000 CDs. Through the bar code on their iStation card, and their ratings of the albums they sample, listeners give record companies feedback on their products. As iStation users, listeners can be targeted for special promotions that bring them back to the stores that have the friendly kiosks. No wonder the iStation has many fans in the highly competitive music industry. Mike Green, vice president of sales at Chrysalis Records, notes that "there is little doubt that a 21st-century information center like the iStation will increase music sales. In fact, our biggest concern isn't pricing, but how quickly every prerecorded music store will be able to have an intouch station."

Inspired by a "listening bar" in a Switzerland record store, in early 1993 Kaplan completed a three-month test run of the iStation in four markets, San Francisco, San Diego, New York, and St. Louis. By spring of 1994, intouch group, inc., had placed more than 130 of the kiosks in record stores around the country; had signed more than 400,000 iStation users, and was enrolling an average of 60,000 new iCard members a month. Each time one of them samples an album, the issuing record company and the retailer pay intouch group, inc., a fee. Since each kiosk costs approximately $18,000 to manufacture, Kaplan's venture required deep pockets. By the end of 1993, the 32-year-old multimedia entrepreneur had raised $22 million from a variety of investors to finance his bold venture.

While that kind of funding may be out of reach for most developers, the innovative approach is not. The powerful combination of interactive multimedia, and networked data collection, puts the iStation in a class by itself and demonstrates the range of services possible with creative, in-depth use of the new technologies. The android-like kiosk is central to Kaplan's business, but he stresses that intouch group, inc., is much more than a kiosk builder. "We're an information company," he emphasized, explaining that the company has designs on the video and software industries. "We poll the machine every night and tell how many previews were made, by what type of person. We tell the record companies not only about what (music) walks out of the store, but also about the customer."

THE OPPORTUNITY: In Tune With Change

In 1988, on one of his frequent business trips to Europe, Josh Kaplan spied something that would change his life. "I spent a lot of time overseas" in a job as a PC industry analyst with Connecticut's, GartnerGroup, he explained. "And on a trip to Switzerland, in Zurich, I walked into a record store, and I saw these kind of listening bars with headphones hanging from the ceiling and vinyl albums playing. They had these ten listening posts." Walking around the

Josh Kaplan: A former PC industry analyst, Kaplan was inspired by a listening bar he used in Switzerland.

store, "I thought, boy if you could bring this about on a broad scale, if you could get this to the mass merchandisers...."

With that inspiration, Kaplan realized that the music industry was faced with major changes that were slowing sales. "The industry was transitioning from six- and eight-dollar products, like cassettes and LPs, to expensive CD audio products," he said. "While the sound quality did improve, and the durability and life of the album expanded, I think it make it much more difficult for people to impulse-buy. Just from personal experience—when I got my CD player, and I wanted to replace my collection, it made it difficult because at that time a CD ran $27. Even when the price came down to $15, it still made for a tough decision." At the same time, he believed, music lovers were daunted by the thousands of titles competing for their disposable income. "Someone walks into a store that has 40,000 choices and you have selection stress," he said. Add that anxiety to the fact that the average record buyer was growing older and was likely to be more discriminating and more cautious than youthful purchasers. No wonder the music industry was in a deepening financial spin.

Back in New York, Kaplan drafted a business plan for a company that would become intouch group, inc. The young investment advisor envisioned "a kiosk that would allow people access to information. I didn't call it multimedia, because no one was using the phrase back then." In a record store, the kiosk would take the concept of the listening booths that were popular in the 1950s and "bring it forward 30 years," Kaplan said. By taking advantage of technological advances, he hoped to enable record shoppers to preview thousands of tunes with ease, regardless of their computer literacy. At the same time, he wanted to collect market data that would aid the sagging industry in assessing its customers and their music preferences. However, Kaplan's vision didn't end there. The same sampling could be easily adapted to the video rental business, by allowing potential customer access to movie trailers and reviews. It could also be a source of concert information and tickets.

Since he had been marketing technology from the early 1980s, Kaplan was up to date on digital advances. One innovation in particular intrigued him, the CD-ROM with its enormous data-storage capacity. With his new plan in hand, Kaplan traveled to California to meet with pioneers of CD-ROM technology at Apple computer, a company that was already preaching the gospel of multimedia. In fact, Kaplan remembers a magazine article an Apple "evangelist" had written around the time of his trip. "It started off, 'Imagine walking into a record store, walking up to an appliance and humming a couple of bars of your favorite album, and up on the screen comes a picture of the album. Then you could listen to the album's music.' That was the picture Apple painted because so much data could be stored on a CD-ROM," he recalled.

Besides being grounded in the potential of CD-ROMs, Kaplan also was exposed to DigiDesign, a company with another technological breakthrough critical to his plan—digitized music. "They digitized music running though their board called Sound Tools, which took all your data, compressed it, and then stored it as binary information," Kaplan explained. "That was the first time I had actually seen the ability to pull the information off a music CD and store it as binary information." With both technological advances at his disposal, Kaplan realized that his kiosk was "something that could be done. I then started looking seriously at how I could pull all the pieces together."

For appeal to users around the world, Kaplan was determined to have an easily-recognized, easy-to-use kiosk design. He likened what he wanted to the Macintosh operating system since once you knew that system, you could use a Mac in any office, anywhere, without additional instruction. Similarly, he wanted an iStation user to feel comfortable with the kiosk whether that user was previewing records or videos, or purchasing concert tickets. Again, new technology would play a decisive role in bringing Kaplan within reach of his goal.

One innovation was touchscreen technology, which was relatively new in 1988-

Simple To Sample: Kaplan wanted the iStation to be easy to use. Innovations like the touch screen and barcode made that possible.

How to
use the

i)station

First, fill out the application and take it to the register to receive your free **i** card. Now, the fun starts. Choose CDs or cassettes that have the **i** sticker. Bring the albums to the **i** station. Take your **i** card — bar code side up — and wave it under the station's bar code scanner until you hear a beep. Now wave your album's bar code under the scanner — exactly as you did with your card.

You can now listen, through headphones or external speakers, to up to five 30-second cuts from each album. You can also see music video clips, read album reviews, and other album information when available, all at a finger's touch. You'll have about three to five minutes to preview all your albums. To keep track of time, watch the countdown clock on the screen.

There's a world of music waiting for you. What are you waiting for?

89. The most significant application adapted to the iStation was the UPC, or bar code, now ubiquitous in supermarkets and other retail operations, as well as record stores. The universal, data-rich code, whether on the back of a CD, or on the iCard of individual iStation users, would activate the kiosk. "I knew that you couldn't have somebody navigate through the system by typing something in it, because most people can't type," he explained. "It can be very frustrating and take too long." If the music lover used a CD to access the kiosk, the potential for a sale was enhanced. "I wanted it to be a tactile thing, where they would go to the bin, grab a product, and have the product in hand, which means they are half way to the cash register," Kaplan said. "The same thing happens in a clothing store. They want you to try on clothing in the dressing room—they encourage that—because you most likely will find at least one item you'll buy. So the iStation was designed so that people could approach the system, scan in an album and get immediate feedback, by way of both graphics and voice-over, so that they know they have done something right."

Data Collection: The barcode on the back of the iCard enables intouch group, inc. to collect information about iStation users.

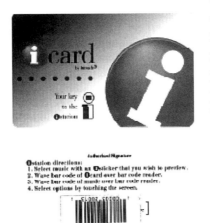

At the same time, since a bar code contains a significant amount of information, Kaplan also wanted to build into the iStation a method of storing and retrieving that data, including a profile of the users, the albums previewed and how the albums were rated. "People don't know a lot about bar codes," Kaplan reminded. "They know that it's something a cashier passes over a scanner to get a price. There are only twelve little lines, but there's a lot of data stored there. At least the way we use it, there's a lot." Thus, while the iStation is "a conduit from the manufacturer to the user," it also is a conduit from the user to the manufacturer, "a kind of Trojan Horse strategy," Kaplan said, and it greatly expands industry knowledge of its customers. "Soundscan (the point-of-purchase system used to compile Billboard's charts) tells a record company what's going out the door," he explained, "but we can tell them who these people are and what's making it from the point of preview to point of sale." As a result, he continued, "we don't consider ourselves in the music industry. We see ourselves as 'place-based media.' In the advertising industry, it is where you deliver advertising at the point-of-sale at the retail store. The value of place-based media is that it reduces the time gap between the exposure to the product and the sale."

As for the iStation's distinctive shape, Kaplan had to return to the scene of his initial inspiration, Switzerland. There, in a picturesque Alpine village, he had tracked down a former colleague, Ueli Mona, who eventually would design the prototype kiosk, and now manages the iStation manufacturing plant in Minnesota. Mona and Kaplan sat at a picnic table in the shadow of the great Eiger mountain and brainstormed. "One prolific symbol over there is the 'i,' which is the international symbol for information," Kaplan recalled. "That's when we decided not only adopt it as a moniker, but to build a kiosk in the shape of the 'i.' That's why it's called the iStation. If you look at a side profile, it's in the shape of an 'i'." At the same time, the two men decided the kiosk would have that shape "whether it's in a record store or a video store...you'd know that if you walk up to a system that's shaped like an 'i' that's where you can see great graphics, get good information, and use your iCard."

i For Information: The shape of the iStation was inspired by the international symbol for information.

THE TEAM: Minding Money and Machines

Since he graduated from college in the early 1980s, 32-year-old Josh Kaplan has marketed technology. In the process, he learned the business and fund-raising skills that brought intouch group, inc., to life financially. For the firm to thrive technically, Kaplan eventually linked up with a high-powered researcher with an entrepreneurial bent.

In 1983, with a degree from the University of Michigan, Kaplan started his own firm, Technology Co., and sold PCs to large corporations. The enterprise proved to be an excellent stepping-stone to his next position at the GartnerGroup, which he joined three years later. As a personal computer analyst for the Connecticut financial company, Kaplan said he "advised Fortune 500 companies on how they should approach buying PCs, clients like General Motors that were buying thousands of PCs at a time." He soon moved to Gartner Securities, the division that advised money managers about investments in information technology stocks. In the process, he became wise to companies on the cutting edge of technology, the workings of the stock market, and the psychology of investors.

Travel was a large part of Kaplan's GartnerGroup job, and it was on one of those overseas visits that he spotted the listening booth in Zurich. Struck by the potential for what would become the iStation, Kaplan drafted a business plan and began researching the technology needed to make it a reality. More often than not, he found himself on the west coast, huddled with Apple "evangelists" and other silicon valley innovators. On one of those trips, he was recruited by San Francisco's Robertson, Stephens & Co. "I wanted to be out on the west coast anyway," he said, reflecting on his decision to move. "I wanted to be closer to the technology."

As an investment banker at Robertson, Stephens, one of Kaplan's jobs was to take technology companies public. Once again, fate dealt Kaplan an ace. One of the companies he took public was video-board maker RasterOps, a firm that would play a major role—technologically and financially—in making his iStation vision a reality. "When I was in London with RasterOps CEO, Keith Sorenson, I said, 'Keith, you have such a neat multimedia board that we've got to do more than just be a board company. I think we can build an industry around it.' And I told him about my model." By this time, Kaplan also had met with Mona, and work on a prototype was underway, funded largely with $143,000 drained from Kaplan's savings.

In January 1990, less than two years after his "inspiration" in Zurich, Kaplan quit his job with Robertson, Stephens to work full time on the iStation. Sorenson made space for him and the completed prototype in RasterOps' Bay Area offices. However, the one-hour commute grew old fast, and except for meetings with potential investors, whom he hoped to impress with RasterOps' spacious offices, Kaplan began working primarily out of his "industrial-looking" loft, south of Market Street in downtown San Francisco. A year later, with $600,000 in bridge loans, including $200,000 from RasterOps, Kaplan opened the first intouch group, inc., office, rented some computers, and hired some part-time help. "We had so little money that when the venture capitalists came in, I scheduled people to come in for work," Kaplan recalled. "If an investor was coming in from 1 to 3 P.M., I'd have my part-timers come in between noon and 5 P.M. We had to make them feel that it was a going concern. It probably would have been better to hire actors at that time."

One of those part-timers was Steve Katz, who is now vice president of product development and Kaplan's techno-right-hand. A "technologist at heart," Katz earned a master's degree from Columbia University in 1986, while he was working at an IBM research lab on a project called QBE (Query by Example), which became the basis for another project called Paradox. "We were

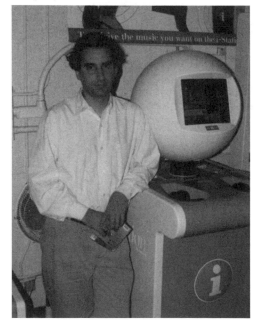

actually a development group within that laboratory, so it was an interesting semi-entrepreneurial effort," he recalled. In 1987, he joined a Wall Street firm as a "rocket-scientist," one of a group of computer "wonks" who worked with mathematicians and physicists on "quantitative models for trading." Eager to return to the cutting edge of technology, Katz moved on, joining Apple in

Steve Katz: A computer "wonk," Katz is now in charge of product development for intouch group, inc.

1988. "First, I worked in their Market Intelligence Group," he said, "where I was conducting competitive analysis research on operating systems and system software technologies. Then I worked in product line management, where I was involved in pursuing the A. I. (artificial intelligence) market and the object-oriented programming market." Almost four years later, he struck out on his own and began assisting Kaplan. Eight months later, Kaplan put him on the payroll permanently.

Now in charge of product development, Katz is responsible for "all the research and development, including software engineering, systems database architecture, interface design, and product planning and specification." "Josh is the main vision guy," Katz added. "He is more on the business side. He still has hundreds of ideas that he throws down. I come up with ideas too, but I am the person who has to make sure that the ideas are going to work well in the product we have."

Two other seasoned executives make up the senior officers of the company. Thomas J. Silinski, chief operating officer, has more than twenty years of management experience. Previous posts included president and CEO of Vernors, Inc., a soft drink company, and CEO of Environmental Technology Group. To help place the iStation with record retailers, and to negotiate agreements with recording companies, Kaplan recruited Dick Wingate. In his two decades in the record industry, Wingate held senior level positions with PolyGram Records and CBS'

Bay Area Base: intouch group, inc's corporate headquarters are in San Francisco.

Epic and Columbia records.

By mid-1993, intouch group, inc., had 84 full-time employees, and another three dozen on the part-time payroll. Kaplan expected that number to double as the iStation moved from a four-city experiment to nationwide use. "When we go into a store, we can have as many as twenty people working there," he said. "and we'll have a greeter in a yellow iStation hat and white iStation T-shirt, who introduces the product for the first 30 days. I think it's money well invested."

PRODUCTION: Crossing T's and Dotting I's

The iStation prototype, which was created in Switzerland according to Kaplan's specifications, is very similar to today's in-store version. For example, the interface using graphics and animations created with MacroMind Director is largely the same. So are the basic i-shaped design and functions. "The prototype did the basic functions of being able to trigger a preview of an album based upon the bar code," Katz said "The fundamental technology of using a CD ROM jukebox gives us the large capacity we needed. We use the laser disc for our video....The audio is stored on the CD-ROMs—five selections per album. That basic structure was defined in the prototypical stage."

In other aspects, however, the current iStation is as different from its predecessor, as a Mac Plus is to a Quadra AV. Though its essential components remain the same, the specific hardware has been upgraded to take advantage of technological breakthroughs. Powered by a mid-range Macintosh CPU, it contains 24-bit video graphics hardware, real-time decompression software, RasterOps Media Time card, including a Digital Signal Processor (DSP) chip for audio playback, a U.S. Robotics 14.4 modem, a relational database, and the SCSI-based CD-ROM changer that holds more than a terabyte of data. In addition, a number of new functions have expanded the iStation's reach. Those, though, had to be balanced with consumer convenience. Katz noted, "One key thing about the iStation...is that it's a listening machine. It allows you to interactively listen to music. The more features you add to the machine that allow people to passively search and look things up, the more it becomes like an electronic Library of Congress catalog. You will have more time spent searching than listening, and you don't want that to happen." As the iStation evolves, he continued, "I keep the vision of the benefits of the machine—who our audience is, who we are trying to please, and who we are trying to benefit."

Katz also has to weigh practical concerns, which were considerable in such a complex, and costly ($700,000 for each prototype), project as the iStation. "It would be a lot simpler to develop a CD-ROM project," he said. "You build the title, you test it, you give it to the customers, and you are done. On the iStation, we have touch screens, a bar code scanner, laser discs, CD-ROM jukebox, electromechanical devices...so there is the pressure of building a system that is going to be reliable and used by people, and has all this different hardware and software integrated. That is really where the risks and uncertainties come in, knowing you are going to deal with all these complexities." As a result, he always strives to keep the big picture in mind. "You have all these different pieces of the pie—making it look beautiful and compelling, giving it added functionality, staying within time frames—all of these elements have to be examined, and there has to be somebody who is always standing above and looking at the entire landscape, making the key decisions."

Graphics

After his meeting with iStation designer, Ueli Mona, Kaplan sketched the kiosk's main screens and faxed them to Switzerland where they were incorporated into the prototype using MacroMind Director. Remarkably, the interface basics in those rough drawings are still in use today. However, with the input of computer artists and the addition of 3D graphics and animation, visually, the prototype and the original drawings are very different.

Compared to the iStations now in the nation's record stores, "the original graphical interface is almost identical," Kaplan reflected. Included were icon-labeled buttons to select music categories, the album covers, and a jukebox-style listing of the tracks to be previewed, as well as icons like headphones for controlling volume and "thumbs" for rating albums. The overall look, though, "was a little bubbly, almost Art Deco," he said. That changed in the hands of another artist, Donald Graham, who was a fan of the German techno-computer artist Giger. "He said 'imagine if the ball were solid and you tore the skin off it,'" Kaplan said of the background design that looks like an abstract circuit board. "That's why it looks like you can see the guts of it— the wires—beneath the user interface."

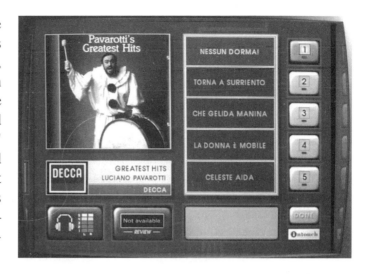

The buttons on the touch screen of the prototype were "very traditional," though, according to Katz, "the three-dimensional representations looked like they pushed in when you touched the screen." Advanced computer graphics and animation changed that, but their use had to be weighed against the performance slowdown such large files could cause. "Richer graphics look great," Katz noted, "but they also can lead to some problems. Our entire application is only 350K, so it's relatively small. However, we have about 18 mega-

bytes of memory devoted to animation and graphics. The richer your graphics and the more animations you have, the more memory they consume. You don't want to be loading too many animations off the disk while the application is running because it will degrade performance. So we preload as much as possible and try to reuse existing elements."

Then and Now: Kaplan's prototype screen, above, and today's iStation screen, below, are remarkably similar.

While striving to make the iStation graphics "striking in appearance," the kiosk's users were topmost in the designers' minds. The high-tech background and the glowing buttons, for example, hold user interest, Katz believes. "Every time you touch a button, it glows, and the glow spills all over the adjoining elements, giving an illusion of dimensionality," he said. "It makes the interface more difficult to create, because every time you make a change in a button, you have to make changes in the set of buttons surrounding that button." Other animations and audio provide user feedback, Katz said. "So when you raise and lower the headphones' volume, the headphone icon rotates, or when you raise and lower the speaker, they (the speaker icons) pop up and down," he explained. "The classical browser sees the conductor with his baton animated. Little touches such as these are not gratuitous because they really help people understand what is going on. The other thing we did was add sound effects and voiceovers everywhere so every screen and every prompt has an accompanying voice that also engages the user."

Another major challenge in refining the interface was "giving the store manager the ability to configure the machine," Katz added. "They might want to set sales promotions, or create their own button for their picks of the week. So we had to design an interface that is as simple for store personnel to use as it is for customers."

Katz generally develops extensive flowcharts and storyboards for his programmers to follow "because there are a lot of things that happen if someone touches here, or doesn't touch here; times out here or doesn't time out here." As features have been added, he sketches screens before turning the job over to staff graphic artists. Although they are now beginning to use Silicon Graphics Indigo workstations with Power Animator from Alias, company designers have used a variety of programs for 3-D imaging. "For most of the project, the main programs we used were Macromedia's MacroModel and MacroMind 3-D," Katz said. "We have used some other modelers for specialized work, but we are trying to standardize so that all the models are interchangeable. This year, we have begun to tap into the full potential of the Indigos by using Alias."

One feature of the Indigo machines Katz likes is that his graphics team personnel can do 3-D creation on their own familiar Macintoshes, then utilize the Indigos for dramatically faster rendering. "You actually use what is called networked RenderMan," he explained. "It executes on the Silicon Graphics machine, but it is initiated from the Mac. It is sort of like going into your printer and choosing a printer. You choose a renderer and then say, 'go and render,' and it actually spools all the render files and then, one by one, renders and stores them." Depending on the size of the graphic, Katz estimates that the rendering time is six to eight times faster on the Indigos as on the Macs. "For shorter renders, it's not really that critical, but when we have a 10,000- to 12,000-frame animation, that gets into some serious rendering time."

Navigation

Simplicity always has been the watchword in iStation design, particularly when it comes to navigation. "I was really taken with the Apple philosophy," Kaplan said, remembering his early work on Macintoshes. "Their advertising always said, if you can point and click, you can use a Mac. They took the fear out of using a personal computer." Another vivid image, from a Public Television special on computers, also shaped Kaplan's viewpoint. "They looked back to when you were a child and what you did when you wanted something—you pointed," he continued. "The idea of pointing and touching and getting interaction, getting immediate reaction, is very powerful."

Thanks to the iStation's state-of-the-art touch screen, point and touch is the basic access to the tens of thousands of albums in its memory bank. "If you watch people around the iStation, the learning curve is about ten seconds," Kaplan said. But as new functions and categories were added, maintaining that simplicity became more and more of a challenge. "Initially, we wanted total simplicity," Katz noted. "Now with all these additional features, the navigation becomes a little more sophisticated. What we really wanted to get away from is layers and layers of menus."

Katz said that since the first prototype was designed in Switzerland, the iStation functions have constantly expanded. "The first station did only one thing," he recalled. "It let you come up to the machine, scan an album and listen to it. That basic function is still used by about half the people who use the iStation today." Katz believes that procedure suits music lovers who "like to have a product in their hands, those who like to walk around the aisles and pick up albums.... Later we found that people might want to go up to the machine without having a CD [in hand]." That led to the addition of albums on Billboard's charts and local radio station playlists. "You would touch a button, go to the Billboard charts, see the different categories, go to a category, and then preview the album from that chart," Katz said. The next feature added was the new release bin, which is similar in design to the Billboard charts in that "you touch a category and see the album covers come up," Katz said.

The next addition, the browse mode, transformed the iStation into a "virtual store," Katz said. "It lets people look up things by musical category and then by artist and title if it's nonclassical, or

Chart Toppers: One new iStation feature lets users preview Billboard's top-selling albums.

To listen to an album, please touch a selection.

THE Billboard 200.

COMPILED FROM A NATIONAL SAMPLE OF RETAIL STORE AND RACK SALES REPORTS COLLECTED, COMPILED, AND PROVIDED BY SoundScan

THIS WEEK	ARTIST	TITLE	LABEL
1	★ ★ ★ No. 1 ★ ★ ★ Snoop Doggy Dogg	DOGGYSTYLE	Priority/Deat
2	Mariah Carey	MUSIC BOX	Columbia
3	Pearl Jam	VS.	Epic
4	Michael Bolton	THE ONE THING	Columbia
5	Meat Loaf	BAT OUT OF HELL II: BACK INTO HELL	MCA
6	Frank Sinatra	FRANK SINATRA • DUETS	Capitol
7	Various Artists	THE BEAVIS AND BUTT-HEAD EXPERIENCE	Geffen
8	Janet Jackson	JANET.	Virgin
9	Various Artists	COMMON THREAD • THE SONGS OF	Giant
10	Guns N' Roses	THE SPAGHETTI INCIDENT?	Geffen

MORE CHOICES EXIT

by composer, conductor, or orchestra, if it's a classical work," he said. To search by artist, title or composer, iStation users spell out their preference on a "virtual keyboard. They tap out the letters and search by name," he explained. "These capabilities allow people to navigate the information by touching preexisting references to other works or actually doing a text lookup.... It's like browsing without going through the racks or bins...and you can listen to a title, whether or not the store has it in stock."

Helping classical music lovers navigate the iStation's vast holdings has proved difficult, Katz said. A recent overhaul of the browse feature for classical music added a "much more extensive searching capacity...because classical music has a more diverse set of information: soloists, instrumentalists, orchestras." A new interface gives the classical music fan access "from basically any point—composer, conductor, orchestra, soloist, or instrumentalist." From that starting point, the search is refined. "For instance," he continued, "after you have chosen the composer, the next thing it's going to ask is what orchestra. It will list all the orchestras and you choose

The Latest Sounds: New releases introduces users to the newest albums in record stores.

one. Then it will ask 'which work of this composer played by this orchestra are you looking for?' And you say, 'I am looking for Beethoven, I'm looking for the New York Philharmonic, and now I am looking for Beethoven's Fifth Symphony.'" This intelligent search method Katz believes is "the way classical music buyers think. So it makes it a lot easier for that customer to use the iStation."

Whether the user is a dred-locked reggae lover or a blue-haired chamber music fan, the iStation has been programmed or "trained," as Katz says, to suggest other albums of likely interest. "After you listen to an album, it asks you, `Would you like to see [other] albums by the same artist? Would you like to see new releases in this particular genre of music?' So it gives you additional opportunities," he continued. "After I listen to one Bruce Springsteen album, I see all of Springsteen's catalog. After you listen to one Beatles' album, not only will it show you all the Beatles albums...it will show you all the albums by each one of the Beatles individually." This feature, programmed manually from the iStation's Oracle relational database, is the kind of complex linkage that Katz believes adds depth to iStation services.

Personal Search: The new browse mode invites users to type in the title of any album he or she wants to preview.

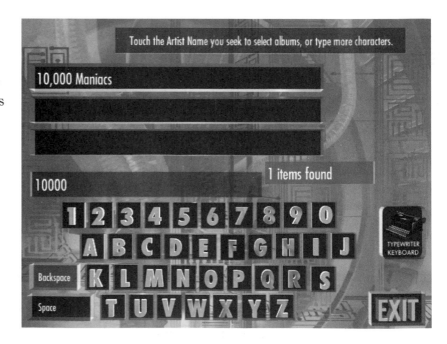

Another recent innovation is a coupon printer, made possible through a joint venture with Catalina Marketing, the premier supermarket coupon delivery company. Now embedded in all iStations in the field, it can be used for in-store promotions. "This is a really nice way for record companies to target customers with value-added coupons," Katz said. It also can help to cinch the sale. "In our market research, we found that the number one reason people walk out of record stores is because they can't find what they are looking for," he pointed out. "Now that either means that the album is out of stock, or, more likely, they just don't know where it is in the store. So we have come up with a way that you can listen to an album and...(get) printed information on it—the name of the artist, the bar code, and where in the store it is located—so you can use that to go find it." If the album is not in the store, the coupon doubles as a special order form.

A second promotion-related feature takes advantage of the time the iStation requires to locate the selected album. "There's a certain amount of dead time while the disc is loading—four to seven seconds," Katz said. "During that period we can put up a message about the artist, or a concert tour, or even a related advertisement." For example, he points to a recent promotion with Sony tied to Sony Pictures' new feature film, "Geronimo." "Every time you scanned in a Sony album, you got a quick clip from the trailer for the movie," he said. For Sinatra's "Duets," he said, "when you previewed an album by an artist who sings with Frank, you got an ad that says be sure to preview 'Duets.'"

Before any new feature is added, Katz carefully considers its impact on the iStation. For example, he points to a proposed link to sales-generating radio station play lists. "The sales force proposed a deal with radio stations to have their logos come up on the screen along with their play lists. You touch any of those, and it goes right to those albums," he said. "So I had to come up with how to do this, how to transmit the data into the machines, what kind of format to use, and what it's going to look like. So we take the idea, find out what the business needs are, and talk to the sales and marketing people about it.... We also look within the iStation, so that it will work with other features, and still be fast."

Audio

Since the iStation is a "virtual record store," the selection of 30-second tracks from hundreds of thousands of albums is an ongoing, major undertaking for intouch group, inc. Fortunately for them, a large, informed labor pool is in the vicinity—the students at the San Francisco Conservatory of Music. As many as five dozen music compilers at a time work in the company's downtown offices, picking samples that are representative of the albums and reinforce industry promotions.

To standardize and simplify this never-ending task, Katz developed a Mac-based software program with a graphical interface, called i-select. After a CD is loaded into an Apple CD-ROM drive, the music compilers scan the album's bar code, which brings on screen an interface similar to the iStation display for previewing albums, except that it shows every track. "Next to each," Katz explained, "is a check box. Using an on-screen menu with play, pause, and back and forth buttons, and a timer...they select up to five tracks and the start and end point of each selection." The average selection is about 30 seconds long, for a total of two, or two and a half, minutes of music from each album. "The classical people have a little more leeway," Katz said. "They may select only one or two tracks but may have longer segments because they are all movements, or parts of movements."

Each compiler then saves his, or her, work on a shared Oracle data base and puts a sticker with his, or her, initials on the album before passing it to a reviewer who checks the work. Next, selections from about 150 albums are compressed, put on digital audio tape, and sent to a CD-ROM mastering plant for duplication and shipment to iStation sites. Some samples are returned to intouch group, inc., where final testing occasionally reveals some errors. "If we find mistakes," Katz said, "we have a technique called exceptions, which are little files we put on the hard drive, that override information inside the disc. So we can make corrections even after the disc has been mastered."

When the business was getting started, Katz said they had music compilers working in shifts around the clock. "At our peak, we compressed 300 albums per day," he recalled. "This level of production is no longer necessary. The number of new releases each month is in the hundreds. Theoretically, if we suddenly signed some new labels that might have large catalogs, like Latin music, we might have to crank up that processing again. But basically, we just keep up with new releases now."

Network

One distinguishing feature of the iStation is that this digital listening booth is also a digital polling booth. Katz believes that the rich demographic and musical preference data collected from iStation users will spur the company's future success. "Our job is not only to come up with new features and capabilities for the iStation, but also to design innovative ways of analyzing and capitalizing on all the data we get back...to create really interesting reports, charts, and marketing surveys that are going to help the record companies strategize their business."

To collect information from iStations across the country, the company has contracted with a third party for an electronic mail and electronic bulletin board system. Using their internal 14.4 modems, the iStations "dial in each night and deposit their daily transaction data," Katz said. They also download any specific data or software updates. In case an individual station does not dial out one night, the information is stored on its hard drive, and two days' worth of information is transmitted the following evening. The next day, intouch group, inc., imports the files collected in its Oracle data base, where they become the basis of standard and custom reports to record labels and retailers.

intouch's job, then, "is to make sense out of all this data," Katz said. While the material is a gold mine of market-related statistics, it

Making Music: Students from a nearby music school select preview tracks for use in iStations.

can be overwhelming "because many record company executives are not familiar with using computer technology to analyze their marketing information. You have to point out the value sometimes; show them how they can use it." Record companies, like Capitol, that already rely heavily on market research, will help demonstrate the value of iStation data to the rest of the industry. "It's also going to help us shape the data and understand what best serves the needs of the industry," Katz noted.

Who's Who: Information supplied by iCard holders is part of the data collected by iStations.

Kiosk Hogs

One unique problem of public kiosks is preventing a single user from monopolizing the machine, without making that user feel rushed, while, at the same time, making sure others feel that they don't have to wait too long for their turn. The intouch group, inc., team tackled the problem by adding a timer to the interface that the store manager sets to limit individual iStation sessions. With intouch revenues tied to the number of albums previewed, Katz said the firm "didn't want someone giving a user an hour to use the machine, nor did we want him to have only ten seconds." Hence a four-minute session was generally approved. If there is not a line to use the iStation, the time limit is "soft," Katz continued. "After your time is up, it says `Sorry but your time has run out, please let someone else have a chance to use the machine. If there is no one waiting, you can come back in a minute.'"

Attempts to prevent abuses by limiting the number of times an iCard could be used in a day, for example, were abandoned in favor of self-regulation. "We thought this would be a nightmare because it's going to hurt the 90 percent of our customers who don't abuse it," Katz explained. "We get daily reports and the average time is usually within a minute of the posted listening time." In addition, the company offers a gold iCard, a premium card that, among other features, offers the consumer a longer preview session in exchange for a small membership fee.

On the average, iStation use is approximately 100 previews a day, although in some stores, previews are double that figure. The more previews on the iStation, the more revenue for all involved—intouch group, inc., the retailer, and the record company, according to Kaplan. "We want to give the customer the necessary information," he said, "but [we wanted to] get them through with enough frequency that people are willing to stand in line wait. The average person samples about two and a half albums per visit to the store...averages about five minutes on the iStation. We find that one out of every three samples converts to a sale. So one of the things we had to consider was the through-put, and that's why we put in the bar code card, which controls the amount of time an individual can take."

Programming

Kaplan and Katz realized early on that a complex array of services and almost constant updating demanded a proprietary program for the iStation. Katz explained that off-the-shelf software did not change often enough to keep up with the kiosk's changes. "It is not like Microsoft Word or something like that, where there are six- or eight- or twelve-month cycles and hundreds of features that you are going to put on the next version," he said. "Here, there is always feedback; there are always people who want to add features. It is very easy to add these things, because of the way we have developed the program. And, because it is easy to modify and customize, it is very seductive to want to add capabilities all the time."

The iStation program, composed of around 300,000 lines of C++ code, had to stand up to rigorous testing before iStations were installed in stores. "You have to go through the same traditional software engineering practices as you would for any commercial product, however, there are two main differences," Katz said. "First, crash and data-loss bugs are totally unacceptable in a retail store. So the reliability of the machine is held to a different standard. Our business depends on not losing data, because we are an information services company. Second, our cycle of releases is much shorter. We don't have a year, or more, to put out a new release. We put out new releases almost every quarter, new software upgrades, featuring new capabilities."

Testing

Unlike the rest of the iStation development, which followed Kaplan's detailed business plan, testing was largely informal and in-house. "We're not really populated by technologists," Katz explained. "Most of the people around here have backgrounds from the conservatory of music. So we have a built-in focus group within the company."

Prior to the test marketing in four cities in early 1993, the company moved an iStation into record stores in San Francisco and New Orleans, for brief consumer tests. "For a couple of days we watched people use the machine," Katz said. As the kiosks have moved into stores nationwide, "we have gotten enormous feedback from consumers in the stores, as well as from store managers and clerks, and through hundreds of demos that we give throughout the country, as well as research studies that we've done."

Mistakes Are Made: Tests revealed that users needed a way to recover when they selected the wrong album from the Billboard charts.

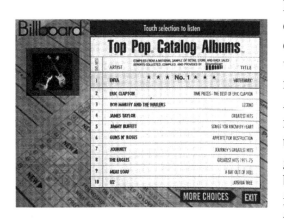

One problem spotted involved the Billboard charts. iStation users often touched the wrong title by mistake. Katz said, "So we had to come up with a way to allow people to recover from mistakes." One potential solution—to delay the response so the customer could change his, or her, mind—was rejected as confusing. Another idea was to make the selection a two-step process, but that "introduced another step and slowed people down," Katz said. "So what we finally did, was that when you touch an album, a picture of the album immediately pops up along with its information and you're asked if you would like to preview this. Then you can touch 'yes' or 'no.'"

Katz, and other intouch group, inc., executives, also make it a point to visit stores, "watching people use the interface and seeing how they react." As a result, "the demand for formal market studies and focus groups isn't as important here," he said.

Kiosk Manufacturing and Maintenance

Ueli Mona, inventor of the prototype iStation, watched his design take shape daily at the iStation's manufacturing plant in Minneapolis, where he now supervises the twenty workers employed there. The location grew out of an early contract with General Pattern, a Minneapolis company that made the kiosk's injection-molded plastic shell. "We used one of their buildings for a while, and then we decided to lease our own building adjacent to General Pattern, and do all our manufacturing there," Katz said. Starting with the prototype, company founder Josh Kaplan has stressed the use of quality materials in the kiosk, which is one reason for its $18,000 price tag. "A lot of kiosks are pressboard and laminate," Kaplan said, "but when you go into mass production, you have vacuum forming and hard tooling, and that's very expensive."

Since the technological sophistication of the iStation is wasted if the machine breaks down, intouch group, inc., created the iTeam of service representatives. "The key to making a successful product of this nature is service," Katz stressed. "It's not like putting a Mac or a PC in a store and leaving it. You have to think of maintenance, updating the machine, transmitting information to it." iTeam leaders, mostly college graduates trained at the iStation factory, are paged, if problems with kiosk hardware or software arise. "If a system goes down," Katz explained, "a number will show up on their pager screen indicting what the potential problem is." Store managers also are given an 800 number to call to report problems. "If needed, we will dispatch a part by plane...so, generally, we can fix the machine in the same business day."

MARKETING: Making Music Together

Josh Kaplan knew he couldn't sell a new idea to record retailers from his San Francisco office. Digital age notwithstanding, he did what generations of salespeople have done, he hit the road. "I would stick the prototype in the back of a truck and drive myself around to all the record shows," he recalled. "I would show the record labels and retailers what this was all about, and try to gain their support." It was an uphill battle; the technology was intimidating to some, while others resisted Kaplan's fee plan. However, changes in the music industry played into Kaplan's hands. By the time of the iStation's national launch in the fall of 1993, many major retailers, and record labels—with some notable exceptions—had agreed to give the space-age kiosk a try.

In-Store Help: To help introduce and maintain iStations, they send iTeam members to stores.

When Kaplan first made his sales pitch, the music industry was riding a sales wave, generated by MTV and the introduction of CDs. "What they didn't realize was, a lot of the growth was from this replacement cycle— people buying CD players and buying CDs for them," Kaplan said, of the short-lived boom. "We found that they didn't build their libraries like they did before. The average purchase, per individual, dropped from twenty-five (CDs a year) in 1983, to six in 1990." Other factors also slowed record store business. "Retailers are forced to carry 20,000 to 30,000 different recordings...and the inventory turnover has slowed considerably to about two times a year, on average," he explained. "And inventory costs have risen because the size of main formats has risen, that's why so many stores are having a hard time. A lot of them have filed for Chapter 11, or are just trying to break even."

With business slumping, Kaplan began to win converts. "I think retailers were fairly convinced that in-store sampling would really help them," he said. "What we had to do was convince the manufacturers to peel off some of their marketing dollars to support this...The labels need to know that making a video, or sending an artist on tour, is not always the best way to sell a product. While they spend $300 million a year making videos, only ten to fifteen percent actually make it to television, and not all of those generate sales." As he made that argument, Kaplan benefitted from pressure on the labels from the retailers. "It's one thing for a start up company called intouch (intouch group, inc.) to try to go up against the record labels," he said, "but when their distribution channels begin to tell them to spend some promotional dollars on the iStation, that has a lot more weight. Some retailers have told the labels, if you don't support the technology in the store, we won't give you the advertising space in-store that you want."

Even so, Kaplan had to juggle iStation fees in his attempt to woo the record labels. "The initial plan was similar to traditional advertising, in that we were going to charge them simply to have their product on the machine. Their response was, 'what if it wasn't in the store, would I be charged for it anyway?'" Instead, both record companies, and retailers, pay a fee each time an album is previewed by an iCard carrier. Labels pay a one-time processing fee to add an album to the iStation catalog, and 30 cents per preview, with a reduced rate for hits, and a cap on daily charges, and additional charges for promotions. Retailers pay a monthly rental fee of $350 per kiosk, which includes maintenance and updating. "The labels felt more comfortable if somebody had their product, scanned it in, and was listening at the point of sale. That was worth 30 cents to them," Kaplan said.

By the fall of 1993, the time the iStation was launched nationally, Kaplan's efforts were beginning to pay off. More than 80 percent of the labels now have their music on the iStation, and have agreed to a pay-per-preview, or special promotions, fees. Among the participants, however, only two—PolyGram and Sima—are major labels. As 1993 ended, talks were continuing with Sony, WEA, and BMG. "We're closing in on them," Katz said. Of the major record retail chains, Wherehouse welcomed the iStation, as did HMV in New York City, which bills itself as the largest record store in the United States. On the other hand, Tower Records opted to create its own listening booths. "We're in a state of market development," Katz added. "We have to strategize what chains, what markets, we want to work on, because it becomes more difficult for us, as we become spread across the United States. It's much better to concentrate on a particular market, like New York or Los Angeles, and saturate it."

To ease the iStation into record stores, Kaplan sends a team of intouch group, inc., employees. "In every store, we have a greeter in a yellow iStation hat, and a white iStation shirt, who introduces the product for the first thirty days." This month-long investment of time is based on record store statistics that show "most people come into the store once a month," Kaplan said. "Those people often train other people, when they come back. Plus (while we're there) we train the store clerks."

To keep interest, and use, high, the company also is developing a variety of targeted sales promotions, to add to the kiosk's appeal. Late in 1993, for example, one was built around the new Frank Sinatra Capitol album, "Duets." "We searched the iStation database, and we had 10,000 iCard holders who had previewed Frank Sinatra, or the artists singing with Sinatra, on the record," Kaplan said. "Each one got a postcard...that had the album on one side and on the other side their iCard bar code, the album bar code, and the address of the iStation, where they could take the card for a $3 discount on the album. ... that's an exact targeted market." A similar marketing effort—cross couponing—is possible with the iStation's coupon printer, Kaplan said. "When you go into a supermarket and buy Coke, often you'll get a coupon for Pepsi," he explained. "We took that idea, and integrated it into the iStation. If somebody scans the rap category, he might get a coupon for a rap label, or a different rap artist.... So we can get cross-promotional, or genre-specific."

Though the overall response is positive—previews now number more than 400,000 a month—Kaplan sees the need for ongoing education about the benefits of the iStation. He is confident that the kiosk will become a fixture in record stores. "It's not a matter of whether the music industry will accept what we have done. It's a matter of when," Kaplan said. Part of his confidence stems from projected growth of kiosks as information purveyors in the digital age. "By 1997, kiosks will be a four billion dollar industry. And ... the fastest growing area is point-of-information kiosks, which will dominate, with about thirty-seven percent of the market."

iSales Promotions: iCard holders were offered a discount on a new Frank Sinatra album.

FINANCE: A Steep Price to Play

After he quit his job to found intouch group, inc., Kaplan initially relied on $143,000 in savings, $400,000 in loans from friends, and a $200,000 bridge loan from RasterOps. However, he knew those funds were far short of what he needed to make the iStation a reality. "The price of admission into this business is about 100 million dollars," he said, matter-of-factly. "An iStation costs about $18,000 per unit. So let's assume you outfit 2,000 stores, with two machines each. That's 4,000 iStations or about $80 million. And that's not counting variable costs. That's just for the hardware."

Fortunately, Kaplan had an extensive background in finance, and with his business plan in hand, he set out to raise the capital he needed from a variety of investors. His big break came when he convinced Suzie Tompkins, co-founder of the apparel company Esprit de Corps, to back the venture. "I knew Summer, her daughter," Kaplan said, "and she said, 'you really should bring my mom in on this.' So Suzie came into the office with some designers from Esprit. She really liked what we were doing, she liked the feel...the energy. And she had a gut feeling, from a retailing standpoint, that the iStation was analogous to people trying on clothes in an Esprit boutique. It's funny because all of the venture capitalists were sitting around wondering what they were going to do until Suzie invested money in us."

By 1992, Kaplan had an impressive lineup of heavyweight investors, many of whom serve on the company's board of directors. Among his backers are Platinum Technology CEO, Andrew (Flip) Filipowski; the Getty oil family; Hewlett-Packard co-founder, David Hewlett; Novell Inc. chairman, Ray Noorda; and RasterOps CEO, Keith Sorenson. Other, anonymous, "angels" from wealthy families, were recruited by Watts & Whelan Capital Management, a prestigious investment counseling firm. As 1993 drew to a close, Kaplan had raised more than $22 million, and intouch group, inc., had more than $8 million in the bank. By the end of 1994, company executives said that the company would be a likely candidate for a public stock offering. Meanwhile, Kaplan said that the fund-raising continues. "We are raising another $15 million right now," he said. "But think of these amounts in the context of other technology start ups. If I were going to start a semiconductor company right now, it would cost me $30 to $40 million a plant."

Even with such substantial fund-raising success, Kaplan's original business plan doesn't predict the company to be in the black until 1995, with pre-tax earnings of $11 million, on revenues of $26.8 million. "The reason for that," Katz said, "is that we're not just a software company; we're a manufacturing company. We have to build these machines, and spend many millions of dollars doing that." Though store lease fees "come close" to covering kiosk production costs, intouch group, inc., has the additional expense of updating and maintaining the machines. "So, it's only when the record label revenue kicks in, that we see good profitability," he concluded.

THE FUTURE: Information Please

In the information age, the iStation could become a symbol for product sampling around the world, Kaplan believes, whether in its present form, or new versions. "Sampling is really the most important thing about the iStation," he said. "Anyone can do an information kiosk—tell me about this, give me the date. The iStation is much more than that."

For the time being, intouch group, inc., is concentrating on perfecting the iStation's music sampling, as it expands into other forms of digital entertainment. "First, we're going to create new versions of the same application," Katz said. "We are going to deliver this technology in other embodiments, such as delivering it to your home with interactive television, or cable. We also are going to make a client-server version, so we will have a media server, and a network of iStations, reducing the cost of individual iStations. We may even have hand-helds." At the same time, as the company becomes better acquainted with its music-loving customers, Kaplan envisions the addition of a "personal" button that would make "intelligent" recommendations. "You keep a profile of what (customers have) listened to available, on-line, so that when they come up to the iStation, we know (for example) they are a Bruce Springsteen nut," he said. "So, a new Springsteen album will come up. In that way, you personalize the iStation."

Given the company's experience with the music industry, the retailers, and the labels, "the most natural next step for us, and next on the agenda, is a video iStation," Katz said. "We would do for video stores exactly what we are doing for music stores. You could preview videos, see other genres, see movies by this, or that, director." Katz also believes a video iStation would be easier to produce than the music version since "the trailers for movies are already done; all you have to do is digitize them. For the music, we had to spend multi-man years compiling the music segments to create what's essentially a trailer for music."

Inspired by the news that some stores are going to preview CD-ROM titles, Katz believes the iStation could be adapted to do that, as well as sample other computer software, such as games and programs. "The customer would scan in the software package bar code, and a demonstration of the software would begin. For instance," Katz said, "it will show you how a spreadsheet works, just as you would sample a song from a Frank Sinatra album." This, and other, digital media are ideally suited to the iStation, Katz believes, because "it has the ability for high-quality audiovideo presentation, vast quantities of storage, a very simple-to-use interface, with bar code scanning and a touch screen. We want to continue to exploit that."

On the other hand, consumers should not expect to find an iStation in their favorite drug store anytime soon. "People have asked us to do wine kiosks, shoe kiosks, drug kiosks." Katz said, with a chuckle. "Some of those things make sense, because you have a large quantity of information to navigate. The problem is, you can't really sample these products electronically. All you're doing is giving information about it."

7

"LEWIS AND CLARK"

Hueneme School District
and TMM

At A Glance

"LEWIS AND CLARK"

Developers: Hueneme School District and TMM.

Client: Originally the Hueneme School District; other educational and home markets.

Personnel: Steve Carr, project leader, chief author and instructional designer; Don Haines, graphic artist; Taylor Kramer, chief technical officer, TMM; Ricardo Amador, school principal and Spanish narrator; Dr. Ronald Rescigno, superintendent, Hueneme School District.

Project Description: "Lewis and Clark" is an educational multimedia CD-ROM with 580 MB of audio, video, graphics, and text. The disc contains primary source maps, journal excerpts, and graphics from the 1804-1806 expedition. Users explore eight different categories—The Louisiana Purchase, The Team of Lewis and Clark, Preparing for the Journey, Encounters with Native Americans, Natural Beauty, Hardships of the Journey, Results of the Expedition, and an Interactive Map.

Development hours: 2,000 hours.

Development period: April 1993–April 1994.

Production hardware: Gateway 2000 4DX-66V, 16 MEG RAM, 1.2 gig Micropolis drive, Media Vision ProAudio board, Sony GVM-2020, UVC Video capture and compression boards, Texel 3034 CD-ROM drive, Maynard Tape backup, Sony CD recordable CDW-W1.

Production software: TMM Producer authoring software, Corel Draw!, Photo Finish, I Photo Plus, Word for Windows, ProAudio-SFX audio recording.

Presentation hardware: 386 or higher, single speed CD-ROM player, 356 color board, Sound Blaster or compatible sound board, mouse.

Cost to Develop: $70,000 to $100,000.

Financing: Hueneme School District, TMM.

Selling Price: $60-$100.

Future Projects: CD-ROM for ESL (English as a second language); other educational titles.

Contact: Taylor Kramer
             Chief Technical Officer
             TMM
             299 W. Hillcrest Drive, Suite 200
             Thousand Oaks, CA 91360
             805–371–0500

             Dr. Ronald Rescigno
             Superintendent
             Hueneme School District
             205 North Ventura Rd.
             Port Hueneme, CA 93041
             805–488–3588

At first glance, Blackstock Junior High seems like a typical California public school. Crouched next to ranch-style homes in a quiet residential neighborhood in the coastal town of Port Hueneme, the low-slung, cinder block building encircles a largely concrete courtyard. As classes change, the 800-plus sixth, seventh, and eighth graders, who pour out of classrooms into the warm September sun, mirror the changing face of the state's population. Eighty percent are minority; the largest group is Latino, but there are numerous Filipinos, Blacks, and Asians as well. Almost twenty percent have no knowledge, or only limited knowledge, of English. Most are from families assigned to one of the area's three large miliary bases, or from families that farm the wide, flat fields that spread inland as far as the eye can see. Many live in nearby government subsidized housing, and almost half need financial aid to buy their school lunches.

Educating an ethnically and economically diverse group of children is only one challenge faced by this and other school districts throughout the state. Like many of his fellow educators, Hueneme School District Superintendent, Ron Rescigno, points to a paradigm shift well underway that is closing the door on industrial soci-

Smart Classroom:
The Hueneme School District is a nationally recognized leader in multimedia learning.

ety and ushering in an information age. Watching the noisy young-sters chattering during class break, Rescigno knows that new skills and new ways of thinking will be needed in the new millennium, now just a few years away, when vast quantities of information will travel down electronic super highways. To prepare a work force for this highly technical tomorrow, demands new approaches to education today, and that is a tough assignment in an era of rising costs, shrinking revenue, and dwindling faith in public schools.

A new class period is about to start, and the quadrangle begins to empty and grow silent as the students file into classrooms. One by one doors close, and teachers prepare to launch into required lessons that harken back to the one-room schools of yesteryear: math, science, social studies and English. First, however, everyone must sign on.

For, while it may appear ordinary, Blackstock is anything but. One of Hueneme's Smart Schools, it is filled with Smart Class-rooms, the technologically sophisticated learning networks that have drawn educators from around the world to this out-of-the-way com-munity 65 miles northwest of Los Angeles. For more than ten years, this district has been an unlikely leader in multimedia educa-tion, a new, interactive approach to learning that integrates the lat-est hardware and software into standard public school classrooms and curricula. From its simple beginnings with one Apple IIe com-puter and links to cable television, this Port Hueneme school now has one computer for every three students, a faculty as comfortable with downlinking satellite programs as with sharpening a pencil, and a student body that navigates software with the same ease as a previous generation connected dots.

History teacher Steve Carr's class on the Louisiana Purchase is typical. Seated in clusters of six, the eighth graders study at work-stations equipped with 286 PCs with 14-inch color monitors, an Apple IIgs, a Mac IIcx with a 20-inch multi-synch monitor, a laser disc player and a VCR. From his workstation, Carr controls a 486 file server and a ceiling-mounted video projector. During the week-long segment on the U.S.'s western expansion, he and the students delve into material about explorers Lewis and Clark, found on video disc and in simulation software. The kids then complete a mock journal about their travels, writing on a word processor. If necessary, they can wrap up class assignments at home by checking out one of the school's laptops.

Measures of Smart Classroom success are impressive. In the all-important area of student achievement, as judged in state-mandated standardized assessments tests for eighth graders, Blackstock students have made stunning gains that paralleled the introduction of multimedia learning. Compared to similar schools, Blackstock was ranked in the 94th percentile in 1992, compared to its 56th percentile rank only eight years earlier. A California Model Technology School since 1988, and the recipient of more than $4.5 million in state grants, Blackstock was honored by the state as a California Distinguished School in 1992. Another of the district's "Smart Schools," E. O. Green Junior High, was picked as a Blue Ribbon School for 1992-93 by the U.S. Department of Education and was the only one of the 265 schools named to be recognized for excellence in science and math. Rescigno, and several of the district's teachers, now serve on state and federal panels dedicated to duplicating their futuristic programs in other schools.

Technology Boon: Hueneme officials point to increases in student achievement that parallel use of technology in education.

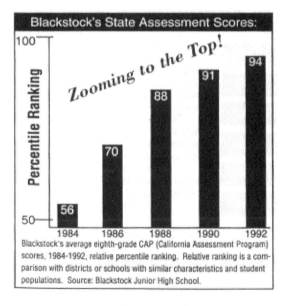

Blackstock's average eighth-grade CAP (California Assessment Program) scores, 1984-1992, relative percentile ranking. Relative ranking is a comparison with districts or schools with similar characteristics and student populations. Source: Blackstock Junior High School.

However, future expansion of this 21st-Century learning mode into all of the district's nine elementary schools, hinges on finding new sources of revenue. "It's one thing to begin to change; it's another thing to maintain the change. I believe the school system's ability to maintain the change is substantially more difficult because you need support systems—people, resources, and money," said Rescigno, reflecting on his 36 years in public education. "As educators, we have to continue to generate exciting curriculum and instructional strategies linked directly to student learning, and maintain those programs over a long period. That's not easy."

If a bold initiative to create educational software succeeds, once again Hueneme may lead the way. Through a foundation created by its board, the district has enabled its teachers to create multimedia educational software in cooperation with a nearby software company, TMM. Proceeds from its sale would be shared by TMM, the authoring teacher, and the foundation, which would pump the funds into Smart Classroom hardware and software. Steve Carr was the first teacher to take advantage of the program, and during a yearlong "artistic sabbatical," he

produced an interactive CD-ROM on Lewis and Clark that contains 580 megabytes of audio, video, graphics, and text. The first multimedia product of the "Hueneme Series," it was scheduled for release in home and school versions by TMM in August 1994. Educational CD-ROMs by other Hueneme teachers also are in the works.

The Hueneme Series: An interactive CD-ROM on the Lewis and Clark expidition is the first in a planned series of educational software.

In the decade since Hueneme moved computer technology into its classrooms, districts across the country have followed suit. In recent months, some enterprising schools even have begun to share noncommercial educational CD-ROMs. Hueneme officials believe the district's joint commercial venture, coupled with incentives for teachers, such as time off and bonuses, is the only one of its kind in the nation. "The Hueneme School District has teachers who have worked in Smart Classrooms since 1986. Now we have teachers who are the best at delivering multimedia instruction and curriculum on a daily basis," Rescigno pointed out. "So, it makes sense for our teachers to replicate their efforts by creating electronic CD-

ROM curriculum that can be used in classrooms and homes throughout the United States, and possibly the world." If the project succeeds, Rescigno believes it could revolutionize and revitalize public education. "I feel that school districts can become public/private corporate entities—modeling the basic tenets of capitalism and entrepreneurship," he said. "I believe that such a program can become the new learning paradigm in the United States."

In the meantime, Rescigno and Carr are encouraged and excited by what they see happening in the classroom. "My goal was to motivate kids, to affect them in the affective and creative domains, so that they would want to come to school, that they would become more creative, more interested in their own learning," Carr said. "And I've seen some real, positive benefits of technology, when kids can learn skills that they then can apply to content—how to search a data base, how to put together multimedia presentations, how to persuade someone, how to express (themselves) in trying to get a concept across. Those are skills that ultimately will carry them into the business world."

THE OPPORTUNITY: An Education in Technology

Apart from the pictures and plaques, the two plump couches, and the paper-strewn desk, Ron Rescigno's office looks more like the control room of a TV station than the hub of a public school district. Centered on a floor-to-ceiling bookcase are four television monitors, VCRs, and a remote-controlled video camera that is focused on the energetic superintendent. The monitors glow with television feeds over local cable company lines from three other classrooms around the district, but although the educators can see each other, they can not hear each other in this experimental four-way link-up. The scene becomes Marx Brothers comical as Rescigno bounces from his desk to his remote control, trying to solve the audio problem that stands in the way of a new interactive teaching style, which would allow one teacher to instruct more than one classroom at a time, and see his or her students' responses. A half hour passes with no progress, when, inexplicably, a noisy football game fills the monitors, abruptly ending the trial. "Technology in action," quips Rescigno, with typical good humor.

Working the bugs out of the district's sophisticated electronics network can be time-consuming and frustrating, but this task is simple compared to others that confront innovative educators in today's public schools. "You gotta have patience," Rescigno says, with strong traces of his native New York and Italian heritage in his voice. It's advice born out of his decade-long efforts to maintain Hueneme's leadership in putting computer technology into the hands of teachers and students in a way that can be copied by other school districts. "The hardest problem they overcame was resistance," notes TMM co-founder, Taylor Kramer, recalling meetings with federal agencies that he attended with the feisty superintendent. " 'Hell yes,' he told them, 'we had resistance. You've got teachers, parents, unions, boards, personalities.' I'm surprised, quite frankly, that they got anything done.... Everywhere you turned, there's a brick wall and a lion."

Dr. Ron Rescigno: The Hueneme superintendent presides over several Smart Schools from his high-tech office.

A major obstacle always was, and always will be, funding. "You set aside so much money for this," said Rescigno. "We did that over the years, and obviously we're constantly fighting a battle between balancing the budget in terms of instructional supplies, against all your other needs." During the past decade, Rescigno and his staff have managed to pay for the needed computer technology with a combination of state grants, district funds (usually one percent of the annual budget), and business deals with various suppliers, who cut prices in exchange for ties to the innovative program. The district's newest Smart Classroom, a $600,000 state-of-the-art math center wired for fiber optics, and outfitted with Pentium-ready computers, cost the district approximately $180,000, thanks to bargain-basement prices negotiated with hardware and software suppliers. "We work on the budget every day. Every day," Rescigno said. "I figure this way, we're not any more creative than anyone else; we just outwork 'em."

Work on what Hueneme calls its Smart Schools began in the early 1980s. In 1983, starting with "glue and wire," and an agreement with the local cable company to provide an Inet and a systems cable line, the school district built its first Smart Classroom—a science classroom—at the second of its two junior high schools, E. O. Green. "We had three concerns," Rescigno said. "One was the management and organization of the school, two was the curriculum, and three was student achievement. And within those areas we wanted to establish models that could be replicated.... Of course we didn't know what the difficulties would be. It pays to be somewhat ignorant, because then you don't have any fear." One year later, the district became part of the Model Technology program of the California Department of Education. A $2.5 million grant, spread over four and one-half years, helped bring smart classrooms to Blackstock. By 1993, the ratio of students to computers—mostly 386s—at that school was an impressive two to one.

Hueneme now has developed more than a dozen different classroom learning environments that use computer hardware and software to help educate students in many diverse subjects. "Our vision has always been to try to prepare our students for what we think the millennium demands. And it's obvious to all of us that electronics aren't going to go away," the 57-year-old Rescigno explained. "I think we're in a paradigm shift; I think all of education is shifting.

One thing that's happening is that the younger people...are more familiar with electronics. And that in itself makes for a significant shift...Our concept is to use technology as an enabling tool." Even the smart classroom design—clusters of desks (designed by the district)

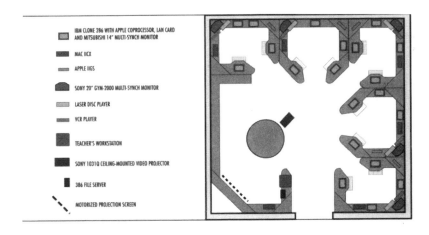

IBM CLONE 286 WITH APPLE COPROCESSOR, LAN CARD AND MITSUBISHI 14" MULTI-SYNCH MONITOR

MAC IICX

APPLE IIGS

SONY 20" GYM-2000 MULTI-SYNCH MONITOR

LASER DISC PLAYER

VCR PLAYER

TEACHER'S WORKSTATION

SONY 1031Q CEILING-MOUNTED VIDEO PROJECTOR

386 FILE SERVER

MOTORIZED PROJECTION SCREEN

with recessed monitors and hideaway keyboards, angled to face the teacher "emphasize people, not machines," he continued. "Our goal is to deliver instruction to the student, to have students have the ability to manipulate materials, so they could not only master what's known, but also get into the unknown."

Delivering Multimedia: A variety hardware and software are utilized in Hueneme's Smart Classrooms.

A Smart Classroom, first and foremost, is a flexible learning center where the growing range of computer technology is tapped to aid students in acquiring academic skills. Multimedia—video, videodisc, cable television, and CD-ROMs—is combined creatively to bring subject matter to life for students, who work alone at individual computer stations or in groups. Textbooks supplement learning in this almost paperless environment. "People say technology has been around," Rescigno said. "Yeah, the machines have been around, but not the stuff that makes things happen. The good software, the multimedia, and the idea of using it (in the classroom) that's where we were one of the first. I think we can take credit for that."

Duplicating the layout of one of Hueneme's Smart Classrooms and outfitting it with the necessary hardware is easier than duplicating the multimedia curriculum content. More often than not, teachers acted as producers, drawing from the whole range of technology-based information to teach required subjects. "It refutes the notion that teachers aren't needed in a smart classroom," Steve Carr said. "These are not what I would call integrated learning systems—completely managed systems that just walk the kids through the software. Most of the software we have in the smart classrooms is third-party software that we integrate and align with our own curricula, which takes even more time and teacher planning." Incorporating a mix of software and multimedia into lessons "gives more flexibility and more teacher creativity, and it offers students a variety. I don't like the systems where all the screens...look the same. I want that variety."

As a result, though, "it's tough to duplicate," Carr admits. "When you try to replicate this at another school, teachers not only have to learn this whole system, but they have to learn all these individual pieces of software." "In the smart classroom, there might be 200 to 300 sources (for curriculum)," Rescigno said. "People say we want your curriculum and you say, 'well, there's 250 pieces of it, and you need a massive switching network,' and it's sort of overwhelming

Multimedia Makers: Hueneme teachers use various media in their classes, as this history lesson plan shows.

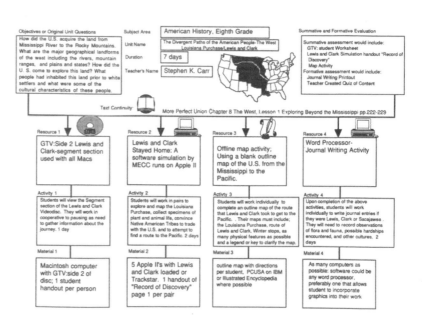

and intimidating." At the same time, district officials realized, "we have teachers who have worked in this environment for seven or eight years...and who have become very good at delivering multimedia on a daily basis," he added.

From this realization, it was a short step "just common sense really," Rescigno said to the district's idea of a partnership with its teachers and TMM, via its five-year-old nonprofit Foundation for Educational Technology. The idea was, Carr explained, "to take some of these various pieces and incorporate them into one medium.... We could replicate the power of a smart classroom on CD-ROM." Or as TMM co-founder, Taylor Kramer, puts it, "It was time for the district to take advantage of their almost ten years worth of intellectual property" to perpetuate its program.

In a memorandum of agreement, unanimously approved by the Hueneme Board of Education in September 1993, TMM agreed to pay the salary of teachers who would substitute for teachers tapped by the foundation to develop educational software; the district would give the chosen teacher a leave of absence. The resulting software would be marketed by TMM, and net profits would be split between the company and the district, which in turn would divide its share with the authoring teacher. "They said yes," Kramer said, of the district's decision, "because they can't lose. The worst case is that they get a disc that can be used through out the district; the best is that it sells, the teachers make more money, and the district gets royalties to enhance the system, and become less reliant upon state funds." Rescigno agreed, calling the pact "good solid business. I don't want them to lose anything, and I don't want the district to lose anything. But maybe together, we can gain something."

A major incentive for teachers is a share of the profits. "It logically fits that if teachers create materials and these materials are good, then they should be able to sell it, and the teacher should be able to make some money," Rescigno said. "I didn't create the lightbulb. Universities have been doing this for years, but in public schools, we haven't." The district would profit, too. Its share of the proceeds would be paid to the foundation, and used to continue its innovative use of technology. The outside revenue would be "a salvation," Rescigno said, especially as government funding shrinks. "We haven't received a cost of living adjustment from the state in three years, and all of the magic I'm supposed to do with the budget is just drying up," he said.

In addition, Carr believes the project will spark teacher creativity. "One of the frustrating things for a teacher in the typical class day is that you don't have enough time to be creative," he explained. "You're dealing with 180 kids a day, and six classes. What good teachers are good at doing is creating new ideas, new instructional strategies. They aren't all computer whizzes, but given the opportunity, I think they will come up with some good things." Besides possible financial gain, Carr emphasizes the "excitement of being published, the strokes from having a product of yours on the market."

Carr and the others are certain there is market for their teacher-created educational multimedia, especially as more and more schools bring computers into the classroom. "Education is an untapped market at this point," he argued. "It's just beginning...and that is primarily because of budget problems.... But money is becoming available. I know of some big projects that have gotten going in other states, because they have been floating bonds, or doing other things, to raise the capital for some of the things we've done. We just consulted with a Phoenix school district and they just floated about $4.5 million in bonds. Not only are they building new schools, but they are also putting a huge Ethernet backbone, plus fiber and a lot of hardware." As schools are wired for technology, a growing number of software companies will be vying to sell to educators. Aware of that potential competition, Rescigno said, "I told my team it shouldn't be content only. It has to be good instructional strategies, and we have to be able to deal with the required core curriculum, bilingual education, English as a second language, and special education. Our original vision must be the prototype!"

THE TEAM: Apples for the Teachers

As part of its computer giveaway to schools in the early 1980s, Apple set up one-day training sessions for instructors new to the machine. When the call went out for a volunteer to attend from the Hueneme district, only one teacher responded, a native New Yorker in his first year of teaching named Steve Carr. "I thought, 'shoot, I'll go,'" he mused. Now, eleven years later, that offhand decision has put this 38-year-old educator on the cutting edge of education in the Information Age, in a partnership with two other unlikely innovators. One, a career educator once named Long Island's outstanding football coach, and the other, a former singer in the rock band The Iron Butterfly.

Steve Carr: The first title in the Hueneme Series was produced by Carr, who earned his M.A. in interactive educational technology.

In addition to his Apple class, Carr saw the potential for technology in the classrooms at the University of California, Santa Barbara, where he worked on the federally-funded Historian Project. The undertaking was the brainchild of professor, Willis Copeland, who wanted to teach teachers, who knew little about computers, how to create social studies software, using a prototype he had developed. "At the end of the project, two and a half years later, we wound up not only very computer literate, at least on Apple IIs, but also learning how to program in Pascal," he said. The resulting eight programs, including Carr's software on two California Gold Rush towns, were later published by Harcourt Brace, "so we even made a little money on the deal." More importantly, the experience "really got

me hooked," said Carr, who enrolled the following fall at UCSB to earn his master's degree in interactive educational technology. "At that time there were no interactive video classes being offered, so a small group of us, about eight students, decided to create this class on interactive video," he recalled. Eventually, that project became Carr's thesis, "a course about Viet Nam on laser disc controlled by a HyperCard interface" that incorporated a variety of video clips designed to help students explain why 1968 was a turning point in the war.

Carr took the lessons he had learned about computers back to his Port Hueneme classroom. "It just kind of mushroomed," he said. "First there was one Apple II, then five, and then more and more. Eventually I got the chance to build my own room." In that classroom, Carr is able to orchestrate multimedia learning segments, from his desk, to clusters of 7th and 8th graders seated around 286 PCs, with access to Macintoshes and Apple IIs. While a knowledge of platforms, computer networks, and a variety of software is essential in this environment, it must be paired with strong teaching ability to be effective. "Good management skills, good organizational skills—things that are effective in teaching—play the most important role," he said. "We've gone the other way, where we hired someone to take over one of the rooms, who was great in technology, but he got eaten alive in there, because he had a tough time managing kids. That's why I say the role of the teacher is even more important in a room like that." And though the district touts rising student academic achievement, Carr insists that higher test scores was not one of his goals. "What I wanted was to motivate kids, to affect them in the creative and affective domains, so that they would want to come to school, and become more interested in their own learning."

By this time, in the mid- to late-1980s, the Hueneme District had become part of the state's Model Technology Program, based on a proposal coauthored by the new superintendent Ronald Rescigno. It built on the district's already demonstrated interest in technology in its first Smart Classroom, by then in operation for more than two years. Rescigno had taken the job to be close to his sons, then students at UCLA, after running a district in Silicone Valley for ten years. "So I'd been into technology for a long time," he recalled. "We had a couple of engineers on the board, and early on I always thought that the best use of technology was word processing. Early on, that was it." Before applying for the state funding, Rescigno, typically, decided "to spend a couple bucks to find out what the rest of the world was doing so we didn't reinvent the wheel" and sent district staff (teachers and administrators) to review computer technology efforts around the country. "The goal was to create a seamless integration of video, audio, and data in the classroom," he explained. "And we wanted the teacher to have time to individualize instruction by engaging students in interactive learning."

In addition to securing state funds, over the years the savvy Rescigno has augmented the district's limited resources through a number of mostly successful business partnerships. A typical deal is with a British furniture company that builds the desks that house the students' computers, at no charge, in exchange for the copyright for the district's unique design, which can be marketed to other schools,

Deal Maker: A British furniture maker supplied desks for Hueneme's new Smart Math Classroom, shown here under construction.

worldwide. Similarly, Softouch Computer Consulting is aiding the school in development of management systems for its Smart Classrooms, in exchange for the right to sell the software. Wheeling and dealing, though, occasionally has its drawbacks, Rescigno admits. "We've had some ventures where there's been an attempt at what I classify as a possible hostile takeover that ended short of adjudication. [At the same time,] we've had some very productive relationships that we think will really help change the way we do things in public education." The keys are shared, mutual interest "...we want something...they want something"; people of good will; and of course "some good solid contract language to protect the public trust," he said.

Hueneme's track record has made Rescigno a nationally-recognized leader in computer-based education. Now called on to address computer industry gatherings as well as fellow educators, he was recently tapped to serve as a special advisor to the education arm of ARPA, the Department of Defense's Advanced Research Projects Agency. This is an unexpected achievement for the former football coach who once thought the pinnacle of his career in education would be his selection as Long Island's Coach of the Year in the late 1960s. "It's not been an easy task, let me tell you," he said, in retrospect. "The nice thing is that I've survived...and the older I get the better I feel about it. I see that maybe, maybe, we started something. Now the object is to take some of our mature models and replicate them around the U.S." And to make that happen, "you have to change the ownership...others have to buy into it," he continued, with a coach's zeal. "You have to have patience, you have to work with people, and...you have to accept the idea of the teacher as entrepreneur and the student as epistemologist, a navigator of knowledge."

Given the rapid rate of change in computer technology, Rescigno and Carr are always on the lookout for advances that will make it easier for the classroom teacher to deliver multimedia curricula. Both were intrigued by a new telecommunications system created jointly by UVC Corporation of Irvine and TMM, a multimedia developer headquartered east of Port Hueneme, over the Santa Monica Mountains, in suburban Thousand Oaks. At a demonstration of the system, they met Taylor Kramer, a former singer with Iron Butterfly, who had founded TMM in 1990 with Randy Jackson, the youngest of the Jackson brothers. "I guess you could say we had a 'mind meld,'" Kramer said, borrowing a phrase from "Star Trek's" Dr. Spock. "I'm fascinated by education and educators that are technologically driven. I was absolutely impressed with them, and I guess they were with me, because we started to work together." The son of two teachers and former national sales manager for Shinano Kensei Corp.'s CD-ROM division, Kramer vividly recalls his first visit to Blackstock Junior High. "I had this incredible feeling...when I saw the kids and the environment. I knew this was it, this was the new paradigm for education.... So I became passionately driven to help them, support them."

Taylor Kramer: A founder of TMM, Kramer had a "mind meld" with Hueneme officials.

As he learned more about the district's accomplishments and finances, Kramer realized it had amassed "ten years' worth of intellectual property" that, like the classroom design, could be replicated on CD-ROMs using TMM's multimedia tools. "What I proposed was to test the concept," he recalled. "TMM would seed it, put money into it, distribute it and return a royalty to the teachers and the district." In negotiating the partnership deal, Kramer said "we came up with guidelines, knowing full well that there are certain costs and overhead involved, so that the teachers and the district could know what to expect per disc." Then they presented the plan to the board. "They stood up and raised their hands unanimously," Kramer said. "I was bowled over. I almost fell out of my chair."

One key element of the joint venture is that the CD-ROMs will be produced using TMM's exclusive fractal technology. Developed and patented by Michael Barnsley of Iterated Systems in Atlanta, now partners with TMM, this "software only" video playback system runs digitized video, full screen, at 30 frames a second. Unlike

AVI or QuickTime movies on most CD-ROMs, that run at half the speed and one-tenth the size, fractal video comes close to feature-film quality when played back. As a result, it has great potential in the entertainment industry, since it would facilitate distribution of Hollywood movies on CD-ROMs and via the emerging electronic highway. For CD-ROMs destined for classroom use, it offers the advantage of video playback without any additional hardware, and it plays that video with the speed and clarity kids are accustomed to seeing. Thus, Rescigno may be right when he calls the development "the most outstanding technology of my generation."

With the agreement in hand, Kramer tested the retail waters to assess interest in the "Hueneme Series" of educational CD-ROMs. "It was phenomenal," he reported. "From a marketing point of view, it's absolutely salable," especially as more schools put computers in their classrooms. "What happens is that other teachers want the same tools," he explained. Also, with the success he is confident the program will achieve, Kramer believes, the district will become a mecca for innovative educators. "They already attract talented people now, but as pro-active education becomes a national mandate, it will bring an upward spiral of positive response, and the system will become self-perpetuating, and be replicated throughout the United States."

THE PRODUCTION: Exploring New Territory

Steve Carr was the logical choice to be the first teacher to produce educational software for the Hueneme Series. On an artistic leave of absence during the 1993 school year, Carr worked out of TMM's Thousand Oaks headquarters, in a corner office with a view of the surrounding mountains. Producing his CD-ROM, while not technically demanding, still was a learning exercise. For the first time, he was confronted with the time consuming, and costly, licensing of many of the materials he had hoped to incorporate into his program on the Lewis and Clark expedition.

Content

The starting point for Carr's, and all future Hueneme titles, is with the state-mandated curriculum. The Lewis and Clark Expedition, a two-year exploration of the Louisiana Purchase in the early 1800s that followed the Missouri River to its source, crossed the Rocky Mountains and ended at the Pacific Ocean at the mouth of the Columbia River, is part of the California framework for social studies and history for the fifth and eighth grades. "The kids have to learn how the U.S. acquired this big chunk of territory in the middle of the country," Carr explained. "The whole point of the expedition was to try to open up the west. From 1803 until the gold rush, what we knew about the west was based on their journals and

Artistic Leave: Steve Carr worked out of TMM's offices as he created his multimedia title.

maps. They did an incredible job, although I didn't realize how incredible until I started building this program." At the end of the unit, Carr said, students should know "the five Ws of the Louisiana Purchase, how to read a map, why Lewis and Clark were sent on the trip, the diversity of Native Americans, and some of the expedition's accomplishments."

From that starting point, Carr said he outlined the multimedia course "creating an original flow of how we expected it to go. I'd like to say it was more organized—it's become more organized—but it was haphazard at first." With an enormous learning curve behind him, Carr said he expects future projects "to go faster and smoother" as a result of more planning and storyboarding, but he acknowledged that "there's something curious about the creation of multimedia" that works against traditional "Plan Ahead" development. "It's almost this synergistic way of creating. It's not a linear process," he explained. "Your links, your branches, come by doing. You all of a sudden say, 'I hadn't anticipated that, but it would make perfect sense to do it this way.' And all of a sudden you've changed the flow substantially." In the case of "Lewis and Clark," Carr said he "had a matrix of where we were going to go, but we ended up taking a lot of stuff from [his Hueneme course], elaborated on it, and added a whole bunch of features that just came to mind as we worked on the project."

Based on his experience with some similar multimedia educational programs, Carr opted for both linear and nonlinear presentations of the material. "There are things out there on the market that do this, and I've found that they are powerful motivating tools that encourage and excite kids about this technology, and the content," he said. "They are going to want to learn about Lewis and Clark, as they start digging into this." Since state education guidelines also emphasize the use of primary source materials, Carr strove to incorporate a variety of historical documents, especially the explor-

Go With The Flow: Although he had a project flow chart, Carr discovered multimedia creation was "synergistic."

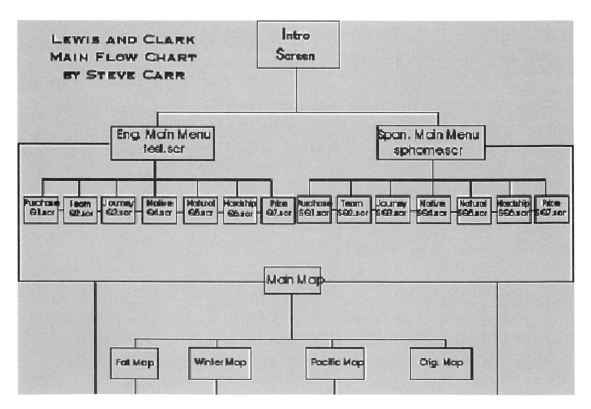

ers' diaries, and extensive maps and drawings. Finally, given the growing number of Spanish-speaking students in the state's schools, he also chose to present the content in both English and Spanish.

However, Carr decided to forego the typical evaluation by not building in a test at the end of the program. Instead, he incorporated a quiz in each of the main divisions of the program "to hold (students) accountable for some content" and a "mini authoring program" to create multimedia presentations that demonstrate their grasp of the subject. "It's like a multimedia report," said Carr, who will make it possible for the students to "re-purpose" any of the data on the CD-ROM. "What we've done is created a really simple interface that will allow the kids...to bring up windows of all the appropriate data they can link to, and then reassemble."

With the subject and thrust of his project clearly in mind, Carr turned his attention to what he believes is the most important aspect of educational multimedia, content. "Content is what makes or breaks a particular program," he emphasized. For the Lewis and Clark CD-ROM, Carr initially focused on the various video, graphics, and audio sources he used in his classroom presentations. "Now," he reflected, "having gone through the lessons I've learned, I would try to do my own content or take things I need from the public domain."

The "lessons learned" were about licensing. A teacher who mixes a few minutes of a PBS special into a class presentation does not need to fret about licensing fees; but, Carr learned, a teacher creating an educational CD-ROM for sale does. Since the school district does not have the resources either to negotiate, or pay the one-time use fees or royalties, TMM's legal department took charge. As a result, Carr said, "I went through and identified all the content that I wanted to use and prioritized it in a number of different ways. That way, if you run across someone who wants to rake you for something, you have the option to say, 'Forget it. We'll go with something else.' But essentially what was most important was the integrity of the program."

This scene shows Sacajawea reuniting with her Shoshone relatives. The Shoshones played a crucial role with the expedition by loaning valuable horses to the party enabling them to make the difficult crossing of the Rocky Mountains. The painting is by Charles Marion Russell, who is best known for his colorful paintings of the American West.

License To Use: Art in the public domain, like this painting by Charles Russell, became a main source of images for Carr's CD-ROM.

By the end of 1993, Carr and TMM's attorneys were still negotiating arrangements with a number of sources, including Oregon Public Television, for excerpts from a program about the Lewis and Clark Trail, the American Historical Society, LucasArts, and the National Geographic Society. "We've had positive feedback," said Carr, of the discussions to date spearheaded by TMM's legal department. "But licensing has been the real devil in all this." One key success was approval from the Coe Collection at Yale University to use the Lewis and Clark maps and diaries in its collection, for a one-time fee of $50 a plate. Paintings by Albert Bierstadt and Charles Russell used to depict the landscape during the 1800s were in the public domain.

In the future, though, Carr said, he will take a different tact in selecting visual content for his programs. "Instead of saying I want this, this, this, and this, I'll say, I ought to take stuff that I know we don't have to go through so many gyrations in order to acquire," he explained. To make this process easier for his fellow teachers, Carr will help them locate content that can be used for free, such as materials in public domain libraries and the Library of Congress, for example. In the end, "because oftentimes what you end up doing in this realm is re-purposing things from various sources to fit them into your concept, you can lose continuity," he warned. In the best of all possible worlds, "you would create your own video," he mused, "but that's not always possible. If I had the opportunity to go back on the Lewis and Clark Trail and take video footage of everything, that would be optimal because it would be exactly what you want."

Interface and Graphics

As the first teacher to try his hand at an educational CD-ROM, Carr wore all the production hats, designing the graphics, capturing video, inputting content, and even recording narration. "Actually, it's the best thing for me to at least have a finger in everything in the beginning, because ultimately I'm going to be a point person, an executive producer of sorts, for other teachers who do this," he said.

Since so much of what is known about Lewis and Clark and the land they explored is from their records of the trip, Carr wanted his CD-ROM graphics to have "the feel of an old journal." The main interface and menus throughout the program rest on a background that resembles aged, torn parchment. "An artist drew the parchment, and we scanned it in," Carr said. "Then we added color to it and blurred the edges a little." Working with a variety of graphics software, including Corel Draw! and Photo Finish, the same look was added to all of the navigation buttons, designed by Carr and artist Don Haines. When students click on them, the buttons seem to depress, as feedback. "To do that, we used TMM's tools interface, which has a built-in button capability," Carr explained.

Begin The Journey: The main interface resembles a picture gallery.

The main interface is built around a group of eight icons that look like pictures in a gallery. They represent the subjects related to the Lewis and Clark Expedition to be explored in the class. "The mini color PICS on each button are representative of the screen you are going to if you click on it," Carr said. "For instance, the first one is background on the Louisiana Purchase. So there's a picture of a map showing the territory of the purchase." Its design was refined many times until Carr was satisfied that it was user-friendly, "really simple for the kids to use," he said. Once inside a specific segment, the student has access to related text, visuals, audio, and videos, via color-coded hot buttons in the text. A phrase or word outlined in green signals graphics; blue, video; yellow, audio; and red, text.

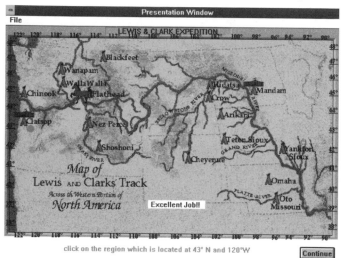

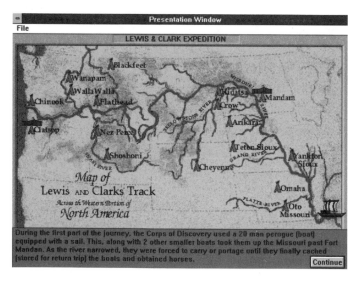

Multimedia Maps: Two screens show Carr's use of Lewis and Clark's original maps.

Working with graphics and video was a learning experience for the youthful teacher, especially in the area of color palettes. "TMM has a tool that allows me to display video on the screen, without having the palettes explode," he said. "It allows you to lock down up to 32 colors, and then the video uses the other 200 plus odd colors. Otherwise, your palettes explode all over the place." As a result, Carr learned "to keep your interface in those 32 colors if you're going to display video with it."

Of all the segments in his Lewis and Clark CD-ROM, Carr is especially pleased with the interactive map that features the explorers' own cartography and sketches and is linked to entries from their journals. From a main screen that displays a map of the Louisiana Purchase, divided into three sections, students gain access to detailed portions of the original maps. "This one," he demonstrated, calling up one of the sub-maps, "is the first part of their journey, from May 1804 to September 1804. Each of the dates you see is linked to a text excerpt. So if you click on one, you hear a narrated excerpt from the original journals along with background music." Clicking on another date, he continued, "This one talks about Sergeant Floyd. He was the only casualty on the trip, and when he died, they named a small river after him. I thought it would be nice to show their annotated map. So here's the actual map, with the Floyd River."

This kind of depth, Carr believes, will expand the potential use of the CD-ROM for other grade levels than the fifth and eighth grade target audience. A Spanish, as well as English, version of the complete program—text and narration—also adds to its versatility. Carr said that the main menu offers the language option, but it is possible to alternate between the two versions throughout the program. In addition, much of the text is narrated, making the program suitable for use as "sheltered English."

Video and Audio

Because of the involvement of TMM in the Hueneme Series, the Lewis and Clark CD-ROM will be one of the first to take advantage of its proprietary fractal technology. Since it allows the playback of video without additional computer hardware, its use should broaden the CD-ROM's appeal to teachers and school districts seeking multimedia materials that are easy to play in the classroom.

The use of video alone—including scenes from a Oregon Public Broadcasting special on the Oregon Trail, "Ft. Clatsop"—gives Carr's educational program an edge over most others in the field. Until recently, very little educational software incorporated video because of its playback difficulties. In addition, Carr has taken pains "to tie the clips back into the content." For example, a segment from a National Geographic Special on the Native American guide Sacajawea is part of the segment on the tribes Lewis and Clark encountered on their trip.

All of the video segments, a total of 18 minutes worth, were digitized using TMM tools and converted to fractal video "the closest you can get to broadcast quality video," Carr said. In addition to being created in software, fractal video is a relatively small file. "That's what's so cool about it," Carr continued. "Fractal is a mathematical equation. All the digital information is shrunk down to this equation, and when you call it up, it blows up (to full size) on your screen. You'd have to talk to a math wizard to understand it all." The digitizing process, on a computer like Carr's 486/33 PC is time-consuming. "About 40 minutes of video would take about four days to create on a station like this," he said. In the future, he expects to work with a service bureau TMM plans to establish in Savannah, Georgia, that will harness a huge IBM mainframe to turn out fractal video.

Though it is possible to play the four- or six-minute long videos, most of the segments will be presented in "little bites" of 15 to 45 seconds throughout the program. "That's deliberate," Carr said, "because what we've found happens with interactive video is that it becomes passive. So the idea was to let kids gain (informa-

Fractal Video: Carr used TMM's tools to digitize video for his program.

tion) from bites that address the particular issue they are looking at." When broken into the short segment, the video was digitized using another TMM tool called PH, which, according to Carr, is similar to QuickTime or AVI but with better resolution. When all of the video has been digitized, it is cut and pasted into the program using yet another TMM tool. "That was one of the things that we liked about TMM," Carr said. "The tools are there for putting together an interactive program, tools that allowed us to do more."

The audio, including narration by Carr in English and a Hueneme principal in Spanish, was recorded at a small studio at the TMM offices. Other sound effects—especially natural sounds likely to have been heard on the wilderness trails—were borrowed from a variety of sources. In all, Carr was satisfied with the program's audio components, until he realized that he had neglected to dub the video audio in Spanish. "What a challenge," he said. "It wasn't that much, but it took time to do this. The dialogue in the videos has to be transcribed, then translated into Spanish, and then you had to do an audio dub."

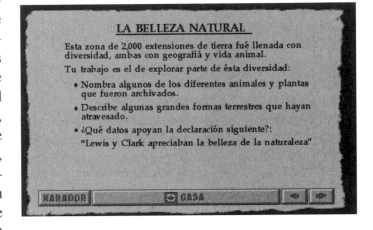

LA BELLEZA NATURAL

Esta zona de 2,000 extensiones de tierra fué llenada con diversidad, ambas con geografiá y vida animal.

Tu trabajo es el de explorar parte de ésta diversidad:

♦ Nombra algunos de los diferentes animales y plantas que fueron archivados.

♦ Describe algunas grandes formas terrestres que hayan atravesado.

♦ ¿Qué datos apoyan la declaración siguiente?:
"Lewis y Clark apreciaban la belleza de la naturaleza"

NARADOR | ✪ CASA | ◀ ▶

Journey in Spanish: The conversion to Spanish was time-consuming.

Programming

To make the many connections that transform his CD-ROM into an interactive learning experience, Carr turned to another TMM tool, TMM Producer, to accomplish much of the authoring. "When we did graphics and scans, we used a lot of Windows products, like Corel Draw! and PhotoFinish. We used Microsoft Word for a lot of the text," he added, then chuckled. "I'm jumping in and out of Windows, is what I'm doing."

By late fall 1993, the authoring was well enough along to press the first three discs. "It was cool," said an elated Carr. But when the first disc wouldn't play on a single speed CD-ROM drive, he found himself recutting everything to play at that rate, without sacrificing the quality of the video or audio. "You can author like crazy on a hard drive, and have it running beautifully," he said, "but the challenge is to then make sure that it adheres to CD-ROM rates. And that's a big impediment." Differences in speed actually pose the greatest problem. "A hard drive runs about five times faster than a CD-ROM drive," Carr explained. "You're trying to pass all that data, and CD-ROMs are notoriously slow.... And what will invariably happen is that the video may maintain, but the audio will drop out. And that's what happened on the first cuts—the data rate was too high."

The first disc would have played on double- or triple-speed players, but Carr was determined to have it run on "a baseline machine. That's one of my goals as an educator, since I realize that schools aren't going to be able to go out and buy 486s and double-speed CD-ROMs. We want it to run on as many machines as possible." Before he pressed a second disc, Carr "cut down the number of frames per second, and cut down on the size of the video screens. It was not fixed entirely then, but by the third one it was." Since he wanted to take the test disc to COMDEX in Las Vegas in November 1993, the last round of changes took a week of "very intensive work."

Testing

Finding a group of junior high students to test "drive" his CD-ROM was no problem for Carr. He simply spent two afternoons back at Blackstock, in a room the school uses as a site for beta testing of products by other educational software developers. "I tried to stay as aloof from this as I could, and just be an observer," he said. "I just let the kids play with it, and took notes. Then I interviewed them afterward."

It did not take an experienced educator like Carr long to spot a problem. "With all these hot-button screens, the kids were just clicking like crazy, clicking everything they could," he said. "They were so enamored of the video and graphics clips, they weren't really focused on what they were trying to pull up." The solution involved the creation of an animated Meriwether Lewis, that kept the kids on track. "Lewis challenges the kids," Carr explained, "saying, for

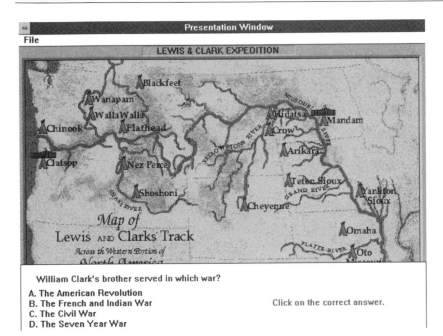

Presentation Window

File

LEWIS & CLARK EXPEDITION

William Clark's brother served in which war?

A. The American Revolution
B. The French and Indian War
C. The Civil War
D. The Seven Year War

Click on the correct answer.

What Was Learned:
Carr built in an evaluation module to measure students' retention.

example, that there are fifteen hidden buttons on the screen, and that they should keep track of how many they find. When they are finished, they then click on a challenge button that tests them." If the students get a certain percentage of correct answers, their "little boat" moves further down a river that Lewis and Clark explored, "indicating their progress in learning," Carr said. As a result, Carr believes, "there's more incentive to hold them accountable for some content. Too often what happens in the exploration of CD-ROMs is that there is not enough accountability, or not enough reason to remember any of the data. So we're trying to build in instructional strategies to encourage that."

Carr's testing of his CD-ROM ends in the classroom. Technical trials will be conducted by TMM at its Savannah, Georgia, offices. Programers there will devise an install program that will ensure the disc is easy to install in classroom situations.

Users' Manual

Since the Hueneme Series is aimed primarily at educators, Carr has drafted a ten-page manual of "instructional strategies" to accompany his CD-ROM. "There will be activities for kids and suggestions for teachers," he said, "along with ideas on how to use this with small groups of kids.... We've also included some off-line assessment activities. You want to hold them accountable, but you don't want to stifle their exploration and discovery."

Although still not finalized, Carr also anticipates that the CD-ROM will be sold for use at home. For that audience, it will be packaged with a shortened version of the manual that is not as educationally based as the school version.

MARKETING: A Bump on the Trail

As 1993 drew to a close, Carr was putting the finishing touches on the first Hueneme title. At the same time, talks continued with a number of potential distributors, who would make the CD-ROM package available to schools, and eventually to parents for use on the growing number of home multimedia computers. But despite a great deal of interest in the product, no deals had been finalized. As a result, related issues such as price and packaging are "on hold," Carr said, although he expects the title to sell from $60 to $100.

One obstacle was a delay in establishing the publishing arm of TMM, which primarily has focused on software development since its founding more than three years ago. "That has been the holdup; it really didn't start to happen until recently," Carr said. "It hasn't slowed me down, because I just keep working on my stuff, but in terms of getting it to market, that's where it's been bogged down." In December 1993, Carr reported promising discussions with Compton's NewMedia to distribute, and with Gateway and other CD-ROM manufacturers about bundling possibilities.

At year's end, both Carr and Kramer were optimistic that a distributor would be found. "The response has been phenomenal," Kramer said of his many discussions with key distributors and retailers. "I've been in meetings, I've been with distributors and I know they want this market. One distributor told me, 'we can sell everything you can make,' and they are talking about 5,000 stores throughout the United States, Mexico, and Canada. Do you know what kind of money that means to the district?"

Kramer expects demand for the Hueneme series to grow as the information highway becomes a reality. Then, "the number one most critical priority is not going to be entertainment, it's going to be survival. And that's what these people represent. They represent the future."

FINANCING: A Purchase of Time

Neither the Hueneme School District, nor TMM could have developed the "Lewis and Clark" CD-ROM on their own. Their forward-looking partnership harnesses the classroom-honed skills of dedicated educators, with the business acumen and technological know-how of an established computer software firm. And both participants believe it could be a model relationship for public and private sectors in the Information Age ahead. "There were 260 schools represented in Washington," Kramer said, referring to ceremonies honoring the nation's 1993 Blue Ribbon schools. "It's not a stretch of the imagination to figure they could all supply content. Two hundred and sixty schools doing this simultaneously can create a wealth of information that, I believe, will sustain the new education paradigm, as well as become extremely profitable."

At present, a memorandum of understanding governs the Hueneme/TMM project. In the document, approved by the district board, the school district agrees to free teachers to work with TMM on CD-ROM development, to identify content for those educational multimedia programs, to facilitate adoption of the program by the State Board of Education and to help promote the joint venture. As for TMM, the software company agreed to provide the additional staff, equipment and TMM technology needed to develop the title as well as legal help in pursuing licensing agreements. TMM also is responsible for distribution and marketing of the learning discs, which it has exclusive rights "to exploit on a worldwide basis, in perpetuity." It's an arrangement that makes sense to Carr since "as a school district, you have enough headaches, so that we don't want to deal with that. So that's why it seemed like a natural partnership."

As part of its "seed money" for the first title, TMM is covering the cost of a replacement teacher for Carr, while he designs the "Lewis and Clark" disc. "The district pays my salary," Carr said, "and TMM pays for the substitute's salary, which is less than mine." They also paid for the graphic art work by Don Haines, and made some programers available to consult with Carr on a number of technical issues. A lawyer is on call to resolve his content licensing. As a result of these financial contributions and the use of TMM software and equipment, Carr estimates that the cost of development to be "extremely low. At this point, it's been basically my time."

When the disc reaches the market, the memorandum calls for a dollar return to the District. What percentage of the district's share goes to the teacher who developed the title is not spelled out in this initial document. "The teacher's share isn't firm," Carr said, "but it's been talked about that 80 or 90 percent would go back to the teacher."

Previous attempts by the district to supplement its budget through activities of the

What Was Learned: Carr built in an evaluation module to measure students' retention.

MEMORANDUM OF UNDERSTANDING
BETWEEN
TMM, INC. AND
HUENEME SCHOOL DISTRICT

The following serves to memorialize the understanding between TMM, Inc. (TMM) and the Hueneme School District (HSD).

A. Goals: TMM and HSD shall jointly work together to develop, produce and exploit a specific number of multimedia interactive educational programs embodied on CD-ROM (the "Subject Programs"), utilizing authoring tools, video compression and other technologies owned or controlled by TMM ("TMM Technologies"). The content of the Subject Programs will be selected and structured in the manner required to conform to curriculum requirements of the State of California.

B. HSD will provide:

1. Teachers employed by HSD to work with TMM personnel to outline, structure and incorporate the content required for each Subject Program;

2. Lists of existing instructional material (i.e., text, audio recordings, video, graphics) which would be appropriate for incorporation in the Subject Programs, inclusive of material heretofore utilized by HSD in HSD Model Technology Classrooms;

3. Its best efforts to cause each Subject Program to be "adopted" by the Board of Education of the State of California;

4. The services of Dr. Ronald C. Rescigno (and others designated by HSD) to promote the TMM-HSD relationship, the TMM Technologies and the quality of the Subject Programs.

C. TMM will provide:

1. All creative and technical personnel (other than the above-described HSD teachers), licenses to all TMM Technologies and the use of all equipment required to develop and produce each Subject Program;

2. Legal services required to obtain the licenses to use the content (audio, text, graphics, video) included in each Subject Program;

3. Its best efforts to cause personalities from the entertainment industry to introduce portions of the subject matter in Subject Programs, where and when appropriate;

4. General distribution outlets to exploit the Subject Programs;

foundation, have been disappointing. "We've had all different kinds of schemes ... and we haven't received a cent yet, except from video tapes, books, and curriculum programs we sell, and that's not enough to make a significant difference." Rescigno said. "The fact is [the partnership with TMM] is truly a breakthrough, and if we can do it here, then entrepreneurship can be done elsewhere. TMM hopefully will be the first example where we will receive significant dollars for our efforts." Though the potential income from the sale of the Hueneme Series titles could be significant, Kramer said TMM took the time "to set up guidelines [with the district], knowing full well that there are certain costs and overhead that are going to be associated with this, so that in broad terms, the district and the teachers would know what to expect, say, per disc." "I told those guys," Rescigno responded, "when you give us the first check." The superintendent paused, looked away with a smile, and sighed.

THE FUTURE: Pioneering Titles

For most of 1993, Steve Carr was out of his classroom, caught up in linking the world of Lewis and Clark to an electronic age neither of the legendary adventurers could have dreamed was possible almost two centuries ago. In 1994, instead of returning to the classroom, he is now coordinating production of the next titles in the Hueneme series. "Other teachers are in the wings," he said. "They have their own projects in mind."

One of those teachers, ESL specialist Pat Newton, regularly shares Carr's TMM office. He has already storyboarded a CD-ROM title that would have Spanish speakers learn English, and created some interactive screens that teach students the names of common supermarket items. Also, the two teachers have met with other district educators interested in "electronic curricula." "We've identified some potential titles and some ways to get started," said Carr. "Basically the first thing you do is storyboard everything out on paper and then start putting life into it. That's what they are doing at this point." Potential titles are likely to include one on oceanography that is structured like a treasure hunt, and one on the Underground Railroad that challenges students to help slaves escape to the North.

Carr hopes that in future months he can put together a production team that would make it possible to develop a number of Hueneme titles simultaneously. "The teachers are essentially going to be on the content and instructional strategy side, because we know what works in a classroom. The idea then would be to have a team of graphics, text, video, and audio people, provided by TMM, who would work with the teacher to put together titles. That's the goal."

Meanwhile, Rescigno, who presided over the opening of the new Smart Math Classroom in early 1994, continues to meet with educators from around the country—and the world—who are intrigued by this district's accomplishments. And through his connections with ARPA, he has emerged as an evangelist for federal support of like projects around the country, in response to the paradigm shift radically altering the direction of public education. But, he acknowledges, the "impact of electronic information technologies" on the nation's schools has just begun. In a keynote speech before a conference on technology and collaborative learning, he exhorted his fellow educators to look forward to "the school of the future," one that will make today's "Smart-School concept seem rudimentary." "The possibilities," he concluded, "are far-reaching. One day, classrooms around the world will be electronically linked, for a truly universal interaction, a global community—that can be accessed at the touch of a student's fingertip."

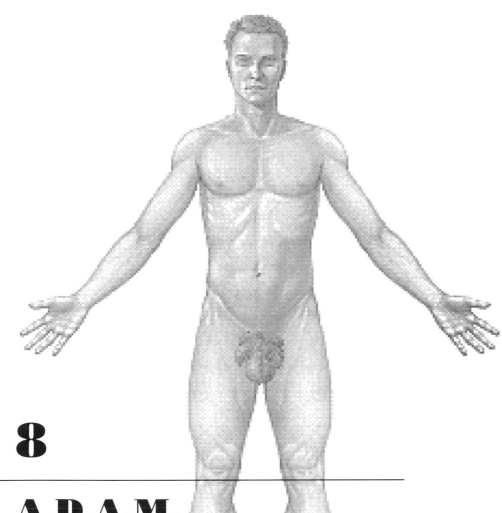

8

A.D.A.M.

A.D.A.M. Software, Inc.

At A Glance

A.D.A.M.

Developer: A.D.A.M. Software, Inc.

Key personnel: Gregory M. Swayne, president and co-founder; Robert S. Cramer, chairman and co-founder; John McClaugherty, chief executive office and co-founder; Curtis A. Cain, chief operating officer; Glen S. McCandless, vice president of marketing, education division; Cary Scott Chandler, vice president of sales; Clay E. Scarborough, chief financial office; Dan Backus and Bill Appleton, programmers.

Description: Interactive human anatomy on CD-ROM for Macintosh and Windows.

Development period: March 1990–April 1993.

Production hardware: Macintoshes and IBM PCs.

Software used: Macromedia Director, SuperCard, Quark, HyperCard, Photoshop, CameraMan, Adobe Premiere and Photoshop, and proprietary imaging and compression software.

Cost: $5 million.

Financing: Privately funded.

Selling price: Approximately $2,295.

U.S. distribution: A.D.A.M. Software, Inc. and reseller partnerships in diverse markets.

Foreign distribution: Matsushita in Japan; Churchill Livingstone in Europe.

Awards: Best of Show, 1993 *NewMedia* INVISION Multimedia Awards; Grand Award Winner, 1992 New York Festival Interactive Multimedia Competition; Frank Hefler Award for Medical Illustration, 1993; Best of Show, MAX awards (marketing award for excellence).

Future Projects: Six related products aimed at health professionals, as well as consumers.

Contact: Amy Woodward Parrish
              Director of Corporate Communications
              A.D.A.M. Software, Inc.
              1600 River Edge Parkway, Suite 800
              Atlanta, GA 30067
              800–755–A.D.A.M.

Meet A.D.A.M., an electronic baby. Unlike most infants, he was born foot first in a painstaking delivery, which took more than three years, and cost his Marietta, Georgia, parents more than $5 million. No small achievement, A.D.A.M. emerged already fully grown, five foot, ten inches of well-toned flesh and bones. No wonder he sports only a fig leaf, and sometimes not even that.

Since 1990, A.D.A.M. has travelled the world, becoming a big man on campuses and a hero to thousands of medical students and their instructors. Fluent in Japanese, as well as his native English,

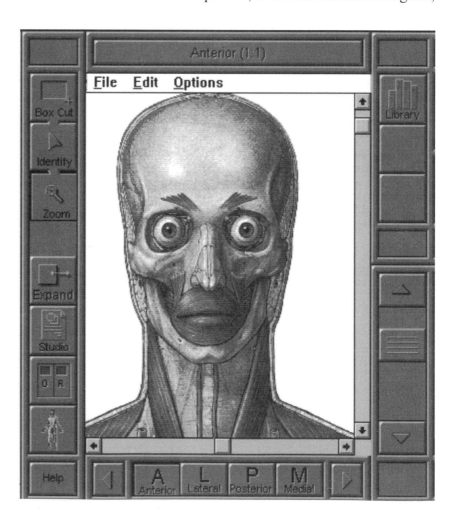

The Digital Man: A.D.A.M. allows users to study human anatomy on a computer screen.

A.D.A.M. has bared all for the sake of modern medicine, submitting to countless operations and medical experiments, often at the hands of novices, and inviting students to get under his skin and learn what makes him tick.

Clearly, A.D.A.M. is a child of the computer age. An acronym for Animated Dissection of Anatomy for Medicine, A.D.A.M. is a true multimedia person, who changes sex and ethnicity with the click of a button. Beneath his skin is a digitized human body with layer upon detailed layer of skin, muscles, bones, organs, nerves and blood vessels, which can be viewed from four different angles.

Thanks to this "computerized cadaver," stored on a CD-ROM, a new generation of medical professionals, and their instructors, interact with the human body on a computer screen, in ways surpassing those in the laboratory. Using a mouse as a scalpel, students can peel away A.D.A.M.'s skin to study his anatomy. They can slice into tissue, practicing surgical procedures over and over again, at their desks. They can view the course of diseases and ailments, and watch their responses to various treatments.

A.D.A.M. also brings users a hyperlinked, customized library of detailed medical information, including X-rays and tissue studies. Plus, the A.D.A.M. multimedia bookshelf gives them access to an up-to-date desktop library of medical references on subjects ranging from histology, to obstetrics, to radiology. Instructors and students alike have the option, through A.D.A.M. Studio, of adding their personal storehouse of interactive information ranging from textbook diagrams, to videos of actual surgeries.

A.D.A.M. is currently in use in 105 medical schools in the United States. The program also is exported to 28 countries around the world, and, as a result of a 1993 agreement with the Japanese company, Matsushita, it is now available in Japan. The software, including A.D.A.M. Studio, books and Support (an annual upgrade), costs approximately $3,000; sales in fiscal year 1994 are expected to top $5 million.

Among A.D.A.M.'s growing number of enthusiasts is Dr. C. Everett Koop, the former U. S. Surgeon General, who now owns the Koop Institute for Advancing Health & Education at Dartmouth.

Medical Educator:
A.D.A.M. has become a fixture in many of the world's medical schools.

He believes this "Gray's Anatomy for the 21st Century" will revolutionize medical education. "In the next five years," he predicted, "A.D.A.M. will become the primary anatomical reference, and the student may only have token experience with a cadaver sometime during his studies."

Surprisingly, A.D.A.M. was not the brainchild of physicians or computer "wonks." Instead, this medical breakthrough originated with a Georgia company that specialized in medical illustration, primarily for lawyers involved in malpractice suits. "We thought, 'wouldn't it be great, to have an anatomy-based program, which would really help doctors explain to patients about the body,'" said Gregory M. Swayne, the 35-year-old medical illustrator, whose vision created A.D.A.M. and who now is president of A.D.A.M. Software, Inc. "The idea itself was an obvious one; we sort of borrowed it from the encyclopedias with the (anatomy) transparencies. It's just that we were the first to recognize how we could do that better in hypermedia."

A.D.A.M.'s achievement in multimedia has been recognized within this infant industry. The product was honored as Best of Show at the *NewMedia* INVISION 1993 Multimedia Awards, and was the Grand Award winner at the 1992 New York Festival Interactive Multimedia Competition, among other major honors.

For potential multimedia entrepreneurs, A.D.A.M. demonstrates the evolution of an interactive project, one that expanded beyond its creators' initial brainstorm both to serve its users better, and take advantage of technological innovations. In a sense, A.D.A.M. took on an electronic life of its own. "As we got into creating A.D.A.M.," Swayne reflected, "we began to realize that we had to do things to the product to let people interact with it in interesting ways. Until that time, people were still caught in the textbook model of creating multimedia. That's an area where we threw away the old model—

we couldn't get locked in electronic page flipping...I think one of the big mistakes people make in multimedia is that they try to copy traditional media such as textbooks. The same thing happened when the motion picture camera was created. The first thing they did was set it up, and point it at a theatrical stage. As that medium developed, you got the close-up, and different camera angles, and what evolved was true motion picture photography...I think that what's required for (multimedia) is totally new definitions, and totally different ways of looking at this stuff."

THE OPPORTUNITY: The Body Online

Since its birth, A.D.A.M. generally has found a home at the world's leading medical schools and undergraduate science courses. Its creators, though, had envisioned that A.D.A.M. would spend more time in examining rooms and courtrooms, than classrooms.

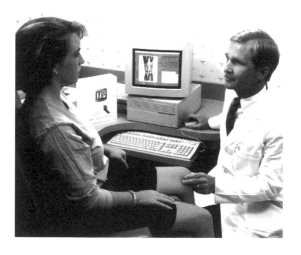

When the notion of a digital anatomy first crossed Gregory Swayne's mind in 1987, he was running an Atlanta medical illustration company which primarily served lawyers who needed exhibits for malpractice and personal injury suits. That company, Medical-Legal Illustrations, Inc. (MLI), today a reseller of A.D.A.M. products, had been founded out of his frustration with the either-or career options for medical illustrators: either freelance for a textbook publisher, or work full time in the illustrations department of a university hospital. Instead, after sales calls on area law firms he was convinced that there was a market. He launched MLI in 1985. Two years later, the company's full-time employees numbered almost two dozen.

In the Doctor's Office: As a universal data base, A.D.A.M. was envisioned as an aid to doctors in their day-to-day medical practice.

During that time, Swayne's exposure to malpractice litigation convinced him that "a lot of what happens in malpractice is a breakdown in communications between the doctor and the patient," he said. "It wasn't that the doctor committed malpractice; it's just that a lot of the risks inherent in some surgical procedures were not understood by the patient, prior to the surgery. And he would turn around after the fact and sue the doctor for basically things the doctor should have communicated to him up front. This happens everyday; in fact, seven out of ten malpractice cases involve known complications and risks."

At the same time, Swayne had been introduced to HyperCard and SuperCard when his firm created some exhibits on a Macintosh. He thought that computer technology could be tapped to develop an interactive anatomy, which could help bridge the doctor-patient communications gap. "We thought it would be a wonderful tool doctors could use to explain things in a way patients could really understand. That essentially is one of the problems. It's not that the doctors don't communicate; it's just that many times the message doesn't get through, because the patient is at one level, and the doctor is at another."

A digital anatomy also could help medical professionals keep pace with medicine's rapid advances, Swayne believed. "One of my first experiences out of graduate school was to illustrate a text-book on foot surgery. It took about two years—I did 400 drawings. The book finally got published, about three years after its inception, and by the time it hit the streets, a third to a half of it was obsolete. That, in a nutshell, is one of the serious limitations of traditional print media in the healthcare market. Technologies change so fast that print media can't keep up. Multimedia, on the other hand, would allow us to send information to physicians, almost in real time."

Based on his studies in medical illustration, Swayne realized a computerized human body would be a welcome addition in medical schools, too. "Part of my training was three years of medical school, and I had to take the same courses as the first-year medical students—gross anatomy, histology, embryology," he said. "I had an exposure to that environment, and I knew immediately that this product would find a home in that marketplace.

In addition to its educational uses, Swayne believed that an interactive anatomy could anchor a much-needed international healthcare data base. Medical providers around the world would have one source for this vital information, that could be accessed via an object—the body—that is automatically, and universally, recognized. "If we come out with 20 different applications for how doctors can access information, then everybody's going to get confused," he noted. "Then everyone would throw their hands up in frustration and say forget it.... However, if it's the body you walk up to and start digging through, eventually you will find what you're looking for."

To realize his multi-purpose vision, Swayne knew "we had to think about this as the human body in the computer, and what people would want to do. Well, they would want to cut on it with a scalpel, scrub it to sterilize it, click on a muscle and get the name of that muscle to pop up." And that demanded thinking outside of circles that confined multimedia to formats identified with traditional media. "We realized early on that this was something that would have to be done very differently. So we strove to really push the envelope on interactivity."

THE DEVELOPERS: Three Partners Plus

Two chance meetings forged the partnership that eventually would emerge as A.D.A.M. Software, Inc. The first occurred in 1985, as Swayne was launching what would become one of the nation's largest private medical illustration companies, MLI. By coincidence, he met a young lawyer who was passing through Atlanta on his way to Dallas, on an assignment for Campaign Strategies, Inc., a New York marketing and political consulting firm. A short time later, that attorney, John McClaugherty, became Swayne's partner in MLI. Over the next two years, the two young men struggled to build a market among attorneys for medical illustrations from their fledgling company.

In 1987, again by coincidence, a mutual friend introduced Swayne to another young businessman, a native New Yorker who had worked for CNN there, and had come to Atlanta to follow his dream of being an entrepreneur, like CNN founder Ted Turner. "I went into business with my freshman-year roommate from Emory

(University) and we started a real estate business," recalled Robert S. Cramer, the grandson of the founder and publisher of Parents magazine. "It was a speculative period here; things were growing dramatically. We were very successful."

After his meeting with Swayne, Cramer became intrigued with his medical illustration business. "I said to them that I would be interested in seeing what the three of us could do," he said. "And over time, that's what happened. I wanted to move out of real estate. It was good business, but it wasn't that challenging." The partnership was formed in 1987 and for the next couple of years, the trio focused on expanding their enterprise.

By 1989, Cramer again felt that familiar entrepreneurial itch. With the approval of his partners, he joined two other men to pub-

A.D.A.M.'s Creators: From the left to right, are Gregory Swayne, John McClaugherty, and Robert Cramer.

lish Atlanta Computer Spectrum, a four-color monthly magazine about computers. After four issues, the publication folded. "We were a real success, except financially," Cramer says with a laugh. "Our advertisers paid way too slow. It was just going to be too difficult."

However, that failed venture, however, proved vital to the birth of A.D.A.M. "What came out of this was exposure to technology," said Cramer. "We learned a lot about desktop publishing...about CD-ROM technology...about Quark and MacroMind Director and other things. So basically we realized that what we were doing in MLI was publishing, and maybe it made sense for us to take what we learned about the technology, and our illustration capacity, and marry the two. And maybe we could create this great product that...would play to both our strengths."

Today, Cramer views the merger as "a marriage of convenience, necessity, and, I guess, good luck. The opportunity and the people all came together at the right time. You could now store large color graphics on a CD-ROM, and manipulate them in a computer. We knew we could produce beautiful graphics. We weren't going to produce the magazine anymore, so we figured we'd better do something else with those people. I certainly was able to see how we could bring the two together, and Greg was instrumental in how we might shape a product out of this. So we had the technology; we had the space; we had people who were good at different facets of this business, which over time has proven to be the key to all multimedia. It requires so many skills to pull something like this off."

One of Cramer's partners in the magazine venture, Ken Lipscomb, contributed his knowledge of computer technology, as the A.D.A.M. team began to develop a prototype. Another major player during this formative time was programmer Dan Backus, although he never joined the staff. "We found Dan through Greg's wife, who worked as a graphic artist at CNN in Atlanta," Cramer recalls. "One day she got a resume in the mail from this guy who professed he could make all of these wonderful animations, and was very skilled in SuperCard. So she gave the resume to Greg. At this time, Dan was living in Tulsa, but he became intrigued with

Dan Backus:
Backus moved to
Atlanta from Tulsa to
work on A.D.A.M.

what we had created and eventually we got him to move to Atlanta.... He was a very important independent contractor, an expert in interactivity, graphics, and making things happen." Later, as A.D.A.M. was assembled from individually drawn body segments, the company called on SuperCard programmer, Bill Appleton, to write proprietary programs that would enable A.D.A.M. users to scroll from head to toe.

The new company was incorporated in 1990. As operations expanded, Cramer said that the initial three partners realized "we couldn't do it all ourselves. None of us had ever built a big business. Our skills had been very complementary, which had worked great, but we felt that if we were going to take advantage of this opportunity, we had to build a team that could run with it." In November 1991, Curtis A. Cain, a Harvard MBA, who was then a regional manager for a national real estate investment firm, joined A.D.A.M. as chief operating officer. Four months later, he was joined by Glen S. McCandless, who had been in charge of Apple Computer's higher education programs in eighteen Southern states. McCandless was charged with running A.D.A.M.'s emerging education division. A third key hire was Clay E. Scarborough, another Harvard MBA, who became A.D.A.M.'s Vice President of Finance, in May 1992. Scarborough had held similar positions with Gerber Alley Heathcare and Digital Communications Associates. Meanwhile, Cary Scott Chandler was hired as vice president of sales for the international markets.

They also pulled together a distinguished faculty advisory board drawn from major medical schools across the country, including those at Stanford, Cornell, Northwestern, and Georgetown universities. The diverse group of academicians was asked to help guide A.D.A.M.'s development, Swayne said.

"It's not easy for entrepreneurs to allow people to come in and let them do the things they are good at," said Cramer, now 33, reflecting on the company's growth in three years to 75 employees. "I think we did very well with that, and that is really a tribute to all three of us. It made a lot of good sense."

THE PRODUCTION: A Foot At A Time

Bringing A.D.A.M. to life was like putting together "...an extraordinary jigsaw puzzle," Swayne said. The mammoth task started with complex drawings that went from skin to bone, layer by layer. This database of thousands of illustrations had to be compiled into parts of the body, and then linked together to form a complete digitized human being that could be viewed from a variety of angles. Where to start?

"It was a fairly inconspicuous beginning," Swayne said. "I basically sat in a room with a guy who knew HyperCard and we created a prototype, of a hand. We illustrated 30-some layers, one layer at a time, on separate sheets of paper, and colored them by hand. Then we scanned them, in and essentially built a HyperCard stack that had multiple layers in it. That was enough to validate the concept in my mind."

The prototype also succeeded in winning investors in the project from the Atlanta medical community. With a few hundred thousand in seed money, A.D.A.M.'s creators forged ahead. "I imagine we were a lot like NASA," Swayne said, reflecting on the company's frenetic early days. "You know you want to go to the moon, but you have no idea how you're going to get there. You start creating, and you build rockets. Some will go to the moon, and some will explode on the launch pad. You learn from both."

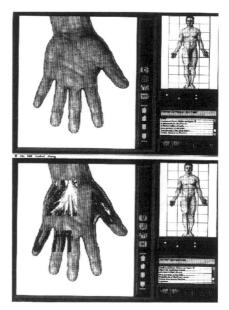

A Handy Prototype: Swayne's first screens for a digital anatomy convinced him it was possible.

The Drawings

Initially, the team responsible for A.D.A.M.'s many layers consisted of Swayne, two other medical illustrators, and two commercial illustrators. To put their ambitious undertaking in perspective, Swayne pointed to bestselling anatomy books that feature only one or two drawings of many body parts. For A.D.A.M. to become a new standard in medicine, the quantity and quality of illustrations was critical.

From the Ground Up: A.D.A.M.'s anatomy began with the foot.

In May 1990, Swayne and his fellow illustrators began the slow process of drawing A.D.A.M. from the ground up. They abandoned the prototype hand and instead focused on the foot. "We couldn't start at the head, and the foot, and work toward the middle, because nothing would have lined up. We had to move from the foot to head and make everything flow," Swayne explained. "You have to try to imagine the problems that were presented in terms of just creating the art work. It was a real challenge from an engineering perspective, because what you really have is a series of structures that flow into other structures. So we had to illustrate the body in very specific regional segments— the foot, the lower leg and knee, the thigh and hip—a trio released as the lower extremities. (This was) followed by the abdomen, the thorax, head and neck, and the upper extremities. All illustrations were done over three years, yet every image looks as if it was created at the same time."

Because of the large volume of drawings, the illustrators eventually were divided into teams, on the basis of the four different viewpoints. Swayne said, "We had a team of anterior illustrators, posterior illustrators, lateral illustrators, and medial illustrators. Each team worked on one view of the body from foot to head."

The drawings of A.D.A.M.'s foot occupied Swayne and the other artists until August 1990. Sketches by the medical illustrators were checked for accuracy by an anatomist, then turned over to the commercial illustrators for final rendering and colorizing. "Near the end of the production cycle, we had about twenty people working on the drawings, so by then it took us about the same amount of time to do the head, neck, and upper extremities combined (as it did to do the foot)," Swayne said.

While it is possible to do anatomical illustrating on the computer, Swayne prefers hand drawing: "At the time we started, Photoshop had just come out, and we could do a lot more outside the computer than we could do inside. I think that's still true. When you look at a scanned drawing, versus one that was completely done in the computer, there are just certain subtleties that you can get with the hand and eye, and the texture of the paper, that are hard to get in the computer. That is changing, though, and we're beginning to do more and more work in the computer."

Before the finished drawings were scanned, Swayne borrowed a technique from movie-makers to insure all the illustrations were aligned "We *had* to have all the layers register perfectly, so we used an animation peg registration system, the same kind Disney uses, so you can flip through all the layers, and be certain everything lines up," he said. "They also were registered on the scanning bed in the same way, so that once they were scanned in, everything came into the computer in perfect registration. The system worked like a

Borrowed From the Movies: Peg registration insured all the layers of the anatomy were aligned.

charm. You didn't have to do any manipulation of the images as they come into Photoshop. They were dead on."

When the anatomy was completed, A.D.A.M. was both male and female; its ethnicity could be changed by changing skin tones. "Since it was called A.D.A.M., everyone just assumed it was male anatomy," Swayne explained, "but from day one, it was developed with both sexes in mind. It's just that, until we got to the pelvis, there were no structural differences, so it took us about a year be-

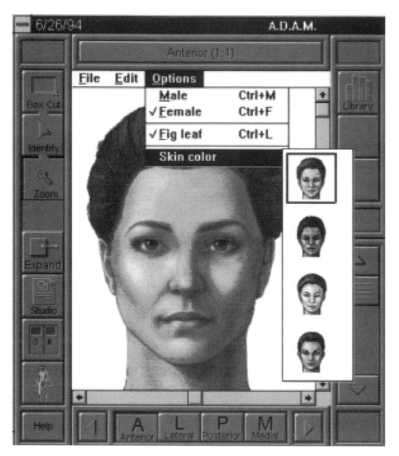

Sex and Race: A.D.A.M.'s anatomy is both male and female. Users can select its ethnicity.

fore we began drawing the female. But you could say that both male and female were drawn from the first toenail." The ethnicity options, added about two years into A.D.A.M.'s development, "seemed like the right thing to do," Swayne added. "It occurred to us that once you peeled the skin away, everything was identical, so why don't we offer the preference. The fun part is that it emphasizes that once you get below the skin, there arc no differences between people."

Those outside the medical professions who think "the thigh bone's connected to the hip bone" may find it hard to believe that human anatomy is still the subject of much debate and research. However, Swayne believes A.D.A.M. will require constant refinement. "The anatomy itself was an incredible obstacle," he said. "There are anatomists out there today who still disagree about anatomy. After this many years, you would think they would understand it, but they still don't.... And we found, in trying to take the body apart, it's like taking an engine apart, and putting it back together without a reference manual. It's not like you can dissect cadavers while you're doing this; it just wasn't practical. So we had to rely on the expertise of a select number of anatomists and the cross-referencing of a number of reference sources."

Storyboarding

In its infancy, A.D.A.M. benefited from its creators' inspired blend of intuition and experience, rather than traditional planning. "At that time in our development," Swayne recalled, "we were more intuitive and less motivated by instructional design. We're very different now; we do a lot more storyboarding and testing of different design concepts, before we go into implementation. Back then it was much more feeling your way through it."

From its inception, A.D.A.M. was an interactive program, since users could peel away the skin to reveal layers of anatomical structures. As the drawings were completed, A.D.A.M.'s interactivity grew in depth and complexity. Swayne, a computer novice, said he called upon his experiences in medical school to arrive at some of the software's most unique features like the scalpel and "box cutting." "One of the problems in med school," he recalled, "is the cadaver. Once you dissect away the skin, it's very hard to get an orientation as to where you are. The same thing holds true for most illustrations and photographs in textbooks. So, I said what if you could create a tool that would let me make a small box and just look down through the box layer to layer."

At other points in A.D.A.M.'s development, Swayne would bounce an idea off his programmers, who would get back to him in a couple of days with a workable solution. "Wouldn't it be cool if you could take a magnifying glass and zoom in on a certain area of the anatomy," he said, recalling the origin of one of A.D.A.M.'s most used features. On another occasion, he remembers telling his team, "I've got to be able to place a pathology on the bottom of the foot— say an ulcer—and then be able to click on it and watch it grow. What the patient needs to understand is, here's how it will look six months from now. And that's what we did.... We had to cre-

Looking Through Layers: A.D.A.M.'s box cutting function grew out of Swayne's experiences in medical school.

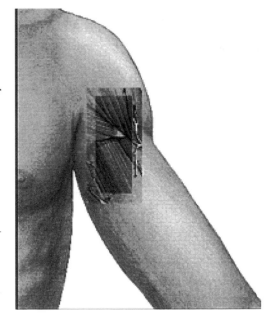

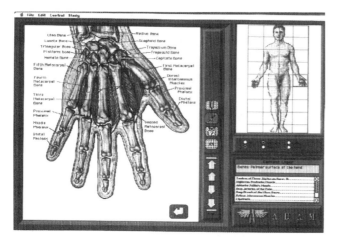

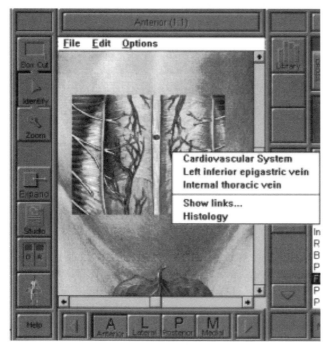

Label Logistics: Leader lines, above, were replaced by pop-up labels that identify body parts.

ate new ways to do stuff like that. But we are first and foremost a medical illustration company, and we have a bunch of creative artists here. Fortunately, we've all been to medical school, which helped us understand how people really learn. And I don't think a lot of what you need to learn can be taught effectively with slides or video—or even cadavers."

Functions also grew out of frustrations, Swayne added: "We were going down a path of having leader lines and labels to identify parts of the anatomy, and I started to realize the logistical nightmare of all these labels. Also you'd never see the anatomy. What if you could just click on a structure and up popped a label, I said. And the programmers just went off and did it." That kind of problem solving was typical. "A lot of the functionality is not from sitting down at the outset and saying here's what this product is going to do," he reflected. "It was stuff that evolved out of overcoming certain obstacles. And obviously, a lot of it was driven by the sheer magnitude of the artwork, and that it all had to be connected together. Just to do that meant that we had to come up with new ways of doing things that forced new functions into the product."

Such collaborative efforts paid off in "a lot of right decisions," Swayne believes. And looking back on those hectic years in the early '90s, he doubts A.D.A.M. could have been created by any other means. "I think that we backed into this whole thing," he says now. "If you set out to create A.D.A.M. and had no core competency, but a lot of money, and you tried to hire the right people and organize them into a real team effort, I think it would have fallen apart. I think you had to feel your way through this, because when we were doing it, we were creating new metaphors for how you get at information, how you interact with it. There were no models; there were no experts. What it required was a lot of imagination, and problem solving ability, and a lot of people who were dedicated—very dedicated—to pushing themselves to the point of solving those problems."

Veteran A.D.A.M. consultant Dan Backus agrees that the seat-of-the-pants approach was necessary in the beginning, but he is a strong advocate of planning, a procedure the company now has adopted. His advice to multimedia developers: "Build prototypes first; before you jump into the creation of a title, do a lot of storyboarding. Spend as much time in storyboarding the production process as you do storyboarding the application of the title. What drives up the cost of a title is not storyboarding, it's the production costs. Have a clear vision of the production process and the type of tools you are going to need. Not only do good tools reduce the time involved in producing the title, but they reduce the number of times the human hand has to touch the application. That is a word to the wise."

Interface Design

Like A.D.A.M.'s interactivity, its interface is the result of an evolutionary process, one Swayne expects to be ongoing. However, while the on-screen design is likely to be simplified, the universally recognized human anatomy will always be the key to A.D.A.M.'s many functions. As a result, the program will be accessible to all health professionals—from nurses to insurance adjusters to pharmacists and consumers around the world. "All these people need to interact with medical information at different levels of sophistication, and it's very difficult to create an interface that everybody can walk up to and understand," Swayne said. "Unless you deal with the body. It's that simple, and I think it really works."

During A.D.A.M.'s development, as Swayne and his team settled on a function, it was added to the interface, which, for the most part, was A.D.A.M., their digitized human being. As a result, "the interface was as fluid as the functionality," Swayne noted. Today, when A.D.A.M. users log on, the interface they see is dominated by a human figure that fills roughly half of the screen. At his feet is a preference panel of buttons that select gender, skin tone, the view (anterior, posterior, etc.), left, and right motion, and, in what must be a one of a kind in multimedia, fig leaf or fig leaf optional. Along the left side of the screen, is the primary tool panel that allows users to identify body parts, magnify them, and box cut, and to enter A.D.A.M. studio, and the A.D.A.M. operating room. At the bottom right are the layer list and depth bar, that enable viewers to penetrate the body layer by layer. At the top right of the interface is the Bookshelf of A.D.A.M. library, with its volumes of reference books. Its addition—a "huge piece of evolution"—enabled the A.D.A.M. team to add more functions to the program without adding to the number of buttons on the screen. "We began to recognize the need for organizing related content, and the analogy that seemed to make sense was the traditional book metaphor," Swayne recalled.

In the future, as the interface is refined, more and more of the program's functions will be stored in A.D.A.M. library. "You will definitely see more changes in the interface. If anything it will get simpler," Swayne said. "We have learned that there's a limit to what people can absorb on their initial utilization of the product. So, functions that today are imbedded in the interface will become imbedded in the library. Users will open up a functionality book and select tools there, as opposed to having all that on the screen." The change, Swayne believes, should reduce user intimidation around a new product with "all those buttons."

A simple interface has another advantage, Backus points out. Speed. "And the faster and more responsive your product is, the

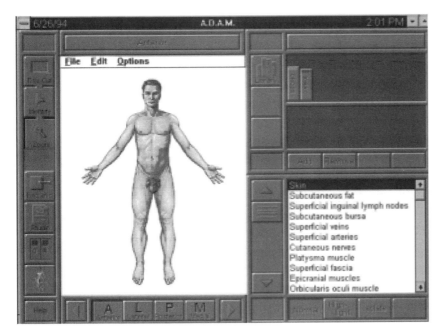

A.D.A.M. Evolving: How to add more functions to the program without adding more buttons to the interface is an on-going challenge.

better it's going to be for the user," he said. "The worst interface is a slow one. You can come up with brilliant ideas that run great on a Quadra 900, but if a user has an SI, the beauty is lost when it clunks along." Slow response is not necessarily the fault of off-the-shelf authoring programs, he added. "There are a lot of techniques and X-objects available that can address some speed issues. It's a question of designing in such a way that you avoid the weakness, not only of the tools you are using, but also of the platform you will be playing on."

Interactivity

Once users select an area of the body to study, A.D.A.M. provides several interactive tools for in-depth learning. One identifies, with the click of a mouse, more than 18,000 body parts. Another scrolls the body, head to toe, following the course of bones, muscles, vessels, and nerves. Both of these features required major problem solving efforts to realize.

Pixel level recognition, developed with proprietary code, met the first challenge of labeling the body's thousands of parts. "Pixel level recognition is a new way of creating hot spots on the program, that aren't really hot spots," Swayne said. "With HyperCard or SuperCard, you have to place invisible buttons on top of things to get interactive functionality. We had to create a totally new way of doing that, simply because we had 18,000 buttons, and if we had had to drag them around the program, it would have been painstakingly slow. So, what we did was create a mapping program that actually looks at where your X and Y coordinates are on your mouse, and when you click an area, the program goes out and matches that to a separate mathematical map, which knows the name, depending upon what layer you are on. It works very effectively and quickly."

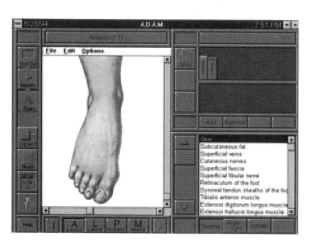

The A.D.A.M. team also had to devise a way to scroll a five-foot, ten-inch image, so that users could move seamlessly up and down the body. The problem, according to Swayne, was linking the body sections, developed one after another over a three year period. "You would start at the foot, but if you wanted to go to the knee, you couldn't scroll to the knee, you had to jump. What you were really doing was launching the knee mod-

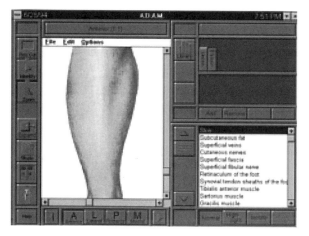

A Major Advance: The A.D.A.M. team overcame a major obstacle when it devised a way to scroll seamlessly through the anatomy.

ule. There was no concatenation between those modules, no seamless scrolling," he said. "One of the biggest challenges was coming up with a technology that, even though all the art work registered, would launch each module seamlessly."

The solution, contained in proprietary code developed by SuperCard creator Appleton, essentially transformed A.D.A.M. from a series of "slides" into a "movie." "Originally, you would launch a module and flip through all these eighteen-inch by ten-inch PICT images," Swayne said. To add the scrolling feature, "we compressed the PICT images into a movie format that doesn't look at the PICT images at all. It just sees a line across the top and it loads each frame of the movie based on where you are. So, essentially it allowed us to create one continuous five-foot, ten-inch person without having a five-foot, ten-inch PICT image, which would be totally unmanageable."

To reformat the PICT images from a HyperCard stack into a QuickTime-like movie, Swayne said they "used a compression algorithm that doesn't see anything but lines of code. It essentially scans about a half-inch wide area of A.D.A.M., and based on which direction you're going, it knows to load the next bar in. So, if it sees that you are going from the knee up to the hips, it says start loading in some of the hip stuff now."

A.D.A.M. also features what Swayne calls a "primitive operating room." This interactive feature, to be expanded in the future, allows users wield their mouse as a scalpel to cut through the layers of tissue. They also are able to cauterize with a laser, sterilize "skin" with betadyne and suture incisions. The effects are "illusions," in which the screen "is repainted with other content. When you scrub the foot with betadyne, what it is really doing is redrawing the skin with a new layer."

Linkage

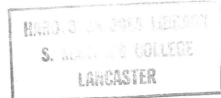

As the project continued to evolve, A.D.A.M.'s medical illustrations, the world's largest database of its kind, became the basis for including even more detailed information to the program. The addition of microscopic slides, X-rays, and eventually video, made A.D.A.M. "a way for educators to organize their content around the human body," Swayne said. "Once you can identify a structure, and you can link information to it, A.D.A.M. essentially becomes a navigational front end for just about everything in medicine."

The added information builds on A.D.A.M.'s pixel level recognition of body structures. "You get directly from the gross anatomy to the histological, or microscopic, anatomy, by clicking on the identification label. That gives you a pop-up menu with the name of the structure, and the option of seeing histology or an X-ray," Swayne said. In the future, as more information is added to A.D.A.M.'s library, that menu will be expanded.

The ability to link additional content to A.D.A.M. is not confined to his creators. Users can add information—slides, charts, video and text—as well, thanks to a powerful tool called A.D.A.M. Studio. It grew out of initial market research that discovered surprising resistance to A.D.A.M. among medical educators. The difficulty, Backus recalled, was "coming to educators, who had built up a lifetime's worth of teaching materials, and telling them that we had something better. It's the 'not created here' syndrome." Or, "I don't do it that way" syndrome, Swayne added. "It's a tremendous barrier.... What we did right, and I have to admit we backed into it, is that we said let's let the user do it, instead of having the A.D.A.M. team create all this content to plug in."

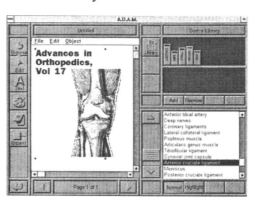

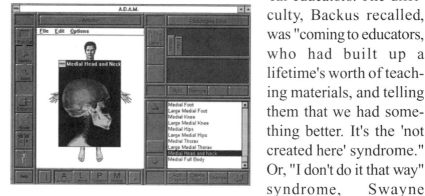

Anatomy Links:
Users can add their own materials to A.D.A.M. or call up information like x-rays stored in A.D.A.M.'s library.

The solution? Transform A.D.A.M. into a filing cabinet, Backus said. "We came up with using the concept of linkage, which has been around since HyperCard days," Backus said. "It's a mechanism for organizing content anatomy professors and educators already have.... Let's say you have an X-ray of a fractured tibia. It's difficult to remember in what folder, or hard drive, or network, I stored it. But if you navigate to the tibia in A.D.A.M. and establish a link there, the next time you need to find it, you'll know exactly where it is."

A.D.A.M. Studio also enables users to create interactive documents, as well. Swayne said, "Let's say you have a QuickTime movie and you want to place it inside a document to show your students where a ligament of the knee is," he explained. "You do that by capturing an image from A.D.A.M.—we actually let you borrow our images. You draw a box around the part of the knee, to capture the image, and then paste it into your project. You can add text, or link to QuickTime movies, or anything else that you've got on the desktop." At the same time, A.D.A.M. also creates the interface for these user-designed documents. "When you link something, A.D.A.M. drops a little blue button into your project so you don't have to spend a lot of time trying to create an interface," Swayne said. "I think that's a powerful tool for educators as opposed to SuperCard or HyperCard, which require you to spend a lot of time on the interface design.... Fortunately, when you're done, it looks and feels like A.D.A.M. to students, and I think that is a real benefit."

This option is one reason "why A.D.A.M. is getting a lot of attention," Swayne emphasized. "It's not because it's an anatomy program. It's really the aspect of the program which allows people in education to take their content and plug it in to A.D.A.M....what's really exciting is that they can take those slides they've been teaching with for the last twenty years, digitize them, and link them directly into A.D.A.M.'s anatomy. So, let's say the students have been using A.D.A.M., they dissect down to the spinal cord, they click on more information and, behold, there's Dr. Smith's slide in a little window totally integrated into the anatomy."

Programming

The original programming took place with HyperCard, in creation of the prototype hand. When production progressed to the foot and on up the body, the programs changed, and A.D.A.M. matured, growing ever more sophisticated. Then, as now, though, software development is done on Macintoshes, then ported over to Windows, Swayne said. "Macintosh is a superior developing tool, though I think that will change, over time. But when we began development in 1988, the gulf between PCs and Macs was enormous."

"Over time, A.D.A.M. practically has become capable of reproduction," said Backus, with a chuckle. It was Backus, who began and still improves A.D.A.M.'s functionality. Although, he now has a team of experienced software engineers and programmers to back him up. "I use the current version of A.D.A.M. to build future versions of A.D.A.M.," he said. "A.D.A.M. 1.5 was created by using A.D.A.M. 1.0. Most of the programming functionality exists in A.D.A.M.. So when I get up in the morning and I'm working on A.D.A.M.-related material, I open up A.D.A.M. studio and begin working on upgrading A.D.A.M.."

Where one program ends and another starts in A.D.A.M. is confusing, Backus explained. "A.D.A.M. is an interface to SuperCard, and, to an extent, HyperCard and Macromedia Director," he said. "Basically, A.D.A.M. is capable of enhancing (itself). I add new content and functionality to A.D.A.M. from A.D.A.M. studio. I write code in A.D.A.M., and that allows me to get in a lot more man hours with the product than I could any other way. So, I have lived in A.D.A.M. for more than a year."

Based upon the thousands of hours Backus has spent programming A.D.A.M., he has definite opinions about each of the programming options. "There are basically three ways that one can create a CD, in terms of authoring tools. You can use one of the off-the-shelf authoring tools like HyperCard, SuperCard, Macromedia Director, or Authorware. You can, and a lot of people do this, build your own tools from scratch. Or you can take off-the-shelf authoring tools that allow for extensions to be added to them, and use externals to extensively address weaknesses that may exist. A.D.A.M. software is written using that approach. A.D.A.M. is a combination of SuperCard and Macromedia Director, with a very extensive library of custom XCMDs and X-objects, that allows us to do things with those authoring packages that you simply can't do any other way."

Of the three main authoring packages, Backus said "HyperCard is probably the easiest to learn, but it has a couple of serious drawbacks. One is that you can only have one graphic playing at a time. You can get around that by using color XCMDs that allow you to bring in color and give the illusion of more than one graphic plane, or graphic object, in HyperCard. But HyperCard is something that is useful for anyone who is just starting out and getting into scripting." Macromedia Director, he continues, "is probably the best multimedia production tool of the three. Its biggest weakness is that it is unable to create an interactive animation that can create other documents, so it's difficult to build a full-fledged application in Director." Though it's more difficult to learn, Backus believes SuperCard, when combined with Director, "can produce some of the best multimedia. The biggest weakness of SuperCard, is the lack of support that it currently has from Aldus, and for that reason we are using SuperCard primarily as a tool to prototype applications, because we can do it so quickly. It allows us to look at ten different interfaces in a fraction of the time we can do that someplace else. For my money it's the best prototyping tool around."

As A.D.A.M.'s software needs expanded, so did the need for highly skilled software engineers. Leading that effort at A.D.A.M. now is a man named—appropriately enough—Adam. "I said, 'This is incredible,'" recalled Adam Hunger, A.D.A.M.'s software engineering manager, when he first saw the anatomy program. "I had spent five years of my life, and generated or worked on over 130 (courseware) projects and had never seen this quality. I really wanted to be a part of this company. So I sent in my resume, and started work four weeks later."

One of the first engineers employed by the company, Hunger hired others "with the right background to take the product from more of a conceptual working prototype in many areas to a fully fleshed-out software. And we're still going through that process now, making sure that A.D.A.M. is truly object-oriented and cross-platform. Now, although most of the Mac version is still in SuperCard, we are spending more of our time converting it into our own C code. On the Windows side, we're using cross-platform codes for our image drivers. The code material that does the pixel-level recognition is identical on both platforms."

Testing

Like many other components of A.D.A.M.'s development, product testing has evolved, growing from feedback from a few paid consultants into a formal program that Swayne credits with "giving us more feedback than we could have dreamed of, to help us refine our product."

A.D.A.M.'s consumer testing dates to completion of the first anatomy segments when the company hired consultants to review the drawings and their usefulness in the medical marketplace. With the release of the lower extremities anatomy, as interest in a computerized anatomy blossomed in the nation's medical schools, A.D.A.M.'s developers sent questionnaires to pioneer users—students and educators—to obtain feedback. Today, in addition to soliciting customer comments, the company has set up usability labs to watch people using A.D.A.M. in hopes of spotting confusing or intimidating functions. "It's been a progression, and each time we've grown a bit, we've pulled in another type of resource, to give us more information," Swayne said.

Based on customer feedback, A.D.A.M.'s features have been modified and expanded over the years, Swayne said. "Those folks have a vested interest in this product, so it has always been the most important conduit of information we've had," he said. "And I think we've done a good job at addressing a lot of their issues." As an example, he explained how one professor's request led to the development of A.D.A.M.'s highlight mode: "Dr. Curtis Wise asked me how students could find structures faster. I told him you could type in the name, and it would come up on the screen; but he pointed out that even though you wanted only one structure, there would be many on the screen. Which one is it?.... It was a fairly obvious thing, but one that we overlooked.... What we needed to do was flash the structure. And from that evolved highlighting, which is one of the most powerful components of the whole program, one that' s gotten lots of acclaim."

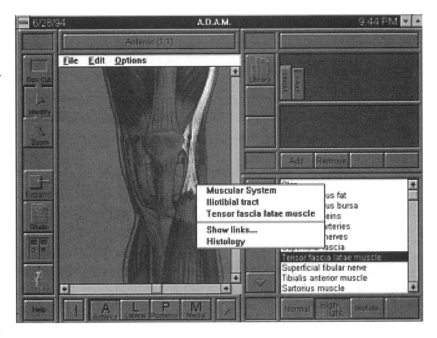

In addition to consumer trials, A.D.A.M. software undergoes a variety of reliability tests. When there are changes in the digital man's functions, a one-off CD-ROM is pressed and sent to the testing department for in and out-of-house trials, which can take up to six weeks. "Software development handles the initial testing to make sure that the software works according to specification on two or three platforms," Hunger said. When that phase is completed, the testing expands to a much broader audience and across multiple platforms. Medical students, and legal groups try out the product, which also is sent to Apple and Microsoft testing centers. "They then pass the product with a bug report back to us, along with any customer feedback," Hunger explained. "We address those areas, and make the fixes. Then we go into production."

The fine-tuning of A.D.A.M.'s database will continue indefinitely, Swayne believes, as knowledge of human anatomy expands. "There's a lot of mystery and debate about what structure runs deep to what structure," he said. "So we had to rely on the expertise of a select number of anatomists who consulted with us. and we had to use a number of standard references. It was an extraordinarily difficult challenge, and I don't think it's finished yet."

Highlight of the Program: Feedback from users led to the creation of A.D.A.M.'s highlighting function.

Online Help

In 1993, the A.D.A.M. team began the process of converting A.D.A.M. to Japanese. The difficulties encountered in the translation ultimately changed the way A.D.A.M. users are helped to interact with the program.

Since nuances in the Japanese language hampered translation of A.D.A.M.'s instructions, Hunger said the company decided to rely on multimedia online help with graphics-based instructions. "We actually show a quarter-sized screen with the interface being used. People can see realistic speed expectations or how a feature should be used, in the context of something being worked on. We now use this system on the Macintosh, and we'll soon be releasing it on Windows."

A multimedia company, Hunger believes, "should have multimedia manuals, because that's the best way of conveying information. We spent the last year dramatically rewriting our manual and are working on increasing the multimedia online help, with over 80 megabytes of real time movies. One of my pet projects is Navigable QuickTime movies that give 360-degree views of pathologies. So that a person can grab it, roll it around the screen, find the angle he wants and then print it out."

A low-priced, off-the-shelf software program called CameraMan makes online help movies a snap, according to Backus. To use it, he said, "just sit down in front of your application and generate one QuickTime document after another. So if you want to show users how to do a certain thing, you make a little 30-second QuickTime movie of it using CameraMan, with a little voice over. The result is great visual help for that particular function. It's a really quick and dirty way of creating multimedia online help."

FINANCE: Finding A Helping Hand

Most of the fund-raising duties at A.D.A.M. Software, Inc. fell to Bob Cramer, who had little fund-raising experience and learned the old fashioned way, by doing it. Early in the company's history, the three partners funneled profits from MLI into A.D.A.M. for start-up funds. But starting with seed money to develop A.D.A.M.'s foot, the company turned to the sale of stock to private investors found through time-consuming networking in Atlanta's business

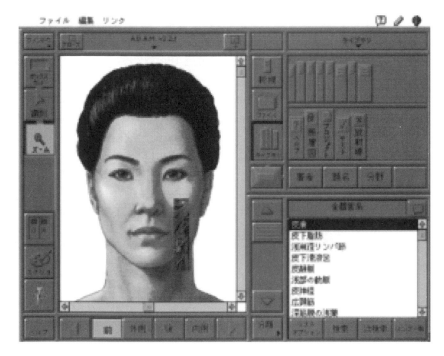

A.D.A.M. in Japanese: Difficulties in translating instructions resulted in the creation of online video help.

community. In the end, they managed to raise what they needed, when they needed it, without outside help.

In his numerous presentations about A.D.A.M. to organizations and potential investors, Cramer believes the digital man was a real asset, especially in a city like Atlanta. "Our product was very visual, and it was appealing to doctors, businessmen and, to a lesser degree, lawyers," he said. Additionally, "Atlanta has a pretty rich history of being an entrepreneurial city. A lot of people had invested in Home Depot and other companies that sprang up here, and did very, very well." Another plus was the personal touch. "A lot of companies turn (fund-raising) over to an outside group, but I think that may not be the best way, because people like to hear from (a company's) founders."

Based on initial interest from "people who wanted to get financially involved in something new," and working only with qualified investors, A.D.A.M. Software, Inc. sold its first stock in the first quarter of 1990 to raise start up funds. Three other offerings followed, each time at a higher valuation, Cramer said.

The young company benefited enormously from its ability to raise money when needed, Swayne believes. "It was the biggest advantage we had," he said, recalling the early years when the anatomy was still incomplete. "It was as if all we had to do was show the product. Doctors, unlike sophisticated investors, who ask about sales and the return on their investment, would look at A.D.A.M. and say, 'I think almost every doctor in the country would use this.' And that's how they would make their decision to invest."

One stock offering, though, grew out of a concern about time,

rather than money, Swayne recalled. "We had a very good planning team, that looked ahead, and said we could certainly make do with what we had," he said. "But here's the real issue. We realized after a year and a half of development that if we stayed with the size of the core team, it would take six more years (to finish A.D.A.M.). So we decided...let's go out and get the people we need to finish. And that is what drove us to raise more money. It's all a function of time and money and we said, 'let's compress that time as much as we can.... Let's get it done.'"

Learning By Doing: Bob Cramer networked Atlanta's business community to find investors.

As the company grew, Cramer said all its positive cash flow, plus profits from MLI, were plowed back into the project. "We just raised the amount of money that we felt we needed as we went along," he said, "which can be kind of risky because if you play it too close, it's possible to run out of money. Fortunately we never did that." At the same time, Cramer said the company worked hard to balance its need for "money to do what we needed to do" and its desire "to hold on to as much equity as possible." Since the company is privately-held, A.D.A.M.'s partners declined to reveal their percent of ownership. "We worked hard to retain control of the company while we were selling stock, and I think we were successful at that," Swayne said.

Having investors keeps a company "on its toes," said Cramer, "You always have people coming through your office, talking to your employees. But you also get their feedback, and a lot of people have a lot of different ideas about the fields we are in, about multimedia and about health care. So we found this a good opportunity to learn from other people with diverse skills.... We wouldn't have had that if we had said, 'let's go raise a bunch of money from a venture capital firm.'"

Today, with the addition of experienced financial managers to the staff, A.D.A.M.'s finances are carefully monitored. But in its formative years, the startup company budgeted its funds as it went along. "That's probably the only way you can get there," Cramer pointed out. "It was a challenge for us in the early days. Then, to tell you the truth, sometimes we didn't know how much money we had. We didn't want to know our financial position. But then we brought in our chief operating officer and, as the payroll got bigger, we got a lot more professional about our budgeting, really controlling what we were doing. We evolved as a management team, and as a company. We really grew up a lot."

Today, the A.D.A.M. Software, Inc., staff now numbers 80 employees; half are in production and half in sales and administrative support. Projected income for the 1994 fiscal year is expected to top five million dollars, doubling the 1993 revenue. Still, Swayne views the firm as "very much an R and D company. We are moving more into the marketing phase of the business. We are meeting our sales goals, and as a result we have to ramp up our ability to manage distribution channels."

MARKETING: Getting a Foot in the Door

Since A.D.A.M. was developed from the ground up, podiatrists were the logical first market for this innovative CD-ROM application. The match was off-target, but the lessons learned pointed the neophyte company in the right direction—away from the doctor's office and into the medical schools.

"A.D.A.M.'s foot module initially was marketed to podiatrists for a variety of sound reasons," Cramer said. "They were a very quantifiable group—there are about 15,000 of them," he recalled. "Podiatrists were a pretty easy group to reach, because they had some established publications and conventions. We also felt that since it was a non-MD marketplace, we could make some mistakes in that market and not really hurt our reputation in the MD market. Also, podiatrists did a lot of elective surgery, and marketing of their practices. But most of all, there wasn't anyone else we thought we could sell (the foot) to."

The product was packaged and priced comparable to an office management system for a medical concern. Including a monitor, a CD-ROM player and a high-end Macintosh with a large amount of RAM, A.D.A.M.'s foot cost more than $15,000. Unfortunately, that price was unaffordable for most of the targeted buyers, who it turned out, were pressed for time as well as money. "We learned a lot," Cramer said of the disappointing sales. "We learned that doctors don't have much time to spend, that they needed to get in and out of information very quickly...that you need a production on a DOS or Windows platform, since most doctors' offices had DOS machines...and that it was going to be very difficult to sell in big numbers to podiatrists at that price point.... Most podiatrists just don't make that much money. The ones who do were the last ones who want to embrace new technology, and change the way their practices are run. I don't blame them."

But even priced right, and on the right platform, a somewhat disheartened Cramer and the A.D.A.M. creators realized then "it would be a difficult sale no matter what," he said. "Technology had not infiltrated the doctor's office in any meaningful way. The doctor never got his hands on the computer, maybe the office manager did, so we learned it was going to be a slow process in that market."

Another market, though, cheered the A.D.A.M. team with their wild enthusiasm for what was still a work in progress. "Our biggest surprise was in higher education," said Cramer. "We thought we had to give them the entire body before they would be interested in our program. I went to a number of different education shows, particularly one in Memphis. We had the foot, and we were working our way to the knee. We were able to show a bunch of educators the program, and they went wild. The fact that we weren't close to having the whole body done didn't really matter to them. They wanted to buy it as soon as they could get it."

Aided by an aggressive public relations program and positive word of mouth, more marketing opportunities began to present themselves, both here and abroad, according to Cramer: "We're focusing on the higher education marketplace, from community colleges to four-year undergraduate programs and nursing, allied health, and medical schools. That's a big group, and it's all around the world. So, we began to focus on international distribution. We currently have distribution in about 28 countries."

In the spring of 1993, after more than a year of negotiations, A.D.A.M. inked a distribution agreement with Matsushita, a major Japanese conglomerate, to sell the software in that country as soon as it could be translated into Japanese. The agreement—the first with an outside firm—makes sense for A.D.A.M. Software, Inc. at this point in time, according to Swayne. "We had been handling distribution on a very opportunistic basis, which is very natural for a software company in the early stages of growth," he said. "But as you grow, it becomes more obvious that you need more strength in those markets, and it just makes sense

to collaborate with a major player, who has the marketing muscle to bring your product the kind of awareness it should command." In addition, a foreign partner can help thwart costly copyright infringements. "If we had ten small companies in Japan, it would be almost impossible to know if there was any leakage going on," he added.

A.D.A.M.'s Fans: The digital anatomy quickly found a home in medical schools around the world.

The distribution agreement also enables Matsushita to become an authorized co-developer of A.D.A.M. Software, Inc.-related products. A.D.A.M.'s founders hope that this partnership will be a model for similar tie-ins around the world. "Clearly there is a need for them to create customized products for their market," Swayne explained "We don't want to encourage all that development to occur here, so we're going to be setting up an authorized developer program in Japan, overseen by A.D.A.M. Software, Inc. and Matsushita with a goal of developing electronic books that can be delivered through the interface, through the anatomy." In the United States, an equivalent program, managed at the company's Atlanta headquarters, encourages developers to use A.D.A.M. software's content to create new "books" for the library, which A.D.A.M. Software, Inc., will publish. Meanwhile, Churchill Livingston, a traditional book publisher has established a similar setup across the Atlantic with A.D.A.M. Software, Inc. "Distribution and developer deals are part of our core business strategy," Swayne emphasized.

A.D.A.M. Goes To Washington: Government agencies are among the new markets targeted for the digital anatomy.

At the same time, the A.D.A.M. partners are continuing to expand their market base. Among the targeted clients are law and health care professionals, he added. "We're still tinkering with the best way to get into the physician's office, clinics, and hospitals," Cramer said. "We think it's important to use leverage to get in there. That means becoming the standard in higher education, so that when students matriculate, they will already have been exposed to A.D.A.M.. But we know that the doctor's office marketplace is going to take time. We're taking the long term approach there.

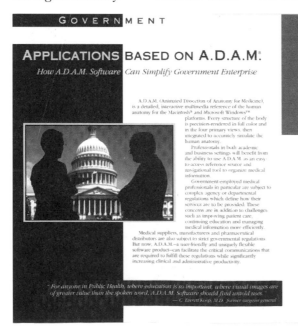

"Finally, there's potential for sales to government agencies, insurance, and pharmaceutical companies. Even the mass media have shown an interest in using A.D.A.M.'s images to illustrate stories on health and medical discoveries," Cramer said.

"A.D.A.M.'s success to date, an uphill battle, an be linked to its subject matter, high quality, and visibility among potential buyers," Cramer said. "Looking back two or three years, CD-ROM multimedia was not as popular as it is today," he remembers, "but we knew that what we were doing was really intriguing to people. It dealt with a subject matter everybody can relate to—everybody gets sick, everybody is interested in the body. Then you add the interactive aspect to it, and people can embrace it in a very visual way."

THE FUTURE: A.D.A.M. On The Air

Having completed the monumental task of digitizing the human body, A.D.A.M.'s creators are planning to use that valuable database as a foundation for a variety of new products ranging from a Nintendo-like game to an in-hospital television channel. Swayne believes that all these things build on the company's initial charter, and it all could impact health care and education, here and around the world. "We are very committed to maintaining our vision for A.D.A.M.," he said. "We are trying to create a standard way for people around the world to receive information. It starts with the anatomy. The rest of our company's charter is to begin to create other information modules for our customers which add functionality or content to their current A.D.A.M. product."

In early 1994, the company added five books to A.D.A.M.'s library and a selection of general merchandise like t-shirts and coffee mugs called A.D.A.M Artifacts. One is a K–12 version of the anatomy; another, the first authored outside the company, covers histology; and a third labels all the body's parts with their internationally recognized Latin names. Students and eductors will have the option of "perusing them as if you were going through a book, flipping the pages," Swayne said. "But what is really exciting is that you can get at those books through links to the anatomy. You could be looking at the heart, want more information, ask for a text bite, and not realize that what you're really doing is opening up a book to page 53. I truly believe that as a reference tool, when you want to get back to something, and you don't remember where you saw it, the most intuitive way for you discover it is by digging into the body."

Another title, the "Examine and Review" book, expands A.D.A.M.'s usefulness in the classroom by allowing instructors to create practical exams using the digital man. "For a practical exam, the instructor pins or flags parts of a cadaver, and the students are asked to identify those structures," Swayne explained. "We've created a tool that lets them pin A.D.A.M., and use him to test the students. It also grades the students, and provides a statistical curve for the class. It's very powerful."

Also, in early 1994, the company began to "stratify" A.D.A.M. Software into new products for both the education and consumer markets. "Imagine, if you will, that A.D.A.M. is one big salami and we're going to cut it into slices," Swayne said. "What we had was a very high-end medical product, now known as A.D.A.M. Comprehensive. [We have] removed some content and made it more suitable for the undergraduate market and renamed it A.D.A.M. Standard. We also reduced the price somewhat." A third version of A.D.A.M., A.D.A.M. Essentials, serves as the K–12 anatomy, Swayne said. "It lets the average person explore the human body," he added. "Plus, there will be some additional features that let you

A.D.A.M. Compre-hensive: New books can be found in the library of this digital anatomy, designed for medical professionals.

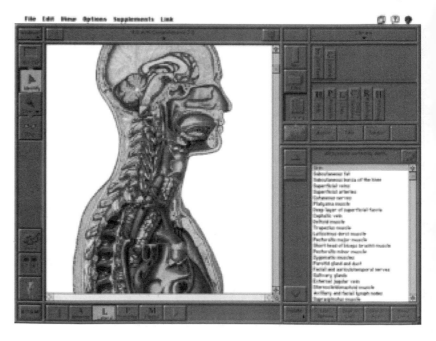

see a heart beating, or lungs breathing. But the best of A.D.A.M. will be embedded in it—you'll be able to peel through layers, rotate views, scroll up and down. It's a fun product."

Other products under discussion are more consumer-oriented. One idea emerged from Dr. Koop's desire to reduce the burden on the nation's health care system, by increasing public knowledge of health risks and preventative medicine. "Dr. Koop thinks that if you can get A.D.A.M.-type products into the hands of the Nintendo-type consumer, the impact will be that more people will stay healthy," Swayne said. "We're talking about a product that lets, say, a 13-year-old, pick a diet and (his or her) activities for a day...if they want to exercise, or if they want to smoke. Once they have made those choices, the product will 'morph' their body over the next 30 or 40 years, as if the child had maintained that pattern every day of their life. Then it will show what your body, your heart, your lungs will look like. Then, the kid could go back, alter his behavior, and see how it would effect him in future years. This can be a powerful message."

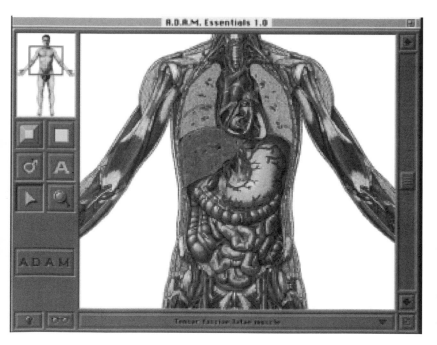

A.D.A.M. Essentials: This version invites elementary and high school students to explore the human body.

Another product on the drawing board, aimed at the general public, will feature the former Surgeon General. "It will be something like, `Mysteries of the Human Body, with C. Everett Koop,'" Swayne said, "and designed to dispel many myths about the body. What you will see is Dr. Koop inside of A.D.A.M. For example, you could click on a button that asks, 'What is heartburn?' and Dr. Koop pops up and explains."

In addition, the company also has set its sights on less traditional media, like the future data highway. "There are great opportunities, we believe, for people who own content to deliver it over electronic highways, be it cable or fibre optics. They can spend millions and billions of dollars building these highways, and eventually they will need stuff sent down them. We think we will have a real niche in that marketplace."

Future communications networks also have captured Swayne's imagination, especially since the timely dissemination of medical news and information is critical in the health care industry. "We're in the content creation business," he said. "Today we're delivering it on CD-ROM, but I don't think that will hold up very long. With telecommunications going in the direction it's going, I can easily see that, one day, you will walk up to a TV set in the hospital, and turn on the A.D.A.M. channel. Content for this channel will come from a variety of sources ranging from companies like A.D.A.M. to CNN," Swayne said, for use throughout the health-care industry—from emergency room nurses, to insurance salespeople, to pharmacists. "All these people, at some level, need to interact with medical information at different levels of sophistication," he said.

Looking ahead, the team will be guided by the lessons learned bringing A.D.A.M. to life. "It's very exciting, the way companies get built," reflected Cramer, on his success in making a multimedia dream a reality. "There's a lot of trial and error. And there's a lot of luck involved; sometimes I've felt we've been lucky, and sometimes, not so lucky. But I think it's perseverance, hanging in there, refusing to say, 'we can't do it.' That's what's really important."

9

STATISTICAL PROCESS CONTROL INTERACTIVE TRAINING

Ben & Jerry's Homemade, Inc.

At A Glance

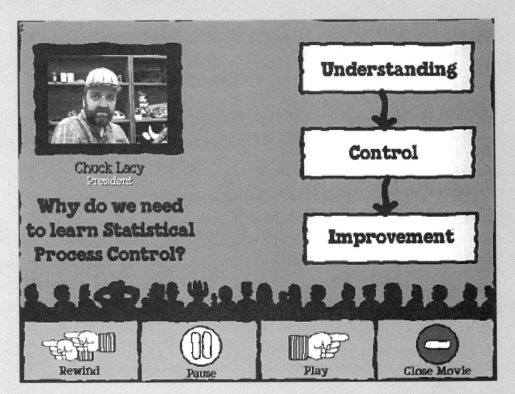

STATISTICAL PROCESS CONTROL INTERACTIVE TRAINING

Developers: Ben & Jerry's Homemade, Inc.

Key personnel: Mary Kamm, director of quality; and Rik Dryfoos, G. U. I. Guy.

Description: A multimedia course on manufacturing process statistics for ice-cream makers, that features QuickTime video and animation.

Development hours: 2,500 man hours.

Development period: May 1992–January 1993.

Development hardware: Macintosh IIfx, Macintosh Quadra 950, Radius VideoVision.

Development software: MacroMind Director, HyperCard, DiVA VideoShop, ADDmotion 2.0, QuickTime.

Presentation hardware: Macintosh Centris 610, 600 MBhard disks, 80-MB internal drive, high resolution RGB monitor, 16-bit Ethernet, trackball.

Cost to develop: $30,000.

Financing: Corporate funds.

Future projects: Multimedia Laboratory Testing Course.

Contact: Rik Dryfoos, G.U.I. Guy
                Ben & Jerry's Homemade, Inc.
                Box 240, Route 10
                Waterbury, Vermont

With flavors like Wavy Gravy, Cherry Garcia, and Dastardly Mash, Ben & Jerry's is no ordinary ice cream maker. The Vermont company's taste for the unconventional does not stop there. Ben & Jerry's Homemade, Inc. may be the nation's third largest premium ice-cream vendor, with sales that topped $330 million last year, yet its founding partners, once "the two fattest, slowest guys" in their seventh-grade gym class, still do not own suits. They give away 7.5 percent of their pretax profits annually to worthy causes. They give away franchises too, insisting that the stores' profits aid the homeless, the disabled, and troubled kids. If you register to vote or write to your congressman, they'll even give you a free pint of ice cream for your patriotic effort.

At the company's Waterbury headquarters, it's anything but business as usual. In this "caring corporation" rooted in '60s activism, top salaries are limited to no more than seven times entry level wages; no one makes more than $130,000 a year. Everyone enjoys profit sharing, paid family leave, and having a say in the company's charitable giving. An annual "social audit" of the company's good deeds is as closely watched as the bottom line at more traditional firms.

Founders With Cones: Ben Cohen (l.) and Jerry Greenfield (r.) have built Ben & Jerry's into one of the nation's largest ice cream makers.

The same philosophy rainbow-colors Ben & Jerry's organization. Where else would you expect to find a Primal Ice Cream Therapist? (Yes, he's the guy in charge of flavors, hired because "he played with his food and kept good records.") Or a Director of Mobile Promotions, as founder Jerry Greenfield once called himself? Or a Chief Taster—another cone of Cherry Garcia, please—the enviable role co-founder Ben Cohen filled to mid-1994?

These days, even Ben & Jerry's has taken its licks at multimedia. That's why there's a Mac Guru on staff. And a G.U.I. Guy. These two computer wonks, Joe Wilkins and Rik Dryfoos respectively, in 1991 created the "Rik and Joe show," an interactive lobby display that introduced Ben & Jerry's to multimedia and introduced the thousands who tour the company facilities to the how-tos of ice cream making. When that kiosk created traffic jams of curious tourists, it was retired. But not Rik or Joe.

Working with Ben & Jerry's Director of Quality, Mary Kamm, Dryfoos went on to create the company's first multimedia training module, an hour-long program on statistical process control rescued from terminal tedium by video, animation, and the company's trademark graphics of black and white Holsteins, green pastures, and puffy white clouds. It was produced in-house with off-the-shelf software on a shoestring budget of approximately $30,000, after Kamm and the G.U.I. Guy managed to convince their somewhat balky colleagues to experiment with this new technology. Since then, all the employees at one plant and 50 others at the Waterbury plant have completed the course. The training program is installed on a Macintosh Centris 610 with a high-resolution RGB monitor and a trackball, and most have found it "pretty simple to use," Kamm said.

At the outset, as first-time multimedia training developers, Kamm and Dryfoos made an understandable, if naive, assumption that Kamm's well liked class on statistical process control could simply be transferred to a multimedia format. They quickly learned that what works in the classroom must be modified to succeed in an interactive format without having an instructor present. They also

Green Grass And Cows: Ben & Jerry's Homemade is based in pastoral Vermont.

admit they failed to establish progress reports to, and reviews by, upper management until production was well along. As a result, even though they had initially blessed the project, their bosses required extensive revisions, and these revisions eventually pushed the job three months past its estimated completition date.

Ben & Jerry's forays into multimedia also demonstrate that the introduction of new technology into small and medium sized business is unlikely to be a straight shot. Kamm envisions future uses for the learning technology and some interactive concepts are being built into the company's new manufacturing plant due to open in mid 1994. However, she says that after the SPC course was completed, multimedia projects became bogged down, detoured by other corporate concerns. "Unfortunately, what we found when we finished the project," Kamm said, "was that no one wanted to go forth from there. So it was at kind of a standstill." Some of the inertia is the result of personnel changes in the company's human resources department, Kamm said. At the same time, the rapidly rising demand for Ben & Jerry's ice cream had temporarily distracted the company. "Training in general had fallen by the wayside as the company got really busy making ice cream." Kamm observed. "We're just now beginning to focus back in on the need to help people with their technical skills."

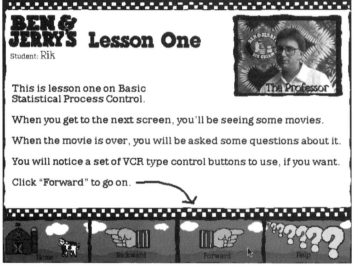

Multimedia Licks:
Ben & Jerry's first interactive training program incorporated the firm's trademark graphics.

THE OPPORTUNITY: A Taste of New Technology

Fans of Cherry Garcia probably don't realize the debt they owe to Mary Kamm and her classes on statistical process control. This training helps maintain the quality and consistancy in the ice cream making production process. "It's a very dry and deadly subject," Kamm admits without hesitation.

A veteran of the food industry, mostly in the area of quality assurance, the 39-year-old Kamm joined Ben & Jerry's three years ago as the company's director of quality. "Our group is responsible for the product from the time it's designed to the time it goes out the door," she explained. "It includes people who would be considered R and D in most organizations." However, she said that since this is Ben & Jerry's, "we call ourselves the tech team."

One of Kamm's duties is technical training, although she has been involved in a variety of training efforts at Ben & Jerry's Waterbury, Vermont, headquarters simply because she "enjoys training." Her class on statistical process control, aimed at the 400 blue-collar workers in Ben & Jerry's two factories, is designed "to give people good decision-making tools," she said. "Specifically it gives the ice cream operators—the people running the equipment that makes ice cream—the tools to say this process is making the product that I want, or it's making a product that doesn't meet our standards." At the heart of the class is a subject that makes most everyone yawn or cringe—statistics. Aware of both the fear and boredom, Kamm always brightened the eight-hour course with charts and graphics which she presented the old-fashioned way, using transparencies and an overhead projector or magic markers on a white "black board."

Then she saw the "Rik and Joe show." "Rik and Joe had gotten together and they wrote this interactive program to be part of a kiosk at our tours operation," she said. "It was a neat little thing that told the story of the company and how ice cream was made." Since the Mac Guru and the G.U.I. Guy knew Kamm was a Macintosh fan, they showed it to her "just for fun." "And I said, 'that's really cool,'" she recalled. After the demonstration, the multimedia experiment stayed on her mind, "and I started thinking to myself, this is a great way to teach people things."

Callling on her decade-long experience with adult learning, Kamm became convinced that an interactive training program would have several advantages over her classroom presentation. In addi-

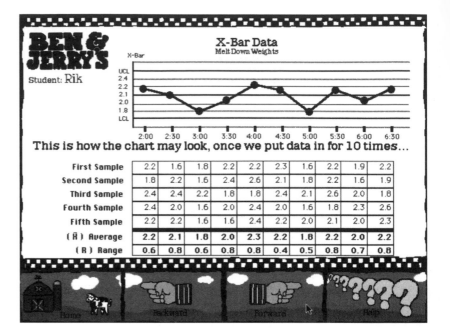

	2:00	2:30	3:00	3:30	4:00	4:30	5:00	5:30	6:00	6:30
First Sample	2.2	1.6	1.8	2.2	2.2	2.3	1.6	2.2	1.9	2.2
Second Sample	1.8	2.2	1.6	2.4	2.6	2.1	1.8	2.2	1.6	1.9
Third Sample	2.4	2.4	2.2	1.8	1.8	2.4	2.1	2.6	2.0	1.8
Fourth Sample	2.4	2.0	1.6	2.0	2.4	2.0	1.6	1.8	2.3	2.6
Fifth Sample	2.2	2.2	1.6	1.6	2.4	2.2	2.0	2.1	2.0	2.3
($\bar{X}$) Average	2.2	2.1	1.8	2.0	2.3	2.2	1.8	2.2	2.0	2.2
(R) Range	0.6	0.8	0.6	0.8	0.8	0.4	0.5	0.8	0.7	0.8

A Dull Topic: Mary Kamm was convinced multimedia would enliven her statistics-filled course.

tion to jazzing up a dull topic, it was highly desirable one-on-one learning. "We read time and time again, that that's the most effective way to transfer information," she said. "The learner learns at his own pace, and the program has pieces in it where, if a learner's not learning a concept, he or she can go another way and learn it. You don't get that in a classroom where you have thirty people go through a course in eight hours." And newcomers to the company "wouldn't have to wait until you have a class full of people again" to take the course, she added. At the same time, the time away from work would be reduced, she believed, since "it didn't slow people down if they were very quick and could pick up the concepts quickly. They could go through the course in two hours, where for other people it might take two days." In addition, Kamm's time teaching would be reduced. "Theoretically there's 40 hours in a week and, if I have to spend 32 of them teaching, it doesn't leave me much time to do the rest of my job."

As the idea jelled, Kamm began to bounce it off her colleagues in the spring of 1992. "I went back to Rik and Joe, and said, 'hey you guys, would this work?' And they said 'yeah,'" she said. Next in line was the head of the information services division, who agreed "it was a wonderful idea" and joined Kamm in proposing the project to the Quality Council, a management group composed of every company executive who reports to the president. The group, Kamm recalled with a sigh, "took some convincing." The biggest objection was to the cost in time and money since Kamm's course was already in place and "most people were more comfortable with the traditional classroom approach," Kamm continued, "but we put together some numbers of what it cost to pull people out in classroom situations versus letting them learn on their own, and we finally got the go-ahead for a pilot project."

THE TEAM: One G.U.I. Guy

In 1989, Rik Dryfoos was a new college graduate, with a degree in economics from the University of Vermont. Rather than chase down a Fortune 500 job in a big city, he found a way to mix work and play. "I started teaching snowboarding," the 27-year-old said. When the snow melted (as it eventually does, even in Vermont), Dryfoos took another seasonal job; he became a tour guide at one of the state's major visitor stops, Ben & Jerry's. Given the twists and turns in his career path, the move from just another guide to the G.U.I Guy was relatively simple.

Dryfoos' job became permanent, and during the three years he shared the mysteries of Wild Maine Blueberry and Apple Pie ice creams with tourists, he also began doing freelance graphic design using the Mac SE his parents had given him as a college graduate gift. "I was a tour guide and a Mac hacker," he said. "And I started doing graphics for cards and brochures. [I] hooked up with a lady who does it in town here." At the same time, he hung out in the Ben & Jerry's art department, fiddling with graphics on their Macintoshes, and getting to know Joe Wilkins, then an Oracle programmer. Hooked on the Mac, Dryfoos wound up at Mac World in San Francisco in 1991, where he was exposed to multimedia for the first time. Multimedia, Macs, tours, it all clicked for Dryfoos, who saw a way to use the new technology to supplement the

Multimedia Partners: Rik Dryfoos, left, and Mary Kamm, right, combined forces to create the company's first interactive training module.

company's guided tours. "I went to the director of information services," Dryfoos recalled, "told him that (a multimedia kiosk) would be cool and asked him if he would like me to follow up on it."

Dryfoos' timing was right. Recently, *the* Ben of Ben & Jerry's had met multimedia industry pioneer, Marc Cantor, the founder of MacroMind. Cantor had offered to make some Macs available to the ice-cream maker for a multimedia project. "Ben memoed that to our director of information services who passed it along to me and said, 'here's a place for you to get started,'" Dryfoos said. A few phone calls later, Dryfoos had in hand a short SyQuest demo from MacroMind. "I didn't even know what SyQuest was at that point," he confessed and took the disc to a local computer company to run. "(The owner) had MacroMind Director and he started tweaking it," he said. "We were pretty amazed at how easy it was to work with, so we (Joe Wilkins and Dryfoos) decided we could make a prototype (kiosk) ourselves."

One year later, at the 1992 Mac World, the "Rik and Joe show" was a reality "and probably the first kiosk there that used QuickTime," Dryfoos said. In the previous months, working mostly on their own time, the two partners had created a multimedia history of Ben & Jerry's using mostly existing graphics and video. The video was digitized into QuickTime using Diva's VideoShop (then in beta tests) and a modified Radius card. The program was authored in HyperCard. When the two developers returned to Vermont, the kiosk was set up in Ben & Jerry's Waterbury factory where it "generated crowds of people in an already cramped lobby. So it got taken down," Dryfoos said. "So that was the end of the 'Rik and Joe show' except that it fits into your story."

Fortunately, Dryfoos and Wilkins had dazzled another in-house Mac fan with their product, and when Mary Kamm decided to give multimedia a try, the G.U.I Guy and the Mac Guru were the logical recruits for her team. However, at the time, Rik was still a guide guy. "To free him up to work on this, we had to get approval," Kamm said. "Fortunately, the director of information services—that's where all the computer development is done-—was very much in support of it...so that piece of it was a fairly easy sell." To complete his transformation, all Dryfoos needed was his own Mac. Ben & Jerry's complied, purchasing a Quadra 950 with a VideoVision card for him to use. *Voila*—the G.U.I Guy.

PRODUCTION: Getting the Flavor of Technology

Working with Kamm's course outline and graphics gave Kamm and Dryfoos a running start on their first multimedia training program, and both expected to finish the project on time, in about six months. However, four months into the production, they displayed a prototype to the Quality Council. "It kinda hit everybody cold," said Kamm, who would work another four-plus months with Dryfoos to fine tune the program to suit her colleagues. In the end, about half of the completed work was redone. "It's not one of my skills," Dryfoos said in retrospect, "but with my next project, we are going to go out and talk to as many people as possible before we actually do any work."

Storyboarding and Scripting

To create the "Rik and Joe Show," Dryfoos had developed a flow chart for its branching and interactivity. However, for the multimedia version of the statistical process control class, Dryfoos and Kamm decided to rely on Kamm's existing course plan for the flow chart, and her overheads for the story boards. "I tend to be somebody who likes to learn using pictures and illustrations, particularly for something like statistics," Kamm explained. "So a lot of the funny cartoons in the training module were elaborations of things I had on my overhead."

Working from Kamm's course materials, the two partners brainstormed on "how to transpose her content into a new medium," Dryfoos said. "It was pretty linear, because each concept builds on the other, and there are conceptual bridges in between." Meeting at least three times a week, Kamm and Dryfoos "kinda chunked through" the information she wanted in the course. "She would talk about the material, and I would take notes, and we would create different screens," Dryfoos recalled. "We did it, just the two of us really, banged it out over lunch a lot of times. Then I would go off over the weekend, and work on bringing it to life."

Kamm said that one major challenge was to teach the concepts without a teacher. "A lot of the course was my teaching, which just didn't come through in the overheads," she realized. "How could someone answer a question and then get feedback and coaching when they didn't get it right, without my being there?" In their meetings, Kamm would pose the questions to Dryfoos, give him different possible answers and show how she would respond to each. "I provided the logic," Kamm said. "Rik found the tools to do it." The solution proved to be putting the questions in a HyperCard stack so that "if you got the right answer, it said, 'yea, you got it.' If you came up with the wrong answer, depending on what you picked, it would take you back and say, 'maybe you didn't consider this.' " The result was "not quite as much feedback as you could get from a teacher," Kamm said, "but we tried to simulate it as closely as we could."

Multimedia Q And A: Kamm and Dryfoos built in feedback to help users learn.

Looking back, Kamm and Dryfoos come to the same conclusion as most multimedia pioneers—plan ahead. "I think we learned a lot about organizing our time," Kamm said. "We should have been a lot more detailed with our storyboards. And we should have gotten a lot more user input along the way."

Graphics

No ice cream named Wavy Gravy belongs in an ordinary container, and, as Ben & Jerry's fans know, the company's cartons are as distinctive as their product. The same goofy, hand-drawn style was a natural for the training program. "It's the look and feel that you see all over the place here," explained Dryfoos. "The green hills and fields, the blue sky with the puffy clouds, Holsteins, checkerboards, no straight lines, chunky lettering that's all part of our art department look."

Gwen Severins, the former freelancer who came up with the distinct look, now presides over eight artists who make up the company's Mac-dominated art department. All were involved in the team effort to create lively graphics for the dull statistics course. "Having the typeface available, and some of the drawings from the art department, really cut down on the art I had to do," said Dryfoos, who takes credit for "the little weevil people" who stand-in for Ben & Jerry's employees in the training program. Other art work was "borrowed," he added, "like the art of the people looking up at the screen when you are watching a movie, that's actually part of a movie festival poster." And some images, like the ice cream container used in the module's many graphs, are "actually video (frame captures) of a pint of Cherry Garcia."

Funky Graphics: The clouds, cows and checkerboards identified with Ben & Jerry's were used in the training program.

For his share of original art work, Dryfoos relied on a Wacom pressure sensitive tablet, "a nice tool for the non-artist." Most illustrations, like the interface buttons and PICT files, were done with

UltraPaint, but "we don't use it any more," Dryfoos said. Midway through the project, he discovered Photoshop, "and that's the only one I have on my machine. I love it. Sometimes I'll use MacroMind Director for simple stuff, but a lot of times you have to jump out and use a real paint program."

Doing the animations, many of which were added after initial in-house reviews of the prototype, was a learning experience for Dryfoos. First, he had to master MacroMind Director, and that meant studying the manuals over weekends. One test of his new-found skills came when he had to replace a "silly" video of Kamm's white "blackboard." "We had videoed a teacher with a white board, which was hard to see and didn't add that much," he said. "So what we did was I turned my screen into that white board, put the information on it, and animated it." The process "took a little more time (than the video) which is why we originally went with the video...trying to save a little time."

Video

Given the goofy graphics that are Ben & Jerry's trademark and the "dry as dust" nature of statistics, one would hardly expect "Terminator" slick video in the training program. However, the resulting "talking heads" turned out to be too funky (i.e., amateur), even for the iconoclastic ice cream makers.

For Kamm's debut in a multimedia program, Dryfoos "put up a sheet behind his desk," grabbed a Panasonic S-VHS camcorder, and taped her lecturing. "If you listen, you can hear the telephone ringing," he quipped about his ad-hoc sound stage. "It was a just-get-it-done kind of thing. It could probably be more professional." Other company executives also were videoed, and their comments were inserted in different segments of the training program. "It was sort of a political maneuver on our part," Kamm said, "so that they felt like they were part of the process and we would get their support."

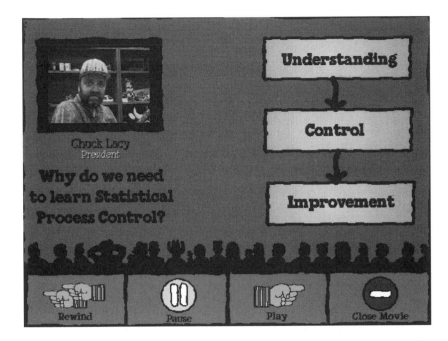

Talking Heads: How to use—but not over use—videos featuring company leaders proved difficult.

Professional or not, videoed or not, Kamm's fellow Quality Council members objected to "the over-use of talking heads," she said, when they first viewed the prototype. "I mean the video was cool and everything, but the talking heads were getting kind of boring." In other parts of the program, the video "seemed like overkill. Just hearing a voice or seeing a screen was enough. When we digitized the videos (with the Radius VideoVision card), they weren't really lifelike," she continued. "There's other software available now that makes it look more like true video, rather than a digitized computer thing." And, even at Ben & Jerry's, vanity reared its head. " 'My nose looks too big so I want you to reshoot this video' was one bit of feedback," Kamm said, with a laugh.

By the time the project was finished, much of the video had been eliminated or replaced by animation. "We were heavy on the videos at first," Kamm said, "and it was an enormous amount of work on Rik's part to take them out." That meant hundreds of adjustments in HyperCard that helped push the project months past its original deadline.

Interface Design and Navigation

Since the statistical process control course has a clearly defined beginning, middle and end, Dryfoos found it easy to keep the interface simple. "There are basically four buttons for navigating," he said. "Home, when you want to go home, or are done with the class; Backwards when you want to see what you just saw; Forward, to see what's next; and Help, to review." All four are spread across the bottom of the screen and identified with an icon drawn "Ben & Jerry's" style. And just to keep novice statisticians—and computer users—alert, many of the moves are accented with music and sounds, like cows mooing.

The simplicity of design is a nod to the program's audience, Dryfoos said. "A lot of the people who will use this have never dealt with computers before," he explained. "It's not like selling a title, where you are selling to someone who is involved with computers and probably has a good idea of what to do. A lot of times, this is their first, second, or third time in front of a computer." Those novice users also dictated the use of a track ball instead of a mouse for navigation. "Believe it or not, not everyone knows how to use a mouse," he continued. One non-computer person Dryfoos tapped to test the program first "touched the screen," he said. "I said, 'well, this isn't a touch screen...so use the mouse.' And he picked up the mouse and started waiving it in the air. So you can't make any assumptions." Except one. "Since Atari came up with 'Centipede,' most people know how to use the trackball."

Easy To Use: Easily understood graphics aid computer novices enrolled in the training program.

Authoring

The "Rik and Joe Show" may be collecting dust in a closet in Waterbury, but its soul lives on in the multimedia training program. "I just copied it and started gutting it," Dryfoos said. "So basically the 'Rik and Joe Show' is the engine that we use now for anything."

For the statistics course, Dryfoos said he had "four elements working together within HyperCard—the playing of MacroMind Director movies, QuickTime movies and the recording of the students' progress—where they left off and how many times they have come in to use it." The actual authoring was done in HyperCard, the animation in Director and QuickTime movies from VideoShop.

Dryfoos had learned the basis of HyperCard on his own, first while customizing his own computer address book and then while doing the "Rik and Joe show." VideoShop proved essential in creating the navigational structure since "you never have to script a button," he explained. "It's pretty amazing. You're in VideoShop, and you take a micon and drag it over your HyperCard stack, drop it on the stack and it scripts its own button. You can actually go in an edit that button if there are other things that need to happen." On the other hand, his use of Director was limited to an animation tool since, Dryfoos said that he didn't have time to learn its author language, Lingo.

Testing

When the multimedia training module was about two-thirds complete, Dryfoos and Kamm scheduled a presentation before the Quality Council. "We took it to the group initially, because those people are very hard to pin down, and we knew they would be in that meeting," Kamm said. The comments from that review sparked a series of extensive revisions that eventually would affect more than half of the prototype's content. "That was a learning experience for both of us," Kamm stressed. "What we did was, as we developed it, we asked people [for comments] along the way. But when they sat down and went through it, and really had a chance to critique it, it was obvious that there were things we had over-looked...questions on how to proceed, points that didn't come across clearly enough."

In addition to objections to too much "talking heads" video, Kamm's colleagues voiced concerns over the program's ease of use. "Some weren't comfortable with computers in the first place," she explained, "so making it as simple, as intuitive to use, was some of the feedback." Others, especially the company's president, co-founder Ben Cohen, raised questions on the content. "Our president tends to be somebody who anguishes over detail," she continued. "He'd go through and say, 'I really think you should make that point this way.' [His comments] were not about the program and the interactivity, but more questioning how I described things."

After the group session, Kamm scheduled individual reviews with many of the Council members, to seek detailed comments and "to watch how they interacted with the program." In the process, Kamm and Dryfoos noticed that some of their instructions generated different responses "so we changed [the instructions] so that people would respond to them in the same way," she said. They also discovered that "the jargon of statistics" was making parts of the course difficult to comprehend. "I guess this happens when you teach anything long enough," Kamm explained. "When I did that live, I could always explain when the students said they didn't understand. We tried to be cognizant of that when we wrote it, but we didn't get it all. So we had to re-make those things so that somebody with absolutely no understanding of manufacturing processes statistics could understand." Lapses in continuity also had to be corrected. "We had to make sure that we used the same terms so that they always translated," she added.

As they played the prototype for their colleagues, Kamm and Dryfoos noticed "redundancies and overkill." "We did this by section or concept," she said, "but when we looked at the whole thing together we edited a lot of stuff out ourselves. We also found some things that weren't emphasized enough." In retrospect, Dryfoos believes "we should have had more formal storyboards, or a listing of content at the very beginning, and then we should have gotten approval from various managers, from people who would be using it, so we wouldn't have had to trash all that stuff and rework it."

At the same time, the prototype also was tested by the factory workers, who were its target audience. "The same kinds of things came up," Kamm reported. As a result, she redrafted the wording of many of the questions and answers raised during the training session. "We had to do a lot more reinforcement, so that people understood why they picked the wrong answer." While she altered and fine-tuned the content, Dryfoos struggled to remove much of the video and add the replacement animations. "Those were probably the two biggest projects in the revision stage," Kamm said.

Before the training program won final approval, Kamm went back to the Quality Council another two times. In the end, "at least seventy percent of the changes were driven more by people's opinions of how things should be done, as opposed to true content changes," Kamm noted. By then, the project was three months late. Fortunately, the delay went largely unnoticed because of some major executive changes and a rapid rise in the demand for Ben & Jerry's ice creams. "That took a little of the heat off in terms of demand for its use," she said. Finally, in early 1993, the finished 150 megabyte program was installed in the company's plant, near its Waterbury headquarters.

In Use

Workers at Ben & Jerry's ice cream factory come to on-site "training stations" to use the new multimedia training tool. They take the course individually, and proceed at their own rate, Kamm said, "based on their schedule and ability to learn." To monitor students' progress, Dryfoos built in data collection that records "who started, who didn't finish, and how far along they got," Kamm said. "When they're done, it automatically prints out a little certificate." The feedback on the program's use is especially valuable since the training occurs away from the management headquarters. "It's hard for a company to drive this kind of training because its really in the hands of operations' people and it may not be a priority for them."

By the end of 1993, all of the workers at one factory and 50 more at the plant in Waterbury had completed the course. While most found it simple to use, Kamm learned that the course could not stand on its own. "The feedback we got was that it wasn't quite enough to make them feel comfortable," she said. "What they really needed was a resource on-site to reinforce what they'd learned." As a result, the company is training a site coordinator to fill that role. "So if a worker sees a particular pattern on a control chart and isn't sure what it's telling them, he has somebody to bounce it off of," Kamm said. This follow-up, she pointed out, isn't unique to multimedia training, "but it's clear, to make it really effective, you need that support and we've had to go back and do it."

One selling point for this innovative form of training was that it would take less time than a conventional classroom course. Kamm still is confident that's the case, although she has not had time to document it. "I suspect that with people who would be pretty comfortable with the basic concepts anyway, that it saved them a lot of time. Someone fairly comfortable with mathematics could probably go through it in a couple of hours rather than

On-Site Training: The finished program was installed in "training stations" at Ben & Jerry's factories.

spend eight hours in a classroom," she said. "A lot of times, in classroom situations, you teach to the slowest person, and everybody else kind of drags along."

Even if there is less time needed, training is still time off-line. "A lot of people like it," Dryfoos said of his visits to the plant, "but when I go up there they get apologetic and say, 'oh, I really haven't had time to finish it yet'.... We are finding that it is not always a priority to get people through this training program. They have their other day-to-day stuff that they are more focused on. We have to realize that we can create all the training programs we want, but until people have time to use them, they won't be implemented all the way." "It's frustrating," Kamm added, "but having been in a role where I've had to train people in operations, it wasn't unexpected."

THE FUTURE: The Scoop on Multimedia

Despite its labored birth, multimedia training is beginning to catch on at Ben & Jerry's. Kamm, convinced that "it works," is eyeing this form of training for another course—laboratory testing. "I don't know if you've ever looked at a standard lab manual, but they are pretty dry," she said, "so what I was thinking about doing for tests that we don't run a lot, or for new people who need to learn a procedure, would be to make these modules interactive where they could see illustrations and clips of video. They would be for training, as well as a refresher."

One group of "true believers," according to Kamm, were the designers of the new Ben & Jerry's plant in northern Vermont, that opened in mid-1994. "They incorporated some of the interactive concepts into online control systems, so that operators running automated processors could take the data that piece of equipment collects and manipulate it while online, using the visual method we used in our training program." To make that a reality, Dryfoos joined them on-site for a time early in the year "just to give them support."

When he isn't out of the office, the G.U.I. Guy, now his own subdepartment of Information Services, has been transforming many of the company's communications with multimedia. "I think we will end up using it as an information dissemination tool within the company," he said. "Everything from current events, to bulletin board, charts and graphs, logos. I see that as a really good niche for the tool...a place where it can add value to what's going on." He's also eyeing a technological update of the slide show that's currently part of the Ben & Jerry's tour, as well as working with Kamm again on her next multimedia training project. And he found time to create a year-in-review video. "We morphed several different plant managers...and had a good laugh."

He'll probably also find time to have a few words with the Primal Ice Cream Therapist. After all, the Information Age deserved its own Ben & Jerry's flavor. Maybe the sign that multimedia is finally mainstream will be found in grocery stores everywhere, as shoppers scoop up pints of Gigabyte.

Multimedia Mailing List: One of Dryfoos' recent projects was an interactive program to update the company's personnel files.

10

HOLIDAY INN WORLDWIDE'S RATE AND INVENTORY MANAGEMENT PROGRAM

MicroMentor, Inc.

At A Glance

THE RATE AND INVENTORY MANAGEMENT PROGRAM

Developer: MicroMentor, Inc.

Client: The Franchise Service Delivery Organization, Holiday Inn Worldwide.

Personnel: For MicroMentor: Eric Vogt, president; and Cindy Steinberg, senior project manager and lead learning designer; Bill Taylor, lead developer; Julie Schlack, learning designer; Jeff Rand, developer; Judy Atwood, graphic designer; and David Willoughby, graphic artist. For Holiday Inn Worldwide: Jewell DeWeese, vice president, franchise service and education; Diane Van Kuren, subject matter expert, property executive training; and Irene Simoneaux, subject matter consultant.

Description: This one-hour multimedia training module challenges the newly hired general manager of a "virtual hotel" to raise revenues by 15 percent over

12 months. After touring the hotel, interacting with personnel and observing operations, the user finds problems and recommends solutions that will increase revenues. Once all these management decisions are made and tabulated, a graph displays resulting revenue gains or losses, and the learner receives a detailed report of his or her work.

Development period: September 1992 to November 1992.

Production hardware: Various IBM 486s and Macintosh IIs.

Production software: Audiovisual Connection (AVC), SuperCard, Adobe Photoshop, and Corel Draw!

Presentation hardware: IBM PS/2 Ultimedia Model 57.

Cost: $125,000.

Financing: Client paid.

Future projects: Conversion of all Property Executive Training programs to multimedia. Courses include training for general managers and guest service, sales, and food and beverage managers.

Contact: Jewell DeWeese or John Lipscomb
             Holiday Inn Worldwide
             Three Ravinia Drive, Suite 2000
             Atlanta, GA 30346
             404–604–2000

             Cindy Steinberg
             MicroMentor, Inc.
             124 Mt. Auburn Street
             Cambridge, MA 02138
             617–868–8500
             617–497–5716 (fax)

I t's your first day on the job as manager of the Placid Valley Holiday Inn. You've been with this huge international chain for almost two years now, working your way up from desk clerk to head of the front office at another Holiday Inn. Your promotion, after only six months in your first management position, took everyone by surprise, but you know as much about how to run a hotel as almost anyone on the staff. After all, you're an old-timer by industry standards.

Before you settle into your office, Jack, the bellman, will take you on a tour, introduce you to your co-workers, and acquaint you

On The Front Lines: Holiday Inns around the country are the focus of the corporation's investment in new technology.

with the community. You have a lot to learn fast. Business has been dropping off, and your boss expects big things of you—like a 15 percent increase in revenues—in twelve months. If you don't do something fast to fill all those vacant rooms, there's going to be another vacancy—your brand-new office.

As you follow Jack from the lobby, a few things catch your eye and your ears. Headlines in the local newspaper announce a new office park opening nearby. The head of catering couldn't be talking to a potential customer with that tone in his voice, could he? In a fax just in, a travel agent wonders how close the hotel is to the dinosaur theme park, Placid Valley's main tourist attraction. That maid wouldn't ignore the do-not-disturb sign on the door of that executive suite, would she?

Back at your desk, you scratch your head. There are some big problems that need to be solved, some basic tenets of the hospitality industry that need to be reinforced, and some obvious—and not-so-obvious—opportunities that need attention. Where to begin? You click pause, and smile. Amazing how like the real world a "virtual hotel" can be.

For hundreds of Holiday Inn managers, the Placid Valley "virtual hotel" has been their training ground, a place where learning one of the industry's driest essentials—rate and inventory management—is almost as much fun as a video game. Since its completion in a whirlwind three months in late 1992, the multimedia program has excited top executives and newcomers alike, many of whom "play" it again and again, hoping to boost their "scores." One enthusiast is Michael Leven, president of The Americas for Holiday Inn Worldwide, who encourages everyone in the company to complete the hour-long simulation because "it's such a good orientation to the industry."

This innovative training program, developed for $125,000 by MicroMentor, a Cambridge, Massachusetts, leader in business learning, is a showpiece of Holiday Inn Worldwide's $60 million investment in new technology and technology-based employee training. The move, a first in the hotel industry, also puts Holiday Inn in the forefront of corporate multimedia users. Central to the change is the installation of new IBM Ultimedia PS/2 computers dedicated to

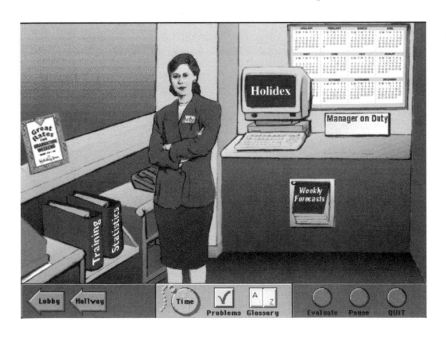

At The Front Desk: Holiday Inn's multimedia training is based on realistic scenarios in a "virtual hotel."

employee training in each of the chain's almost 1,800 hotels around the world. By mid 1994, approximately one-third of these multimedia terminals with CD-ROM drives, color monitors, and 16-bit audio were in place. In addition to the Rate and Inventory Management Program, the hotel chain also is developing multimedia instruction for its new custom global property management and reservation systems. In the future, multimedia training modules on planning and revenue management for key hotel managers will be created as part of the company's effort to both standardize training and reduce its cost.

Jewell DeWeese, Holiday Inn Worldwide's savvy vice president for franchise service and education, helped pave the way for the hotel chain's substantial commitment in time and resources to multimedia desktop learning. In the process, she confronted all of the predictable obstacles in a large organization to this type of innovation—resistance to change, funding, departmental in-fighting. Her need to produce a successful model program subsequently pushed MicroMentor quickly into overdrive, initially without the benefit of clear direction. The tense three months that followed exemplify challenges of doing multimedia business in the high-stakes corporate world where a program often has to succeed on a number of levels if technological innovation is to continue.

DeWeese would be the first to argue that the risks she took were outweighed by the potential benefits of effective training, however. More than other traditional forms of training, she believes, interactive multimedia lessons capture and hold the student's attention. "The thing that makes the learning so superior is the fact that you are engaged," she said. "That's the magic that you cannot get in the classroom."

THE OPPORTUNITY: Finding Room to Learn

Jewell DeWeese couldn't possibly know all of Holiday Inn's employees. After all, the chain spans the globe, and its staff—from franchise owners to bellboys—numbers in the tens of thousands. But she knows a lot about the challenges they face as a home-away-from-home for millions of travellers annually. "I went around the world four times for Holiday Inn," she said, in a brief summary of her career with the international innkeeper. "I opened hotels in Japan, Singapore, Hong Kong, Sri Lanka. I worked in Europe, and in about forty states. My experience was the one that I am now in charge of doing something about." As vice president for franchise service and education, her post since 1991, DeWeese spearheads "what we can do for hotels, for hotel management, and for owners" from the company's North American headquarters in Atlanta. "How can you service a system that has almost 1,800 units, in 58 countries? It's awesome beyond words," she said. "You could get overwhelmed in a hurry."

Most of her efforts in education have been colored by some unavoidable facts of life in the hospitality business. Foremost is the high turnover of employees. "I know that people take jobs in hotels until they can get jobs in something else," she said. "I know that they hire lots of students, lots of immigrants. We have a very diverse work force, basically with low skill levels, and often with low education levels, especially in certain areas of the hotel. I'm not sure we should look at it as a problem. It's just the way life is." At the same time, many of these workers are on the hotel's "front lines"; they are the ones serving guests and influencing whether or not the guests enjoy their stay. "Obviously, the demand for job proficiency is high," she said. Frequently, under-prepared staff members advance simply because they have more longevity than anyone else, DeWeese said, again speaking from personal experience. At one hotel, she recalled, "I worked in guest services and then became a front office manager. Then—get this—in six months, I was the manager. Not because I was extraordinary, but because I was the only one who had been there. I happen to have been conscientious, but there is no doubt in my mind that people who are not qualified get these jobs everyday. And what price do we pay for that? It's huge. It's huge."

Jewell DeWeese: Holiday Inn Worldwide's vice president for franchise services and education worked in inns around the world.

Because staff come and go so quickly, training often gets short shrift. "Owners and hotel managers hesitate to make tremendous investments in people who won't be around for very long," DeWeese continued. "So it has always been a part of life that people neglect the training that should happen. You could spend millions, millions, millions and millions, and it would be like falling in a black hole, because people change incredibly fast. You just get someone where you need them to be, and they're gone. So that is why you start saying, is there any way to get it done faster, more effectively?"

During its 41-year history, Holiday Inn executives repeatedly have grappled with the dilemma of training a high-turnover staff. "It has changed a myriad of times," DeWeese said, as she flipped through an inventory of seminars, training materials, and job aids made available by the hotel's corporate headquarters. "There have been times in our history when we have had a great deal more [than we have today]." In the past, most of the efforts involved off-site classes, that often proved a hindrance to training since sending an employee was generally costly and left a crucial staffing gap for days, even weeks, at a time. "On-site training never really existed; it's just a void," she admitted. "We created job aid, we created training programs. And in some of those, we would do area workshops to get the general manager and the guest service manager trained to go back and implement the customer service program. We still sort of do it that way." Implemented in April

Trying To Teach: Over the years, the giant innkeeper has tried a variety of training programs.

1993, a new program, the franchise service delivery organization (FSDO), sends a consultant to each hotel four to six times annually to focus on revenue and service management. "This again is management training, rather than employee training," DeWeese noted.

In the past, the company also has experimented with new technology to expand training opportunities. "We were the first chain to do videos," DeWeese pointed out. "We put VCRs in every hotel fifteen years ago for training purposes. It was called Vidnet, video network training. We don't even use those things anymore. I think it was a great idea, video training. It served us very well at the moment." In the '90s, multimedia will play a similar role, DeWeese continued. "Video was the best way to cope at that time, just as multimedia is the best way to cope with this time."

The opportunity to introduce multimedia into Holiday Inn's training grew out of the company's decision to upgrade its company-wide computer system. In March 1992, the chain, owned by Bass PLC of the United Kingdom, announced a $60 million investment in two new software programs and the advance computer hardware

to run them. "Mike [Leven] and I were both saying, there is no way in hell that this is going to fly [without training]," DeWeese recalled. "The people who sell that system walk away from that hotel with things running well, [and] six weeks later they will have had a turnover. Who will teach the new guy what he needs to know?" Concerned, the two executives "contacted the guy in charge of the project, and told him it may be his responsibility to get the system in, but it was our responsibility to live with it," she continued. "The only way to survive would be to help the franchisees live with it. They *must* be trained. So it put us in a spot where we've never been before. There was no way to do without. There was no way to survive."

DeWeese immediately focused on multimedia-based training "as a way to save a lot of money on the implementation of this $60 million system." Other options weren't even considered, she said

Computer Update: When Holiday Inn introduced new computer hardware and software, DeWeese immediately saw a need for high-tech training.

after consultations with the firm's Information Technology and Emerging Technology departments. "They were comfortable with multimedia," she said. "There are a lot of creative things happening. And it was pretty solidly here, not off on the horizon somewhere." There were concerns about obsolescence since the training sequences developed would have to "stay in service" for several years, but DeWeese was convinced "there would be ways to enhance and upgrade them without throwing out hardware."

The advantages of computer-delivered, interactive training were numerous. Regardless of the site or the diversity of employees, the training message would be consistent. Employees would be able to learn at their own pace, yet, would probably spend fewer hours with the interactive lesson than they would have in the classroom. Since most of the learning would take place at individual hotels, there would be less disruption of hotel operations and a reduction in training costs. "Those are some of the reasons a multimedia system is going to be such a savior for us," DeWeese said. "I really look at it that way. We've said it is insurance, a savior. With those kind of words, you know our expectations are great. They are just awesome."

With the urging of several key executives, the Holiday Inn Worldwide Board of Directors agreed to hire a nearby firm to produce a multimedia training program to introduce its far-flung staff to the new computer and reservation system. However, when those multi-hour modules were delayed, DeWeese grew concerned that the company's commitment to interactive training would waiver. That was when she proposed moving ahead with the first of two multimedia management courses that would be funded out of the franchise services budget and would be completed by the end of the fiscal year—less than three months away. It was a high-stakes risk, but at year's end, it had paid off. Said a proud John Lipscomb, the company's project manager, "We're now the poster child for the way these projects should be done and done effectively,"

THE TEAM: In Training for Learning

Jewell DeWeese needed a showpiece multimedia training demonstration, and she needed it fast. One man came immediately to mind: Eric Vogt, president of MicroMentor. "I knew Eric because we have been to several conferences together," she explained. "I'm responsible for education, for training—but learning is probably the right word. I'm into learning big time, and he is too. He helped us establish a vision for our division. Plus they do this kind of work, so he was a natural."

The fortysomething Vogt brings backgrounds in education and business to his work at MicroMentor, the "business learning" firm he founded in 1982. A former consultant who specialized in corporate strategy, Vogt joined the faculty at the Harvard Business School and taught MBA students, before striking out on his own. "Basically we blended together work and learning, rather than separating them from each other," he said. "We borrowed some techniques from the Harvard Business School, and there are some principles we believe in, like discovery learning, and case-oriented grounding of the learning experience." What he doesn't like is *training*, a word

Eric Vogt: Business learning is the focus of the firm this former Harvard professor founded in 1982.

he believes should be "used only as an adjective for wheels and bras." The difference, he believes, is that "training is something you do to people; learning is something that is insightful, that comes from the participant. ... So the training mentality says, 'I can identify twelve things you need to learn, and I'm going to open the top of your head and pour it in. Then you're done. You don't need to think.'" A learning design, on the other hand, is "much more like saying, 'hey, this is wide open, we're just scratching the surface, but here are some models for continuing to learn.'"

In the learning process, multimedia is one of several available tools and its effectiveness depends on the right combination of "the principles of learning and the principles of using multimedia effectively." "Multimedia can be an extraordinary tool, but we spend a lot of time talking about the discipline of learning design," he said. "One problem is that most corporations are unconsciously following an implicit learning methodology from 1904. It is entirely possible to take multimedia mindlessly and to codify all those archaic practices. So, I predict you're going to see some really terrible implementations of multimedia over the next decade. But for those people who think outside the box, who redesign the learning process conceptually, who think differently about what they are up to—from [these people] you will see some really nifty multimedia implementations."

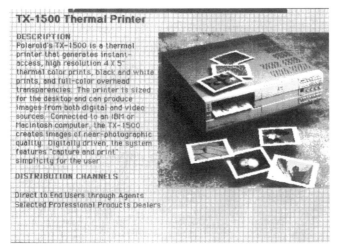

Desktop Learning: MicroMentor's clients include Polaroid, which uses multimedia to teach quality control.

In MicroMentor's early days, multimedia learning consisted of using computers and computer software—games, simulations, etc.—in workshops the company conducted for Citibank, Ernst & Young, and other major clients. Then, about four or five years ago, Vogt said, he saw the power of multimedia in the classroom. "The business school was given a gift, simultaneously, by Apple and IBM," he recalled. "IBM gave them about $5 million in PS/2 equipment to be used as a creative exchange. Apple gave them about $5 million in Macintoshes. The business school said thank you very much and then came to us and said, 'how might this change the way we learn?' So we started experimenting." One trial linked the digitized voice of a professor to an Excel spreadsheet. "Suddenly we had our first talking spreadsheet," he said. "The professor spoke at appropriate times and explained the conceptual material." When executives in Harvard's advance management program tried it out, "they had a different kind of learning experience," Vogt said. "The business-school professor said he had never seen a group so well prepared. So right away, we noticed the difference from spending two hours with a paper-based case, as they were normally doing at the Harvard Business School, to spending an hour or less in an early interactive multimedia learning experience."

The other lesson learned from this seminal experiment has shaped MicroMentor's approach to multimedia programs. "We noticed that a lot of learning can in fact be accomplished by using the voice creatively, as opposed to investing in full-motion video," Vogt said. "If you think about what experiences have shaped your own learning as you grew up, often you remember a voice—a friend's, your parent's, a teacher's. So our bias as a firm is to move at right angles to a lot of what we call the glitzy full-motion development and exploit all we can from a blending of the voice with the visual, with the interactivity, in such a way as to engage the human mind at a higher level." The resulting programs are less expensive, and easier to update than those with extensive video clips. Vogt does not rule out the use of video, but he believes that its role in multimedia learning needs "some exploration and reflection, which is all a part of learning process, which I highly endorse."

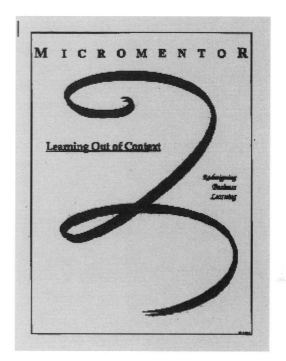

For The Information Age: Vogt argues that Industrial Age learning techniques won't work today.

When Vogt and DeWeese first worked together, the focus was "shifting the organization to a learning organization," he recalled. As a consultant to the worldwide innkeeper, Vogt knew DeWeese also had set her sights on desktop learning. What he couldn't have foreseen at the time is that his firm would be picked to develop the prototype course—or that it would be such a demanding assignment. "Our basic challenge," he said, "was to take something that was quite dry, that always received the lowest scores in live classroom, and figure out how to convey it in less time and in a more engaging manner—with better results." The choice of Rate and Inventory, he remembers, was outside his hands. "They picked it," he said. "Jewell and I had come up with five potential topics, and I remember meeting with Mike Leven just before dinner. He looked over the five and made his pick. That's how Rate and Inventory became what we were going to do, and do in a very fast turnaround time as well."

Under normal circumstances, when approached by a new client or one new to multimedia, Vogt shows them what he calls "the seven to nine flavors of desktop learning" to open their eyes to options. "In the past, we erred when we just showed people one example and then went into design and production, and three months later, realized that they had only one example in mind," he explained. "Obviously to us there are seven to nine different flavors of desktop learning, but to them, there was only what they had seen. Then they wanted to know why we weren't building exactly what we showed them." By introducing clients to the range of "architectures" available, Vogt believes he "engages their mind's eye in building a vision" of what they want. He also closes the sophistication gap about current desktop learning. "Some [clients] come already knowing what they want; others honestly don't know anything about it or how it fits in the context of an overall corporate learning process."

With customers like Holiday Inn, Vogt prefers to work in what he's dubbed "a committed co-creative process. Which is to say," he continued, "we prefer that our clients give us a couple of people who are going to be part of the team." That working relationship "establishes the knowledge, understanding, and trust between the client and the MicroMentor team" that enhances the brainstorming and design phases ahead. As the Holiday Inn project got underway, Vogt negotiated hard with DeWeese to put a Holiday Inn staff member on the MicroMentor team. Eventually, Diane Van Kuren, a member of the Holiday Inn's property executive training staff who taught rate and inventory classes, among other subjects, became the project's content expert and a key member of the MicroMentor team. In the heat of the development process, she spent days at a time at MicroMentor's Cambridge headquarters.

The MicroMentor team was headed by thirtysomething Cindy Steinberg, a learning designer who had joined the company a year earlier. Her interest in "how technology and media can facilitate learning" dates to the late 1970s, when she was a graduate student studying cognitive psychology. Her work for a number of visionary research firms and startup companies in the early and mid-1980s included the development of management training programs on videodiscs, artificial intelligence expert system software, and an award-winning interactive videodisc that helped medical students learn about the cardiovascular system. Among her teammates were two freelancers who had worked on a number of previous MicroMentor projects: David Willoughby, a Princeton University-educated engineer who switched to graphic design and desktop publishing in the early '80s, and Bill Taylor, an experienced programmer who had assisted Vogt with previous projects.

The Holiday Inn team was typical of MicroMentor's approach, Vogt said. "We have a project manager to act as a liaison with the client and lead the team," he explained. "That person may or may not be the learning designer. If not, we have a learning designer. Then we will have a lead software architect, a graphic designer and possibly an interface designer and at least one of those two will be involved early on." In the early phase, "what we try to understand is what this deal is all about what knowledge and skills do we need to imbed in the learning experience." MicroMentor's team, then, must be adept at "honing in on the key pieces of understanding quickly," Vogt said. "I credit people like Cindy Steinberg for having the capacity to guide the design process and extract from Holiday Inn professionals the requisite perspective and knowledge."

Before pulling her team together, Steinberg and her associate, learning designer Julie Schlack, flew to Holiday Inn's Atlanta head-quarters for a crash course in rate and inventory management that included sitting in on classes taught by Van Kuren, talking with their fellow students, and interviewing key executives. That kind of involvement paid off, not only in the product but in client relations. The rate and inventory course "is so on target," DeWeese said. "And I give the credit to MicroMentor and the project manager. They lived with us. ... and we did almost as much work as they did. They knew their business and we knew ours, and I tell you it can't be done without both."

PRODUCTION: Just Inn Time

The clock was ticking rapidly toward deadline as the MicroMentor team began the feverish round of brainstorming meetings on the Holiday Inn multimedia course. With less than three months to develop the segment, "Jewell had asked for almost the impossible," Vogt said. "She had this pot of money that had to be spent by October 1 [1992]. So we had to work pretty hard to be 'substantially complete' by then when the concept was only being sketched out in late August."

Confronted with that deadline, Steinberg and her crew first responded with a healthy "no way, no way at all," Taylor recalled. "The first thing we did at the meeting was to ask Cindy to go back to the clients and tell them that they are not going to get it in four weeks. It turned out that they really did have a hard deadline, but Cindy worked with them on how best to satisfy their accounting needs and give us an extension of a couple of more weeks to smooth out the development process." Even with the slight give in the deadline, Steinberg's team "did a lot of things simultaneously," Taylor continued. "We would have meetings once a week, then all of us would go off and start doing various parts of the project," he continued. "She would be talking with the client and developing content with them."

During the ensuing seven weeks of almost round-the-clock work, there would be some tense moments as the project came together. Three weeks before the "outrageous" deadline, Steinberg made an emergency trip to Atlanta. "I wasn't getting enough of Diane (Van Kuren's) time; she was under a lot of pressure to deliver in other areas," Steinberg recalled. "I told Jewell (DeWeese), 'if I don't have Diane next week, we can't make this date.'" Consequently she freed Diane to work on the project. With that obstacle removed, the team, remarkably, was able to complete the project in November and unveil the interactive course before Holiday Inn's management group in December. And just in case you think that all's well that ends well, Vogt puts it all in perspective: "It was a ball-buster."

The Script

Start with a topic that's dull, dull, dull. Add a mandate to bring it to life. Spice with an impossible deadline. And bring in a creative team to mix it up. The result? In Holiday Inn's case, it's an engaging, funny, challenging take on a key area of hotel management, that now seems more like a detective game than a required course. The key leavening agent is humor, a natural outcome of the tight development schedule, Vogt believes. "When you have a team working around the clock, under pressure, you have a lot of humor," he said.

For a grounding in rate and inventory, the skill that keeps a hotel full and thriving, Steinberg dropped in on a class Van Kuren was teaching. "I didn't know what she was there for at first," Van Kuren said. "I knew that she was a consultant, looking at some of our training materials. But that was all." When she learned what was planned, Van Kuren, who had never seen a multimedia presentation, responded with a mix of skeptical enthusiasm—"gee, it would be neat if you could do that,"—and dread—"you're going to replace me."

"It was a brief feeling, because they're only doing one part of the course," Van Kuren continued. Previous efforts to incorporate computers into this curriculum had failed. "My other thought was,

Diane Van Kuren:
Since she had taught the rate and inventory class, Van Kuren was MicroMentor's content expert.

'how are you going to make this exciting?' Because it's dull and mundane; it's very tedious and a lot of work. It's something that has to be done." In the day-long training sessions, without a lot of group interaction and activities, "you'll have them yawning; you'll put them to sleep," she said.

After class, when Steinberg and Van Kuren got together, the Holiday Inn teacher was very impressed with her new student. "She had picked up the concepts really fast," Van Kuren said. "I would have no problem letting her run one of our hotels." "One of the things I specialize in," Steinberg acknowledged, "is in learning diverse information really quickly and trying to structure it for presentation to a novice audience." Steinberg also recognized almost immediately that Van Kuren was the content expert she desperately needed. "Diane knew the content best, had the hotel experience I wanted, and could explain things clearly," she recalled.

Based on her class experience, Steinberg was determined to make the multimedia version "more engaging. They were teaching rate and inventory with some arcane overheads that had tons of number in them from computer reports so when it came to rate and inventory, class size would dwindle, everyone's eyes would glaze." She also experienced first-hand the diversity of Holiday Inn's audience for this course. "Some people had been on the job for ten years and some for ten days, so I knew that the program we would build required a really rich environment, one in which the more you worked on it, the more you got out of it." Based on conversations with Mike Leven and other executives, she knew she wanted to "foster a long-range view of hotel operations that expands the context in which rate and inventory operates since a lot of the concern was that the franchisees were taking a really short-term view of their businesses. They needed to do better business planning and long-range forecasting to coordinate what was happening in the hotel with what was going on outside in the community."

With all of those diverse demands to meet, Steinberg clicked on the idea of "a fictitious hotel" and the Placid Valley Holiday Inn was born. "Julie and I thought of a Midwestern hotel in a university town that had a decline in corporate market share, but had a leisure business potential that could be developed. Julie is very creative and funny, and she came up with the dinosaur [theme] park idea before anyone had heard of *Jurassic Park*. There were a number of things that she thought of that were great." Eventually they would create the characters who fill the hotel lobby and its executive offices, including the new manager faced with increasing revenues by fifteen percent, and the "old director of sales, with a bad attitude." Finally, they "added realism" by giving the new manager twelve months to turn the hotel around.

Still in Atlanta, Steinberg remembers "locking Diane and her associate Irene Simoneaux in a conference room for four days" and papering the walls with problems and solutions at what would become the "virtual hotel." Van Kuren focused on scenarios "that happened most frequently in a hotel, although I would hate to see a hotel with that many problems. I wanted to make sure that the problems were real-world ones, [ones] that we most often consult on or that I experienced when I ran a hotel." In addition, Van Kuren strove to underline procedures "that we're always trying to encourage our hotels to do. A lot of our hotels don't do business planning, even though it's something we preach to them. So we wanted to give them an example of how, if you had a business plan, it would help you out. Hopefully that would peak their interest." The use of an imaginary hotel, she believed, was very effective in helping managers "see problems with fresh eyes, without all the baggage that comes with their own property."

A "Virtual Hotel": Steinberg and her team created a fictitious hotel with real-world problems.

Because of the tight deadline, Steinberg had to push everyone. "It was a lot of work, it really was," Van Kuren recalled. "They were very demanding in terms of time, but they had a very aggressive schedule." At one point, Steinberg "called in two experts in rate and inventory and had them look at everything we had written up. They liked it, and could find very few things wrong with it. So we knew we were on the right track."

Steinberg also knew her concept was "radically different from anything Holiday Inn had ever done since they, like most corporations, teach in the traditional mode, the way we were taught in school." On the other hand, MicroMentor's programs generally use simulations "to get people involved. We talk about this circular diagram where content or information is the inner circle, the next circle is process or how it applies to your job, and the outer circle is context or why is this important anyway. Usually what goes on in a classroom is content at the expense of process or context. We try to create context." In the case of Holiday Inn, that meant showing how to get the big picture and use that information to build hotel revenue. "If you don't integrate it with work, people won't retain it.

It's that simple," Steinberg said.

Back in Cambridge, surrounded by her team and with major assistance from Van Kuren, Steinberg and Schlack fleshed out the content into storyboards, after considering all the ramifications of each problem the new general manager would face. "We had a couple of really key group meetings that everyone contributed to," Steinberg said. "Julie and I wrote the specific [dialogue], but a lot of the ideas for the humorous scenes came from our meetings." Building light moments into serious study is a major tenet of Steinberg's personal philosophy of learning. "I have a personal life-long commitment to learning," she stressed. "And my entire life view is that learning should be fun—always." So should the team experience, she added: "I think you have to trust that everybody has good ideas." Another of Steinberg's tenets is that no one can develop a multimedia project on his or her own: "If anyone ever tells you that, don't believe them. It's just too complicated, too many pieces of information [must be incorporated], and if it's going to be good, if it's going to work, you need a team."

With the pressure of an "outrageous deadline," Steinberg benefited from an informal review process. "Lots of times on projects, there will be these review cycles that really delay things and take a lot of the creativity out," she said. " What happened here, probably because of the time constraints was that Jewell trusted me that we knew what we were doing. She gave us a lot of leeway." In return, Steinberg kept her client well informed at every stage of the production. "I gave her updates, storyboards, documents showing what the fictitious hotel was going to look like," she said. "I also touched base with key people who have a stake in content, so we had their blessing."

In the end, Van Kuren became a multimedia believer. "I think the approach is really neat," Van Kuren said, reflecting on the finished product. "I think it's a fun learning experience. We really achieved that. It's almost like a game. But I wouldn't have believed it on that first day." Now, she admits, she's eager to work on more multimedia learning projects—"with a little more time, of course."

Interface Design

The first screen that students see in the multimedia course on rate and inventory is the entrance to the mock hotel, with its familiar green Holiday Inn sign. To begin, they click on the door and move into the lobby. There, instead of a menu of functions and instructions, they are greeted by Jack, the bellman, who takes them on a tour of their new property. In the process, he explains how the program works.

This user-friendly approach grows out of one of Steinberg's standards for interactive programs: "If it's going to take me anymore than three minutes to figure out the interface, it's too complicated, it's not elegant," she insists. "The point is, I'm trying to teach rate and inventory, not how to interact with the program." Steinberg believes that too many multimedia programs "spend an inordinate amount of time trying to teach the user how to use them. I think that just gets in the way. I remember this great application I saw a year or two ago. It was graphically gorgeous and got a lot of buzz in the industry. But I couldn't believe how difficult it was to use. So I was frustrated. I didn't have the time to figure out how to use it."

Working from this philosophy, Steinberg began the Holiday Inn module with disarming simplicity: "You click on the front door and you're in." The explanatory tour with Jack—the result of a brainstorming session—"keeps everything in the context of the hotel and makes perfect sense, because the first person you see when you go into a hotel is the bellman," she said. As the students make the

A Familiar Guide: Jack, the bellman, tells users how the program works.

rounds, they are introduced to the many hot-spots that position them for "discovery learning." "You move from room to room simply by clicking on doors," Steinberg said. "To get behind the front desk, where all the offices are, you click on the door, and behind it is another set of doors that say sales manager's office, general manager's office."

The bellman also explains that "the student" can interview people, poke into files and read newspapers, brochures, and even incoming faxes. He also points out the clock that times the course— twelve months at the fictional hotel, but only an hour in real time— and the glossary button, that, when clicked, explains unfamiliar phrases or terms. Finally, he introduces the problem checklist, which amounts to a simple way of keeping score. Anytime one of the almost two dozen problems in the hotel is discovered, the students check it off on that list. That click in turn opens a pop-up window with a number of right and wrong solutions to the problem. Responses to these choices ultimately affect the hotel's revenue, and the student's score in the game.

The clock, checklist, and glossary are centered in an unobtrusive gray stripe at the bottom of the full color screens. When students leave the lobby, an arrow appears to the left, that, when clicked,

A Simple Interface:
A strip of buttons across the bottom of the screen is user-friendly.

will take them back there or to whichever office they last visited. At the far right, in addition to the buttons for pause and quit, is one for evaluation. This button produces a graph displaying the percentage of revenue growth. Seeing that percentage turns the course into a competition, Vogt notes. "I re-

member playing for the first time, in the prototype mode," he said, "and I only had 8 or 9 percent, instead of 15. And my immediate reaction was, 'I want to do that again.'"

Graphics

Two of the flashy components of multimedia presentations are missing from the rate and inventory course-—animation and digitized video. "There wasn't anything in this application that warranted them," Steinberg said. "The way I feel is that if there is a place for them, and if you really need them, use them. If not, don't." As a result, the Holiday Inn project relies on computer graphics for its visual impact.

Because of that emphasis, Willoughby and graphic designer Judy Atwood experimented with a new graphic style, "the use of illustrations, instead of photographs, to create a real environment." The resulting screens, scanned-in pencil drawings that were shaded in gradations of color using Corel Draw!, look a bit like panels in the Sunday comics—realistic, but obviously not real. And while many of the settings, including the paintings on the walls, were copied from brochures supplied by Holiday Inn, many were "made up," Willoughby admitted. "A couple of the people included in the scenes, were people—key people, as a matter of fact-—from MicroMentor. We just photographed them and drew from the photographs." Some other faces were "borrowed" from stock photography, while the remainder were just invented.

In selecting colors for the office and guest room interiors, Willoughby said he aimed for a reassuring consistency. "There was a lot of green used, from Holiday Inn's green logo, but otherwise it was just what felt good," he said. "I did try to keep the colors the same so that the rooms don't look substantially different from each other, though. As a person went through this we didn't want him to get disoriented. If there were a jarring transition, he would feel like he was in a completely different place. We tried to make it feel like it was all one place and that they were just moving around to different parts of it."

Like Sunday Comics: Scanned-in pencil drawings are realistic, but obviously not real.

Pressured by the deadline, the graphics team developed a two-pronged process for handling illustrations to keep things moving, Willoughby said. "We would make graphics quickly to get something to the programmers so that they could work with it, and then take the time to refine and polish it," he explained. Often that meant handing off a black and white version or even a sketch. "So they would work with a sketch of the lobby, for instance, while I was finishing the final drawing," he continued. "Then when the coding was finished, we could just swap out the sketch for the finished full-color graphic."

To assemble his graphics, Willoughby worked in SuperCard, even though the Holiday Inn project was being developed on the OS/2 multimedia platform using AVC as the authoring software. "SuperCard allows you to have background- and foreground-level graphics, so you can establish a common control panel or a common title area on the background and have it be on every card," he explained. SuperCard also allowed Willoughby to test the navigational structure before it was put in the final product. To bring these images back to the PC, he converted them to .TIF files and transferred them with a SyQuest drive. "We were able to bring large quantities of graphics across the two platforms that way," he said, "but it was key that the color palettes stayed consistent through the whole process."

Willoughby and Atwood also used SuperCard to create some text-heavy graphics—like the open file folders and hotel documents. "They were done with the paint and draw tools that are built into SuperCard and then captured and screen shot," he said. "That let us save all the text in text format within SuperCard so that if we needed to, we could edit after we had already handed it off." SuperCard also facilitated creation of images like file folders "that were just straight lines and solid filled color," he added. "We didn't have font problems because we were using bitmapped screen shots of the text."

Willoughby admitted that the project "became stressful toward the end." Except for meetings twice or three times a week, he and the other freelancers frequently worked on their home computers "for a more quiet environment than at MicroMentor with interruptions, people asking questions." But as the clock ran down, some of the freelancers' time ran out. "A number of people on the team only had a limited amount of days they could put into the project ... so those people weren't available to finish it off," he said. "We also lost a couple of people because they didn't fit into the budget. It was stressful in terms of finishing off things that weren't quite finished, especially toward the end," he said.

Audio

In keeping with MicroMentor's philosophy, sounds—from the voices of the characters to the noises in a busy hotel—play a prominent role in the training program. But, Steinberg stressed, sound was used only when it was appropriate, "so when a person has something to say, [he or she] will talk to you when you click on [that person]. But there's no narrator or disembodied voice that talks to you all the time."

Other sounds "are in context to the people and the situation," Steinberg said. For example, students can eavesdrop on a conversation between a travel agent and a salesman for the hotel, by clicking on the phone. As they talk, the agent tells the salesman she is sending a fax. "When you click on the fax, you hear the fax machine, and a fax comes up," she said. "That happens throughout this program. When you click on a door, you hear the door. The same with file drawers." To capture the sounds they needed, Jeff Rand "went around our offices recording sounds." The 16-bit digitized audio files were automatically compressed by AVC for integration into the program.

Programming

In doing his work on the Holiday Inn project, programmer Bill Taylor and MicroMentor's Jeff Rand, faced a double challenge: "the time was condensed and difficult." So while Steinberg and her team worked on content and Willoughby and his team sketched out the mock hotel, Taylor and Rand studied the software that

would be used to drive the OS/2 authoring system. "We would look at what we ultimately would have to do, and we would build tiny little prototypes," Taylor said. "In a way, we worked through the programming process, so that we felt comfortable." The programmers also explored the AVS software "trying to figure out what its strengths and weaknesses were...which worked out well, because it has strengths and weaknesses, as all products do. That helped us avoid serious pitfalls, by knowing in advance some of the problems we might encounter."

Program prototypes: To meet their deadline, Taylor and Rand built prototypes using the OS/2 authoring system.

Even with all his advance work, Taylor became concerned about the project's flow. "Everything was not falling in place so that we could meet targets." So he took advantage of Steinberg's open management style that allowed anyone working on the project to call a team meeting. "I was really concerned that a whole lot of stuff was going to be dumped on me toward the end," he said. "So we talked about the whole schedule again and we were able to stop and make mid-course corrections and avoid a lot of problems that other people would have encountered by not being willing to stop and say, this isn't working for me." "We were under a fair amount of stress," Steinberg deadpanned. "So what I try to do is eliminate as many roadblocks as I can—to run interference."

Still there were obstacles as the project rushed toward deadline. "The only thing that I got burned on personally," Taylor recalled, "was the scoring module, which was a lot more difficult to do in AVC than it would have been in a lot of other programs. I had estimated that it would take me three days, and it took me about seven. Initially, I just scoped it out and said, 'yeah, that's where this goes.' After I started doing it, though, it was more difficult to get exactly what we wanted, so it took a lot more time."

Though it has since been replaced by a new product called Multimedia Builder, Taylor became a fan of AVC. "I would use it again for a lot of different things," he said. "AVC did some things really well. It handled images really well, and it integrated audio really well."

Testing

With Van Kuren at their sides and time rapidly running out, the MicroMentor team "spent some heavy nights," Steinberg recalled. Part of that time was spent in a "rigorous quality assurance stage because you don't want it to bomb when it gets to the client, and God knows what can go wrong with a program." Normally that process takes at least three weeks. But for the Holiday Inn Project? "Well we had nights and weekends," Steinberg said with a rueful laugh. For the QA of the Rate and Inventory Management course,

Steinberg relied on several MicroMentor student interns drawn from the Cambridge college community. Their assignment was to "test for functionality, for content errors, storyboard deviations, misspelling—to catch anything you can." Fortunately, the necessary corrections were only minor.

Regardless of the fine-tuning, Steinberg was nervous-—and not only because she was now seven months pregnant. "We were working like crazy, with this outrageous deadline, just bombing ahead, "she said of those last hectic days. "And everyone was believing in me, that I knew what the audience would like. I had an idea that they would like it, but they could have said that's stupid—who wants to look at pictures of a hotel?" Then after two Holiday Inn executives who were uninvolved with the project saw a prototype and raved about it, DeWeese called for a demo for Leven and her fellow executives in Atlanta. "So I have to give this demonstration," Steinberg recalled, "and the first time out of the box, you never know what is going to happen. It's like a live animal act—you never know how the animal is going to behave."

When Steinberg arrived in Atlanta in mid-December, her worst nightmare seemed to be coming true. At 9 P.M, the night before the demo, when she went to check out the corporate presentation room, "the projection screen wasn't working and I was freaking out," she said. "Finally, I got it to work; it was wired wrong." The next morning, she continued, "all the chief honchos stroll in. We started. And when we finish, everyone is looking around and I can't figure out what their reaction is going to be." After what seemed like a long time, "Mike [Leven] stands up and says, 'This is fabulous. I want everyone at Holiday Inn to take this course, even the secretaries.' It was unreal."

As the congratulations flew back and forth between Atlanta and MicroMentor, Steinberg sighed with relief and satisfaction: "Jewell immediately called Eric— she was absolutely ecstatic. She told him 'It served the purpose that I hoped it would, that people would see it and go, "Wow," that they would see it and say that multimedia is not something for the future. It is for right now. Today.'"

FINANCE: Rate and Inventory Management

In these days of re-engineered, leaner, meaner corporations, funding for multimedia is a hard sell. "[Your board] will say 'what does it do for us,'" DeWeese said, speaking from experience. " 'How does it reduce costs?' 'What are the advantages?'...You proceed as if it's locked and loaded, but every day we fight the battle." But it's equally difficult for multimedia pioneers to price their work, whether they are developers trying to estimate a complicated project in advance or freelancers wondering what hourly fee to charge. "It's one of the art forms in this business," Vogt said, "because for any given piece of multimedia you can spend 75,000 dollars or you can spend 175,000 dollars to build it. And the tricky thing is to make an estimate *before* you've built it."

The impossibly tight deadline for the Holiday Inn course was tied to the end of Holiday Inn Worldwide's fiscal year for a very good reason, Vogt points out. DeWeese was funding the project from her capital budget using dollars that would go back into the general fund if they weren't spent by the end of October 1992. Does training qualify as a capital expense? Not usually, Vogt said, "but generally accepted accounting principles allow you to capitalize software. Therefore it's a way of using investment dollars and depreciating them in the future, rather than coming up with an expense budget to do that."

To determine what to charge Holiday Inn, Vogt relied on a formula he devised about three years ago. All of MicroMentor's multimedia courses are billed on the basis of what he calls, a desktop learning hour, which costs $75,000. "Now that has some real weaknesses to it," he admitted. "How do you define an hour? What if some people go faster or slower? What level of treatment is this? Are there full-motion clips, high quality art? There are probably at least five dimensions of ambiguity when you get into multimedia pricing." Still, he argues, even with its drawbacks, a per-hour fee gives clients "a way to think about multimedia and that way is via time."

To calculate an estimate, Vogt starts with a company's existing education program. "We ask how many hours of learning were in that course," he said. "Let's say the response is about four hours. We divide that by two, because desktop learning works twice as fast as classroom learning. We now have data on that, so we are comfortable in predicting time compression. So that leaves two hours of desktop learning. We multiply that times $75,000 and our quote is $150,000." In return, clients get a worldwide license to use and duplicate the software, an average of twenty to forty megabytes in size per hour of desktop learning, within their organization. To help them understand in advance what they are buying, Vogt shows them his "flavors of multimedia," a variety of programs that "both stimulate their imagination and bound their creativity at the same time." And when the program is delivered, MicroMentor provides installation and initiation support.

Recently, Vogt believes, other companies have begun to use per-hour fees. "Some potential clients come back and say, 'we're talking to people who say they can do it for $50,000 a learning hour.' And I say, at least they are talking per learning hour, at least we are comparing the same things." His hourly rate, he says, was fixed, based on his experiences in this field. "We've done a number of different things and lost a lot of money," he said. "So we had to think about at what level we can reliably manage the process and the client, to deliver satisfaction, and not lose our shirts in the process."

Like many multimedia companies, Vogt holds MicroMentor's custom development staff to less than two dozen people. Their skills and availability for any given project are supplemented from a pool of another two dozen freelancers, including computer artists and programmers. Payment to freelancers can be either based on a per hour fee or a fixed-rate contract. An experienced programmer like Bill Taylor warns that both methods have pitfalls. "You can get burned on a fixed priced contract if you haven't worked with [a company] before," he explained. As a result, Taylor avoids fixed-priced contracts with new clients, if possible. "I would almost never work on a project with a fixed contract with someone I don't know," he emphasized, "because in the middle of the project they may say they want this or that. And you're in a funny position because you want them to be happy because that can lead to referrals and more business. If you say, 'wait a minute,' you could have a disagreement over what was in the original specs."

Because of his five-years of experience, Taylor says he charges $90 to $100 an hour for his programming services. But sometimes, based on the project, he accepts a lower fee. "You should talk to a client about what the project is to see if you can manage the process a little bit...manage them away from the pitfalls and manage them into areas that are relatively easy to do. If you're good at managing that process, you can still get your billing rate out of it, by making sure they are not going to do stuff that is going to cost you a lot of time."

Despite all of his accomplishments, Taylor still finds it hard "to develop multimedia leads as an individual." Companies that want costly multimedia applications prefer to work with other companies, "one they can call up and see their offices. I think companies are shy about investing a huge amount of money on an individual unless they have a track record with that person." As a result, Taylor generally works for companies like MicroMentor, a business relationship that has some real advantages. "It's a nice way to work, because you get to know a lot of creative people out there, who have different strengths. And you can draw on them for a lot of different things—if they aren't busy when you need them."

THE FUTURE: Room to Learn

In the year after MicroMentor delivered Holiday Inn Worldwide's first interactive training course, more than 750 managers and corporate staffers have completed the course, according to Lipscomb. "It's been fantastic," he said, of the students' response. All have tried their hand at raising revenues at the Placid Valley Holiday Inn at the giant innkeeper's Atlanta offices, since installation of the IBM Ultimedia computers in individual hotels was delayed. "As soon as our new reservation components are in place," Lipscomb said, "we will put the course on CD-ROM and put it out in the field."

With such top-to-bottom enthusiasm for the first course, Lipscomb said the company is proceeding with plans to transfer all of its property executive training programs to multimedia. At the top of the list are modules for such critical personnel as the general managers, guest service managers, sales managers and food and beverage managers. A request for proposal went to likely developers in early 1994, and Lipscomb hoped to have the first of the new courses in hand by the end of the year. "I only hope that the production of these courses will be as smooth as Rate and Inventory and will be as well received," he said.

Among the bidders, of course, will be MicroMentor. Founder Eric Vogt shares Holiday Inn's enthusiasm for CD-ROM-delivered learning, which he believes is building "a level of trust" throughout the corporate community. In the course of doing similar programs for such giants as Polaroid and Ernst & Young, though, Vogt has begun to see another alternative to custom learning programs. "After the fourth client asked us to develop something in total quality management, we've begun developing some standard products," he said. "We think one way we are going to market it is bundled with a color laptop. Imagine if I gave you a color Powerbook that has everything you need to learn about total quality management, it speaks to you and coaches you through the process, and you can take it home with you to use." Vogt envisions these in-demand courses would be leased for approximately $3,000 a month, and passed from executive to executive during that time.

By the end of the decade, Vogt predicts there will be "a desktop learning market" among small businesses. "Larger businesses are going to figure out how to take large portions of what people are learning in the classroom today and put it into desktop learning for use any time in a variety of circumstances," he said. That concept is particularly appealing to companies like Ernst & Young, whose employees face constant changes. "Last year we put a large portion of the corporate tax code into desktop learning for them," he said of

Multimedia Supporter: Holiday Inn Worldwide executive, John Lipscomb hopes future multimedia projects are as well received as Rate and Inventory Management.

his work for the international accounting firm. "They shortened their off-site consultant training from two weeks to one. And then they found out that during their busy season, during February and March, periodically the people would be reaching for modules as they were in the process of doing work. Obviously you need to keep learning in accounting." He paused briefly, then added: "Show me a business where you don't."

11

"Illuminated Manuscripts"

Interactive Arts & The J. Paul Getty Museum

At A Glance

"ILLUMINATED MANUSCRIPTS"

Developer: Interactive Arts (formerly Interactive Production Associates).

Client: The J. Paul Getty Museum.

Personnel: For Interactive Arts: Peter Bloch, executive producer; David Schwartz, producer/director; Michael Yampolsky, associate producer; Jim Kealy, art director; John deLancie, host/narrator. For the J. Paul Getty Museum: Bret Waller, producer; Thomas Kren, project director/script; Ranee Katzenstein, administrative coordinator/script.

Description of project: This interactive videodisc information system helps visitors learn about the museum's renowned collection of illuminated manuscripts. Segments, illustrated by 600 still images, 22 minutes of motion video and a hour of narration and medieval music, courtesy of Harmonia Mundi, explain the history, types and making of these manuscripts. Visitors also may browse page by page through five outstanding examples of this complex art form.

Development hours: Impossible to calculate.

Development period: Design, October 1987-April 1988; Production, May 1988-May 1989.

Production hardware: Sony DXC 3000H CCD camera, TARGA 16/IBM 386, Macintosh IIx, motion control camera, 16mm and 35mm camera, Betacam and 1-inch tape VTRs.

Production software: TIPS, Studio 8, Lumina, various C libraries.

Presentation hardware: Sony VIW 3015, Sony LDP 1550, Sony PVM 1271A display, Carrol IR touchscreen.

Cost: $300,000 (including two delivery systems).

Financing: The J. Paul Getty Museum.

Awards: Bronze medal, 1989 New York Festival; Gold, AVC CINDY, 1989.

Contact: Peter Bloch or David Schwartz
               Interactive Arts
               3200 Airport Avenue, No. 16
               Santa Monica, CA 90405
               310–390–9466

               Thomas Kren
               Curator, Manuscripts
               The J. Paul Getty Museum
               P. O. Box 2112
               Santa Monica, CA 90406
               310–459–7611

Visitors to the J. Paul Getty Museum in Malibu are time-travelers. Just minutes away from frenetic Los Angeles and the sunny California coast, high on a tree-shaded bluff, they enter the world of ancient Rome. A long reflecting pool and sculpture-filled garden welcome them to a Roman country house, an exact replica of a villa that overlooked the Bay of Naples, until it was buried by Mt. Vesuvius in A.D. 79. Inside rooms, rich with marble and frescos, are displays of antiquities from Greece and Rome, as well as Renaissance, Baroque, and nineteenth century paintings and European decorative arts, collected by the late billionaire, who built the museum two decades ago.

Amid these treasures from bygone times is some very modern technology. Tucked in a corner of a second floor room, an interactive information system helps visitors learn about and appreciate, one of the museum's most renowned collections, illuminated manuscripts from the Middle Ages and Renaissance. At the touch of a screen, they can study the decorative details of these rare, hand-

An Exact Replica:
The J. Paul Getty Museum was modeled after a Roman villa.

painted books, see how they are embellished with brilliant colors and precious metals, and browse page-by-page through five stellar examples of this complex art form. A narrator introduces each of five sections that visitors can then explore in depth, if they choose, with the aid of a touch-screen menu that gives them access to some 600 still images, 22 minutes of motion video, an hour of narration, and medieval music, courtesy of Harmonia Mundi.

Magnificent Manuscripts: The Getty Museum has an extensive collection of illuminated manuscripts, richly illustrated with miniatures like this one of Saint Hedwig.

This $300,000 interactive videodisc program is the result of a twenty-month collaboration between museum officials and Interactive Arts, a Santa Monica-based multimedia developer. Its achievement has been recognized by the multimedia industry. "Illuminated Manuscripts" was awarded a Gold CINDY by the Association of Visual Communications and a Bronze medal at the New York Festival Interactive Multimedia Competition in 1989. While its hardware and software are no longer state-of-the art, this program has become a model for museums around the world that are seeking to tap the power of multimedia for art education. Its creation, often a stormy process, also reveals the often unavoidable strains and stresses encountered when an emerging technology is introduced into a wary traditional institution. Working on the cutting edge of new technology, both developers and their clients must be prepared for daily, time-consuming, give-and-take in the mutual learning process that is part of multimedia development.

Today, thanks to peer recognition and positive user response, museum director, John Walsh, lauds the program as "an extra visual aid" that enhances the museumgoers' experience with the actual works of art. Like an earlier, similar interactive program done

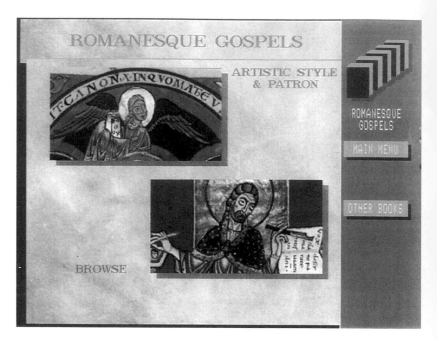

Page by Page:
The "Illuminated Manuscripts" interactive display allows the viewer to study details of these complex art works.

for the museum's collection of Greek vases, "Illuminated Manuscripts" was designed "to provide an incentive" for people to look at little-known art forms. "Greek vases are something that everybody recognizes but nobody knows. A case full of Greek vases does not grip the imagination of large numbers of people," he explained. "But they will grab the attention of anybody who knows what these things are, what they are used for, what their shapes signify...what the pictures are saying. If you can just get a visitor to understand what's going on, that is really thrilling for people." In the case of both programs, studies showed that after using them, visitors "really did spend more time with the works of art."

Because of the Getty's insistence that multimedia technology serve its collection, aesthetics were of primary importance as this project evolved. "Museums are unique institutions—the ultimate corporation," noted Interactive Arts vice president, David Schwartz, who coordinated "Illuminated Manuscripts." "Not only do they have business concerns, but their design and information concerns are at a high and very refined level." As a result, the project benefited from what Schwartz called "executive aesthetic oversight that added incredible gloss and value to a program. It also added to the time and effort.... But we were willing to go the distance. This was a project we all realized was going to be ground-breaking, a feather in everyone's cap, and it's proven to be that way."

THE OPPORTUNITY: A New Page in Art Appreciation

When Thomas Kren, the Getty's curator of illuminated manuscripts, saw the museum's interactive exhibit on the Greek vases collection, he immediately knew that illuminated manuscripts were "an ideal application" for this new technology, despite his general aversion to high-tech gadgets, like television and video games. "Manuscripts are an unusual art form, in that they are books that are often decorated front to back," he explained. "However you can only open them to display two pages at any given moment. It's difficult to make them fully accessible as works of art."

Thomas Kren: The Getty's curator of illuminated manuscripts wanted this art form to be accessible to the public.

Kren's cluttered office is located two floors below the small, dimly lit room in the villa that houses displays from the museum's extensive manuscript collection—140 books, or codices, and an additional 50 single leaves, or groups of leaves, from the same book. At any given time, fewer than two dozen manuscripts are on view, their covers opened to reveal only two, side-by-side vellum pages. Both religious and secular, and mostly from the middle ages, these books are "illuminated" or adorned with decorated letters, borders, and figurative scenes called miniatures. Painted in vibrant hues of ultramarine blue and vermilion, accented with gold leaf and other precious metals, these works of art are rich in symbolism and detail. They demand close scrutiny to be fully understood and appreciated.

While highly regarded in the art world, illuminated manuscripts are little known among the general public. "This was a tradition that lasted a thousand years and it's very rich," said Kren, "but

there's a widespread viewpoint today that dismisses small objects as minor arts. But these weren't minor arts in their time. The best artists painted them. They were artistically sophisticated objects in every respect. They had their own traditions, and the value

Side By Side: Only two pages of an illuminated manuscript can be displayed at a time.

society invested in them is reflected in their materials—gold and silver, and very expensive pigments. As museum curators, one of the things we endeavor to explain to the public is, 'yes, they are small, even readily portable, but no, they are not just books. The are in fact much more than that. They rank among the artistic treasures of their time.'"

Kren believed an interactive videodisc could help present "the brilliant character" of this complex art. "While you're still dealing with reproductions, the videodisc allows you to go through a whole book. You could show every page, if you wanted to, or felt the need to. A lot of these books tell stories through pictures, so we wanted to show the sequence of that story, because that's part of the aesthetic experience," he said. "Another issue is complexity. A manuscript is a very complex object. We have one book that has more than 300 illustrations in it, while the program of illumination will take, necessarily, into account the variety of texts that some books contain. (An example is the popular private prayer book called the book of hours.) In addition to the text, the subject matter of miniatures, the patron, and the artist all hold interest for visitors to the galleries. With artworks of this complexity, there are many kinds of questions that the 'man on the street' will rightly pose. How do you anticipate these questions, and how do you present the answers? It struck us that the interactive videodisc was a ideal for galleries. (People) come in, they see a book, they find absolutely wonderful, and they want to know more about it The videodisc can provide answers in part by showing them more."

What the public saw had to be visually precise, Kren insisted. "This program would succeed, in part, based on the quality of the images," he said. "We wanted the color to be as faithful to the originals as possible. We wanted the crispness to echo the originals. We did not want people to look at images that glamorize what they see, but to show them as accurately as possible.... We don't want the reproductions to be more beautiful, more rich, more exotic or exciting than the real thing. We don't want them to become a substitute for the objects."

Kren believes that ultimately, the use of new technology could enlarge the audience for this important collection to include the video generation. "The Getty Museum, as an institution, is committed to finding new ways of educating the public. We want people to come in and enjoy the objects, but we also want to educate them if they are interested...and the Getty Trust is very interested in the use of technology, especially advanced technology, in the arts and humanities. So the videodisc fit very much with their concerns. And we saw it as a new way of reaching an audience. I don't watch television, and I don't play PacMan, so it isn't entirely my sensibility, but I could see the usefulness for the public and for a younger audience familiar with this technology."

Five Great Manuscripts: The interactive display allows users to study five complete manuscripts, page by page.

THE TEAM: Art and Technology Joined

Since the firm that had created the "Greek Vases" had been re-structured, Kren and the Getty's education department drew up a project description based on that exhibit and a request for proposal (RFP) and distributed it to some fifteen companies around the country. Many had completed interactive projects for other museums, or large corporations like IBM.

Among the local firms vying for the contract was Interactive Production Arts, now known as Interactive Arts. The Santa Monica company, based near the Santa Monica airport and only a few miles from the museum, came highly recommended by one of the key architects of the "Greek Vases" project, an artist named Jan Sircus, who had taken a job with the Walt Disney Company. The IA team stood out, president Peter Bloch believes, "because the experience of the people on our team was unmatched." In addition to work in film and video production, as well as some earlier videodisc displays, the then two-year-old company had just completed a major videodisc exhibit, with computer-controlled lighting, for the Los Angeles County Museum of Natural History.

An Englishman with an extensive experience as a special effects producer for films such as *Romancing the Stone* and *Starman*, Bloch prefers to convince potential clients to first undertake a design phase with the company. "What many institutions expect is that interested vendors will respond to an RFP and we very rarely do that because, quite frankly, to do one properly is a huge amount of work," he explained. "A museum RFP will cost us anywhere from $5,000 to $15,000. We have to design the entire

Interactive Arts Partners: David Schwartz, left, and Peter Bloch, right, brought backgrounds in film to their multimedia work.

application and figure it all out and, hey, that's what we do for a living." Instead of RFPs, Bloch suggests that potential clients select three or four companies and pay them to participate in a design competition, similar to those held with architectural firms for major buildings. "Like architects, we want to be paid to design the product," Interactive Arts vice president, David Schwartz, explained. "Interactive exhibits are very much like houses...and what clients don't realize is that design is 60 percent of it. If you design something, you've solved the problem."

Interactive Arts did respond to the Getty's RFP because "it was very brief, and there wasn't a huge amount of work involved in it," Bloch said. As a result, the company was selected to make a presentation to museum officials. Having narrowed the field to four or five companies that "were extremely impressive and all seemed as though they could do the job," Kren said they decided to go with a local firm and picked Interactive Arts to proceed with the next step in the project, its design. "The decision was pretty much mine," he recalled. "We felt that we would have to work with them so intensely that commuting long distances would be a nightmare. And in fact, it was the right decision, because there are periods when all you do is work on the videodisc, and you need to go back and forth daily, whether you're going over a few pages of script, or the images, or what ever. It's enormously labor intensive, a consuming project that dominated the activities of my professional staff of four for two years, and engaged the collaboration of the Getty Education Department."

During that time, Kren worked very closely with Schwartz, who became the project manager. He was a freelance film editor whose credits include the feature films *Sunset Strip*, *Walking After Midnight*, and *The Jupiter Menace*, as well as award-winning documentaries and educational films. Schwartz met Interactive Arts' founding partner Peter Bloch in 1982, when both were working on the same movie. He had worked on some projects for Interactive Arts, and as the company began work on the Getty project design, he was hired full time as a staff producer.

During the next five months, Interactive Arts' staff was paid an hourly rate as they worked with museum officials to hammer out the project design and test a variety of potential delivery systems. It also gave the museum and the high-tech company a chance to get acquainted. "This makes a lot of sense to me," Bloch said, "because an institution might decide that vendor X was the best and go into a design development agreement with them, but while working together on that, they might find out that these people are impossible. Well then, once the design period is over, they can say *ciao*."

At the end of this phase, Interactive Arts presented the museum with an in-depth plan that included an overview of the project and its organization, a discussion of hardware and an all-important explanation of costs and some budget options. "You guide clients through the budget line-by-line. You give them a commentary," Schwartz said. "This is a service business and you have to help the client understand how you arrived at your figures." On the basis of that report, the Getty awarded Interactive Arts the contract for the project and fixed a budget for it.

Schwartz drew heavily on his experience in film production to organize the "Illuminated Manuscripts" project. "I look at multimedia as filmmaking put through a sieve," he said. "Filmmaking uses so many arts and there are so many complex tasks to accomplish; when you get into multimedia, you add another level on top of it—file

Planning Ahead:
Schwartz organized the Getty project along a detailed time line.

management, file conversion, programming, interface design, and so on. So Peter and I approach making interactive projects in a very methodical way, much in the same way that we would go about making a film or a video. What I also find, though, is that the narrative thrust that is so very important in filmmaking often gets lost in all the discussion of slick graphics and windows."

As project manager, Schwartz was responsible "for keeping the project on budget and on schedule, and making sure that all the key production team members worked well together." Another Interactive Arts vice president, Michael Yampolsky, who has designed and produced more than 40 interactive videodiscs, took charge of production design, with help from staff graphic artist, Valerie Lettera, and from Sircus, who served as design consultant. Art director Jim Kealy, another graphic artist, Alan Ridenour, and programmer Steven Cohn, worked on a freelance basis. When faced with an unfamiliar aspect of the production, Schwartz said that he often hired consultants for a day to get the benefit of their knowledge.

As a first step in organizing the team, Schwartz worked with Kren and assistant curator, Ranee Katzenstein, to create a flow chart using Claris' MacProject, a program that tracks every production task along a time line. "Since my forte is film and video production, I go in and break apart all of the production pathways...." scripting, animation, shooting live action, music, and sound effects, art direction, computer graphics, editing, etc. "Then I indicate how many days for each activity. I do that in Microsoft Excel first, and then I use MacProject to create the time track."

In the course of the project, both the museum's and Interactive Arts' staffers learned from each other—a sometimes thorny process. "We used to have terrible fights. We'd get furious at each other and there were times when we were exasperated with each other," Kren recalled. "I didn't really want to know all the technical stuff. I wanted to get our message out, and I felt as if I shouldn't have to absorb all that information, because it took away too much time from other pressing responsibilities. In that sense, Interactive Arts was terrific, because they genuinely did their best to fulfill our needs and try to make possible what we desired." Bloch has similar memories. "Thom really gave us a hard time initially. He really made us prove ourselves. And, we did. We proved we could be sensitive, that we could support him in the way he wanted. And he changed. He became our friend."

THE PRODUCTION: In Touch with Ancient Books

Using the "Greek Vases" videodisc as a point of departure, museum officials envisioned a "more complex" treatment of its collection of illuminated manuscripts. But, in the end, limits of technology, budget, and the intended audience refined that ambition. A frequently frustrated Thom Kren and David Schwartz ultimately settled on a simple design and pared-down content that allows users the options of a brief overview, or an hours-long immersion in this little known art form. The process turned out to be a grueling learning experience for both.

Scripting

Kren, and other members of the museum staff, drafted the script, paring down their extensive scholarship into the exhibit's four modules: types of manuscripts, keys to understanding (manuscript subjects and symbols), materials and techniques (creating the manuscripts), and a page-by-page look at five great manuscripts. This distillation proved to be one of the project's most difficult and frustrating tasks.

"You have to remember that curators tend to be specialists, and we've been working in a fairly narrow field for years. We're often off working on some arcane aspect trying to solve a highly focused problem," Kren said. "And you have to remember what interests you at the moment isn't necessarily what the public is going to get excited about." The challenge then, he continued, "is for curators to get off their high thrones. That's difficult in the sense that you have to re-imagine a time when you knew nothing about this material, and since I do this 10 hours a day, six days a week, it takes some effort. But it's also good for us because we are teachers. We need to think about our audiences."

Drawing on their experience mounting manuscripts' exhibits four times a year, Kren and his staff talked at length about the content of the script and how to make it accessible to the general public. After six months of writing and rewriting, Kren felt they had pared the information down to "as lean as it could possibly be" only to dis-cover that the draft script was almost twice as long as the tech-nology could accommodate. "We had to edit the script down to fit on the disc," Schwartz ex-plained. "On the disc there are 30 minutes, or 54,000 frames of video, and we were using both soundtracks, channels 1 and 2. So there's 60 minutes of audio. Everything had to add up to one hour tops. Anything else would be relegated to text pan-els on top of video stills."

Kren and Schwartz met al-most daily, and faxed revisions flew between the two offices as they cut the script to fit, or al-tered sections to mesh with ani-mations, or video. During the process, "there was a sense of mutual education," Schwartz believed. "We learned a tremen-dous amount about manu-scripts, and Thom and his staff learned a lot more about video and multimedia production. So this was give and take, a col-laborative effort in terms of massaging the script."

One frustration, for both Kren and Schwartz, was the difficulty in determining the right length of the script. "I couldn't tell Thom

---

2. TYPES OF MANUSCRIPTS - INTRO

[Manuscript inserts]

There were different types of illuminated books in use during the Middle Ages. Some of these... are still used today... the Bible, for example.

[Host on camera with English Apocalypse (no move)]

Now we live in a secular society.... and most religious texts from that time are no longer widely known. The Sacramentary, the Lectionary, and the Book of Hours...once at the center of religious life... are today studied only by specialists.

Here are three major types of illuminated manuscripts....

[Ms. IX 18 fol. 260 v]

Liturgical Manuscripts... books used during the religious

[Ms. VIII 1 fol. 16]

celebrations of the Roman Catholic Church...

[Ms. V 2 fol. 22]

Devotional Manuscripts.... books used by

[Ms. 22 fol. 137]

individuals in their own daily meditation and worship....

[Secular Manuscript detail #1]

Secular Manuscripts... books on non-religious subjects....

[Secular Manuscript detail #2]

from law to science... from literature to games.

[Choices appear on screen:

Liturgical Manuscripts, Devotional Manuscripts,

Secular Manuscripts]

Touch the type of manuscript you want to see...

January 19, 1989   Page 4

So Much to Say: Paring down the script was frustrating to all involved.

when we had cut enough," Schwartz said. "We would whittle the script down, and he'd say, 'Are we done?' And I wouldn't know until I went back, read it myself, timed it, and added up my times. I did that for months. I remember once we had reached a certain milestone and I thought we had made great progress. But, I had to call and tell him we had to throw out ten more pages. He went nuts, but I don't blame him."

Another concern that, in the end, colored the entire project was the perceived attention span of the exhibit's users. "The issue is how much new information can you hand over to the novice," Kren said, "since almost anyone who is going to use this will probably be completely uninformed about illuminated manuscripts. After all, they are not an art form that's even commonly talked about. So, it's not just the technology.... If you figure that the average visitor is going to sit with this exhibit for ten to twenty minutes, you are talking about providing fairly basic information." Even with that understanding, Kren remained dissatisfied with the amount of information finally conveyed. "It was never enough as far as we were concerned, simply because there are so many kinds of questions we have heard from the public."

Unlike the "Greek Vases" display, which features a seven-minute introduction, "Illuminated Manuscripts" starts with a brief one minute, 45-second overview. "The 'Greek Vases' intro was deadly," Schwartz said, "and there was no way to get out of (exit) it. They (museum officials) knew they didn't want an introduction that long. They wanted to get people into the program quickly, but you still need to explain it." But how short is shorter? "We felt it took quite a bit to set the stage in terms of information," said Kren, "and they (Interactive Arts) kept saying—and they were absolutely right, but we fought them all the way—'It's much too long. It's got to be shorter.' I have to say, I don't love the introduction today. It seemed to me then, that it was saying almost nothing. But, when I watch it now, it seems much too long. It seems to go on forever. This is an issue that someone, who works with TV and media, really will understand, that we did not, which is how much can people take in?"

Not surprisingly, Schwartz would have preferred an ever shorter introduction for "Illuminated Manuscripts," but more importantly, he wanted to give users the option to skip over it. "In an interactive program, you want people to have the option to get right into the program," he added. "In all of our programs now, we make the introduction selectable off the menu. We didn't do that with this intro, but we should have."

Since the introduction is critical in grabbing viewer attention, Schwartz brought in an experienced script "doctor" to polish Kren's final draft. "In the end, we wanted the make the introduction more poetic and cinematic," Schwartz said. "This took it to a level of poetry that people could hear im-

In The Beginning: Introductions for the program and each segment were rewritten again and again.

mediately." Even so, during the video shoot when the narration was recorded, Kren and the others continued to fine-tune the script. "When we were working with the actor, even though we had whittled it down and made it simpler, you could see him stumble over certain things and you'd realize that maybe you hadn't written it in a way that was suitable to be spoken. So we would play with it to make it work."

Interactivity

The interactive depth and complexity of "Illuminated Manuscripts" initially was another point of contention. After numerous arguments and discussions, Kren came around again to believing that the simple approach advocated by Interactive Arts was best.

Following the brief introduction, which includes an explanation of its interactivity, the program begins with an overview of the three types of manuscripts: secular, liturgical, and devotional. Each of those topics then is subdivided at least four times. For example, under Secular Manuscripts are sections on books about history, natural history, law and literature, and leisure. The next major topic, Keys to Understanding, explores common manuscript subjects and symbols, which also are broken down into three divisions. The third major segment, one that has proved extremely popular with users, is materials and techniques. Four subsections, parchment, writing, decoration, and binding, demonstrate how a manuscript was created and illuminated.

The most important segment, from Kren's point of view, was the final one on five great manuscripts. It allowed users to view them leisurely, one page at a time, from front to back. "If we ever expanded the disc, the first thing we would do is 20 great manuscripts," he emphasized. " As they browse through each book, viewers also have the option of focusing in on details of decoration.

Originally, Kren said he wanted more depth, "basements and subbasements" that would be linked horizontally as well as vertically. Interactive Arts argued against that format. "They would say that's too complex. If you go this far down into this subbasement, you're never going to get out," Kren recalled. "In fact, we originally wanted to be able to cross subbasement...and in retrospect I realize that they were right. You can't make it too complicated." As the project evolved, Kren said, "everything was made simpler." For

In Depth: There was much debate over the amount of branching to include, as this early outline reveals.

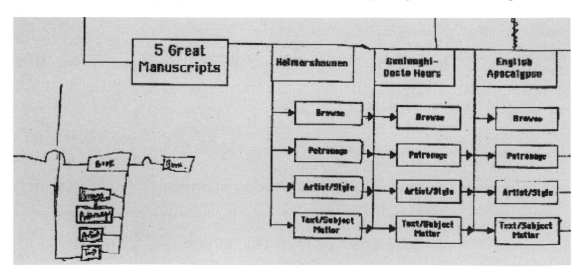

example, plans originally called for an introduction to each of the five great manuscripts, plus segments on the patron, artists, and subject of each. Instead, those topics were combined into one. "We just simplified it," Kren said. "We tried to reduce the number of choices so as not to overwhelm people. I think that works."

Interface

Design of the main menus for "Illuminated Manuscripts" was determined as much by the art form on the screen, as by the needs of the art lovers who would use the program. And, because of some unexpected quirks in the playback system, the museum's "aesthetic oversight" is much in evidence in the polished final panels.

When users approach "Illuminated Manuscripts," they are greeted by an "attract mode," still frames dissolving one into another of side-by-side pages from famous books. This loop of video continues moving until someone touches the screen and returns after users depart and/or no one has touched the screen for about forty seconds. The main menu appears first, toward the end of the mandatory introduction, where its use is explained in a brief animated sequence. On it are buttons labelled with icons that symbolize the program's four main divisions. When one of them is selected, the next screen appears, featuring a control panel of navigational buttons, generally, in a vertical column on the right that fills twenty percent of the screen.

The control panel design reflects the Getty's concern "that the technology not compete with the works of art," Schwartz said. "The works of art come first. So our idea was that, like the televisions of the '50s, you'd have a control panel that appeared by and large on the right side of the screen. After a while, you would just forget (about it). You would have all the buttons you need, but your eye would be drawn to the full-color image on what remains of the screen." He added that the right side was chosen because most people are right-handed.

In addition to advancing them through the program, the control panel also serves as a "bookmark for users"—a vital function,

Schwartz believes. Always present, at the top, is the icon of the segment; when a branch is selected, its name appears in text below the icon. Continue, Skip Ahead, Pause, and, in most cases, Return to Main Menu buttons complete the user options available. "You don't want people to move in such a way that they lose track of where they are, and you don't want them to get lost in the program," Kren said. "At the same time, you can only have so many buttons without people totally freaking out. I think Interactive Arts did a pretty good job of reminding us that there were limits to the degree that you could clutter the screen."

Many of the details in the interface design are a result of Kren's desire for quality and clarity of symbols. The Getty's art director, Patrick Dooley, worked with Yampolsky and Kealy to perfect the icons, which began as pencil sketches, before being transferred to TARGA files and to select the shade of gray for the control panel. The main menu was superimposed against a parchment in the attract mode. Manuscripts were displayed against the same velvet used by the museum for its exhibits. "When we chose a symbol to represent a section," Kren said, "we wanted to be certain that symbol was meaningful. I also was very concerned about having an authentic feel to the program. If you are going to have something that deals with vellum, you want to get the texture of vellum. You want people to realize that this isn't paper. You want consciously, and unconsciously, to convey the specifics to your audience so that they realize that they are looking at something with its own personality, its own integrity."

Main Divisions:
The main menu allows users to select one of the four major topics discussed in the program.

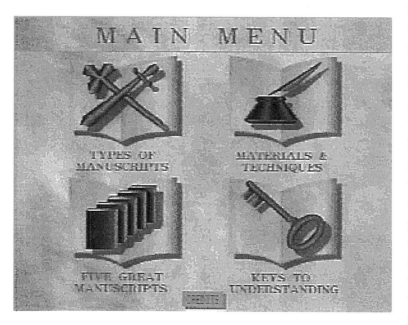

Unexpectedly, the Sony system used to play the program had a mind of its own when it came to displaying the parchment background. "There were certain artifacts in the system that affected what the authoring code did, in terms of delivering items to the screen," Schwartz said. "What we found was that it wouldn't give us the parchment all the way to the top of the screen. So we had to make an aesthetic fix. Getty art director, Pat Dooley, helped us pick the color of a border line and additional parchment to fill in that top space."

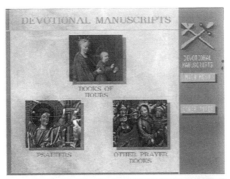

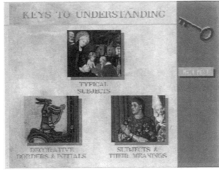

In Place: Icons on every control panel serve as "bookmarks" for users.

Images and Video

The bulk of the manuscript images in the exhibit were provided by the Getty. Museum staffers had transparencies shot, or rounded them up from other museums. It was an extremely labor intensive process. "There are hundreds and hundreds of images in this," Kren said. "We faced the technical problem, even in-house, of getting all the objects photographed properly, of getting high color quality. We are fortunate that the museum has on its staff Charles Passela, a great photographer, with a particular gift for photographing illuminated manuscripts. The photography required a lot of checking, a lot of going back and forth. We also used about 50 comparisons from other collections and getting that material together...the man-hours were imposing."

Because of limits of technology at the time, most of these transparencies were transferred from film directly to video tape. Only the pages of the five great manuscripts were digitized, making the finished program an "analog-digital hybrid," Schwartz explained. "At the time, there wasn't a system available that made doing it (all digitally) financially feasible at the quality level they wanted...or that would provide the functionality desired." Some Getty staffers had argued against going ahead with the program, preferring to wait for the digital technology to evolve and drop in price. "But eventually, they decided they needed something out there now, not later," he said. As a result, he continued, "the majority of ('Illuminated Manuscripts')—80 percent—are essentially images that we shot on either 16mm or 35mm film and then laid on to the disc and programmed. Then we digitized the Five Great Books section—they're TARGA files—and in terms of the technology of the time, it was state-of-the-art."

A Hybrid: Only the images from the five great manuscripts were digitized. The others were transferred directly from film to video tape.

To convert the other transparencies to video, Interactive Arts first had them filmed by motion-control experts "who shoot animatics," he said. "You go into a facility that has a 16 or 35mm camera mounted on a special tripod that enables it to do computer-controlled moves—move-ins, pans, etc.—in a precise sequence. It's like shooting filmstrips, except portions of the strip are single frames; but all of a sudden you might do a 10-second move-in. So once the script was done I had to plan all that out."

Working from the completed script, Schwartz drew heavily on his experience in film editing to coordinate the camera's moves with the narration. At the same time, he strove to give each image its due. "There were hundreds of images, and I had to space out the narration so that people could see them," Schwartz said. "A lot of massaging was done in the linear editing of these segments so that each image got the time it needed." In addition, Schwartz had to accommodate the control panel, which filled 20 percent of the screen. "What we did was shoot everything normally, but then in video post (production), we shifted it so that it would be centered (on the remaining 80 percent of the screen)."

After the animatics work was completed, the filmed images from the five great manuscripts were captured to a TARGA R16 graphics board. Next the TARGA frames and the filmed images were laid off onto a Sony component Betacam and put into NTSC 1-inch video format. At this point in the process, it was possible to color correct the images, a task that preoccupied Kren for more than a week including late night sessions. "Having Thom there was essential," said Schwartz, "because he knew what the real book looked like under natural lighting. They were very fun sessions because he got to tweak this, change that." "We were very, very concerned about the level of fidelity," added Kren. "In the end I discovered that it was very difficult to control, but we spent a lot of time trying to make sure that the color quality was right."

At one point in the making of "Illuminated Manuscripts," Interactive Arts proposed to the museum that it digitize all the images for an additional cost of $50,000. The Getty Trust decided against the added expense, Kren recalled. "I think everything is digitized now, but in those days, not everything was, and it was much more expensive. But the truth is it could be done so much better today because digitization is much more affordable, much more common." Given the limitations of the time, light years ago in terms of technology, Kren says he is "satisfied" with the program. "One of the compromises we made is that we used more details, because the smaller the images, the crisper they were," he added. "This worked well for us, because this is partially an art about detail. You want people to look closely, and the videodisc enables you to do that."

The filmed segments in the segment introductions and the manuscript making demonstrations were directed by Schwartz, who hired a film crew for four days of shooting. Juilliard-trained actor, John deLancie, who, now, is familiar to "Star Trek: The Next Generation" fans as the perverse Q, was chosen as the narrator after a series of screen tests. "The selection of the narrator was a big thing," Schwartz said. "We zeroed in on deLancie, who was a big character actor at the time, and who had just begun to have a guest spot on the new 'Star Trek.' They liked (the fact) that he was young, and the way he sounded. But, when the rest of the museum staff saw him, they were divided."

Schwartz believed that having a narrator was important for continuity. "We wanted to have someone on camera who would knit the whole thing together. And, in the introduction to the various manuscripts, we wanted to show a human being next to these books to show their size." At the same time, Schwartz wanted to avoid "on-camera-itus where you're constantly seeing the host, rather than the works of art. So when we go to the section on the five great manuscripts, we only cut to him to show how big or little the book is."

One day of shooting with deLancie was done on a Hollywood sound stage; a second day was done at the museum under cool fluorescent lights in order not to damage the manuscripts. The demonstrations of book binding and manuscript illumination were shot over an additional two days. "We shot a lot of stuff to get this fabulous section of 10 to 12 minutes of

On The Set:
Schwartz, above, and Kren were present for the video shoot with a professional crew.

material," said Schwartz, who used 16mm film and later transferred it to video. "Everybody loves these sections, because you get to see how it's actually done."

When the completed video and film segments were transferred to the disc, Schwartz got another unwelcome surprise from the Sony system. It shifted the video again, leaving a space between the image and the control panel. "We had to take the whole program and shift the video a second time," he said. Such unexpected technical glitches and the resulting time-consuming problem solving, givens in most multimedia projects, have an impact on costs. "There's a lot of technical figuring out that you can only do on the fly, so you have to build in that experimentation in time and money," Schwartz said. "That's why you build in contingencies." (There were none in this case.) "Filmmakers usually put in 10 to15 percent for acts of God, or mistakes. Here, it's for your learning curve."

Programming

All of the programming was done in C programming language, written specifically for this application. One reason Interactive Arts chose this route was that at the time, off-the-shelf authoring systems were extremely expensive and they wanted to avoid paying royalties. "When you write the code yourself, you take up less disk space," Schwartz added. "All of our applications are customized, because, sometimes, authoring systems have certain parameters— they become another limit."

This and other decisions grew out of the company's philosophy that "content rules the hardware and software," Schwartz said. "A lot of people feel the opposite, but we couldn't disagree more. One of our hallmarks, along with our concern for design and navigational ease, is that we want the subject matter to come through. The technology is a means toward understanding the subject. We're not there to entertain through the hardware. We're there so people can get to the subject at hand really easily."

Testing

Getty and Interactive Arts staffers tried and fine-tuned the program as it neared completion, but there was no test run of "Illuminated

Manuscripts" before its installation in the museum. "Because the program is so complex...because it is so video and menu intensive, you have to work out your assumptions in HyperCard or in a series of drawings," Schwartz explained. "When there is a predominate scripting language for interactive applications, then maybe you can finish a program and have the time or wherewithal to play with it. But, here you had such a degree of work on the graphics, and the videodisc elements, that to make changes would have been financially prohibitive."

Shortly after the exhibit was placed in the museum, Getty officials commissioned an evaluation of public use and satisfaction with the interactive display. While overall response was extremely positive, users singled out two annoying problems. Because there was no pause button, when the screen remained dormant for 40 seconds, as users browsed the great manuscripts segment, the program automatically returned to the attract mode. "People would have to go all the way back through the program, and they hated that," Schwartz said. "So we made pause an unlimited thing...especially in the browse mode. This is a case where evaluation really helped, because we saw real world use and how people were stymied by this function."

The second complaint concerned the small size of the menu buttons. As a result, viewers often wound up in a section of the program they had not selected. "We knew that the buttons were small from the beginning," Bloch said, "but that was because of aesthetic considerations that the museum felt strongly about. There was nothing that could be done about that."

Survey Says: A museum poll of users revealed overall satisfaction with all aspects of the videodisc presentation.

Table 2
Opinion of the Videodisc Program (Means and Standard Deviations)

The presentation: $\overline{X} = 4.7 (\pm .61)$	Boring 1	2	3	4	Interesting 5 ----X----
The presentation: $\overline{X} = 4.6 (\pm .75)$	Confusing 1	2	3	4	Clear 5 ----X----
The information: $\overline{X} = 2.9 (\pm .48)$	Too Superficial 1	2	3 ----X----	4	Too In-Depth 5
Educational value: $\overline{X} = 4.5 (\pm .72)$	Very Poor 1	2	3	4 ----X----	Excellent 5
Visual quality: $\overline{X} = 4.4 (\pm .77)$	Very Poor 1	2	3	4 ----X----	Excellent 5
Overall rating: $\overline{X} = 4.6 (\pm .65)$	Very Poor 1	2	3	4 ----X----	Excellent 5

N = 75; post-test respondents only

Installation

Nowhere is the Getty's ambivalence toward interactive technology more evident than in its choice of a site for the completed "Illuminated Manuscripts" exhibit. Keeping public focus on its impressive collections is an admirable and understandable goal, but relegating an educational program—albeit a high-tech one—to a room away from art objects and viewers, seems self-defeating. The exhibit's two viewing stations are tucked in a corner of the museum's second floor Browsing Room. The room is located two rooms away from the manuscripts exhibit, and is home to a mini-library of catalogs, art books, and other educational materials. Each station consists of a Sony VIW/3015 interactive workstation, a Sony LDP/1550 videodisc player and a Sony 13-inch color monitor with Carrol IR touchscreen. There's seating for two users at each station, with cramped standing room behind the chairs.

A small, easily-missed sign inside the entrance to the manuscript gallery points museum visitors to the installation, which is two rooms away. However, the interactive display is noted on a floor-plan map made available to visitors as they enter the museum. The "Greek Vases" interactive display, located on the first floor, is similarly signed. Each is well used despite the challenge to find them.

Out Of Sight: The "Illuminated Manuscript" display is installed in out-of-the-way corner room.

The placement of both exhibits was determined by the Education Department in consultation with the curators who didn't want the technology to compete with the art on display. "My feeling is that the museum's primary function is to show its collections, and even if they were shown with relatively little information, it would actually achieve something of its goal," Kren said. "The objects are primary. At the same time, I think it's helpful to make educational information available to anyone who's interested. For those people (who are interested), we want to make that information available without competing with the collections." While he is opposed to housing the educational technology with the art, Kren believes that ideally it should be in an adjacent room. "There's a conscious attempt not to make educational materials a focus of people's visit," he said. "We want people to know that they are there. We want them to be accessible, but the collection is meant to be what you come across first and enjoy first."

MARKETING: Multi-Uses for Multimedia

In addition to offering museum visitors a detailed view of its rare manuscripts, Getty officials had hoped that the "Illuminated Manuscripts" exhibit would be the basis for other related products aimed at scholars, educational institutions and other museums. This goal was abandoned early in the production, when it became clear that the necessary changes in the format, to facilitate multiple uses, would take a toll on the resolution of the images. "What the museum is hoping to do in the next few years is to take the videodisc and turn it into something linear. To make that work, we've discovered we need a bit more information, images and transitions," Kren said. "Ideally, someone would be able to take what we have and update it technologically into something affordable."

From Schwartz's point of view, ancillary uses of a multimedia project could be built in from the beginning of production. "We have learned that these are very expensive projects to produce, and that even institutions like the Getty want more than one product, in order to justify the costs," he explained. "It's one thing to have an

From The Beginning: Schwartz believes ancillary uses of a multimedia project should be built in at its start.

installation in the museum, it's another to have a HyperCard-driven laser disc for use in schools, and a linear video version to sell in the museum gift shop. Had we known that (with the Getty), we would have said for an extra $25,000, we'll do all that, or we'll prepare the assets in such a way that we can do that simply." To make the changes now, "a lot of technological things would have to be done to the master tape to adapt it. That's a very expensive process," he added.

FINANCE: A Film Model

In the search for clients for multimedia, Bloch has attended all the right trade shows and made a significant number of difficult cold calls, to no avail. Both he and Schwartz agree that the best sources of new business have been their business partnerships with hardware manufacturers, and the recommendations of past clients. "We've done at least a half a dozen major projects because of our status as a business partner with IBM," said Schwartz. Interactive Arts also has a similar relationship with Philips, in which both hardware manufacturers recommend their business partners to potential clients and allow the partners to sell their equipment.

Equally valuable is a good word from a previous customer. "When people call the Getty, they give them our number. We've gotten tremendous mileage out of that," Schwartz said. "I have to say this—none of our jobs has come from cold calls or trade shows."

Bloch generally encourages potential clients to enter into a design contract with the company, that will result in a preliminary proposal. Another option is a design competition among several potential contractors. "We have learned how to give a taste of the program, but not do all the work in advance, in order to get the job," Schwartz said. Since most potential clients want more features than they can afford, a significant portion of the resulting proposal spells out costs, which are estimated on a filmmaking model. "A film budget has line items for staff, production equipment, production staff, location expenses, graphics production, audio production, post-production, and office help," said Schwartz. "I analyze the tasks that have to be done, estimate their difficulty and the time they will take, and then I'm able to come up with a figure for every line item. So you make educated guesses going into it." Despite institutional resistance, he insists on building in a line item for contingencies. "Every project is an evolutionary process, but a fixed price contract negates that true nature," he added. "It's very difficult to talk to institutions about this, though. They look at the project as a line item. Period."

Schwartz believes that filmmaking also offers a useful model for putting together a staff for a multimedia project. "You'd be hard pressed to find a film company that has enough work to keep a director of photography on staff at the pay scale they are accustomed to getting. The same for a film crew and film equipment," he said. "Also every project has different visual needs. So when you're looking for a certain look or feel, you bring in freelancers to fit your material. You select from the available pool of talent."

The Getty project cost $300,000. Bloch notes that Interactive Arts' budget for it "was extremely accurate. The problem always is the client wants something extra. In fact, the definition of a client is someone who wants more than he's going to pay for. It's a bit of a game and you sort of have to play it." While the Getty Trust is one of the wealthiest institutions in the world, the budget for the museum's interactive display was closely monitored. "Everyone said, 'Oh the Getty, they have unlimited money,' but it's not true. The Getty is like any other organization. All the departments have budgets and they have to stick to them." Funds for the project were disbursed at agreed upon milestones during the 20 months it took to complete.

While there's much talk about a multimedia boom, Bloch and Schwartz caution potential developers. "The projects are time-consuming and very expensive, given the current state of technology," Schwartz said. "Peter has done a study that found it's five years on the average from the initial contact to actually going into production." "Since multimedia became such a major buzzword, we're finding there are a lot more companies doing multimedia work," Bloch said. "The only market that is viable is the business market, so that every project that comes up there is hotly competed for."

Item	Rate	Unit	Qty	Cost	Subtotal
TELEPROMPTER	$300	DAY	2	$600	
DOLLY	$225	DAY	2	$450	
FIBER OPTIC LIGHTS	$100	DAY	5	$500	
DIMMER	$250	DAY	3	$750	
LIGHTS/GRIP		FLAT		$3,750	
EXPENDABLES		FLAT		$300	
DUMMY PROPS		FLAT		$750	
BLACK FELT		FLAT		$500	
EMULSION TESTS				$600	
FILM STOCK	$95	ROLL	10	$950	
4000' DEV./WP				$2,350	
CREW MEALS				$1,000	
CRAFT SERVICES				$500	
MISC.				$750	
CAMERA VAN	$50	DAY	6	$300	$45,700
AUDIO					
PRODUCER	$150	DAY	6	$900	
NARRATOR	$180	HOUR	6	$1,080	
STUDIO	$100	DAY	7	$700	
EDIT				$1,500	
SWEETEN				$1,000	
MUSIC (STOCK)				$1,200	
MUSIC RIGHTS				$500	
TRANSFERS				$300	
WINDOW DUBS				$200	
MISC MATERIAL				$200	$7,580
VIDEO POST					
TELECINE(Live action)	$700	HOUR	3	$2,100	
OFF LINE EDIT	$100	HOUR	30	$3,000	
MISC EXPENSES				$500	
EDITOR	$800	WEEK	3	$2,400	
ON LINE	$350	HOUR	18	$6,300	
TAPE STOCK				$700	
DUBS				$900	
CHECK DISC	$350		2	$700	
DISC MASTERING				$2,000	
REPLICAS	$15		40	$600	$19,200
GRAPHICS					
GRAPHIC DESIGNER	$300	DAY	5	$1,500	
TARGA SYSTEM	$50	HOUR	10	$500	
ARTIST	$20	HOUR	160	$3,200	
MISC MATERIALS				$200	
COMPUTER SUPPLIES				$250	$5,650

Movie Model: Schwartz drew on his experience in film-making to budget the Getty project.

THE FUTURE: Multimedia In-House

While user response to the "Illuminated Manuscripts" exhibit has been positive, The Getty Museum has not produced, nor does it have plans for, another similar interactive system. However, that does not mean the museum has abandoned educational multimedia. "They are thinking multimedia," said Kren, referring to the Getty Trust's construction of a major museum complex near Santa Monica. "The Education Department here is now extremely involved with a range of media for presenting information about the collections. They have discovered that people learn in different ways. For example, multimedia is ideal for self-directed learners. They will be in charge of information centers located strategically in relationship to the galleries throughout the new museum. These centers will be places for interactive videodiscs and various kinds of multimedia installations. The museum maintains a strong commitment to interpretive materials and to technological applications."

Getty Museum director, John Walsh, is confident that "some form of interactive video will come here [to the museum] again," but he expects "this next step to be towards programs that can be used in the museum and also have an afterlife—commercial or noncommercial—but in any case, [it will have] a wider use in either schools or homes." He believes that soon, "it will repay us many times over to digitize the entire collection," a time-consuming task that is now underway.

While Walsh is uncertain whether future multimedia projects will be produced in-house, by outside firms, or in a partnership between the two, Bloch expects the museum and other nonprofit institutions to "start making their own multimedia programs because you can make simple multimedia programs very easily with off-the-shelf software." Museums that do choose to hire outside "will probably look at the experience and track record of that company. Companies that take on these projects without the experience of dealing with these complex issues and client needs could find themselves getting into all kinds of problems."

Museum Multimedia: Getty Museum director, John Walsh, expects multi-purpose interactive programs to be part of the museum's future.

Meanwhile, the Getty has taken "some technological steps backward," Walsh admits. "We are making some little in-house videos of some demonstrations—how a piece of furniture is made, how a piece of art, like a bronze statue, is made. You could never explain these things in words, because who could follow that. But all you have to do is show them three minutes of video, and boom, they have the point. It's old fashioned, but it works."

12

"THE MULTIMEDIA CASEBOOK"

Black Cat Interactive

At A Glance

"THE MULTIMEDIA CASEBOOK CD-ROM"

Developers: Black Cat Interactive; Altura Software, conversion and CD-ROM mastering.

Key personnel: For Black Cat Interactive—Ron James, producer, art director, graphic designer, and programmer; and Mary Hellman, assistant producer, editor, and graphic designer. For Altura Software—Phil Faris, technical consultant; Lee Lorenzen, president; and technical staff.

Description: A multimedia, hybrid CD-ROM version of *The Multimedia Casebook*.

Development hours: 500 hours.

Development period: January 1994 to August 1994.

Development hardware: 486DX2 66 PC, 486DX 33 PC, VideoSpigot, Epson 800c scanner, Canon A1 Hi8 camcorder, Sound Blaster Pro sound card, and assorted household appliances.

Development software: Altura QuickView, Atimira Composer, Microsoft Viewer 2.0, Micrografx Picture Publisher 4.0, Adobe Photoshop 2.5, Corel Draw! 4.0, North Coast Software Inc. Conversion Artist, Adobe Premiere, ATI Media Merge, Lenel Multimedia Works, Microsoft Video for Windows 1.1, and Microsoft Word 5.0.

Presentation hardware: Certain PCs and Macintoshes.

Cost to develop: $2,500-plus

Future projects: Saturna's "Edible Garden" and "Seed Packet;" "Doc Adventure and The Discovery Street Kids."

Contact: Ron James
              Black Cat Interactive
              4674 Del Monte Avenue
              San Diego, CA 92107
              619–223–5337
              619–223–9238 (fax)

              Lee Lorenzen
              Altura Software
              510 Lighthouse Ave., Suite 5
              Pacific Grove, CA 93950
              408–655–8005
              408–655–9663 (fax)

There are two ways to qualify to be in this book. The first is to be the developer of a multimedia product that illustrates important areas of this new industry. The second is to be the authors of the book. We meet the latter criterion. We do not claim to be in the same league as the multimedia pioneers profiled in the previous chapters. However, our undertaking—the creation of a cross-platform, hypermedia version of this book, on CD-ROM—provides a glimpse of an aspect of multimedia development not covered previously. Specifically, we have documented the production of a sophisticated, multimedia title from a tiny in-home studio, with a laughable budget, very limited, although inspired, person-power, and a very tight deadline. Warning! If you attempt this in your home, the authors and publisher assume no responsibility for damage resulting from stress, fatigue and frequent falls off the learning curve.

Black Cat Interactive, our multimedia production company, is the quintessential "mom-and-pop" operation, named for our magnificent blind, three-legged black cat, Bix. Thousands of dollars of hardware, software, and video and audio equipment are crammed

The Casebook CD-ROM: The CD-ROM with this book was designed to highlight the multimedia elements of each project discussed.

into a space about the size of a walk-in closet, in our home in the San Diego community of Ocean Beach. In this "office," just three blocks from the Pacific Ocean, we put together the included CD-ROM version of this book.

"The Multimedia Casebook CD-ROM" was part of our initial proposal to our publisher. It seemed like a good idea at the time. After all, most computer books being published today have a floppy disk or CD-ROM packaged inside the front or back cover. However, too many of these "bonus" floppies or discs are little more than gimmicks to make the book buyer feel as though he or she is getting some added value with his or her purchase. The majority contain little of consequence—a few shareware programs, a couple of software demos, etc.

However, from the beginning, we saw how a multimedia version of this book could be an ideal complement to the text. The video and audio excerpts from the programs profiled, plus four-color photographs and screen shots, would bring those programs to life for the reader in a way that still photography and words cannot. Given our limitations of time, equipment and money, we envisioned a simple, but dynamic, multimedia program.

It did not quite work out that way. Our modest demo disc took on a life of its own, and, during the six months it took to complete, almost without our knowing, it grew into a complex and powerful software product that can stand alone, unaccompanied by the pulp version. "It's alive!" Ron often felt like shrieking, as the digital monster consumed more and more of our time, resources—and hard drive. In the end, like the other multimedia developers showcased in this book, we survived—scarred but wiser. Next time, we'll follow all that good advice about planning, teamwork, and project management.

Since we work in both the traditional publishing and the multimedia industries, we have been part of the great debate on the fu-

Writers At Work: Research for this book took authors Mary Fallenstein Hellman and W. R. James on location to the J. Paul Getty Museum, shown above.

ture of books. Will they soon be collecting dust on library shelves, as we climb into bed with a multimedia lap top, which weighs less than a Anne Rice novel? Or will multimedia "books" be a flash in the pan, which never had a chance to outshine "real" books in popularity?

"The Multimedia Casebook CD-ROM" has shown us this does not have to be an either-or debate. Instead, publishers of text and multimedia have the opportunity to package the two together, creating "books" for the Information Age. In many cases, a CD-ROM—with its video, audio, and animation—augments text, and enriches the "reading" experience. Consider a hypertext version of "Hamlet," with videos of famous actors reading the most famous lines; or an interactive map, included with an atlas; or cooking demonstrations, included with Julia Child's new cookbook.

We expect to see more "bundling" along these lines, as the installed base of multimedia PCs expands. These products will fit on shelves in book and computer stores, in home and school libraries, in briefcases and backpacks. They will give users options, without great additional expense. Eventually, as some futurists have predicted, they will become one and the same: The product will look like a book, but have a computer inside. Now, that's a project we'd like to work on.

THE OPPORTUNITY: A Power Book

As this multimedia project took shape, we were interviewing the developers featured in this book. Each related all too common development horror stories (rarely revealed to the mainstream trade press). Many times we shuddered, thinking about the ugly multimedia moments in store for us. On the other hand, we got caught up in the joys of the creative process, just as these pioneers recounted how they pushed pixels in ways not imagined. Inspired by their enthusiasm, we eagerly booted up our trusty PCs to work on the multimedia version of this book. We knew we would skin a few digital knuckles in the process, but we hoped we would finish with the same great sense of accomplishment (and relief) shared by the pioneers we had interviewed.

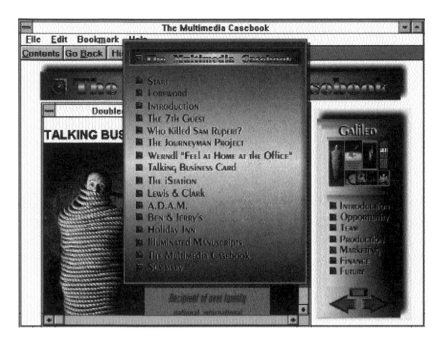

Take Your Pick:
James wanted the CD-ROM to allow users both linear and non-linear access to all of the book's content

As we began our work on this project, it became obvious that the best way to explain the power of multimedia was to use it. A book about exceptional multimedia projects, filled with audio, video, special effects, and animation, was a logical subject for a multimedia application. What better way to understand the essence of a multimedia project than to hear its sound, and see it in motion? In this case, the limitations of print could be mitigated with a digital version, which would allow readers, to see, hear, and, we hope, better appreciate the projects discussed.

Having reviewed a wide variety of multimedia "books," we knew what we wanted to avoid. Shovelware, the dumping of text on to a CD-ROM, was out of the question, since it would defeat our purpose of showcasing multimedia. So was electronic page flipping, the endless scrolling of text, without the benefits of interactivity. On the other hand, we did not want multimedia for multimedia's sake—the temptation to litter the text with flashy multimedia elements without regard to content. Nor did we want to become so interactive that users would lose their bearings, as they moved from subject to subject, chapter to chapter.

Early in our discussions, we decided to make the content of the CD-ROM accessible in both linear and nonlinear ways. Users would have the option of moving, chapter by chapter, from beginning to end. At the same time, if they were interested in a particular subject, certain software, or a development issue, such as marketing, we wanted to give them the option of easy access to just those topics. Thus, we could play to the strengths of both media.

As developers, working out of our homes, we had no choice but to do this project on our home PCs, using off-the-shelf software. Given the variety of powerful programs now available, this limitation, initially, did not seem to be a drawback. In fact, we hoped we could demonstrate what is possible with technology within reach of almost everyone. However, as the project grew, we longed for more hard drive storage, more RAM, more on-line assistance from software firms. Many times we also dreamed of adding programming whiz Graeme Devine to our team.

This project also gave us the opportunity to create a CD-ROM title for mass distribution. For our national debut, we faced the curse, and the blessing, of being associated with many of the industry's acknowledged stars. Since our work would stand along side theirs, we felt a great sense of responsibility to create a product that would not diminish their exciting applications. Fortunately, we had the benefit of their experiences to help us.

THE TEAM: An Old Dog Learns Some New Tricks.

Baby boomers, take heart. While it may appear that this new industry will be shaped by twenty-, and thirtysomethings, there should be plenty of room for your generation, as well as members of almost any other generation, to get in on the multimedia action. The only regret many of us middle-aged developers have is that we often wish we could have found this niche a couple of decades earlier.

In 1989, at the age of 43, Ron was semiretired from The James Gang, a graphic arts company that he had started with his brothers in 1976. That summer, Mary (now his co-author) asked him to

Raising The Flag: A virtual company flag James created using 3D Studio. James and Hellman named their multimedia firm after their cat, Bix.

design a flyer to help sell her condominium and steered Ron to her son Aaron's Mac Plus. "This was my first experience with a computer graphics program," Ron recalled, although he had worked with three graphic artists for a dozen years in his old business. After fooling around with MacDraw for an hour or two, he produced a pretty professional looking document. "This was fun," he said. "Soon I had my own graphic design studio and was producing logos, brochures, and newsletters for companies in the San Diego area."

W. R. James: This California developer started his multimedia career with a project for kids.

About a year later, San Diego City college offered an honors animation class that taught the use of Macromind Director. On a whim, Ron enrolled in the class. "I was blown away by this program. I knew from that first class that multimedia was my future," he said. By the time the course ended, he and his classmates had produced a sophisticated multimedia project for the Metropolitan Transit Board, designed to help tourists get around San Diego using buses and trolleys.

Ron then looked around for an opportunity to put his new-found skills to work. Unfortunately, at that time, there wasn't much call for local multimedia talent, so Ron decided to develop his own title. Inspired by one of the first "hit" CD-ROM titles, "National Geographic's Mammals," he thought, "Hey, we have the greatest zoo in the world here in my backyard, The San Diego Zoo. So I went to work on 'ZooCrazy.' "

Ron envisioned "ZooCrazy" to be an animated "info-tainment" for the whole family. In it, Doc Adventure, a combination tour guide, scientist and wacky grampa, would lead a diverse group of children, as they learned about zoos around the world, and their animals. Their tour bus would make three stops—the program's three modules—at ZooU, ZooTour and The Animal Hall of Fame, home of Hollywood's apes and literature's lions. Unlike many of the titles available at that time, Ron wanted to spice "ZooCrazy" with plenty of humor and off-beat information.

Dale Sedenquist: The Ocean Beach artist helped James bring Doc Adventure, and other "ZooCrazy" scenes to life.

With storyboards in hand, Ron enlisted Ocean Beach artist, Dale Sedenquist, to sketch characters and scenes. "From his scanned pencil drawings, I filled in color and animated the characters using Autodesk's Animator Pro," he said. "For the demo, I used a basic authoring program; Tempra Show, knowing that a more sophisticated program would be needed for the finished product. After about six months of work we had a prototype."

The ordeal of trying to market "ZooCrazy" was a valuable learning experience. During the roller coaster ride of rising expectations and dashed hopes, Ron's and Mary's eyes were opened to the realities of this new and volatile business. "One small-time publishing company loved the program, and dazzled us with talk of big sales and big money, both of which were ridiculous at that time, and promises were broken," Ron recalled. Slowly the reality of the multimedia consumer market—or the lack of it at that time—began to sink in. At about this same time, The Software Toolworks debuted the outstanding zoo program "Animals," featuring the San Diego Zoo. "The retailing mentality was that there was only room for one or two CD-ROM titles in a given category. Even if it was great, what chance would another zoo title like ZooCrazy have to get into the stores?" he wondered.

Next, a large four-letter corporation expressed an interest in the program, now wisely repackaged as the first installment in a series, called "Doc Adventure and the Discovery Street Kids." Simultaneously, Ron began drafting the second title in the series, "DinosaurCrazy." "Kids love dinosaurs, and there were no dinosaur CD-ROMs on the market then," Ron said. "At least there weren't any for about two weeks after we had gotten underway." Within a month, it seemed, the trade magazines were filled with news of new and about-to-be-released dinosaur titles. "And the large company just kind of forgot about me, Doc, and the kids," Ron remembered.

Ron was discouraged, especially as the media buzz about multimedia and the information highway began to grow louder and louder. "However, these experiences made me want to learn even more about this business—about marketing channels, competition,

'ZooCrazy' Screens: James envisioned a lively adventure CD-ROM for kids that would be set in the San Diego Zoo.

alliances, techniques and technologies," he said. "So I began writing about it for The San Diego Computer Journal. If you can't do it, or at least sell it, then write about it, I reasoned." His quest for information about how other developers took a good idea to market eventually led to the idea for this book.

In the process, Ron didn't forget about Doc Adventure and the kids of "ZooCrazy." They have their day in the CD-ROM sun at last as part of the digital version of this chapter.

During these years, Mary took a keen interest in Ron's early multimedia work, cheering him on "while sometimes wondering what he was talking about and why we were always buying a computer this, or that, instead of adding to our collection of Native American pottery," she said. Saturdays often would be spent previewing CD-ROM titles, and slowly she got a grounding in this new art form, and its vast possibilities. "Occasionally, I'd feel bold enough to join Ron in talking multimedia, something he would do at the drop of a hat," she said. "Plus I couldn't ignore the flood of ink on this topic. Ron, I decided, was on to something."

While she may not have been a computer expert, Mary gives herself credit for recognizing a good idea—Ron's proposal for this book. "I encouraged him to put his plan in writing and run it past our agent," she said. "I admit that, in the back of my mind, I wasn't sure it would find a buyer. I didn't believe we were going to be coauthors until the day we signed the contract. Then, talk about a learning curve." A veteran journalist, now the Books Editor for *The San Diego Union-Tribune*, who viewed computers as word processors, and little more, Mary found herself talking with a wide range of multimedia experts, about the intricacies of development. "It was frightening, especially the first time I had to do an interview by myself," she recalled. "I was convinced I'd use the wrong term, or ask a question that revealed how much I still had to learn. I was lucky, in that I had the opportunity to learn from some of the legends of this industry."

Mary Fallenstein Hellman: The Books Editor for a San Diego newspaper got a fast introduction to multimedia technology.

Ron patiently endured Mary's initiation into the Information Age. "Soon she was talking the talk, walking the walk, and even offering me creative criticism on the CD-ROM," Ron said. "I can't get away with handing down my old equipment to her any more. She's been talking seriously about a 90 mhz Pentium PC." These days, both Ron and Mary scan newspapers and magazines for multimedia news, keeping each other abreast of developments. He attends trade shows; she doesn't. She reads software manuals; he doesn't. The couple are proof positive of Cindy Steinberg's observation that multimedia development is a team effort.

To complete "The Multimedia Casebook CD-ROM," Black Cat Interactive joined forces with a northern California software firm. The alliance grew out of Ron's desire to create a hybrid or cross-platform version of the CD-ROM, for Windows and Macintosh. "A cross-platform title was appealing, because of the huge installed-base of Windows, and because most multimedia developers, as well as many potential readers of this book, are Mac people," Ron said. "The idea also scared the hell out of me, after hearing horror stories regarding the conversion process. Fortune smiled on me when I virtually ran into Phil Faris on CompuServe."

In response to an inquiry on the on-line multimedia forum, Faris mentioned an upcoming program, from Altura Software, a small company in Pacific Grove, California. Altura's software would convert programs designed in Microsoft's Viewer 2.0, into titles that would run on Macintosh computers. "Soon, I was talking with the president of Altura Software, Lee Lorenzen, who kindly offered me his new program, QuickView, and his help in the conversion process," Ron said. Faris, a consultant, who now works with Altura, was instrumental in the conversion process, which took place at the company's Pacific Grove facilities during August 1994.

Altura Software, Inc., was founded in 1990. Its original goal was to develop database publishing software on the Macintosh, to be sold as a vertical market solution for the mail order industry. In doing so, the company began initial research and development of the technology that would move Macintosh source code to the Windows platform. In 1991, Altura used this technology to port Fractal Design Corporation's Painter to Windows.

Help From Altura: The northern California firm, including consultant Phil Faris, left, and Lee Lorenzen, right, helped convert the Windows CD-ROM into a Macintosh version.

Before he helped found Altura Software, Lorenzen worked at Xerox on a PC-based prototype of the early Star computer. He continued his ground-breaking work at Digital Research where he contributed to the development of GEM Application Environment Service and GEM Desktop. Later, as a cofounder of Ventura Software, he designed and wrote large portions of Ventura Publisher, and developed the porting mechanism for moving Ventura Publisher to Windows and OS/2.

Faris retired from the Air Force in 1992 after serving as a Middle East Intelligence Analyst. He also was project manager for Educational Technology at the Defense Language Institute, where he established a large project to develop foreign language training software for CD-ROM distribution. In 1992, he founded LE Centre Inc., a consulting business to support publishers of multimedia and multilingual educational software. He is currently co-located with Altura, where he is supporting Windows, and Macintosh multimedia CD-ROM, publishers with authoring tools and techniques, as well as custom CD-ROM production.

PRODUCTION: A Case of Multimedia

Navigation and Interface Design

Starting from Scratch:
James sketched out the interface while sipping margaritas in Mexico.

High on a seaside bluff, at a patio table outside a favorite Baja California restaurant, Mary and Ron sketched the flow of "The Casebook" CD-ROM on a legal pad, in between sips of margarita. "Multimedia production isn't so bad, I thought to myself," Ron remembers. "Our goal that day was to devise a program that would be simple and easy to use. We wanted the user to be able to use the program in linear fashion, much as he, or she, would a book. However, we also wanted to take advantage of the power of interactivity to navigate easily between chapters, and parts of chapters."

Cooled by an ocean breeze, Ron sketched, again and again, the control panel and its many buttons and arrows. Initially, there was a button for every chapter on the main menu screen. Each button would sport a screen shot,

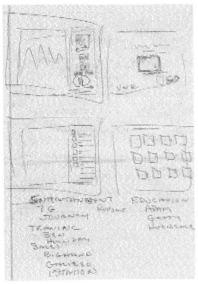

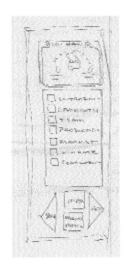

representing the project described in the chapter. Then the buttons would be grouped by category—entertainment, business, and education—just as the chapters are in the book. When a button was clicked, the chapter would appear along with an on-screen controller, much like a television remote control. The controller would enable users to navigate inside the chapter, via the subtopics (The Opportunity, the Team, etc.) listed on the controller. Another button on the controller would access the book's table of contents, enabling users to move easily from chapter to chapter. A final button would take them back to the main screen. "It looked pretty good to us," Ron said. "Even my drawings on the yellow pad looked impressive. So we called it a day and congratulated ourselves on a fine brainstorming session."

Navigating the Book:
Two stages of controller development.

A few days later, in the Ocean Beach studio, Ron began to try to decipher his chicken scratches on the salsa-stained tablet. "Using Corel Draw!, I drew a box representing a 640 x 480 screen and began drawing very basic interface elements," he said. "When I started drawing the main screen with button icons representing each chapter, I knew I had a problem. Busy, busy, busy...too many buttons." His initial solution was to add another layer, devising a screen for each category. "But I decided against that too," he said. "Then it

dawned on me that the answer was the red table of contents button, one I had already labelled 'Index' on the controller. It would always be present, and any time a user wanted to get anywhere in the program, all he or she had to do was to click that button." Ron also eliminated the icons for each chapter, opting instead for "Hot Words" on the index. "If the user can't read the 'Hot Words,' then they're in the wrong program. They should go boot up 'Doom' or something," he reasoned.

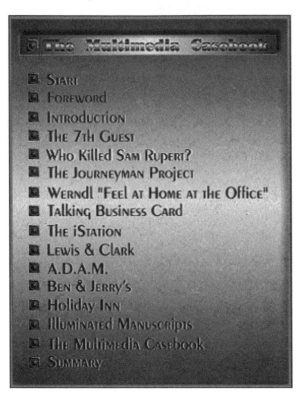

Navigation Popup: "Hot Words" in this pop-up allow the user to go anywhere in the book, at anytime.

The index button fulfills another important function in the program. It enables the user to exit at any time. "That's critically important information for the user," Ron said. "That ever-present red button is their ticket to travel anywhere in the book." Used in combination with the controller arrows, which allow users to move forward and backward in the program, these features provide linear and non-linear access to all the information in the text. "It's up to the user, to decide what suits his, or her, needs best," Ron said.

Based on interviews with other developers, Ron and Mary also were determined to provide users with a "bookmark," that tells them where they are in the program at all times. "I designed the controller to feature a screen shot from that particular chapter, and I put the name of the chapter above it," Ron said. "To facilitate quick access to various parts of each case chapter, 'Hot Words' for each main subtopic in the chapters were added on the body of the controller. Using this feature, the user wouldn't have to scroll the entire chapter to get to an area of interest."

As the program evolved, Ron continued to fine-tune the navigation and interface. "I discovered there was no way to get to the beginning of the chapter without either leaving it and returning to the index, or scrolling it back to the beginning," he said. "To remedy this, I simply made the screen graphic on the controller *hot* and programmed it to jump to the beginning of that chapter, when it was clicked."

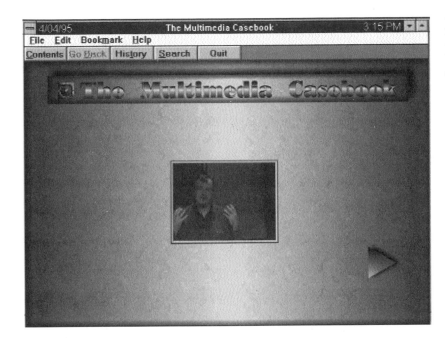

Before and After: Early(top) and final versions of the chapter interface.

Graphic Design

Like the navigation design, the program's graphic look evolved through several stages. Again, the goal was to keep the graphics clean and simple, so they did not interfere with the chapter content or use of the multimedia program. "Initially I made the controller, scrolling windows, and header out of simple rectangles in Corel Draw!, in order to plug them into the authoring program to see their size in relation to each other," Ron said. "Then using Corel Draw! and Micrografx Picture Publisher 4.0, I designed the elements to echo the cover design of the book I had submitted to the publisher (VNR)." This design was used in the first program demo, "in order to see, first of all, if the program would work, and second, to show VNR's staff what they could expect on the CD-ROM," Ron explained.

The program worked, and the graphics looked good, but Ron felt the design needed more work. "I felt the interface needed more depth and texture," he said. "I wanted a high-tech look that suited the subject matter, and the flat screens just didn't have that look." He said that the solution emerged during an interview with Trilobyte's graphics guru, Robert Stein III, "who told me he was very impressed with Altimira Composer, a new graphics program for the PC. I decided to take a look at it, and at first blush, the program seemed very difficult to use. The interface was unlike any paint programs on the market and it definitely wasn't intuitive...at least to me. However after going through the well-designed tutorials, I realized what a powerful and useful program this was."

Highlights and Shadows: James used Altimira Composer to give depth to the interface elements.

The next day, Ron used Composer to redesign the interface, and other graphic elements. "The tools in Composer enabled me to get the subtle shading and shadowing I was looking for," he said. "Its ability to anti-alias text and imported graphic elements also helped give the overall composition an integrated look. Although I still use

**Chapter Introduc-
tion Screens:**
Short video se-
quences introduce
each chapter.

Photoshop and Picture Publisher 4.0 for certain jobs, Composer now is my main program for design."

While the graphic look was being polished, Mary and Ron began gathering the materials needed for the program's graphic and multimedia elements. This process turned into one of their biggest headaches in producing both digital and print versions of "The Casebook." "We ended up getting every conceivable type of format from our casebook developers, from little-known—to us—OS\2 files, Mac files without file extensions, to very low resolution .GIF and very large .TGA files," Mary said. "We were supplied with photographs—black and white, and in color—Kodak photo CDs, slides, transparencies, negatives, rolls of film, video tape, floppies, removable cartridges, tape and brochures. The task was daunting at best." As a result, the images in the book, as well as the CD-ROM, vary widely in quality. So do the audio and video elements in the digital version. "The only quality control possible would be to create all of the graphics needed, using one format and strict guidelines," Mary said. "That would up the production costs so high, that projects like this would become out of reach for most publishers."

Initially, Ron and Mary relied on a hand-held color scanner to digitize the brochures and photos. "We quickly found out that this was very time-consuming, because we would usually have to scan the image two or three times before we could get a decent image," Mary said. "Even then, we often couldn't get the quality we felt was necessary for the book, as well as the CD-ROM." A first solution was to use the scanner at a local copy shop, but that proved time-consuming and frustrating, since it required many trips as materials arrived in the mail. "So we decided to blow our budget on an Epson 800c scanner," said Ron. "We now preach that a good quality scanner is absolutely necessary for at-home multimedia production."

In order to use the graphic images in Viewer 2.0, Ron and Mary had to convert all of the graphics files into 256-color .BMP files. "Fortunately, we came across a great little program, Conversion Artist, from North Coast Software, which reduced most of the various 24-bit graphics files into 256 colors, using an optimized palette and dithering system," Ron said. "It was so good that it was difficult in most cases to tell the millions of color images from the 256 versions. I also used the Bit Edit and Pal Edit programs to merge a special pallet, supplied to us by Phil Faris at Altura, to reduce pallet flashes in the CD-ROM program."

To simplify the sizing of the graphics and illustrations, already digitized for use in the print version, Ron decided to scale all of them down to three inches wide. Mary used the batch function in Picture Publisher 4.0 to convert the images into three-inch wide, 256-color, .BMP files, ready to insert into the authoring program.

Audio and Video

Most of the audio and video in the CD-ROM was obtained directly from the titles, or from promotional videos, supplied by the developers. All audio, including music, is digitized .WAV files. "We decided not to use MIDI," Ron said, "because there was plenty of room on the disc for the larger .WAV files, and there's still a lot of compatibility problems with MIDI drivers, and standards used in the many sound cards on the market. The highlight of the game chapters is the original musical scores, showing how important music and sound effects are in the future of title development.

All of the video was digitized, shot in the Black Cat Interactive studios, using available light from the one, west-facing window and the two 60-watt bulbs in the overhead fixture. Using a SuperMatch VideoSpigot card for the PC, the video was digitized and then compressed using the SuperMatch Cinepac compression codec. A Canon A1 Hi8 camcorder was used to shoot introductory video sequence for each chapter. "Because of budget constraints, we used non-union actors in these sequences," quipped Ron, who joins Mary in her national video debut. "We borrowed our video strategies from the Rik Dryfoos 'let's-just-get-the-damned-thing-done' school of videography."

Authoring

After some hand-wringing, Ron decided to use Microsoft's Viewer 2.0 to author the CD-ROM, for two reasons. "First, it was the most powerful off-the-shelf multimedia program with a sophisticated hypertext engine," he explained. "Second, I received a free, reviewer's copy just as I was starting the project. As learning curves go, the one for Viewer 2.0 runs from, 'hey, that's pretty easy,' to 'there's no #@%% way.'"

After a first run through the tutorial, Ron mistakenly thought, "This is going to be a piece of cake. This, and many other tutorials, are misleading because the tutorial programs on them are almost finished, and they walk you through only a few of the tasks it took to do that. Wham, bam, the tutorial is over. That was easy. Now how do I really put together a multimedia title from scratch? Where are the land mines in the program? Why doesn't it do that, or this? Without the benefit of lessons, or a programming Yoda next door, I could only slog along, step by mucky step, until I beat the rascally thing into shape."

Altura Software to the Rescue:
Lee Lorenzen's team help the authors convert the Windows program to Macintosh.

To start, Ron used the scripting code from the tutorial to author a chapter, using a window of "Hot Words" to jump to various sections of the chapter. "I went into the script, and substituted my text for their text, and my images, audio, and video, for theirs," he explained. "That worked to a point, making me somewhat familiar with a few primary scripting techniques."

The next step was to adjust the panes, which, in Viewer, are the windows that hold graphics, video and text. Panes are used to design screens throughout the program. "The panes were a royal pain," Ron said. "For nearly three weeks, I futilely attempted to create or change the size of the panes in the program. They just wouldn't cooperate, even though I went through the tutorial dozens of times, and even read the manual." It took a minor disaster—the crash of Ron's hard drive—to help solve "the riddle of the reluctant panes," he continued. "I reformatted my hard drive and reloaded Windows, which defaulted to 640 x 480, 256 colors. I loaded Viewer 2.0 and began to rebuild my primitive program. Shazam, the panes were working. When I positioned a pane, it stayed exactly where I had placed it." Before he reloaded, Ron said he had been working with his video set to 640 x 480, with 64-K color. "But Viewer would only cooperate when it was in the 256 mode," he continued. "It only pretended to work in the bunch-more-colors mode. It was a lesson I will never forget."

Ron recalled many other little struggles along the learning curve for this, and most other, arcane software programs. "Some of the solutions and warnings are hidden in the manuals, but just as many are not," he said. "One little annoyance occurred as I first attempted to imbed graphics into the text. I would get these nasty little pop-ups, telling me that I was not authoring correctly. I wish they had been a little more specific, but it only took me a few minutes to figure out, that the images I was trying to imbed were 24-bit, and Viewer only allows for 256-color images. That information was tucked in the manual...my fault."

Some procedures and techniques in the manual about preparing a title for CD-ROM production were either questionable, or practically impossible to figure out, Ron noted. "When I finally found my Viewer 2.0 Yoda, in the form of Phil Faris, the guy I ran into on CompuServe, he would tell me, 'Forget that way of doing it...it doesn't work. I have a program that will do that. If you do it (Viewer's) way, you'll never get done.'" Finding Faris was "a god-send," Ron believes, and he encourages other developers to take advantage of on-line multimedia forums. "They can save you a whole lot of time and money," he said. "Every time I log on, I find something interesting, or useful, and in the case of this book, the means to go cross-platform."

One suggestion from Faris saved Ron hundreds of hours of compiling time. "Viewer 2.0 allows you to store all of your multi-media files within the master file, in what they call baggage," Ron explained. "At first, this was really cool, because I didn't have to search my drives, trying to locate the graphics, audio, and video files. But the more multimedia elements I added, the longer it took to compile the program—and you had to compile the program every time you made a change in the script." Some chapters, he recalled, required hundreds of little changes and to preview each meant "compiling up to 30 megabytes of media files, which took 20 or so minutes on my 486 66DX2. This nightmare would only get worse when I put all the chapters together."

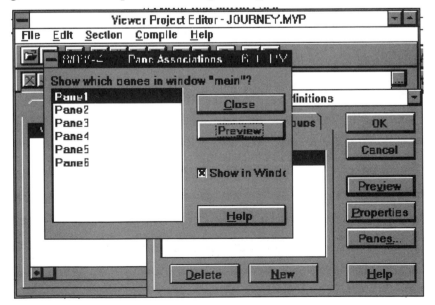

A Paneful Interface: James had a difficult time getting the panes to follow instructions in Viewer 2.0.

All Aboard?:
Viewer 2.0 allows you to store your files in baggage, but the author found that may not be the best solution.

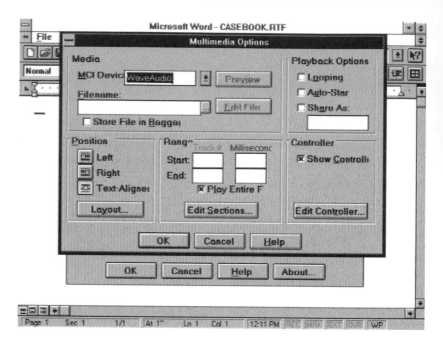

Instead of storing the files in baggage, Faris told Ron to put them in folders on the hard drive. Each element—.AVIs, .WAV, etc.—had its own folder. "This method was a real time-saver," Ron explained, "because when you compiled a change, only the text was compiled, instead of all the graphics and audio files. Phil also said this step would make the master process more efficient."

Time, of course, was a precious commodity, as the CD-ROM was being built. Van Nostrand Reinhold wanted the CD-ROM master just two weeks after the final editing of the manuscript was completed. "Since the text in the CD-ROM had to be the same as in the book, I couldn't actually insert text, or any of the multimedia elements, until we received a final OK on the copy," Ron said. "In order to get a head start, I did as much of the program as I could using placeholders, such as a short video file representing all of the video, and topic headings representing entire chapter segments. I tested the navigation using these 'lightweight' place holders, so all I would have to do was substitute the final text and multimedia elements for the finished version." Ron also programmed the controller for each chapter, which he nicknamed "shorties," and the "Hot

Spots," so they would jump to the target chapter section. "Each controller was named: ShortyJ for 'The Journeyman Project,' ShortyG for the Getty's 'Illuminated Manuscripts' chapter, and so on," he said. "Then I would test it, using the placeholders. When I was finished, I would move on to the next chapter."

Since each chapter was similar in structure, Ron relied on a template he created to hold the placeholders. "I would rename each of the jump spots and pop-ups in the script, so they would take instructions from the controller programmed for that particular chapter," he said. "It got very confusing at times, especially when I would quit working on it for a week or two, to focus on writing or editing the book. When I'd go back to the CD-ROM, I would have to relearn how to 'rewire' my template." As a result, Ron doesn't recommend "trying to write, design and layout a book and develop a multimedia title at the same time."

Since he had heard horror stories about converting Windows to Macintosh, and vice versa, months earlier, Ron had arranged for help from Altura. "I practically begged Phil Faris and Lee Lorenzen to lend a hand," he admitted. "I only had two weeks to put this all together, a daunting task for an experienced developer, an insane task for me. Graciously, they took pity on me and invited me to Altura's Pacific Grove headquarters. They said they would help with the conversion, and even burn my worm." Prior to that, Faris asked Ron to send him a couple of chapters so that he could check the authoring.

At this writing, Ron and Mary still haven't received a final version of the manuscript. Thus, the hectic two weeks of final development cannot be part of this chapter, since it must be turned in before the manuscript can be finalized, before the CD-ROM can be finished. However, below are the conversion procedures as Faris explained them to Ron.

The Windows version of "The Multimedia Casebook" CD-ROM first will be transferred to a large hard drive. Then Altura's QuickView program converts the Windows files into Macintosh files. "Then, we will do some tweaking," said Faris. "For example, the type will look smaller in the Macintosh version, so we will have to change the type faces to either a bolder style, or large font, or both." After each tweak, the program is recompiled, which takes up to an hour and a half. "Hopefully, we will only have to compile the program three or four times," he continued. "When we're satisfied with the look of the Macintosh version, we check to make sure all of the Windows files are there, and functioning."

After the program is tested, Faris imports the Macintosh and Windows files on to a large newly formatted Macintosh hard drive The files are arranged in order to facilitate optimum playability, by keeping the seek times minimized. When everything is in place, including Macintosh and Windows CD-ROM player software, the CD-ROM is burned. "This is an abbreviated version of the process Phil described," Ron said, "since the unabridged explanation was a bit on the arcane side, given my limited technological capabilities. I'm just glad Phil will be there. It gives me a good feeling about the final authoring and conversion. Both probably came off without a digital hitch. Besides, if there is a shiny, silver disc stuck to the back of the book, everything must have gone great. Thanks Phil. Thanks Lee."

One final detail: Ron and Mary hope the CD-ROM works on your computer; but if it doesn't, don't call them or Van Nostrand Reinhold. Neither has tech support. Instead, follow Ron's advice and "keep changing computers, until you find one on which it works."

FINANCE: On A Used Shoestring

Ron and Mary wondered why most of the developers they interviewed for the book laughed when they were asked how many hours it took to complete their project or title. Now, both authors understand. "Do you count the hours you spend working on the project, while staring at the ceiling from three to five in the morning? Do you count the time learning new programs and techniques? Or even the hours spent reading trade journals and browsing CompuServe and America Online forums?" Ron asked. "It is almost impossible to know, much less try to estimate beforehand."

Even the best predictions tend to meaningless, since most developers push themselves, without regard to time or money, to do a good job on a title or project. "No wonder, most of us end up making two bits an hour," Ron quipped. "Although, if the CD-ROM helps sales of this book, which will increase our royalties, our effort will start to pay off."

While there are benefits to devising a realistic budget for this and other multimedia projects, Ron believes that "breaking even or even losing money on early multimedia projects is not unusual in this business. This can be justified, assuming you can handle the financial ramifications, because it takes experience and exposure to command budgets that include a profit for the developer. As the market for all types of multimedia applications dramatically increases in the coming years, the experienced developer, with a portfolio of quality work, will be able to write his, or her, own ticket."

FUTURE: Case After Case of Multimedia

Even before this book was finished, Ron and Mary already were involved in new projects in the multimedia arena. Both agreed to co-author a second book on multimedia, focusing on the process of development, rather than individual projects. They also have proposed volume two of "The Multimedia Casebook." Both titles would be packaged with related CD-ROMs—cross-platform, of course. "At this stage in the development of this new industry," Mary said, "it is exciting to get to know the pioneers who are bringing an art form to life. Their stories and projects, in a few years, will comprise a valuable history for future gen-

Future Projects:
One of the many screens designed by James for Saturna Interactive's Edible Garden CD-ROM title.

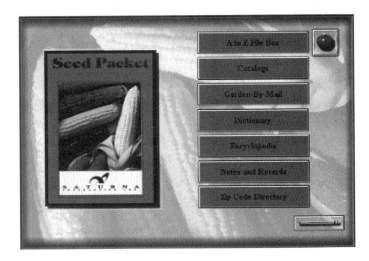

erations, as well as serve as an inspiration for up-and-coming developers and entrepreneurs."

At the same time, Ron has managed to fit in some multimedia projects that are not book-related. He recently completed, involved two CD-ROM demonstration gardening titles, authored in Asymetrix Multimedia ToolBook, for Saturna Interactive. He is now working on a marketing CD-ROM for the Hotel Del Coronado. "Regardless of where this all leads," Ron said, "I know our future is wrapped up in multimedia. We have a chance to make our mark in this limitless, powerful business, because we are among the pioneers, exploring new ways of communication, creating new paradigms. And, who knows, `Doc Adventure and The Discovery Street Kids' may someday have their own CD-ROM."

PLAYING THE CD-ROM

For best performance, we recommend a big, fast 486 PC or Macintosh Quadra computer with a double or triple-speed CD-ROM player, a video card that displays thousands of colors, 8 megabytes of RAM and a really cool amplified sound system. The program was designed for 640 x 480 viewing, but it works in higher modes as well.

WARNING: Before installing the CD-ROM on a PC, you should back up your system.ini file so you have an extra copy in your Windows directory. In case of any system defects, restore your original system.ini file and reboot your computer.

To setup in Windows insert the CD-ROM disc into the player, go to the Program Manager, click the File menu, click the browse button to select the drive your CD-ROM drive is installed on. Then click the file folder titled **setup** and finally select the **setup.exc.** The computer will automatically setup Video for Windows player and an icon in the Program Manager. Click the icon to start the program.

Mac users should first make sure they are not using virtual memory. Once this feature is turned off, they should insert the CD-ROM into the player, an icon will appear on the desktop. Click on the icon and several files will be visible. Click the QuickTime update icon first for further instructions. After you are through setting up, click *The Multimedia Casebook* icon to get started. Have fun!

SUMMARY

Writing this chapter brings to mind the 19th-century poem about the six wise men "who went to see the elephant, though all of them were blind." Touching a part of the beast convinced each that he has found its identity. One feels the side and is certain it's a wall; another grabs a tusk and is convinced he's found a spear. The knee? Well, that's got to be a tree. And the ear? A fan. The tail? A rope. And that undulating trunk must be proof the men have met a snake.

We have attempted a similar feat, that is, trying to give a human, real-life dimension to the term *multimedia* by examining several cases. It's a task made more difficult by the fact that multimedia—our elephant—refuses to stand still. Instead it's moving at warp speed, propelled by technological change, unbridled imagination, and burgeoning public interest. Not only is it hard to get the whole picture, but what you see today is likely to be very different tomorrow. As a result, as anyone attempting to keep pace with this new medium knows, generalizations about the industry are quickly dated, and for the most part solipsistic. No wonder multimedia continues to defy easy definition.

Even so, an industry and an art form are emerging. Like early filmmakers, challenged and fascinated by the potential of a motion picture camera and film, multimedia pioneers are experimenting with new technologies, finding new ways to combine their power. And while there are how-to guides for using certain software, or thinking about key characteristics, like interface design, there's no guide yet —nor is there likely to be—to the application of human energy and imagination. This is what separates the genius, say of Thomas A. Edison from that of director D. W. Griffith. One made the motion picture camera, while the other invented the fade-out, cross-cut, close-up, and long shot and made "The Birth of a Nation."

The pioneering multimedia projects in this book reveal much about the business and practice of multimedia during the past five years, which may be useful to makers and/or users of multimedia applications. In the creation of these real-life applications, ranging from bestselling games to Talking Business Cards, one can glimpse the emerging marketplace for multimedia, its commercial applications, and the blood, sweat, and tears that make those projects a reality. Through the frustration of vanished gigabytes or dust-gathering training programs, discerning the emerging discipline of multimedia management is possible. While this industry seems to thrive on individuality and risk-taking, it is no longer the province of solitary hackers, or fantasy game players. Increasingly, it demands as firm a grasp of business practices and public relations as it does of programing to prosper.

Finally, these innovators, regardless of the scale of their undertaking, share a restless creative energy that fuels the multimedia elephant's forward motion. They are to be admired for recognizing the power of these tools, especially in the service of entrepreneurial and/or artistic vision, and for having the courage to try them out. As in the rough-and-tumble early days of the film industry, every project is an adventure, making what goes on behind the scenes almost more interesting than the finished product. "We don't know what we're doing when we start a lot of projects," admitted Big Hand's Lance Lyda. "We are pushing it, we are out there, saying 'yeah, we can do that.'" D. W. Griffith, we suspect, said the same.

THE OPPORTUNITY: Vision with Purpose

"As we got into creating A.D.A.M., we began to realize that we had to do things to the product to let people interact with it in interesting ways. Until that time, people were still caught in the textbook model of creating multimedia...we threw away the old model...we couldn't get locked in electronic page flipping."
—*Gregory M. Swayne, A.D.A.M. Software, Inc.*

Perhaps the biggest challenge in this new industry is to apply innovative multimedia technology in useful, functional ways, rather than use it simply for novelty's sake. Even at this early stage, clearly multimedia does not work as an add-on—"bells and whistles for the sake of bells and whistles," as Galileo's Jackie Goldstein is fond of pointing out. Mindless or meaningless "window dressing," even though technologically advanced, is simply confusing clutter.

Multimedia succeeds when developers, and/or users, harness powerful digital tools and techniques to solve problems, communicate, educate, and entertain. In training, for example, MicroMentor's Eric Vogt insists that multimedia augments "sound learning strategies." In its CD-ROM games, Presto Studios enlists animation and video to propel a story and some devilish puzzles into, what seems like, an interactive movie. In the classroom, a hot-spot must educate, not be the digital version of make work. Every time it is used, multimedia must enhance, enable, expand, involve. If it does not accomplish this, another medium, another tool, may be a better vehicle, a better solution.

On the other hand, simply confining multimedia's powerful attributes in the strictures of other media seems a shame, even if it is an understandable pitfall of working with new tools. A.D.A.M.'s Gregory Swayne, who dismisses such uses as "electronic page flipping," recalls the example of early filmmakers who pointed a camera at a stage production and tried to call it a movie. Attempts to create a multimedia art form are ongoing. At this early point in time, most applications mesh the standard or traditional forms with the new. The iStation, a listening booth for the '90s, and the Talking Business Card, are good examples of this hybrid. These enterprises benefit from familiarity and tend to be effective.

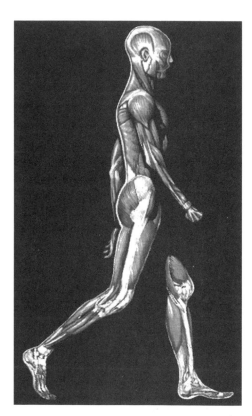

Form And Function: Multimedia must move beyond "electronic page flipping," as A.D.A.M. did.

The most experimental work of late has been nonlinear, which pushes the parameters of interactivity to allow highly personal usage. However, the confusion and disorientation that plague these freewheeling titles have frustrated and baffled many users. As a result, some developers who have experimented with nonlinear formats are returning to the proven beginning, middle, and end storytelling, as the best way to get any message across. The differences between "The 7th Guest" and its upcoming sequel, "The 11th Hour," mirror this changing viewpoint.

These pendulum swings about how to use multimedia are typical of new art forms. Over time, multimedia, like the film industry, will find its own voice and vision, most likely in ways some of its pioneers could never have imagined. Along the way, the uses of multimedia need to be both considered and imaginative, while conforming to time-tested tenets of education, entertainment, business, and communications. Here are some views of what is working, and why, in the four broad areas of multimedia represented by the preceding cases.

Education and Training

The use of multimedia in the classroom—whether the students are third-graders or middle managers—is certain to grow in the Information Age. On the job, well-developed multimedia training applications excel, solving a number of problems that have plagued companies, their in-house training specialists, and long-suffering students. Members of a diverse work force can learn a standardized curriculum at their own rate, and usually at their job site. Even with time to practice until perfect, multimedia training tends to cut the time away from work to half of what is demanded by traditional classroom presentations. No wonder executives, like Holiday Inn Worldwide's Jewell DeWeese, laud this interactive training as "a savior."

᾿ In the elementary or secondary school classroom, multimedia takes on a bigger role. It will not only help today's students in the age-old struggle with algebra, but it also will prepare them for the digital world of tomorrow. Dr. Ron Rescigno, superintendent of the Hueneme School District with its award-winning model technology schools, points out that educating today's students for tomorrow means ensuring they are computer literate. Convinced that the world is in the midst of a paradigmatic shift from a manufacturing-based, to an information-based economy, and society. He stresses, "Our vision has always been to prepare our students for what we think the millennium demands. And it's obvious to all of us that electronics aren't going to go away."

How to put multimedia in the classroom has been a challenge to both public and private school educators, and their business counterparts. Resistance to change, and the hefty investment required, keep DeWeese and Rescigno on their toes, battling for money and support. On the other hand, teachers like Hueneme's Steve Carr, or learning designers like MicroMentor's Cindy Steinberg, strive to create successful learning modules that are not so interactive that students miss the point, or become intimidated by the technology. Developers and clients alike must seek feedback from the target audience, as well as company executives, to avoid costly revisions or, worse yet, a product that is never used.

Regardless of the intended audience, training and educational multimedia need to conform to established classroom demands: ease of use, flexible learning strategies, built-in measures of student progress and low cost, to name a few. In programs destined for public school classes, content should fit into core curricula. Similarly, corporate training programs must suit the corporate culture, and each must be of high technical quality, so that its use does not interfere with the learning process. Thus, educators and multimedia experts generally must work hand-in-hand to bring these projects to fruition.

Solving Problems: Multimedia training, like this one for Holiday Inn staffers, eliminates many drawbacks to on-the-job learning.

When all of these factors succeed, students are the winners, and they know it. An often-cited landmark study of a multimedia class on the campus of California State University at Fullerton revealed that its students learned 40 percent faster, scored 10 percent higher on standard tests, and remembered what they learned longer than those in a typical classroom. The experience made believers out of the doubtful participants. Before the classes started, 78 percent of the students said they expected the classroom session to be superior. After they had experienced both multimedia and traditional learning, they were given a choice of a third class. Ninety-eight percent opted for multimedia learning.

Business and Sales

The advent of corporations fully wired for multimedia is right around the corner. While multimedia is used today by companies mostly for training and presentations, in the near future it will be commonplace in practically every facet of corporate life, from the boardroom to the lunch room. As multimedia becomes a standard tool of corporate communications, in-house multimedia departments will soon become the norm. Or, as Big Hand's Jay Wolff, predicted, companies soon will retain multimedia firms for large jobs and ongoing projects—much as they retain advertising agencies.

At present, most companies are in the midst of transition. They have seen the power of multimedia sales presentations, the effectiveness of CD-ROM product catalogs, the ease of online purchasing. They even may have contracted with a multimedia firm for a multimedia version of the annual report, or for a training module. They also may have an in-house committee looking into ways to access the ballyhooed information highway. At the same time, they are wrestling with some of the same issues that confound every multimedia user: the confusion of platforms, diverse hardware and software, and the rush of technological change. Executives of large companies face making costly financial commitments to technology that could be obsolete before it is delivered to headquarters. The resulting wariness generally limits many a firm's investment in new technology, and keeps an equal number on the sidelines, with a nervous wait-and-see attitude.

The impact of this push-and-pull psychology on in-house multimedia proponents and outside developers is the same. Both may need to ease companies, project-by-project, into the information age. And both must educate each other on issues of technological innovation to facilitate informed decision-making. At the same time, both may need to devise creative ways to finance, purchase, and implement new technologies, to lessen the risk of expensive blunders, and to provide for upgrades. Finally, each must urge leaders of the multimedia industry to formulate standards that will simplify purchasing new technology.

Fortunately for all interested parties, on the frontlines, or on the sidelines, there are an increasing number of multimedia success stories in the corporate world. Multimedia presentations, like the one Big Hand developed for Werndl, are becoming the sales force of the 1990s. Standard business documents, from business cards, to catalogs, to in-house newsletters, are coming to life with multimedia. In the future, as more and more companies around the world are linked to each other and their customers by compatible computer systems, more and more business will be done online.

In-Store Helpers: Businesses and consumers alike benefit from multimedia kiosks, like the iStation.

In retail establishments, kiosks are already proving their worth. Because of their familiarity with ATM machines and early multimedia displays in museums, consumers are comfortable seeking information from these multimedia workhorses. Kiosk users are confident they can ask a naive or repetitive question without getting a rude response from an overworked clerk. With their ability to playback numerous product catalogs housed on CD-ROMs, a kiosk can transform the corner store into an international department store, without shouldering its mom-and-pop proprietors with additional costly inventory.

For some products, as the iStation has shown with music, kiosks allow the consumer to sample before slapping down a credit card. The iStation also has demonstrated the previously untapped ability of these sophisticated machines to collect information about customers and their preferences. As they proliferate into globe-spanning networks, kiosks could become business's jack-of-all trades. Other uses are limited only by the imagination—and the pocketbooks of developers and their investors, since the start-up costs can be hefty.

Institutions

Kiosks, and other multimedia applications, offer similar options to museums, hospitals, and other institutions. As the "Illuminated Manuscripts" project at the J. Paul Getty Museum revealed, multimedia can be harnessed to enrich visitors' appreciation of little-known subjects, from artwork to a period in history, to a type of animal or a medical procedure. As space in many institutions is limited, multimedia also can be used to display little-exhibited, but valuable, parts of their collections. In addition, when these presentations, or a museum's collection, are transformed into multimedia consumer products, the institution becomes literally a museum without walls, and it gains a potential new source of income.

At the local, state, and national level, multimedia kiosks are becoming fixtures in government offices. Planning departments rely on them to convey permit and zoning information. State motor vehicle departments use them to answer questions about driver's license requirements. By 1995, the Internal Revenue Service hopes to offer multimedia tax information to befuddled citizens. In each case, the kiosks lessen the burden on overworked civil servants, and convey accurate and uniform information. Also, when laws or procedures change, these "government workers" can be quickly, and inexpensively, reprogrammed with the new information.

Developers who work with institutions, like museums or government agencies, will encounter some of the same obstacles they face with businesses: resistance to new technology, confusion over hardware and software, and concern about costs. In addition, they can expect added red tape from government bureaucracy or institutions' boards and committees. Approval processes alone add significant time and expense.

Confronted with the cost of multimedia production, institutions frequently want maximum bang for their multimedia bucks. In most cases, they expect their multimedia assets to be multipurpose. Information prepared for a kiosk, for example, would be transferred to a CD-ROM for sale in the gift shop, to schools and libraries, or to similar institutions. To be cost-effective, though, multiple uses need to be part of the initial planning and budgeting, since conversion of assets after a project is completed is quite costly.

Entertainment

With the installed base of CD-ROM players now in the millions, computer entertainment is no longer the exclusive domain of computer wizards. They now have to share the field with everyone from 3-year-old kids to 70-year-old seniors, all of whom are fueling a skyrocketing demand for consumer titles. After years when programmers by-and-large created games that amused themselves, developers now are challenged to produce diverse titles for a diverse audience: computer golf games for dad, interactive storybooks for kids, and gardening books for mom.

As with any new industry, there has been a painful shakedown period in CD-ROM title development. Unfortunately, many multimedia users soured on this technology when they tried some of the CD-ROM junk bundled with their new computers, sound cards or multimedia upgrade kits. Often, the titles were "shovelware," a book or reference dumped on a CD-ROM without the saving grace of meaningful video, animation, graphics, or interactivity. Even if the titles were first rate, some were practically impossible to boot up because of incompatibility problems with hardware and software. Then there are those nightmares where the CD-ROM demands more memory than is possible to squeeze out of a computer, without tinkering with scary items like autoexec.BAT files.

For this market to continue to grow, plug-and-play must become a reality. Fortunately, there have been significant steps in that direction. Some computer manufacturers are already featuring fully integrated multimedia computers. Soon, all new computers will have these features built-in. Developers, too, have learned from their early mistakes, and they are producing products that are easier to play. Additonally, the multimedia industry is slowly setting standards leading toward universal compatibility.

However, this will not mean title developers will rest on their laurels. They will continue to seek out the cutting edge and push beyond it. Each of the game developers featured previously, is

On The Cutting Edge: Game makers like Graeme Devine and Rob Landeros push themselves and the industry to new heights.

tinkering with new entertainment paradigms, out-of-this-world combinations of animation, video, audio, and interactivity. For the most part, they have rediscovered the power of traditional storylines, and yet they are tapping the power of interactivity to inject the unexpected, the discovery, the power of choice in a virtual world. Within a few years, the small digital QuickTime or AVI movies as we now know them will be a memory. Even now, games entertain and amaze with full-motion video, special effects and production standards worthy of Hollywood.

THE TEAM: Multimedia Is People-Powered

No one can develop a multimedia project on their own. It's just too complicated, too many pieces of information. If it's going to be good, if it's going to work, you need a team."
—*Cindy Steinberg, MicroMentor*

Making a major multimedia application requires a convergence of talented people who just say yes to the challenges—anticipated and surprise—inherent in a new industry, a new art form. It is a rarity, especially in these early, pioneer days, to find all of the skills needed for multimedia development embodied in a single person. How often, for example, is someone a crack C++ programer and a brilliant proposal writer; or, an animation wizard and a bottom-line genius; or, a master of client relations and digital video production? And even if, somewhere, sometime, "Multimedia Person" were to spring into being, it would still take a half dozen of these wunderkinder to meet the tight deadlines most developers face. Steinberg had barely two months to devise a training program for Holiday Inn Worldwide. Big Hand's team revamped a CD-I sales presentation in just a few weeks. Even game makers, like Presto Studios and Trilobyte, live with market pressures for new state-of-the-art products delivered in time to take advantage of holiday spending sprees.

So many people, so little time (and money), is hardly a lament for multimedia work alone. Just as there are parallels in the evolution of the multimedia and movie industries, there also are emerg-

A.D.A.M.'s Makers: Three men with diverse backgrounds combined their talents to create and market a digital anatomy.

ing parallels in their production. Think about the special effects credits in a blockbuster like *Jurassic Park* and you'll get the idea. A standard operating procedure in Hollywood is to tailor a cast and crew to suit the film. The model makes sense for multimedia production too, especially since fluctuations in business make it almost impossible to keep a production team on payroll. MicroMentor regularly supplements its staff from a group of twenty freelancers. Interactive Arts hired a sophisticated crew when it was time to shoot video. Trilobyte turned to an outside script writer, music maker, and computer artists to make its award-winning game.

So who are the people who make multimedia? It's risky to generalize about such a diverse group, but there are some shared characteristics. Most have a fascination with computers. For some this love affair began in childhood, when they were addicted to computer games. Others were bitten by the bug later in life. Some developers eased from computer-related careers into multimedia, but, increasingly, they have come from wide, unpredictable backgrounds—filmmaking, psychology, real estate, finance, graphic design, education, advertising, writing, and in the case of Ben & Jerry's GUI Guy, snowboarding. What moves them into multimedia tends to be an introduction to the power of these new tools,

Twentysomethings: Most of The Journeyman Project's creators have played computer games since they were in high school.

combined with an eye to exploiting them. Medical illustrator, Greg Swayne, saw the potential of a digitized, interactive human anatomy. Josh Kaplan moved the '50s listening booth into the Information Age. Teacher Steve Carr turned his classroom experience with multimedia learning into a product for other educators.

The people who chance bringing multimedia into their institutions are equally hard to categorize. Thom Kren, the Getty's curator of manuscripts, "doesn't watch TV or play 'Pac Man'," but he accepted multimedia as another way to share his passion for a little known art form with the general public. Veteran educator Dr. Ron Rescigno once thought computers were best as word processors, but now he champions his school district's leadership in multimedia education. Holiday Inn Worldwide's Jewell DeWeese, who worked her way from the front desk to the international corporation's executive offices, enthusiastically embraced multimedia as a tool for learning, not merely for training. What they may lack in computer literacy or hands-on experience, these leaders more than deliver with vision and/or conviction, not to mention political savvy.

Once an idea gels, or a contract is signed, the team pulls together, drawn largely from networks of friends and colleagues that can stretch back to high school. Given the pressure of multimedia production, the bonds of friendship or shared previous business experience seem invaluable during the inevitable, nerve-wracking, budget-grinding moments. As projects take shape, some teams literally live together, as Presto's crew of twentysomethings did while making "The Journeyman Project." Others are spread across the country and, in Big Hand's case, the world. From tiny Jacksonville, Oregon, Trilobyte linked up with a scriptwriter in New York, a music man in Tulsa and a graphic artist in San Diego. Such tele-multimedia is likely to be the norm as the information highway spans the globe.

Companies and institutions that contract with outside firms for multimedia projects seem split on the need for proximity during production. Other things being equal, the Getty Museum preferred to work with a company only miles away. "We felt that we would have to work with them so intensely that commuting would be just a nightmare," curator Thom Kren argued. Holiday Inn Worldwide in Atlanta, on the other hand, linked up with a Cambridge, Massachusetts, company, turning key executives from each company into commuters between the two headquarters. "I don't think you need that proximity," project manager, Cindy Steinberg, said.

Regardless of their backgrounds or working arrangements, co-workers on multimedia are in for a wild ride. Almost all set high standards and are determined to push the limits of the technology and their imaginations. Almost all find themselves working with unfamiliar hardware and software on projects far larger, or more complex, than anything they had previously undertaken. More than one project manager said that if they had known what they were getting into, they would have been frozen with fear. Looking back, though, most tend to agree with Big Hand's Jay Wolff: "It was painful, but it was worth it."

PRODUCTION: Making Multimedia Happen

"I imagine we were a lot like NASA....You know you want to go to the moon, but you have no idea how you're going to get there. You start creating and you build rockets. Some will go to the moon, and some will explode on the launch pad. You learn from both."
—*Gregory M. Swayne, A.D.A.M. Software, Inc.*

There are as many ways to approach, and produce, multimedia applications, as there are developers and clients. However, if there is one constant in multimedia production, it is to expect the unexpected. Since developers constantly break new ground, use new software and hardware, this is no nine-to-five job. Breakneck schedules and impossible deadlines are the norm. Clients change their minds, equipment breaks down, software does not do the job.

Friends On The Inside: Holiday Inn's Jewell DeWeese, above, and the Getty Museum's Thomas Kren, below, backed multimedia projects within their respective organizations.

Murphy's law is ever present. So why do very intelligent individuals put themselves through nightmares on Multimedia Street?

At this point in the multimedia revolution, pioneer developers seem to thrive on adversity. "Some people would say that something goes wrong every day," said Lance Lyda. "We think of it as learning something new everyday. And when working with a new medium, unknowns are a given." To cope, and Lyda's Big Hand team did plenty of that, "the best thing is patience," he counselled.

Take A Deep Breath: Big Hand's Lance Lyda and his fellow pioneers know it takes patience to make multimedia.

Still, there are some lessons to be learned from the gut-wrenching experiences explored in the previous chapters. Eventually, they may become tenets of the new discipline of multimedia production management. No, they will not eliminate 11th-hour problems, but they may lay a groundwork that makes it possible not only to cope, but to flourish.

The Plan

"A really good rule of thumb is to come up with a production schedule, make it accurate, and give yourself enough time, and then double it."
—Shannon Gilligan, "Who Killed Sam Rupert?"

There was a familiar refrain when each developer said what they'd do differently if they could do their projects again: Plan Ahead. Plan the project from script to authoring, and do not forget client relations and finances along the way. This up-front work, everyone agreed, could save thousands of dollars, hundreds of hours work— and even, in some cases, the project itself.

In a new industry like this, it's hard to find multimedia veterans. Most developers learn a lot as they go. For Ben & Jerry's Mary

Kamm, the lessons were about "organizing our time. We should have been a lot more detailed with our storyboards. And, we should have gotten a lot more user input along the way." Others draw on their experiences in the meat grinders of other industries, like InterActive Arts' David Schwartz, who traded the pressure-cooker of film editing for the pressure-cooker of multimedia production. "There's a lot of technical figuring out that you can only do on the fly, so you have to build in that experimentation in time and money," he said. "That's why you build in contingencies. Film makers usually put in 10 to 15 percent for acts of God or mistakes. Here, it's for your learning curve."

Still, perhaps more so in multimedia than in other industries, best laid plans are put aside in favor of something better, bigger, or just discovered. "There's something curious about the creation of multimedia," teacher Steve Carr noted. "It's almost this synergistic way of creating. It's not a linear process. Your links, your branches come by doing. You all of a sudden say, 'I hadn't anticipated that, but it would make perfect sense to do it this way.'" Up in Oregon, Trilobyte's founders planned to film the haunted house setting for "The 7th Guest," but they changed their minds—and dramatically altered their production schedule—when they saw Robert Stein's 3-D creations. And down in Atlanta, many functions of A.D.A.M., the digital man, grew out of casual conversations between his inventor and the company's crew of creative artists and programmers.

Making Connections: Steve Carr learned that multimedia production often is filled with serendipity.

So, the moral is "plan ahead," as much as possible, then, when the creative light bulb flashes on, there is time and energy left to respond. This plan may take the form of a project calendar as it does at Interactive Arts; a comprehensive script, like Presto Studios' story for "The Journeyman Project" and/or detailed storyboards, as is the norm at MicroMentor and Galileo. All are the subjects of brainstorming meetings and client briefings before technical work begins. Equally

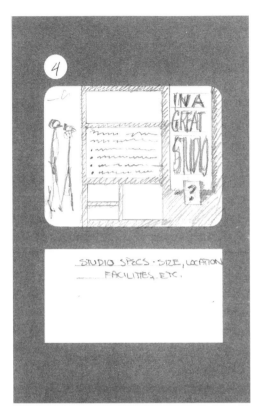

Plan Ahead: Storyboards help developers and clients think through a project before time-consuming, costly production begins.

important are realistic project deadlines. Shannon Gilligan laughs now at her naive boast that she would finish three of her virtual murders in a year's time. Until there are more established, reliable patterns and tools for multimedia production, her adage—to build in double the time you think you'll need—is a word to the wise.

The Script

"In an interactive script, you take the storyline and pick out locations and dramatic scenes so that the isolated events are linked together...and each scene has a beginning, middle and end throughout the story."
—Matthew Costello, "The 7th Guest"

Scripting an interactive multimedia application means going where linear writers fear to tread. Whether for a training program, game or museum kiosk, the interactive script is the soul of the project. It must have a strong beginning, middle, and end, like conventional written works. It also must deal transparently with the parallel worlds available through interactivity.

No wonder, for most of the preceding applications, scriptwriting was a job for a professional, either a writer, content expert, or both. Shannon Gilligan drew on her experience as a successful children's book author to create her interactive murder series, while the Trilobyte partners, both experienced game makers, turned to professional horror writer Matthew Costello to plot "The 7th Guest." Curator Thomas Kren's, expertise made him the logical person to draft the script for the Getty's "Illuminated Manuscripts." Similarly, MicroMentor's Cindy Steinberg worked with Holiday Inn's in-house expert to outline a training program for rate and inventory management.

Regardless of the project or the creative crew's experience, script development includes give-and-take between the artist and the developer, between the client and the project manager. Experienced writers, or specialists in a specific field, also face numerous revisions to tailor content to this new medium. Gilligan overwrote, Costello penned a dozen revisions, Kren fretted as his script was whittled down to size. Arriving at a final version can be a tense, painful period, especially since so much of the product's success and the subsequent production rides on its ability to tell a story or communicate a message.

Interface Design and Navigation

"Believe it or not, not everyone knows how to use a mouse."
—Rik Dryfoos, Ben & Jerry's

Skilled multimedia developers use the full power of interactivity, without resorting to interactivity for its own sake. This skill is immediately evident in the design of an elegant, easy-to-use, intuitive interface. Sound simple? It's not, as the majority of multimedia products, and their thick user manuals, reveal.

In the industry's early days (that's just a few years ago!), many early multimedia developers, wild-eyed with the potential of interactivity, went button and branch crazy. (Remember when desktop publishers, with font after font at their fingertips, mixed and matched them with reckless abandon?) Today cooler multimedia heads prevail and, now, there's an industry understanding that there should be enough interactivity—no more and no less—to make the program work effectively. "Interactivity based on old schools of thought is a mistake," Galileo's Mike Wittenstein reminds. "To make people click a button just to see the presentation—press here to continue—is an old CBT [computer-based training] metaphor that doesn't make any sense. As Jackie [Goldstein, his partner] said, 'if adding buttons takes away or interferes, then they just don't belong.'"

Interface and navigation design also must be user-friendly. In multimedia applications, that catch phase means the user always knows where he or she is and how to get where he or she wants to go. At Big Hand, interactivity is confined to no more than three layers deep. At Interactive Arts, a "bookmark" on every screen identifies the section being explored. At Presto Studios, sensory feedback tells a user "your command is being processed." In the CD-ROM version of this book, a button on every screen takes users back to the main menu at any time. Generally, clean, simple graphic and navigation systems make a user feel in charge, without the aid of an inch-thick instruction manual. "If it's going to take me anymore than three minutes to figure out the interface, it's too complicated; it's not elegant," MicroMentor's Cindy Steinberg said. "The point is I'm trying to teach rate and inventory, not how to interact with the program."

Since an interface is a window on a program, design details can, and do, set a tone for functionality and content. As conventions of interface design emerge, such as locating control panels on the right side of the screen (because most users are right-handed), these elements subtly and not-so-subtly identify a program with an

A Quick Study: The best interface designs are clear and simple to use, like this one from the iStation.

established series, a corporation, or a particular subject. For the Getty's "Illuminated Manuscripts," Interactive Arts backed introductory screens with the same parchment used to make these medieval books. Holiday Inn Worldwide's training program is brightened with the familiar green of the company logo. Big Hand's presentation for Werndl utilizes the furniture maker's modern graphics. And Steve Carr picked a yellowed parchment for backgrounds in his educational CD-ROM on the Lewis and Clark Expedition.

3-D Graphics and Animation

"Everyone out there knows that this is a benchmark they will have to surpass. And we're going to surpass it. We want to go leaps and bounds beyond it. "
—Michel Kripalani, Presto Studio

With all the affordable, hardware and software on the market now, artists are making their mark on multimedia in a big way. In all of the cases described, artistic polish was a prime concern of the developers, many of whom combined computer skills with an art background—graphic design, animation, video and film, writing, and even theater. In fact some companies, like Big Hand, make it a point to hire artists, not computer technicians, to create their award-winning applications.

One consequence is that computer graphics, 3-D, and animation are being pushed to new heights of excellence and innovation. Among entertainment titles, in particular, graphic one-upmanship is a must in this increasingly crowded, highly competitive market. Creators of both "The 7th Guest" and "The Journeyman Project" aimed for a cinematic photorealism that is light years away from the flat, jerky images of early computer games. Yet both are determined to best themselves in their upcoming sequels. In turn, the state-of-the-art graphics in these and other bestselling titles tends to raise consumer expectations and, thus, set graphic standards for most all new multimedia applications.

Key to this rapid evolution are powerful computer paint and draw, photo-manipulation, and animation software. Among the most popular are Corel Draw!, Adobe Photoshop, Kai's PowerTools, Altimira Composer, Aldus PhotoStyler, and Autodesk's Animator Pro and 3-D Studio. All enlarge artists' capabilities and reduce the effort needed to achieve spectacular effects. Want to replicate the style of the great Impressionists? No problem. Prefer "Star Trek" effects? Sure. Even with these powerful tools, production of advanced computer graphics still is time-consuming and staff-intensive. As such, these graphics add substantially to the cost of title development, and need to be budgeted for accordingly

Great Graphics: Animation and 3-D graphics are a hallmark of best-selling games like "The Journeyman Project."

Video

Video, even if it is the size of a postage-stamp, is now considered a must for consumer multimedia. New video compression software soon will make full-screen, full-motion playback possible without the use of acceleration hardware. Accelerator boards that already allow for full-motion video are already on the market, and soon these accelerators will be standard in computer configurations and eventually integrated into the motherboard itself. In the not-so-distant future, today's itty-bitty AVI and QuickTime movies will be as passé as silent movies.

Then developers, especially for consumer titles, will no longer be able to get away with home-movie-quality video shot with VHS camcorders in available light. Multimedia video will have to equal the production quality of television. Many developers already are turning to professionals to mount their video shoots. Having learned some hard lessons producing video for "The 7th Guest," Trilobyte has vastly improved the quality and professionalism of the video for the game's sequel. Presto Studios, too, opted for a professional crew and actors on a sound stage, when it shot video for "The Journeyman Project II." Other developers, like Hueneme's Steve Carr, have wrestled with difficult licensing questions to acquire clips from television programs and movies for his educational CD-ROM.

As the emphasis on quality video grows, watch for professional videographers and editors to play major roles in multimedia production. Future projects also will get a boost from the talents of well-known actors, stars who also can be touted in ads and on the packaging. Shannon Gilligan's use of Sheryl Lee, "Twin Peaks'" Laura Palmer, in her next

murder mystery, is a case in point. New, improved, standards will also be fueled by new alliances between developers and "video content sources" like public television stations, television production companies, and Hollywood studios.

On Location: Video shot by professionals, like these working on "Illuminated Manuscripts," is rapidly replacing amateur endeavors.

Audio

"Sound design is under-used and overlooked. It's an incredibly important way of communicating with your audience. It can make up for a lot of rough edges."
—Shannon Gilligan, "Who Killed Sam Rupert?"

With the arrival of powerful computer sound cards, quality audio—music, voice-over narration, and sound effects—are a must for exceptional multimedia productions. Sound adds a sense of realism, as office noises do in MicroMentor's "virtual" Holiday Inn; or the nature sounds do in Steve Carr's "Lewis and Clark." It can also add drama and tension, as the creepy score does in "The 7th Guest" or suggest mood and compliment the subject, as the medieval music from Harmonia Mundi does in "The Illuminated Manuscripts."

As the industry has grown, multimedia audio specialists and musicians are coming to the forefront. Often, like Presto's Geno Andrews, they milk existing audio technology for all its worth and force the development team to take sound quality seriously. "There wasn't a choice," remembers Michel Kripalani of Andrews' memorable work on "The Journeyman Project." "His biggest thing was wrestling with the programmers to get the music sound quality better in the game. The Mac has a real good sound output, but he just wanted it better." As technology elevates multimedia sound to that of film or television, The Fat Man (a.k.a. George Sanger), the reigning king of game soundtracks, believes "a developer will be able to hire anyone they want to work on music—us or ex-Beatles, African master musicians, or an a capella choir, or whatever they want."

This emphasis on audio reinforces the growing belief that in multimedia, what counts is not just how well it manipulates the bits and bytes, but how well it pulls the heart strings, or sends chills down the spine. "It won't be the guy who can model a 3-D dragon with a naked lady in his mouth that makes it," warns The Fat Man, looking ahead. "It will be the person who makes facial expressions that mean something." That's why it's important, he continued, for developers to "budget the time and space on your title for good music. The more music that's in there, the better."

Sounds Serious: Composers like The Fat Man are playing a growing role in multimedia production.

Authoring/Programming

"The faster and more responsive your product is, the better it's going to be for the user. You can come up with brilliant ideas that run great on a Quadra 900, but if a user has an SI, the beauty is lost when it clunks along."
—Dan Backus, A.D.A.M. Software, Inc.

As with most everything in this industry, there is no one way to program multimedia. Why program a title in C++ if a hundred dollar, royalty free, off-the-shelf package will do everything necessary? In the near future, new versions of standard authoring tools will offer more speed and do more tricks, while being easier to use and cross-platform compatible. On the other hand, if you need speed or unusual features, as Trilobyte did, or constant upgrades of your product, as intouch or A.D.A.M. Software, Inc. did, proprietary code, or a modified software package, may be the only choice. Some game developers now are having an engine, or template program, written for them for use in a series of titles. Thus the substantial cost of the initial programming is spread out over a series of products.

Facing a market where users have a choice of platforms, most consumer title developers, including the three game firms in this book, are producing both Windows and Macintosh titles, while keeping an eye on 3DO. Developers working for outside clients often are tied to the client's platform, as MicroMentor was to Holiday Inn Worldwide's OS/2 system. In the future, the platform dilemma confronting both consumers and developers may be eliminated by powerful new computers that play both Windows and Macintosh programs, which are now beginning to be marketed. For now, however, new cross-platform authoring programs eventually should take some of the pain out of the platform conversion process.

Once the platform and authoring tool is selected, what is the best approach to getting the job done? Big Hand's Lance Lyda suggests that the authoring team make up the program using dummy screens, while the actual assets are being created. "As you produce assets, you simply drop them off at the authoring station and they replace what they have," he said. "Then toward the end of the project, the authoring is minimal." A similar approach helped MicroMentor complete their Holiday Inn project on time. Lead programmer Bill Taylor built "tiny little prototypes," and, in the process, "worked through the programming process, so that we felt comfortable...That helped us avoid serious pitfalls, by knowing in advance some of the problems we might encounter."

Programming Programs: A growing number of today's multimedia developers, like Trilobyte's Graeme Devine, often create proprietary code for their multimedia projects.

Regardless of the advance preparation, or the experience of the team, this final stage of multimedia production is a challenge, if for no other reason than huge files are being moved up and down their computer network. While tape backups are a lifesaver when systems crash, they are no substitute for file and project management at this critical stage of production. In the future, this job will be a key position on every multimedia team.

Testing

"We brought in some kids, friends of friends, everyone we knew. We were bringing in people off the street...We gave them T-shirts and popcorn to sit there all night and play."
—Michel Kripalani, Presto Studios

Big Hand's Jay Wolff said it all when he warned that when you develop multimedia, you are developing software; thus there are almost always problems. Experience with the hardware and software, and a seasoned production team means fewer bugs at deadline. However, even the most conscientious developers need to test-run their products before clients or customers get their turn.

Currently, there are as many testing procedures as there are developers and publishers. A.D.A.M. Software, Inc., visits medical schools around the country to collect data used to refine its digital anatomy, while another educational developer, Steve Carr, simply walked back into his California classroom to test-run his CD-ROM. In the beta testing of "The 7th Guest," Rob Alvey, and some colleagues, played the game around the clock, phoning in needed fixes to Trilobyte's Oregon offices. Similarly, Big Hand's staff is enlisted to "abuse" an application, "go through every branch...view every screen...click as fast as you can" before it was turned over to a client.

For a stressed-out developer on deadline, testing may seem like a never-ending obstacle course. "With the amazing variety of PCs on the market, a bug-free consumer title is almost out of reach," Virgin's, Robb Alvey admitted. Depending on the application, this process can take from a few days to weeks and even months to complete. However, while there's an uphill struggle for consumer confidence in this technology, it's a step that can't be skipped. By the time it reaches a client or consumer, many of whom haven't mastered setting the clock on a VCR, multimedia should be simple to use.

MARKETING: Selling Multimedia

Some pundits are fond of dismissing today's multimedia on CD-ROMs as nothing more than "training wheels" for the future information highway. Regardless of their fate, undoubtedly today's emerging market for these silver discs and their channels will shape tomorrow's business practices and strategies. At this early stage, the multimedia market seems generally divided into consumer products sold to the general public, and service applications—sales, training, information management, and communications—aimed at businesses, government and other institutions. In both arenas, selling multimedia has become a job for marketing professionals who know the particular "ins and outs" of each sector.

Consumer Multimedia

"As a small company, it was really crucial to get our message out. If you don't educate the public about that you are doing, then you get lost in the shuffle."

—Robert S. Cramer, A.D.A.M. Software, Inc.
"Because of the word of mouth on this game, the hype was so strong that we could have put the game in a brown paper bag and it would have sold."
—Rob Alvey, Virgin Games, on "The 7th Guest"

Each of the five consumer titles chronicled in the previous chapters took different roads to market. Presto Studios initially did their own marketing and distribution for "The Journeyman Project," only to decide the time-consuming effort kept them from their first priority, game-making. So almost a year after their game was released, they signed up another San Diego County company, Quadra Interactive, to expedite sales. Quadra, in turn, handed off PC and Mac versions of the popular game to an established nationwide distributor, Game Tek, and eventually distribution was handed over to Sanctuary Woods. In contrast, Trilobyte's first game, the eagerly anticipated "7th Guest," was marketed by their co-producer, Virgin Games, while Shannon Gilligan's first virtual murder mystery was published by a growing Oregon multimedia firm, Creative Multimedia Corporation. Both Virgin and CMC utilize a variety of established distributors, including Baker & Taylor, and Merisel, as well as the mail-order catalog outlets. A.D.A.M. Software Inc., one of the two educational titles profiled, continues to market its digital human anatomy in the United States, but has contracted with a Japanese firm to handle sales there. The Hueneme School District preferred to turn over marketing of what it hopes is a planned series of educational CD-ROMs for home and school use to its partner TMM.

The sales potential for these products has multiplied in recent months. Media hype about multimedia and the information highway, has broadened consumer awareness of multimedia. However, more importantly, the critical installed base of multimedia-capable computers has skyrocketed since these projects were conceived. Estimates of the number of multimedia-capable computers in homes by the end of 1994 range from eight to fourteen million. At the same time, industry watchers are predicting a drop in CD-ROM retail prices, yet another boon to sales.

As consumer demand grows, the channels available to multimedia marketers will expand to include bookstores, music/video stores, discount department stores, and even grocery chains. This expansion will make obsolete the conventional wisdom that 5,000 in sales equaled a successful CD-ROM title. Instead, sales of 30,000 to 50,000 will be the measure of success, while sales of 100,000 and 1,000,000 will not be uncommon. To appreciate the impact of just one additional channel, consider an experiment by Blockbuster Video during the 1993 holiday season to rent and sell CD-ROM titles in 58 stores. If the company decided to stock CD-ROMs and put ten copies of a particular title in each of its 3,600 stores, the initial buy would equal 36,000. And that's just one chain.

On Their Own: Presto Studios initially handled distribution of "The Journeyman Project" themselves.

Affiliates

A relationship with an affiliate publisher makes the most sense for inexperienced developers hoping to break into this rapidly growing industry. Affiliate publishers co-develop, or publish and market, titles as CMC does with Shannon Gilligan's CD-ROM mysteries, and TMM does with the Hueneme School District. Even the experienced game-makers at Trilobyte benefited from a partnership with Virgin Games to bring "The 7th Guest" to market. Affiliate publishers have the advantage of experience in the marketplace, professional accounting systems, a seasoned sales force, and/or established distribution networks. In most cases, they help finance, develop, and package the product, as well as handle the time-consuming conversion to different platforms.

Financial arrangements, publishers and developers agree, are negotiable, and tend to depend on the status of the project when the partnership is formed. Generally, affiliate publishers demand exclusivity on the current and future Windows and Mac titles for at least two Christmas selling seasons, and generally will keep 70 to 90 percent of the price to the distributor. The percentage pocketed by a developer depends on what he, or she, brings to the table. A finished product, packaged and ready to go, returns more to the developer than an idea, or demo, in the early stages of design that requires investment from the publisher to complete. Other considerations that effect the developers share include their experience and creative talent, plus the content he or she owns. In the case of the Trilobyte partners, their impressive track record as game designers enabled them share the publishing credits, and a substantial portion of the profits, with Virgin Games.

Packaging

As Presto Studios discovered bringing its game to market, many buyers for retail outlets often are as concerned with a title's packaging as with its content. Unless you are Trilobyte, and customers are waiting in line for your game, this is a cynical fact of life in the increasingly hard-fought competition for consumer multimedia dollars, and retail shelf space. Buyers not only judge a title's value by its packaging (and weight), but they also determine whether it fits on the store shelves, generally designed to hold software products. Until outlets for multimedia entertainment expand, the industry standard probably will remain what CMC calls the Compton's box, which measures 8.25 inches by 5.75 inches.

Once inside a store and in a customers' hands, the graphics and copy on the box have to make the sale. If the title is part of a series, especially a successful one like Shannon Gilligan's "Who Killed...?" mysteries, similar packaging builds product identity and consumer recognition, as CMC discovered. The Hueneme educational series, as well as sequels by Trilobyte and Presto Studios to their top-selling games, are likely to adopt a similar strategy. In the future, as the market becomes more crowded, packaging and other sales strategies increasingly will be turned over to marketing professionals in-house, or to outside agencies.

Pricing

Even veterans of the multimedia marketplace agree that today's product pricing strategies can seem like a game. With few exceptions, consumers do not pay the suggested retail price (SRP). The SRP is important to developers and publishers, however, since the distributors' cost for the product generally equals 55 percent of the SRP. Retailers pay the wholesale price, which includes an additional markup, by the distributor, for the title, and then they add on their

profit-margin before putting the title on store shelves. To remain competitive and attract new buyers, the store, or street price, of a title is usually substantially discounted from the SRP.

Other factors that influence price point are SRPs of similar titles, product positioning, trends in multimedia entertainment, the length of time the product has been on the market, and the individual developer's or publisher's bottom line. Over all, the sale price positions a title in the marketplace, vis á vis similar titles. Industry-wide, prices have

Too Many Messages: The packaging for this, and all of Shannon Gilligan's murder mysteries, was simplified to build on her first success.

THE MAGIC

DEATH

VIRTUAL MURDER™ 2

A MULTIMEDIA MYSTERY ON CD-ROM

been dropping, a reflection of market competition and growth. As the industry matures, prices are likely to stabilize and pricing policies, especially SRP, may become a more realistic reflection of actual costs and expected profit.

Timing

Caught up in title production, the first-time developers profiled in this book had only one goal: to finish their work. Now, given the rise in consumer demand, they must amend that goal—to finish their title so that it arrives in stores in time for the busy holiday buying season. Industry experts agree that means the product must be ready to ship by September 15.

Business and Institutional Multimedia

"We had this incredible sales presentation; and the client was absolutely floored....They saw how multimedia might revolutionize their company and that they should have it. We had talked to some big, big people, but basically the project became too large for anyone in the room to have authority over. Then nothing happened."
—Jay Wolff, Big Hand

"Some (clients) come already knowing what they want; others honestly don't know anything about it...or how it fits in the context of an overall corporate learning process."
—Eric Vogt, MicroMentor

Marketing their services has challenged the pioneering companies attempting to convince corporations and institutions to invest in multimedia. The flood of trade and mass media news about multimedia in recent months should make that task easier, but it still will be far from a snap. "You proceed as if it's locked and loaded," said Holiday Inn Worldwide's Jewell DeWeese of her efforts to introduce multimedia training there, "but every day we fight the battle."

With the tremendous growth in networks, information systems, and multimedia platform bases, opportunities for multimedia companies with businesses and institutions of all sizes will increase dramatically. As a result, new multimedia service companies will spring up, while established enterprises, like advertising agencies, film and video companies, and graphic design firms will incorporate multimedia into their service mix. The increased competition will force established, pioneering multimedia firms like Big Hand, Interactive Arts, and Galileo to become more aggressive and sophisticated in marketing their services. One likelihood is harnessing the technology they sell for self-promotion. It is not too far-fetched to imagine every multimedia company with versions of Galileo's "Talking Business Card." Another viable option is soliciting new business outside of their city, region, or nation. As Big Hand proved, with its project for a German furniture maker, today's communications technologies make it possible to service a client anywhere in the world.

Currently, when potential clients decide to try multimedia, networking plays a dominant role. All the developers interviewed for this book agreed that most of their new business was the result of referrals by satisfied former customers. As Peter Bloch of Interactive Arts reported, "cold calls" rarely brought in new business, although they may not be as unrewarding in today's multimedia-aware climate. Nonetheless, multimedia companies still have to follow the age-old practice of good client relations to survive and grow. Often, that process will begin with education, since, as Eric Vogt points out, potential multimedia clients come to the table with vastly varied knowledge about these sophisticated new tools.

When wooing new clients, Big Hand's veteran, Jay Wolff, notes that a sales pitch should match the company's multimedia needs and funds. Overselling multimedia can lead to major problems and even to losing a sale. As Wolff realized, "We thought we were going to land these huge jobs, and because of our thinking at the time, we literally have no clients from that stage of the business. After about a year, we started recognizing that no one is able to buy these big projects." Big Hand aims to keep the first project small. "Now at every (sales presentation), we jazz them up, and then we talk them back down to the ground," he said. At the same time, Wolff and his colleagues also look for ways to enhance each application's value to the client, an approach that is especially appealing to institutions that often want income-producing consumer versions of their multimedia projects.

As familiarity with multimedia grows within the corporate community, Big Hand and other companies hope to establish long-term working relationships with their clients. Instead of developing multimedia piecemeal, they encourage their customers to integrate it into their overall communications effort. "We don't want it to be just a novel, fun project," Wolff said, "where a company comes to us, throws some money at an application, gets some nice press for it and then goes back to the old way of doing things."

FINANCE: Excuse Me, Mr. Banker

"We wanted to stay away from venture capital. And we wanted to own the program outright. For investment capital, we went to our parents first and our friends second."
—**Michel Kripalani, Presto Studios**

"It's one of the art forms in this business, because for any piece of multimedia you can spend ten dollars, or you can spend fifty dollars to build it. And the tricky thing is to make an estimate before you build it."
—**Eric Vogt, MicroMentor**

Announcing the FIRST Truly aLTeRNatiVe music StATiON.

Music To Their Ears: The intouch group, inc. had to convince record companies and retailers to back the iStation.

Reading the headlines made in 1993, it is hard to believe the multimedia industry is not a millionaires' club. After all, the moguls fighting for lanes on the digital highway are rich, and to join in their vision of 500 cable television channels takes some very deep pockets. But a broad range of multimedia firms exist, stretching from mom-and-pop operations with back-to-back computers in the upstairs bedroom to corporations in high-rise offices. All will attest that being on the cutting edge of an industry can take its toll financially. Yet using the same inventiveness found in their products, they manage to make money—and multimedia—at the same time.

Many of these developers can relate to Presto Studios' bargain basement beginnings. This group of young adults borrowed money from family and friends to fund creation of "The Journeyman Project," because they were determined to hold sole rights to the game. In the final months, with deadlines looming, all of the team members had quit their day jobs to work day and night building the game. "If we were married and had kids, we couldn't have done it," Presto's, Michel Kripalani, admitted.

Other multimedia developers used already established businesses to launch their new endeavors. Gregory Swayne financed his dream to create a digital human anatomy with profits from his established medical illustration business, as he and his partners raised investment capital from the Atlanta medical community. Josh Kaplan, who launched the intouch group with money from his savings and some substantial startup loans, also sought investors who would back his venture to place digital listening booths in record stores around the country. By the end of 1993, he had raised a cool $22 million.

Developers of consumer titles also seek out potential investors, in the form of publishers or co-developers. A successful children's book author with a good idea, but no experience in multimedia, Shannon Gilligan convinced CMC to bankroll her first title. When Rob Landeros and Graeme Devine wanted to develop CD-ROM games with their employer, Virgin Games, the company president said no to their in-house project, but agreed to co-develop an outside project with an initial investment of more than $350,000.

Developers like these, who risk their own funds to make multimedia, may envy companies paid "in full" for their efforts by clients. That avenue, while seemingly less risky, is pot-holed with its own problems. The major one is agreeing on a price tag with a client, most likely inexperienced in the many contingencies of multimedia for a project that undoubtedly will have unexpected expenses. Grappling with this issue led MicroMentor's Eric Vogt to devise a fee structure for his learning program, the desktop learning hour, which costs $75,000. "We have done a number of different things and lost a lot of money," he explained. "So we had to think about at what level we can reliably manage the process and the client, to deliver satisfaction, and not lose our shirt in the process."

Even when the price is set, developers often wrestle with clients for timely payment. Dissatisfied with 30-, 60-, or 90-day terms, Big Hand now asks for 50 percent down; 20 percent to start producing; 20 percent to start authoring; and the remaining 10 percent when the program is delivered. Other companies make certain that contracts spell out a mutually agreeable payment plan.

When working on their own projects, or for clients, most developers hire freelancers to get the job done. It's a relationship that makes sense, since business tends to ebb and flow, but it, too, is built on the quicksand of evolving financial arrangements. Some freelancers accept flat fees for their services, while others, such as the script writer and composer for "The 7th Guest," are paid a flat fee plus royalties for their services. "God forbid the royalties don't work out, at least we get something for our work," explained The Fat Man. Given his background as a published horror author, "Guest" writer Matthew Costello based his royalty demand on the book industry's standards, but, he acknowledged, "in this industry, everyone's just finding their way."

If royalties are not an option, most experienced freelancers prefer to charge an hourly fee, which generally is $100 or higher. Developers, on the other hand, would rather contract for a specific job at a fixed price. "You can get burned on a fixed-price contract if you haven't worked for [a company] before" warns freelance programmer Bill Taylor, as it's hard to know how exacting or demanding the job will be. Freelancers also tend to be out of the running for large corporate assignments, since companies venturing into this emerging field prefer the security of working with an established firm. With luck, hard work, and a lot of networking, though, freelancers can land steady work, either with companies like MicroMentor, that draw from a pool of freelance talent, or with consumer-title developers, like Shannon Gilligan, who are committed to a series of related projects. Sometimes, out of the blue, they'll score a "hit," as did Alan Iglesias, a 3-D graphics designer for the high-profile "7th Guest." Since that game became an industry sales leader, Iglesias said he's had "offers to work every other day. I'm turning stuff down left and right."

As multimedia companies prosper and grow, financial management generally becomes a full-time job for an experienced executive. When the intouch group moved from a four-city experiment to nationwide distribution of its digital listening booths, the San Francisco company hired the former CEO of Vernors, Inc. to be its COO. A.D.A.M. Software also added a vice president of finance and a chief operating office to its management team.

On Their Terms: Big Hand's management team has devised a payment plan for its multimedia clients.

As A.D.A.M. partner Robert Cramer notes, "It's not easy for entrepreneurs to allow people to come in and let them do the things they are good at." But, he continued saying, it made good business sense and contributed to the company's ongoing success.

THE FUTURE: Sequels and Variations

Within weeks after "The Journeyman Project" began its climb to the top of the Mac game sales charts, its creators had already begun work on a sequel to the time-travel adventure game. The same was true of the Trilobyte duo, now well along on the production of a second haunted house game, and of Shannon Gilligan who is due to deliver her third and fourth "Who Killed...?" murder mysteries this year. Even though Steve Carr is still wrapping up what will be the first of the Hueneme Series of educational titles, several of his fellow teachers are waiting in the wings with projects of their own. While Holiday Inn Worldwide installs its new multimedia computers in its hotels around the world, the company is moving forward with three more interactive training programs like its debut multimedia venture, "Rate and Inventory Management."

Clearly, one project is not enough when it comes to multimedia. Most pioneers in this industry, blessed with the imagination and fortitude to produce one successful title, are eager to move on to another, and yet another. Since none had an easy time bringing the first one to life, it must be true that time erases pain, or that multimedia masochism can't be cured. More to the point is the fact that one successful title, or program, paves the way financially and politically. "Actually, we ran out of money toward the end [of making 'The 7th Guest"]," Landeros said. Devine added that the game's success has resulted in a very secure environment at Trilobyte. At Holiday Inn Worldwide, the success of the first multimedia training program made the sponsoring division "the poster child around here for the way these projects should be done and done effectively," said John Lipscomb.

For some fortunate developers, their original multimedia idea is a candidate for many variations. A.D.A.M. Software, Inc., now

"The Journeyman Project II": Presto Studios wants the sequel to its best-selling game to set a new standard for photorealistic graphics.

that this Georgia company has put all of human anatomy into an interactive program, is working on a variety of versions that will take the digital man into elementary school classrooms, doctor's offices and even the family den. One variation could be an entertainment-type game that teaches kids about health maintenance. Across the country, the intouch group has visions of other data-collecting, networked kiosks based on its original iStation. Topping the list are iStations for video, CD-ROMs and other computer software—ideal "sales people" for the information super stores on the horizon.

Other developers, with track records in a variety of multimedia presentations, have the advantage of high profiles in what has become a hot industry. Their pioneering efforts should pay off in more business for more clients, who are understandably drawn to experienced developers. Since its Werndl project, Big Hand has done work for numerous corporate clients including Mercedes-Benz. Galileo, playing their "Talking Business Cards" right, has developed multimedia projects for Coca-Cola USA, AT&T, and the 1994 Goodwill Games in Atlanta.

While many of these developers seem to have found their digital niche, all continue to toy with the possibilities opened up by this new media in the coming digital age. Gregory Swayne envisions the A.D.A.M. channel, serving doctors and patients in hospitals around the world with health education and medical news. Shannon Gilligan is fascinated with the prospect of multiple-user games played across networks that could span the globe. Eric Vogt wants to package standard executive learning courses into laptop computers and rent them to companies and business students. Jay Wolff is intrigued with interactive cable, which would allow home viewers to interact with programs, like movies, delivered to their televisions.

A.D.A.M. Essentials: This new product brings the digital man to a new market.

With so much on the horizon, the multimedia elephant of the future is likely to look vastly different than today's beast. Not even the boldest of the new media gurus expected this industry to take off as it has. New hardware, software, techniques, and technologies are unveiled daily, and new talented developers, with vision and tenacity, will be there to apply them. So, it is with a great sense of excitement that the growing legion of us, who would be a part of this revolution, wake up every morning to see what the multimedia elephant will look like on this particular day.

Index

PLAYING THE CD-ROM

For best performance, we recommend a big, fast 486 PC or Macintosh Quadra computer with a double or triple-speed CD-ROM player, a video card that displays thousands of colors, 8 megabytes of RAM and a really cool amplified sound system. The program was designed for 640 x 480 viewing, but it works in higher modes as well.

WARNING: Before installing the CD-ROM on a PC, you should back up your system.ini file so you have an extra copy in your Windows directory. In case of any system defects, restore your original system.ini file and reboot your computer.

To setup in Windows insert the CD-ROM disc into the player, go to the Program Manager, click the File menu, click the browse button to select the drive your CD-ROM drive is installed on. Then click the file folder titled **setup** and finally select the **setup.exc.** The computer will automatically setup Video for Windows player and an icon in the Program Manager. Click the icon to start the program.

Mac users should first make sure they are not using virtual memory. Once this feature is turned off, they should insert the CD-ROM into the player, an icon will appear on the desktop. Click on the icon and several files will be visible. Click the QuickTime update icon first for further instructions. After you are through setting up, click *The Multimedia Casebook* icon to get started. Have fun!